# DICTIONARY OF BORROWED WORDS

A WYNWOOD LEXICON

# DICTIONARY OF BORROWED WORDS

LAURENCE URDANG AND
FRANK R. ABATE, EDITORS

WYNWOOD® Press
New York, New York

WYNWOOD PRESS EDITION 1991

*This edition published by special arrangement with*
*Gale Research Company*

**Library of Congress Cataloging-in-Publication Data**

Loanwords dictionary.
  Dictionary of borrowed words : over 6,500 foreign
words and phrases used in English contexts / Laurence
Urdang, editorial director ; Frank R. Abate, editor.
      p.      cm.
  Reprint. Originally published: Loanwords dictionary.
1st ed. Detroit, Mich. : Gale Research Co., c1988.
  ISBN 0-922066-62-0
  1. English language—Foreign words and
phrases—Dictionaries.   I. Urdang, Laurence.
II. Abate, Frank R.   III. Title.
[PE1670.L58   1991]
422'.4'03—dc20                                      90-20528
                                                         CIP

Copyright © 1988 by Gale Research Company
Published by WYNWOOD® Press
New York, New York
Printed in the United States of America

# Contents

# Preface

The English language has by far the largest stock of words of any language ever known. Users of English have freely and copiously borrowed terms from foreign tongues whenever their own vocabulary, imaginations, or circumstances seemed to suggest that "native" possibilities were wanting. Evidence of borrowing can be found throughout the historical record of English, as speakers and writers sought to capture the essence of a phenomenon or some facet of experience. Hence, the lexicon of the language bears witness to the diverse cultural contacts and influences that have shaped it.

Borrowings from other languages into English manifest themselves in various guises. A great proportion—particularly those many thousands of words adopted from Latin and Greek since the sixteenth century, known as "inkhorn terms"—were assimilated into English at or very near to the time of borrowing, taking on simplified spelling and English morphology. These words look, sound, and feel English, and do not, without study, manifest their foreign origin. Examples, from words used above, are *copiously, vocabulary, circumstances, experience, proportion, lexicon,* and *morphology.*

Another class of derivatives are those, from several sources, that have been in the language so long that they no longer can be deemed foreign. Such words as *wine, wall, vale, camp, bishop* (all from Latin, or, for *bishop,* Greek via Latin); *skirt* and *kindle* (from Old Norse); or *admiral, shampoo, canoe,* and *boss* "supervisor" (from Arabic, Hindi, Cariban, and Dutch, respectively), all were borrowed into English, but have become so familiar and natural that they give no one pause.

## Focusing on Borrowed Words

A third group of borrowings are the subject of this dictionary. Like other derivatives, they have a foreign source, and many have been used in English for centuries. What distinguishes these borrowed words, however, and allows treatment of them as a subset of the English lexicon, is that despite their use in English contexts, they still, in some regard, *seem* or *feel* foreign. Clearly, this determination can be subjective, so the editors have striven to follow certain criteria in the selection of terms to be defined:

1. The term maintains some measure of its foreign orthography, pronunciation, or flavor. Put differently, the term has a widely recognized association with a specific non-English language or culture.
2. The term is freely and commonly used in English contexts; that is, it is employed by users of English as if it were part of their language.
3. The term, if originally specialized or technical, has become generalized in application or is from a field that attracts broad general interest (such as cookery or literature).

The first criterion is inclusive—many thousands more terms than are defined in this dictionary fit this description. When speaking or writing about another country or culture, it is natural if not necessary to use foreign words that describe things not naturally encountered in the experience of English speakers. Examples abound in the pages of many popular periodicals whenever they focus on foreign culture: Brazilian barbecue restaurants known as *churrascaria* (*National Geographic,* March 1987, p. 370); *palabas,* a Filipino word for ostentatiousness (*New York Review of Books,* June 11, 1987, p. 10); *makiwara,* a punching post used in karate training (*The Atlantic,* April 1987, p. 80). Many such uses are essential in their contexts but can be regarded as nonce words—not, as far as English is concerned, a customary part of the lexicon.

This leads to the second and third criteria, which are excluding or exclusive in nature. The constant intention of the editors was to create a dictionary that is essentially English, one containing words that are used in English contexts with some degree of naturalness or frequency, so that a wide-reading and curious English speaker likely to encounter them in English sources may use them. These criteria exclude highly technical or specialized terms of occasional interest mainly to experts or aficionados in certain fields. Also excluded were many words from widely studied languages—French, German, Italian, Spanish—that are of high frequency in those particular languages (and hence well known to anyone who has studied them), but not common in English.

We have tried to focus on those terms that are likely to be encountered, either in speech or in writing, by a person who is attuned to literature, culture, and society. We have included words borrowed from certain technical areas, such as cookery and music, on the grounds that these and other such areas are familiar to a broader audience than terms from, say, medieval philosophy and pharmacology.

We have avoided including the thousands of botanical and zoological taxonomic names, many based on Latin and Greek, as these were felt to be technical, of low frequency, and better covered by other sorts of dictionaries.

Also generally avoided were short quotations, mottoes, and proverbs (common in some collections of foreign expressions), as these were deemed to be outside our chosen area of focus.

## The Development of Borrowed Words

How do these words develop and grow in use so that they merit lexicographic attention? There are several ways. Perhaps most telling is the fact that many terms for conceptions, devices, institutions, and other products of culture are so closely associated with or well denoted by their "native" term that they can be only lamely, gracelessly, or verbosely expressed using English words. Examples of such words would be *cursus honorum, objet d'art,* and *Weltanschauung.* Literal translations of such terms into English simply do not carry the same connotations as the originals. English has traditionally been liberal in borrowing words from other languages, and speakers of English have had intimate (if not always peaceful) dealings with people in all quarters of the globe—factors that have led to the assimilation of such words into English.

Another, perhaps more subjective reason for the wide use of borrowed words in English has to do with simple vanity. Familiarity with a foreign culture and language, whether directly or through education, is taken by some as a mark of sophistication, refinement, even erudition. Terms from French and Italian (particularly the former) have been so used and exploited for centuries by speakers of English (and of other languages, as well). So, to address one's beloved as *mon cheri* or *bellissima* (with whom one might have an *intime* conversation), to speak familiarly (perhaps with an imitative pronunciation) of such things as *la dolce vita* and *vin de table,* to be able to use such terms as *raison d'être* and *poco a poco,* these are signs of one's background and character. Whether used pretentiously or, as often they can be, naturally and gracefully (out of an effort to find the *mot juste*), borrowed words impart a certain cachet to a conversation or passage, an air of the exotic and the cosmopolitan.

Certain words or phrases have survived because they capture, with economy and grace, a bit of the human condition. Such are:

> *embarras de richesses*
> *esprit d'escalier*
> *mutatis mutandis*

One would be hard pressed to capture the full sense of these phrases in pure English terms of equivalent pith and moment. Similar are expressions that, owing to their familiarity in certain contexts, are pregnant with (metaphorical) meaning, hence difficult to paraphrase:

> *papparazzo*
> *alma mater*
> *Realpolitik*

As borrowed words grow in general use and usefulness, they tend to become partially assimilated into their new language, such that they are subsumed into the new language's rules of pronunciation, syntax, and word formation. Words such as *data, criterion,* and *media* are used by some writers and speakers with scrupulous attention paid to their native singular or plural form. Are they any less English for this? How many native speakers of English would consider *finesse, venue, morgue,* or *naive* to be words borrowed from French? What are we to say about *cameo, macaroni, casino,* or *confetti,* from Italian? Is there any German-ness remaining in *kindergarten, kitsch,* or *zwieback? Smorgasbord* may retain a slight Swedish air for some, but can it be anything but English when shortened to *smorgie?* In English, *laissez-faire* is an adjective, usually hyphenated, the plural of *concerto* is *concertos,* and practically no one would nasalize the *os* in *bonbon.* Such is the result of assimilation. We could mention hundreds of other examples of words that are felt by some to be more or less assimilated, but by others to be totally foreign. Our selection has tended to be a bit open-ended, in that we have included terms such as *adobe, naïveté, aloha, de facto,* and *junta,* words that still bear some hint of their foreignness, though they are quite familiar and widely used in English. With such borderline cases, inclusion was based on a sense that a good proportion of potential users may attach specific cultural connotations to the terms.

*Borrowed Words and Cultural Influence*

The contributions of words assimilated from particular languages into English offer insights into cultural influence. Although a large percentage of American English speakers claim some German ancestry, the influx of German words is not nearly as great as that of terms from French. Reasons for this are difficult to argue scientifically, but we might surmise that the far greater contribution of French than German can be attributed to the following:

1. The direct infusion of Norman French into the English court, law, and manners
2. The long supremacy of French as the language of diplomacy worldwide (though now having given way to English)
3. The close ties with France in the history of the development of the North American continent
4. The remarkably large contribution of the French to Western culture in general—in lifestyle, fine and applied arts, cookery, wine, literature, fashion—far more influential than German culture in European-based societies

Latin, too, has contributed a great number of words to English, but the circumstances are notably different from the situation with French. Many of the Latin terms used in English, like *et cetera, bona fide, de facto, per diem,* and others, have been in use for centuries, but still seem to be recognized by most educated speakers as from Latin. Latin stands, of course, as a linguistic heritage common to much of Europe, and it was the *lingua franca* in the West into the seventeenth and eighteenth centuries. Its influence is long and deep, yet many of the terms Latin has contributed still seem unassimilated, like memorials graven in stone. No doubt the influence of Latin on the law—an area known for linguistic stability—can explain in part why Latin terms survive so long in their original form. Nor can we forget that Latin was the official language of the Roman Catholic church and its liturgy for many centuries. Latin, because of its associations, seems to have an aura of permanence and an air of solemnity. And it is precisely to evoke these qualities that English speakers make use of words borrowed from Latin.

The contributions of words from two other Romance languages, Italian and Spanish, are also significant, with certain areas of particular influence from each. Italian words are most notable in the realm of music, with a strong influx, too, from art and cookery—again, as with so many French words, fields of cultural sophistication.

Increasingly important, especially in American English, are contributions from Spanish, particularly Spanish-speaking America. True, many of the words from bullfighting can be said to be from Spain itself, but in other categories—cookery, dance and music, cattle ranching, and landscape and vegetation—entry was via Spanish colonial influence on America, especially the western and southwestern regions of the United States. A unique quality about the Spanish contribution is that the influence remains strong today and very likely will continue into the future, owing to the close relations of the United States with Hispanic countries and peoples. Indeed, Spanish is the second most common language among United States citizens (by a comfortable margin over French), and the continuing presence of Hispanic language and culture suggests that there may be an ever-growing number of borrowed Spanish words in the future.

## Style and General Features of the Dictionary

Each entry begins with the headword or entry word in boldface type, along with common alternate forms, if any. Thus, plural forms of nouns (labeled *pl.*), and gender-specific forms of nouns and adjectives (labeled *fem.* or *masc.*) are given for feminine and masculine forms in the headword, as are any other frequently used alternate forms.

The language of origin is shown in parentheses after each headword.

Where it was felt to be instructive or interesting, the literal meaning of the entry in its language of origin is shown in parentheses, preceding the definition(s).

To delineate specialized or technical terms and senses, restrictive labels, such as *Law*, *Cookery*, and *Music*, are frequently used, in each case immediately preceding the definition(s), with the label in italic type and followed by a period.

Each entry is defined according to its typical sense in English. In cases where multiple senses are clearly distinguishable, definitions are numbered. The great preponderance of borrowed words are phrasal elements or nouns, with quite a few adjectives and nouns that are used attributively. There is a smattering of other parts of speech, with verbs and prepositions being the rarest of all. Where essential for clarity, definitions are accompanied by a label for the part of speech (*n.* = noun; *adj.* = adjective; *adv.* = adverb; *interj.* = interjection; *v.* = verb; *conj.* = conjunction; *prep.* = preposition).

If a term used in a definition is in boldface type, that item is itself an entry in the dictionary, and the user may consult further under that entry.

Other features, found in many entries, are cross references, abbreviations, and alternative spellings.

Cross references are of two types. Some entries are simply cross references to another entry where a definition is given. In these, the headword is immediately followed by a period. The cross reference reads, "See [**other entry**]"; the user is directed to that entry for a definition. Another type of cross reference follows a full, defined entry and directs the user to another entry for further or related information. These cross references read "See also [**other entry**]."

Abbreviations are given for those entries where they apply. They are preceded by the label *Abbr.*, and the abbreviated form is shown in boldface type.

Please note that, as an added convenience, all abbreviations for borrowed words found in this dictionary have been compiled into a single alphabetic list, with reference to the fully spelled-out form for each. The List of Abbreviations follows this Preface.

Alternative spellings are shown in boldface type at the end of the entry or with the definition to which they apply. They are preceded by the word "Also." In most cases the differences are slight, involving a difference of a letter or the presence or absence of hyphens and diacritical marks.

Entries have been arranged and defined for simplicity and ease of use, with *usage in English* or *among English speakers* being the overriding principle. Alphabetic placement and definition are according to English usage. The standard practice in alphabetization is to ignore *all* articles, but in the case of borrowed words the editors felt that technicalities of foreign grammar are of little concern to an English speaker when trying to look up the term. Hence, the full entry for **La Belle Epoque,** for example, is in the *L*s, because that is the form of the term most often encountered in English contexts. In the interest of convenience, a cross reference to the full entry is also given in the *B*s, at **Belle Epoque, La,** serving those users who might first look there.

Alphabetic order is according to the standard English alphabet, using the letter-by-letter method. All words are shown with English spellings; items taken from languages that employ non-Roman alphabets have been transliterated.

One of the most obvious distinguishing features of many a borrowed word—often a strong suggestion that the term has not been fully assimilated—is the presence of diacritical marks. Use of diacritics is quite rare in English generally, so borrowed words that do have them tend to stand out. Aside from making this observation, we add that, in this dictionary, alphabetization involving diacritics is on the tried-and-true principle "Nothing precedes something." This means that of two words spelled identically, except for diacritics, the one *without* diacritics precedes the one *with* them.

For words taken from Latin, the post-classical convention of using *v* for consonantal *u* has been maintained throughout this dictionary. Also, *j* has generally been used for consonantal *i;* cross references are provided as needed. As for Latin word order, which is much freer than in English, words have been defined under their most common form, as determined by the editors. Thus, there is a definition at **jacta alea est;** for convenience, there are cross references to it from **alea jacta est** and **iacta alea est.**

Precedence has been given to senses as used in English, both in individual definitions and in the ordering of multiple senses. Thus, at **alma mater, maître d'hôtel,** and **sine qua non,** it is the English sense (frequently metaphorical) that is given prominence, with parenthetic reference to the literal meaning.

## Acknowledgments

Contributions to the completion of this project were from so many quarters that it is difficult to give them priority or even hope to duly thank each. The expertise with specific languages provided by our associate editors—David M. Glixon (Latin) and Emily Mitchell (French and Italian), and our assistant editors, Peter M. Gross (German), Pamela Korsmeyer (Spanish), and John Landry (French)—as well as their sound judgment and numerous additions, all were indispensable to the editorial effort. Their wealth of experience is reflected throughout these pages, as is their dedication and industry. Emily Mitchell is particularly to be noted for her significant editorial contributions in the critical closing months of the work. Jacquelyn Goodwin did the bulk of the keyboarding, coding, and corrections, diligently carrying on amid the difficulties of the manuscript, frequent deadlines, and the manifold eccentricities of the editors.

## Suggestions Welcome

A dictionary, however modest or narrowly defined its subject area, is a compilation of many thousands of bits of information from numerous sources, dependent on the technical and administrative talents of many for its success. But it is the judgment, experience, and human limitations of the editor that are manifest in the final product. Hence, responsibility for any errors on these pages must rest with the editor, who can only hope that the concept and presentation will prove valuable in general use. The comments and suggestions of users of this dictionary are welcome, with the further hope that such improvements as may be noted will see their way into future editions.

Frank R. Abate

# Abbreviations

The following abbreviations are used in the definitions:

| | | | |
|---|---|---|---|
| *Abbr.* | abbreviation | lit. | literal meaning |
| *adj.* | adjective | *masc.* | masculine form |
| *cap.* | with initial capital letter(s) | *n.* | noun |
| *conj.* | conjunction | *pl.* | plural form |
| *fem.* | feminine form | *prep.* | preposition |
| *interj.* | interjection | *sing.* | singular form |
| *l.c.* | with initial lower case letter(s) | *v.* | verb |

The following are common abbreviations for entries that are fully defined in the text:

**A.B.** See **Artium Baccalaureus.**

**ab ex.** See **ab extra.**

**ab init.** See **ab initio.**

**abs. feb.** See **absente febre.**

**abs. re.** See **absente reo.**

**A.C.** See **ante Christum.**

**a.c.** See **ante cibos.**

**A.D.** See **Anno Domini.**

**ad ex.** See **ad extremum.**

**ad inf.** See **ad infinitum.**

**ad int.** See **ad interim.**

**ad part. dolent.** See **ad partes dolentes.**

**ad val.** See **ad valorem.**

**aet., aetat.** See **anno aetatis suae.**

**Ag** See **argentum.**

**A.G.** See **Aktiengesellschaft.**

**a.h.c.** See **ad hanc vocem.**

**a.h.l.** See **ad hunc locem.**

**A.H.** See **Anno Hebraico.**

**A.H.** See **Anno Hegirae.**

A.H.S.   See Anno Humanae Salutis.

A.L.   See Anno Lucis.

alt. hor.   See alternis horis.

A.M.   See Anno Mundi.

a.m.; A.M.   See ante meridiem.

A.M.   See Artium Magister.

A.M.D.G.   See ad majorem Dei gloriam.

A.O.C.   See appellation d'origine contrôlée.

A.R.   See Anno Regni.

Au   See aurum.

A.U.C.   See ab urbe condita.

B.A.   See Baccalaureus Artium.

b.i.d.   See bis in die.

c.   See circa.

Cantab.   See Cantabrigiensis.

cant.   See cantoris.

cf.   See confer.

cito disp!   See cito dispensetur!

Cu   See cuprum.

cum div.   See cum dividendo.

C.V.   See curriculum vitae.

D.D.   See Doctor Divinitatis.

dec.   See decani.

D.F.   See Distrito Federal.

dieb. alt.   See diebus alternis.

dieb. secund.   See diebus secundis.

DIN   See Deutsche Industrie-Norm.

div.   See divisi.

D.O.   See denominaciones del origen.

D.O.C.   See denominazione di origine controllata.

D.O.M.   See Domino Optimo Maximo.

D.V.   See Deo volente.

e.g.   See exempli gratia.

et al.   See et alii.

etc.   See et cetera.

et seq.; et seqq.; et sqq.   See et sequentia.

et ux.   See et uxor.

excud.   See excudit.

ex div.   See ex dividendo.

f.   See forte.

Fe   See ferrum.

fec.   See fecit.

ff.   See forte forte.

fl.   See floruit.

fp.   See forte-piano.

f.v.   See folio verso.

fz.   See forzando.

GmbH   See Gesellschaft mit beschränkter Haftung.

GT   See gran turismo.

h.c.   See hors concours.

Hg   See hydrargyrum.

h.s.   See hora somni.

ibid.   See ibidem.

i.c.   See inter cibos.

id.   See idem.

i.e.   See id est.

I.H.S.   See Iesus Hominum Salvator.

imp.   See imperator.

infra dig.   See infra dignitatem.

in pr.   See in principio.

I.N.R.I.   See Iesus Nazarenus Rex Iudaeorum.

J.D.   See Juris Doctor.

J.U.D.   See Juris Utriusque Doctor.

ktl.   See kai ta loipa.

Litt. D.   See Litterarum Doctor.

loc. cit.   See loco citato.

loq.   See loquitur.

L.S.   See locus sigilli.

m.   See mane.

M.A.   See Magister Artium.
m.d.   See mano destra.
M.D.   See Medicinae Doctor.
mf.   See mezzo forte.
m.o.   See modus operandi.
mod.   See moderato.
more dict.; mor.dict.   See more
dictu.
mp.   See mezzo piano.
m.s.p.   See mortuus sine prole.
Na   See natrium.
n.b.; N.B.   See nota bene.
nem. con.   See nemine contradicente.
nem. diss.   See nemine dissentiente.
n. et m.   See nocte et mane.
n.l.   See non liquet.
noct.   See nocte.
nol. pros.   See nolle prosequi.
non cul.   See non culpabilis.
non pros.   See non prosequitur.
non rep.   See non repetatur.
non seq.   See non sequitur.
ob.   See obiit.
omn. hor.   See omni hora.
omn. man.   See omni mane.
op. cit.   See opere citato.
o.s.p.   See obiit sine prole.
Oxon.   See Oxoniensis.
p.   See partim.
p.   See piano.
p.a.; per an.   See per annum.
Pb   See plumbum.
p.c.   See post cibos.
pf.   See pianoforte.
Ph.D   See Philosophiae Doctor.
pinx.   See pinxit.
p.m.; P.M.   See post meridiem.
p.o.   See per os.

p.p.   See per procurationem.
pp.   See pianissimo.
p.r.n.   See pro re nata.
pro et con.   See pro et contra.
pro tem.   See pro tempore.
prox.   See proximo.
P.S.   See post scriptum.
pt.   See perstetur.
PX.   See Pedro Ximénez.
q.; qq.   See quisque.
Q.E.D.   See quod erat demonstrandum.
Q.E.F.   See quod erat
faciendum.
q.i.d.   See quater in die.
q.l.; q. lib.   See quantum libet.
q. pl.; q.p.   See quantum placet.
qq. hor.   See quaque hora.
q.s.; quant. suff.   See quantum
sufficit.
quot. op. sit   See quoties opus
sit.
q.v.   See quod vide.
q.v., qq.v.   See quae vide.
ren. sem.   See renovetur semel.
rept.   See repetatur.
R.I.P.   See requiescat in pace.
R.S.V.P.   See répondez, s'il vous
plaît.
S.A.   See Société Anonyme.
S.A.   See Sturmabteilung.
s.a.   See sub anno.
Sb   See stibium.
sc.   See scilicet.
s.d.   See sine die.
seq.   See sequens.
sesquih.   See sesquihora.
sf.   See sforzando.
s.l.a.n.   See sine loco, anno, vel
nomine.

**s.l.p.**   See sine legitima prole.

**smorz.**   See smorzando.

**s.n.**   See sine nomine.

**Sn**   See stannum.

**s.o.s.**   See si opus sit.

**s.p.**   See sine prole.

**S.P.Q.R.**   See Senatus Populusque Romanus.

**Sr.**   See señor.

**Sra.**   See señora.

**Srta.**   See señorita.

**S.S.**   See Schutzstaffel.

**ss.**   See semis.

**stat.**   See statim.

**s.v.**   See sub verbo.

**S.V.P.**   See s'il vous plaît.

**TGV**   See train à grande vitesse.

**t.i.d.**   See ter in die.

**trid.**   See triduum.

**ult.**   See ultime.

**ult.; ulto.**   See ultimo.

**u.s.**   See ubi supra.

**usw.**   See und so weiter.

**V.D.M.**   See Verbi Dei Minister.

**verb(um) sap.; verb(um) sat.**   See
verbum sapienti sat(is) est.

**vesp.**   See vespera.

**viz.**   See videlicet.

**vox pop.**   See vox populi.

**z.B.**   See zum Beispiel.

# DICTIONARY OF BORROWED WORDS

# A

**aba** (Arabic)   1. a fabric of camel's or goat's hair.   2. a sleeveless outer garment made of this fabric or of silk.  Also **abba**.

**ab absurdo** (Latin)   *Geometry*.  from the absurd.

**ab actu ad posse valet illatio** (Latin)   inference from what has happened to what will happen is valid.

**abaculus** (Latin)   a small tile used in mosaics.

**abaissé** (French)   lowered; reduced.

**abajo** (Spanish)   down; downwards; below.

**abandon, à l'**.   See à l'abandon.

**abanico** (Spanish)   a fan.

**à bas . . .** (French)   (lit., 'to the bottom')  down with . . . .

**ab asino lanam** (Latin)   (lit., 'wool from an ass')  equivalent to *(get) blood from a stone*.

**abat-jour** (French)   a device, such as a reflector or skylight, that allows daylight to enter an interior space.

**abat-sons** (French)   a device for deflecting sound, such as a louver in a belfry.

**abattis** (French)   giblets.  Also **abatis**.

**abattoir** (French)   a slaughterhouse.

**abat-vent** (French)   a device that deflects wind without preventing the passage of air or sound.

**abat-voix** (French)   a sound reflector, as behind a band stand.

**abbacchio** (Italian)   baby lamb.

**abbadia** (Italian)   *Architecture*.  an abbey church.  Also **badia**.

**abbandonatamente** (Italian)   *Music*.  passionately.

**abbandone** *or* **abbandono, con**.   See **con abbandone**.

**abbandonevolmente** (Italian)   *Music*.  unrestrainedly.

**abbandono** (Italian)   (lit., 'abandon')  *Music*.  an impassioned, free style.

**abbé** (French)   an abbott; priest.

**abboccato** (Italian)   sweet or semisweet, often applied to **Orvieto** wine.

3

**Abend** (German)   evening.
**Abendlied** (German)   *Music.* evening song.
**a beneplacito** (Italian)    *Music.* at the will or pleasure of the performer.
   See also **beneplacimento**.
**Aberglaube** (German)    belief in things beyond experience; superstition.
**abesse** (Latin)   (to be) absent.
**ab extra** (Latin)   from outside; from without. *Abbr.* **ab ex.**
**à bientôt** (French)    see you soon!
**abilità, aria d'.** (Italian)    See **aria d'abilità.**
**ab imo pectore** (Latin)   from the depths of the heart. Also **imo pectore.**
**ab inconvenienti** (Latin)   (lit., 'from the inconvenience')  *Law.* used to
   state that a position is untenable because of the hardship or inconvenience
   it would create.
**ab incunabulis** (Latin)   from infancy.
**ab initio** (Latin)   from the beginning. *Abbr.* **ab init.**
**ab integro** (Latin)   (starting) anew or afresh.
**ab intestato** (Latin)   *Law.* from a person who died intestate (without a
   will).
**ab intra** (Latin)   from inside; from within.
**Ablaut** (German)   *Linguistics.* vowel variation or gradation, as seen in
   different forms of certain verbs in  Indo-European languages.
**ab officio et beneficio** (Latin)   (suspension) from duties and remunera-
   tion.
**à bon compte.**   See **à bon marché.**
**à bon droit** (French)    with good reason; justifiably.
**à bon marché** (French)    at a bargain price; cheaply. Also **à bon compte.**
   See also **bon marché.**
**à bonne raison** (French)    with good reason.
**ab origine** (Latin)   from the beginning or origin of something; from the
   creation of the world.
**abortus** (Latin)   something aborted.
**à bouche ouverte** (French)   (lit., 'with mouth open') over-eager; gullible.
**ab ovo** (Latin)   (lit., 'from the egg') from the very beginning.
**ab ovo usque ad mala** (Latin)   (lit., 'from the egg right up to the apple')
   from the very beginning through to the very end (alluding to the typical
   first and final courses at a Roman banquet); equivalent to *from soup to
   nuts.*
**à bras ouverts** (French)   (lit., 'with open arms')  cordially.
**abrazo** (Spanish)   an embrace; hug.
**abri, à l'.**   See **à l'abri.**
**abricot** (French)   apricot.

4

**abruzzese** (Italian)    designating something, as a song or dance, in the style of the Abruzzi mountain region.

**abruzzese, all'.**    See all'abruzzese.

**absence d'esprit** (French)    absentmindedness.

**absente febre** (Latin)    *Medicine.* when fever is absent. *Abbr.* **abs. feb.**

**absente reo** (Latin)    *Law.* with the defendant absent. *Abbr.* **abs. re.**

**absit invidia** (Latin)    may there be no ill feeling (used as a formal apology).

**absit omen** (Latin)    may this be no omen (alluding to the superstition that the mere mention of some evil may help to bring it on).

**absolvo te** (Latin)    (lit., 'I absolve you') *Roman Catholicism.* the formal declaration of absolution from sins, as given by a priest.

**absque hoc** (Latin)    *Law.* without this (fact).

**ab uno disce omnes** (Latin)    from (this) one thing learn all.

**ab urbe condita** (Latin)    from the founding of the city, especially in reference to Rome; used by Romans as the starting point of an era for calculating dates. The traditional date of the founding of Rome is 753 B.C. *Abbr.* **A.U.C.**

**a capite ad calcem** (Latin)    (lit., 'from head to heel') from head to toe.

**a cappella** (Italian)    *Music.* **1.** unaccompanied.    **2.** in the style of old church music. Also **a capella; alla capella; alla cappella.**

**a capriccio** (Italian)    *Music.* according to the fancy of the performer.

**acariâtre** (French)    irritable; petulant.

**accarezzevolmente** (Italian)    *Music.* caressingly.

**accelerando** (Italian)    *Music.* quickening the tempo gradually.

**accent aigu** (French)    a diacritical mark (´) over the letter *e* in many French words, indicating that the sound is close; the acute accent.

**accent circonflexe** (French)    a diacritical mark (ˆ) over a vowel in many French words, indicating that the sound is long and of a certain quality; the circumflex accent.

**accent grave** (French)    a diacritical mark (`) over a vowel in many French words, indicating that the sound is of a certain quality; the grave accent.

**accentué** (French)    accented; emphasized.

**accentus** (Latin)    *Church music.* the part of the traditional liturgy of the Mass that is chanted by the celebrant alone. See also **concentus.**

**accessit** (Latin)    (lit., 'he (*or* she) came close') said of a runner-up in an academic competition. Also **proxime accessit** ('he (*or* she) came nearest').

**acciaccatura** (Italian)    (lit., 'bruise') *Music.* a short grace note.

**accidenti!** (Italian)    damn!; I'll be damned! (an expression of aggravation or annoyance).

**accipe hoc** (Latin)    take this.

**acciuga,** *pl.* **acciughe** (Italian)    an anchovy.

**accompagnamento** (Italian)    *Music.* accompaniment.

**accordamento** (Italian)    (lit., 'agreement; concordance') *Music.* in tune.

**accouchement** (French)    1. childbirth. 2. confinement owing to child-birth.

**accoucheur,** *fem.* **accoucheuse** (French)    one who assists at childbirth; an obstetrician; (*fem.*) midwife.

**accrescendo** (Italian)    *Music.* increasing; building up of sound.

**aceite** (Spanish)    oil.

**aceituna** (Spanish)    olive.

**acequia** (Spanish)    an irrigation ditch or canal. Also **asequia, cequia, zequia.**

**acequia madre** (Spanish)    main irrigation canal, usually the property and responsibility of a community.

**aceto** (Italian)    vinegar.

**aceto balsamico** (Italian)    an aged wine vinegar made in Modena.

**acetum** (Latin)    vinegar.

**acetum Italum** (Latin)    (lit., 'Italic vinegar') the characteristically harsh, biting wit of the Romans. See also **sal Atticum.**

**à chacun son goût** (French)    (lit., 'to each his own taste') to each his own. Also **chacun à son goût.**

**achar** (Persian)    a type of salty relish or condiment.

**à cheval** (French)    on horseback.

**acht** (German)    eight.

**Achtelnote** (German)    *Music.* eighth-note.

**Achtung** (German)    attention!

**acini di pepe** (Italian)    a granular **pasta** used in soups.

**a cinque** (Italian)    *Music.* for five voices or instruments.

**à coeur ouvert** (French)    with open heart; generously.

**à compte** (French)    on account; in partial payment.

**à contre coeur** (French)    reluctantly; against better judgement.

**à corps perdu** (French)    (lit., 'with body lost') with abandon; desperately.

**à couvert** (French)    under cover; sheltered.

**âcre** (French)    sour; tart; bitter.

**a cruce salus** (Latin)    *Christianity.* salvation (comes) from the cross.

**acta** (Latin)    deeds; used in ancient Rome of an account of actions or achievements.

**acte gratuit** (French)    an impulsive act with no apparent cause.

**actum est** (Latin)    it is done; it is all over.

**actus** (Latin)    *Drama.* act.

**actus curiae** (Latin)    *Law.* act of the court.

**actus Dei** (Latin)    act of God.

**actus purus** (Latin)   *Thomistic philosophy.*  Aquinas' concept of God as pure act, without matter or form.

**acus** (Latin)   needle.

**acushla** (Irish)   dearest; darling (a term of endearment).  Also **macushla.**

**ad absurdum.**   See **argumentum ad absurdum.**

**adage** (French)   *Ballet.*  1. a series of exercises performed to a slow musical tempo.  2. a portion of a **pas de deux** in which a ballerina performs various maneuvers while supported by her male partner.

**adagio** (Italian)   *Music.*  1. *n.* a slow movement.   2. *adv.* slowly; leisurely.   3. *Ballet.* a designation for a slow dance.

**adagissimo** (Italian)   *Music.* extremely slow.

**ad annum** (Latin)   up to the year (used with a specific date).

**ad arbitrium** (Latin)   at will; as one pleases.

**ad astra** (Latin)   to the stars.

**ad astra per ardua.**   See **per ardua ad astra.**

**ad astra per aspera.**   See **per aspera ad astra.**

**a datu** (Latin)   from the date.

**ad baculum.**   See **argumentum ad baculum.**

**ad captandam benevolentiam** (Latin)   for the purpose of winning good will.

**ad captandum** (Latin)   for the purpose of pleasing.

**ad captandum vulgus** (Latin)   for the purpose of pleasing the common people; to win the favor of the masses.

**ad cruminam** *or* **crumenam.**   See **argumentum ad cruminam.**

**addendum,** *pl.* **addenda** (Latin)   something to be added on.

**ad Deum** (Latin)   (lit., 'towards God')  *Christian ritual.* facing the altar with one's back to the congregation (said of the celebrant).  See also **ad hominem, 2.**

**addio** (Italian)   farewell.

**additum** (Latin)   something added.

**à demi** (French)   half; in part.

**a Deo et rege** (Latin)   from God and the king.

**à dessein** (French)   by design; on purpose.

**Adeste Fideles** (Latin)   title of a popular Christmas carol; English version is "O Come, All Ye Faithful."

**ad eundem** (Latin)   to the same (degree); of equivalent value.

**adeus** (Portuguese)   goodbye.

**à deux** (French)   for two; two at a time.

**à deux mains** (French)   *Music.* played with two hands.

**ad extra** (Latin)   in an outward direction.

7

**ad extremum** (Latin) **1.** at last; finally. **2.** to the last; to the point of death. *Abbr.* **ad ex.**

**ad fidem** (Latin) in allegiance.

**ad finem** (Latin) to the (very) end.

**ad gloriam** (Latin) for glory.

**ad gustum** (Latin) *Cookery.* to one's taste.

**ad hanc vocem** (Latin) at this word. *Abbr.* **a.h.c.**

**ad hoc** (Latin) (lit., 'for this') for a specific purpose or occasion (used of temporary committees appointed to accomplish a set task).

**ad hominem** (Latin) (lit., '(directed) to the man') **1.** maliciously critical; directed at a person's character, not his logic or record. **2.** *Christian ritual.* standing behind the altar and facing the congregation (said of the celebrant). See also **ad deum**.

**ad horrorem** (Latin) to the point of horror.

**ad hunc locem** (Latin) to this place. *Abbr.* **a.h.l.**

**ad idem** (Latin) *Law.* to the same (point or effect).

**a die datus** (Latin) dated from a certain day.

**adieu** (French) goodbye; farewell.

**ad ignorantiam.** See **argumentum ad ignorantiam**.

**ad infinitum** (Latin) to infinity; endlessly. *Abbr.* **ad inf.** Also **in infinitum**.

**ad initium** (Latin) at the beginning. *Abbr.* **ad init.**

**ad instar** (Latin) like; after the fashion of.

**ad interim** (Latin) for the meantime; meanwhile. *Abbr.* **ad int.**

**a Dio** (Spanish) an exclamation, similar to *for God's sake*, to indicate surprise, disgust, etc.

**adiós** (Spanish) goodbye.

**adiratamente** (Italian) *Music.* angrily; furiously.

**à discrétion** (French) with discretion.

**ad judicium.** See **argumentum ad judicium**.

**adjuvante Deo** (Latin) with God's favor or help.

**ad Kalendas Graecas** (Latin) until the Greek Calends, that is, never (*Calends* being a Roman convention for dating).

**ad libitum** (Latin) at will; as one wishes. *Abbr.* **ad lib.**

**ad litem** (Latin) *Law.* for the suit (said, for instance, of a guardian appointed to represent someone incapable of acting for himself).

**ad lit(t)eram** (Latin) to the letter; literally.

**ad locum** (Latin) at the place (indicated).

**ad majorem Dei gloriam** (Latin) to the greater glory of God (motto of the Jesuit order). *Abbr.* **A.M.D.G.**

**ad manum** (Latin) at hand.

**ad misericordiam.**  See **argumentum ad misericordiam.**

**ad modum** (Latin)  after the manner of.

**ad nauseam** (Latin)  to the point of disgust or nausea (said of something that goes on too long).

**adobe** (Spanish)  **1.** bricks made of sun-dried clay.  **2.** buildings made of this construction material.

**ad oculos** (Latin)  before one's eyes.

**Adonai** (Hebrew)  the Lord; God.

**Adon Olam** (Hebrew)  (lit., 'Lord of the world') *Judaism.* a prayer expressing the faith of Israel in God.

**ad partes dolentes** (Latin)  *Prescriptions.* to the painful parts. *Abbr.* **ad part. dolent.**

**ad patres** (Latin)  (lit., 'to the (fore)fathers') to the ancestors; to the dead.

**ad populum.**  See **argumentum ad populum.**

**ad quem** (Latin)  to whom; to which (point).

**ad quod** (Latin)  to which place or point.

**ad rem** (Latin)  to the matter at hand; to the point.

**adriatico, dell'.**  See **dell'adriatico.**

**à droite** (French)  to the right; on the right.

**adsum** (Latin)  I am here; present (response to a roll call).

**ad summam** (Latin)  in short; in sum.

**ad summum** (Latin)  at most.

**a due** (Italian)  *Music.* for two parts in unison.

**ad unguem** (Latin)  (lit., '(down) to the fingernail') to the minutest detail.

**ad usum** (Latin)  according to custom.

**ad utrumque paratus** (Latin)  prepared for either alternative.

**ad valorem** (Latin)  according to value (used especially of taxes levied on the basis of the stated value of goods). *Abbr.* **ad val.**

**ad verbum** (Latin)  to the word; verbatim.

**adversa** (Latin)  things noted.

**adversaria** (Latin)  notes; random comments.

**ad vitam** (Latin)  for life.

**ad vivum** (Latin)  to the living.

**advocatus diaboli** (Latin)  *Roman Catholicism.* the devil's advocate, the official appointed to the task of finding objections to a proposed canonization. Also called **promotor fidei.**

**aequisonae voces** (Latin)  *Music.* tones and their octaves.

**aequo animo** (Latin)  with an even temper; with equanimity.

**aere perennius.**  See **exegi monumentum aere perennius.**

**aes alienum** (Latin)  debt; borrowed money.

**aetate.**  See **anno aetatis suae.**

9

**aetatis suae.** See **anno aetatis suae.**

**affabile** (Italian) *Music.* in a gentle manner.

**affaire d'amour** (French) a love affair.

**affaire de coeur** (French) (lit., 'affair of the heart') a matter involving deep emotion; a love affair.

**affaire d'honneur** (French) (lit., 'affair of honor') a duel.

**affaire flambée** (French) (lit., 'a burned affair') 1. a ruined love affair. 2. an unsuccessful business deal.

**Affektenlehre** (German) *Music.* doctrine of aesthetics.

**affettivo** (Italian) *Music.* causing emotion; affecting.

**affetto, con.** See **con affetto.**

**affettuoso,** *fem.* **affettuosa** (Italian) *Music.* with warmth. Also **affetuoso.**

**affiche** (French) a poster; public notice.

**afflatus** (Latin) inspiration.

**affrettando** (Italian) *Music.* hurrying.

**aficionado** (Spanish) a devoted and knowledgeable follower of a particular activity or pastime.

**afikomen** (Hebrew) *Judaism.* a piece of **matzoh** broken off by the leader of a **Seder,** later hidden to be searched for by the children present.

**à fond** (French) to the bottom; thoroughly.

**a fortiori** (Latin) with stronger reason; with all the more certainty.

**aga** (Turkish) 1. a title of honor, equivalent to *lord.* 2. a Turkish general. Also **agha.**

**agal** (Arabic) the cord that is tied around the head to hold the **kaffiyeh** in place.

**agapē** (Greek) 1. unselfish, brotherly love. 2. *Christianity.* the love of Christ for mankind. 3. a meal of fellowship; love feast.

**à gauche** (French) to the left; on the left.

**agent provocateur** (French) a secret agent hired to lure an unsuspecting person into committing a crime.

**ager publicus** (Latin) public land; public domain.

**agevole** (Italian) *Music.* easily; lightly.

**Aggadah** (Hebrew) *Judaism.* the nonlegal or narrative background material of the **Talmud** and other rabbinical literature, as distinct from the legal material of the **Halakah.** Also **Aggada.** See also **Haggadah.**

**aggio** (Italian) a fee or premium paid for the exchange of currency. Also **agio.**

**aggiornamento** (Italian) modernization; a bringing up-to-date.

**aggiunta, aria.** See **aria aggiunta.**

**agha.** See **aga.**

**agilità** (Italian)　　*Music.* speed and skill in execution.

**agilità, aria d'.**　　See **aria d'abilità.**

**agio.**　　See **aggio.**

**agiotage** (French)　　1. foreign exchange dealing. 2. speculation.

**agitato** (Italian)　　*Music.* fast and with agitation.

**aglio** (Italian)　　garlic.

**agneau** (French)　　lamb.

**agneau du printemps** (French)　　spring lamb.

**agnello** (Italian)　　lamb.

**agnellotti** (Italian)　　*Cookery.* dumplings stuffed with meat or herbs. Also **agnolotti.**

**agnomen** (Latin)　　nickname.

**Agnus Dei** (Latin)　　*Christian liturgy.* Lamb of God, a metaphor for the Savior; the first words of a prayer in the liturgy of the Mass.

**à gogo** (French)　　to your heart's content (especially popular in the 1960s in the names of nightclubs and **discothèques**).

**agon** (Greek)　　(lit., 'contest')　1. a public competition of ancient Greece in athletics, drama, music, etc. 2. *Greek drama.* a formal debate between two characters. 3. *Literature.* a conflict between two characters, especially the protagonist and the antagonist.

**agora** (Greek)　　the public square or central market place of an ancient Greek city.

**agostadero** (Spanish)　　pasture land; open prairie.

**à grand choeur** (French)　　*Music.* in full chorus; in full song.

**à grand orchestre** (French)　　*Music.* with full orchestra.

**à grands frais** (French)　　at great expense.

**agréable** (French)　　agreeable; pleasant.

**agréation** (French)　　*Diplomacy.* a procedure through which a government determines the acceptability of a proposed envoy. See also **agrément, 3.**

**agréé** (French)　　a lawyer.

**agrégation** (French)　　an admission to a fellowship after an examination.

**agrégé** (French)　　a degree awarded by a French university after a competitive examination qualifying the recipient for certain teaching positions.

**agrément** (French)　　1. agreeability; charm; pleasantness. 2. **agréments,** *pl. Music.* grace notes. Also **agremens.** 3. *Diplomacy.* official government approval of a proposed envoy from a foreign government. See also **agréation.**

**agua** (Spanish)　　water.

**agua caliente** (Spanish)　　hot water.

**aguada** (Spanish)　　a watering hole; water supply.

11

**agua fría** (Spanish)   cold water.

**aguardiente** (Spanish)   (lit., 'burning water') any of several colorless alcoholic beverages, especially anisette or rum. Also **aquardiente.**

**à haute voix** (French)   with a loud voice; at the top of one's lungs.

**ahimsa** (Sanskrit)   *Hinduism.* the principle of nonviolence and sacredness of life.

**ahora** (Spanish)   now.

**à huis clos** (French)   behind closed doors; **in camera.**

**aide de camp** (French)   a confidential assistant, especially to a military commander. Also **aide-de-camp.**

**aide mémoire** (French)   1. an aid to memory; mnemonic. 2. a memorandum. Also **aide-memoire.**

**ai ferri** (Italian)   (lit., 'on the iron') broiled; grilled. Also **alla griglia.**

**aigre-doux** (French)   sweet-and-sour; bittersweet.

**aigrette** (French)   egret.

**aigu** (French)   1. *Music.* high-pitched; shrill. 2. acute; pointed. See also **accent aigu.**

**aiguière** (French)   ewer.

**aiguille** (French)   (lit., 'needle') 1. *Geology.* a needlelike rock formation. 2. a tool for making holes in stone.

**aiguillette** (French)   1. an ornamental braid, as that on a military uniform; aglet. 2. *Cookery.* long, thin strips of meat, especially from a breast of fowl.

**ailes de pigeons** (French)   (lit., 'wings of pigeons') *Ballet.* a step in which a dancer leaps and flutters the legs.

**aimable** (French)   likable.

**aimé,** *fem.* **aimée** (French) loved; beloved.

**aîné,** *fem.* **aînée** (French)   elder; eldest.

**air à boire** (French)   a drinking song.

**air détaché** (French)   *Music.* a single melody extracted from an opera or symphony.

**air, en l'.**   See **en l'air.**

**air varié** (French)   *Music.* a melody with variations; an ornamental or elaborate melody.

**ajarcara** (Spanish)   *Architecture.* decorative brick relief.

**ají** (Spanish)   chile pepper.

**ajo** (Spanish)   garlic.

**à jour** (French)   decorated with an openwork pattern, as embroidery.

**ajutage** (French)   the nozzle of a water fountain.

**Aktiengesellschaft** (German)   a joint-stock company; corporation. *Abbr.* **A.G.**

**akvavit** (Scandinavian)    a dry, distilled spirit flavored with caraway seeds. Also **aquavit.**

**à la . . .** (French)    in the style of . . . .

**à l'abandon** (French)    with abandon; recklessly.

**à la belle étoile** (French)    outdoors, as in referring to sleeping outdoors.

**à la boitelle** (French)    *Cookery.* cooked with mushrooms.

**à la bonne heure** (French)    (lit., 'at the right moment') great!; good!

**à la bordelaise** (French)    *Cookery.* designating a manner of preparation in which **Bordeaux** wine is a chief ingredient.

**à la bourgeoise** (French)    in middle-class fashion.

**à l'abri** (French)    take cover!

**à la broche.**    See **en brochette.**

**à la campagnarde** (French)    in country style; in rustic fashion.

**à la campagne** (French)    in the country; rustic.

**à la carte** (French)    (lit., 'according to the bill of fare') designating restaurant dishes that are served and priced separately, not part of a fixed-course order.    See also **prix fixe; table d'hôte.**

**à la chinoise** (French)    in the Chinese manner.

**à la créole** (French)    (lit., 'in Creole style') *Cookery.* prepared with rice and Creole-style seasonings.

**à la diable** (French)    *Cookery.* deviled or highly seasoned.

**à la fin** (French)    at last; finally; in the end.

**à la forestière** (French)    *Cookery.* prepared with mushrooms, bacon, and diced potatoes.

**à la française** (French)    in the French manner or according to French custom.

**à la grecque** (French)    in the Greek style or fashion.

**à la hollandaise** (French)    (lit., 'in the manner of Holland') *Cookery.* prepared with a rich sauce made of butter, eggs, lemon juice, and seasonings.

**à la jardinière** (French)    *Cookery.* prepared with a garnish of vegetables.

**alalá** (Spanish)    *Music.* folk music of northern Spain.

**à la maison** (French)    *Cookery.* in the house style.

**à la maître d'hôtel** (French)    *Cookery.* prepared with a seasoned butter sauce containing parsley, lemon juice, salt, and pepper.

**à la marengo** (French)    *Cookery.* designating a style of preparation in which meat is browned in oil and cooked with mushrooms, tomatoes, garlic, and wine or brandy.

**alambrado** (Spanish)    *Wine.* a wine bottle wrapped in open wire netting, a procedure used with high quality wines.

**alameda** (Spanish)    **1.** a cottonwood grove; poplar grove.    **2.** a road or path lined with these trees.

**à l'américaine** (French)    (lit., 'in American fashion') *Cookery.* designating a particular manner of preparation, as in *lobster à la américaine.* See also à l'amoricaine.

**à la militaire** (French)    in military fashion; disciplined; soldierly.

**álamo** (Spanish)    the cottonwood or poplar tree.

**à la mode** (French)    (lit., 'according to the fashion') 1. *Cookery.* designating a dessert, especially pie, served with ice cream. 2. in style; fashionable.

**à l'amoricaine** (French)    (lit., 'in the manner of Brittany') *Cookery.* served with a sauce of white wine, tomatoes, shallots, and cognac. A̦o (by corruption) à l'américaine.

**à la napolitaine** (French)    *Cookery.* in the Neapolitan style, especially designating desserts served with ice cream of various flavors and colors.

**à l'ancienne** (French)    in an old fashioned or traditional manner.

**à l'anglaise** (French)    1. in the manner of the English. 2. *Cookery.* prepared by cooking in water or stock.

**à la parisienne** (French)    1. in the manner of Parisians; Parisian. 2. *Cookery.* designating a style of preparatiion for potatoes, boiled in stock and served garnished with parsley.

**à la pointe d'archet** (French)    *Music.* with the point of the bow, in playing a violin, viola, etc.

**à la printanière** (French)    *Cookery.* garnished with spring vegetables.

**à la provençale** (French)    (lit., 'in the style of Provence') *Cookery.* designating preparations that feature garlic or garlic and tomato.

**à la régalade** (French)    designating a manner of drinking from a bottle in which the liquid is poured directly into the mouth without the bottle touching the lips.

**à la rigueur** (French)    in a rigorous way; harshly; severely.

**à la russe** (French)    in the Russian style or fashion.

**à la seconde** (French)    *Ballet.* referring to a movement carried into the second position.

**à la sourdine** (French)    in a stealthy way; secretly.

**à la suédoise** (French)    in the Swedish style or fashion.

**à la suisse** (French)    in the Swiss style or fashion.

**à la vapeur** (French)    steamed.

**à la viennoise** (French)    in the Viennese style or fashion.

**à la villageoise** (French)    in the village fashion; rustically.

**albariño** (Spanish)    a variety of dry, white wine produced in Galicia in northwestern Spain.

**alberca** (Spanish)    a water hole; pond; cistern.

**albergo** (Italian)    a hotel; an inn.

**alborada** (Spanish)    1. dawn. 2. serenade at dawn.

**alcalde** (Spanish)　mayor; justice of the peace.

**alcázar** (Spanish)　a fortified castle or stronghold, especially of the Spanish Moors.

**al dente** (Italian)　*Cookery.* firm to the bite, used especially to describe the state of doneness for boiled pasta.

**alea jacta est.**　See **jacta alea est.**

**aleichem shalom** (Hebrew)　(lit., 'peace to you') a traditional Jewish expression of greeting, used in reply to **shalom aleichem.**

**Alella** (Spanish)　a wine district near Barcelona in northeastern Spain.

**à l'espagnole** (French)　in the Spanish style or fashion.

**à l'estragon** (French)　flavored with tarragon.

**à l'étuvée** (French)　stewed.

**à l'extérieur** (French)　on the outside or exterior.

**à l'extrémité** (French)　at the extreme; at the final point.

**al fine.**　See **alla fine.**

**alforjas** (Spanish)　saddle bags.

**al forno** (Italian)　(lit., 'in the oven') baked.

**al fresco** (Italian)　out of doors; in the open air.

**alguacil** (Spanish)　constable; bailiff; law enforcement officer.

**Alhambra** (Spanish)　a Moorish palace and fortification in Granada, Spain.

**alhuana** (Spanish)　*Architecture.* a niche; recessed space.

**à l'huile** (French)　in oil; cooked or packed in oil.

**Alianza para Progreso** (Spanish)　The Alliance for Progress, an initiative of the Kennedy administration for economic development in Latin America.

**alias dictus** (Latin)　otherwise called; alias.

**alieni generis** (Latin)　of another sort. See also **sui generis.**

**alieni juris** (Latin)　*Law.* under another's authority (said of a minor or ward). See also **sui juris.**

**alimenta** (Latin)　food; means of support.

**à l'impromptu** (French)　at a moment's notice; suddenly; without rehearsal.

**à l'improviste** (French)　without warning; unexpectedly.

**à l'intérieur** (French)　on the inside; within.

**aliquando bonus dormitat Homerus** (Latin)　(lit., 'sometimes even good Homer nods') even the greatest occasionally lose their mastery (from Horace, *Ars Poetica* 359).

**à l'irlandaise** (French)　in the Irish style or fashion.

**alis volat propriis** (Latin)　it flies on its own wings (motto of Oregon).

**à l'italienne** (French)　in the Italian style or fashion.

**aliud et idem** (Latin)　other and yet the same; the same thing but in a different light.

15

**aliunde** (Latin)   from elsewhere.

**aliyah** (Hebrew)   *Judaism*. the act of going up to the reading table during a synagogue service to read the blessing or recite from the **Torah**.

**alla bolognese** (Italian)   1. the style of Bologna.   2. *Cookery*. designating a sauce of ground meat, herbs, and vegetables. Also **bolognese**.

**alla breve** (Italian)   (lit., 'by the breve')  *Music*. a direction to make the half note a unit, not the quarter note. Also **tempo alla breve; tempo maggiore**.

**all'abruzzese** (Italian)   (lit., 'in the style of Abruzzi')  *Cookery*. made with red peppers.

**alla caccia** (Italian)   *Music*. in the style of the hunt. See also **caccia**.

**alla capella, alla cappella.**   See **a cappella**.

**alla carbonara** (Italian)   (lit., 'coal dealer's style')  *Cookery*. a pasta dish served in a sauce of beaten eggs, diced bacon, olive oil, and garlic.

**alla casalinga** (Italian)   *Cookery*. in homemade style. See also **cucina casalinga**.

**alla ciociara** (Italian)   *Cookery*. a pasta dish served in a seasoned meat sauce with fresh butter and grated Parmesan cheese.

**alla contadina** (Italian)   (lit., 'peasant style')  *Cookery*. a pasta dish served in a butter-based sauce made with onion, mushrooms, and tomato.

**alla diavola** (Italian)   (lit., 'in the devil's style')  *Cookery*. a pasta dish served in a highly spiced tomato and meat sauce. See also **fra diavolo**.

**alla fine** (Italian)   *Music*. to the end, a direction to play to the end of a section, used with **da capo** or **dal segno**.

**alla fiorentina** (Italian)   (lit., 'in Florentine style')  *Cookery*. 1. a dish of poached eggs served with spinach and cheese.   2. designating a pasta sauce of tomatoes, meat, herbs, and peas.

**alla genovese** (Italian)   *Cookery*. in Genovese style, that is, in a sauce made of fresh, crushed basil leaves, garlic, olive oil, and pine nuts. See also **pesto**.

**alla griglia** (Italian)   (lit., 'on the grill')  broiled; grilled. Also **ai ferri**.

**Allah** (Arabic)   *Islam*. the Supreme Being; God.

**Allah akbar** (Arabic)   *Islam*. God is great.

**alla marinara** (Italian)   (lit., 'sailor's style')  *Cookery*. 1. designating a manner of preparing various dishes in a spicy tomato sauce.   2. shellfish cooked in broth with oil, garlic, wine, and parsley.

**all'amatriciana** (Italian)   (lit., 'in the style of Amatrice')  *Cookery*. prepared with onion, ham, and tomatoes.

**alla milanese** (Italian)   (lit., 'in the style of Milan')  *Cookery*. designating a manner of preparing meat by breading and frying in butter.

16

**alla napolitana** (Italian)    1. in the style of Naples.    2. *Cookery.* a style of preparation in a sauce of oil, tomatoes, garlic, and onion.

**all'antica** (Italian)    in the manner of the ancients.

**alla Palestrina** (Italian)    (lit., 'in the style of Palestrina,' a 16th century composer) *Music.* unaccompanied, referring to choral music. See also **a cappella.**

**alla parmigiana** (Italian)    (lit., 'in the style of Parma') *Cookery.* designating dishes prepared with Parmesan cheese.

**alla pizzaiola** (Italian)    (lit., 'pizza style') *Cookery.* a designation for a dish that is cooked in oil and served with tomato sauce, garlic, and oregano.

**alla Posillipo** (Italian)    (lit., 'in the style of Posillipo,' a suburb of Naples) *Cookery.* designating a **pasta** dish served with a sauce of seafood, tomato, and herbs.

**alla prima** (Italian)    *Fine Arts.* the technique of finishing a painting at one sitting.

**alla sarda** (Italian)    (lit., 'Sardinian style') *Cookery.* designating **pasta** served in a brown tomato-meat sauce with red wine and basil.

**alla siciliana** (Italian)    (lit., 'Sicilian style') 1. *Music.* in the style of the **siciliano.** 2. *Cookery.* designating a **pasta** dish served in a sauce containing eggplant, tomatoes, anchovies, and olives.

**alla tedesca** (Italian)    (lit., 'in the German style') *Music.* in the style or tempo of the waltz.

**alla Valdostana** (Italian)    (lit., 'Valle d'Aosta style') *Cookery.* a method of preparing veal with **fontina** cheese.

**alla vostra salute.**    See **salute.**

**alla zoppa** (Italian)    (lit., 'with a limp') *Music.* syncopated.

**alléchant** (French)    alluring; attractive.

**allegretto** (Italian)    *Music.* fairly lively, though not as fast as **allegro.**

**allegro** (Italian)    *Music.* 1. *adj.* in a fast tempo. 2. *n.* a designation for a movement or composition to be played in a fast tempo.

**allegro di molto** (Italian)    *Music.* very quick.

**allegro furioso** (Italian)    *Music.* quick and in an angry manner.

**allegro moderato** (Italian)    *Music.* moderately quick.

**allegro non tanto** (Italian)    *Music.* not too quick.

**allemand,** *fem.* **allemande** (French)    of or pertaining to Germany; German.

**allentando** (Italian)    *Music.* slowing down.

**alle vongole** (Italian)    *Cookery.* designating a **pasta** dish served with clam sauce.

**allez** (French)    go; move quickly.

**allonge** (French)   1. an extension piece, such as a leaf for a table. 2. an added clause or attachment to a document.

**allongée** (French)   *Ballet.* elongated; stretched.

**allons** (French)   let's go.

**allo spiedo** (Italian)   *Cookery.* (cooked) on the spit.

**all'ottava** (Italian)   *Music.* an octave higher than written.

**alma mater** (Latin)   (lit., 'fostering mother') the school, college, or university from which one graduated.

**al Marsala.**   See **Marsala, 2.**

**almena** (Spanish)   battlements.

**almendra** (Spanish)   almond.

**almuerzo** (Spanish)   lunch; mid-morning snack.

**aloha** (Hawaiian)   love; hello; goodbye.

**aloha oe** (Hawaiian)   farewell to you.

**à loisir** (French)   at leisure; in spare time.

**à l'ordinaire** (French)   as usual; ordinarily.

**alouette** (French)   a lark; skylark.

**à l'outrance** (French)   to the extreme; to excess.

**aloyau** (French)   sirloin.

**Alpenstock** (German)   a long staff with an iron tip, used for mountain climbing.

**al pesto** (Italian)   *Cookery.* served with **pesto**.

**alpha kai omega** (Greek)   the beginning and the end (the first (*alpha*) and last (*omega*) letters of the Greek alphabet).

**al piacere.**   See **a piacere.**

**al più** (Italian)   at the most.

**al pomodoro** (Italian)   (lit., 'with tomato') *Cookery.* designating a dish of pasta served with a tomato sauce.

**al-Sahih** (Arabic)   (lit., 'the right') a compilation of **hadith** deemed to be genuine.

**al segno** (Italian)   (lit., 'to the sign') *Music.* a direction to play to a certain mark, the **segno**.

**also** (German)   thus; so.

**al solito** (Italian)   as usual.

**al tedesco** (Italian)   in the German style or manner. See also **alla tedesca**.

**alter ego** (Latin)   another self; a very close friend.

**alter idem** (Latin)   another exactly the same.

**alter ipse amicus** (Latin)   a friend is a second self.

**alternativa** (Spanish)   *Bullfighting.* a ceremony in which a young man takes the matador's oath.

**alternis horis** (Latin)   *Prescriptions.* every other hour. *Abbr.* **alt. hor.**

18

**Altertumswissenschaft** (German)   the study of ancient civilizations and their culture.

**altiora peto** (Latin)   I seek loftier things.

**altiplano** (Spanish)   a highland; high plateau, especially of Bolivia and Peru.

**altissimo** (Italian)   *Music.* highest.

**alto,** *fem.* **alta** (Italian)   (lit., 'high') *Music.* **1.** the lowest of the three types of female voices.   **2.** the highest of the male range of voices.   **3.** an instrument with a high tonal range.

**al tonno** (Italian)   *Cookery.* designating a **pasta** dish served with a sauce of tuna, garlic, tomato, and olive oil.

**alto rilievo** (Italian)   *Fine Arts.* high-relief sculpture, in which the figures are cut so as to project strongly from the background. Also **alto relievo, alto-rilievo.** See also **basso rilievo; cavo rilievo; mezzo rilievo; schiacciato rilievo.**

**altra volta** (Italian)   *Music.* another time; encore.

**alumna,** *pl.* **alumnae** (Latin)   a woman who has graduated with a degree from an educational institution.

**alumnus,** *pl.* **alumni** (Latin)   a man who has graduated with a degree from an educational institution.

**amabile** (Italian)   (lit., 'lovable') **1.** *Music.* sweetly; gently.   **2.** a designation for a variety of wine that in certain vintages is quite sweet.

**amah** (Portuguese)   an Oriental nursemaid.

**amain** (Hebrew)   (lit., 'so be it') amen (said at the end of a Jewish prayer).

**à main armée** (French)   (lit., 'with armed hand') by force of arms.

**amande** (French)   almond.

**amandine** (French)   *Cookery.* prepared with almonds.

**amantium irae** (Latin)   lovers' quarrels.

**amaretto,** *pl.* **amaretti** (Italian)   **1.** an almond-flavored cookie.   **2.** an almond-flavored **liqueur.**

**amarezza, con.**   See **con amarezza.**

**Amarone** (Italian)   a variety of red wine produced in Piedmont and Veneto.

**amatriciana, all'.**   See **all'amatriciana.**

**a maximis ad minimis** (Latin)   from the greatest to the smallest.

**ambiance** (French)   the atmosphere or characteristic feeling evoked by a place.

**ambulant** (French)   (lit., 'strolling') a strolling musician.

**âme** (French)   **1.** soul.   **2.** *Music.* the sound post of a violin, fancifully considered the "soul" of that instrument.

**âme damnée** (French)    (lit., 'a damned soul')  a person who is willingly manipulated by another.

**âme de boue** (French)    (lit., 'soul of mud')  a mean person.

**amende honorable** (French)    a public apology.

**a mensa et t(h)oro.**    See **separatio a mensa et t(h)oro.**

**âme perdue** (French)    a lost soul.

**américaine, à l'.**    See **à l'américaine.**

**americano** (Spanish)    American, either North, Central, or South.

**à merveille** (French)    marvellously.

**a mezza di voce.**    See **mezza voce.**

**ami,** *fem.* **amie** (French)    a friend.

**amicus curiae** (Latin)    *Law.*  a friend of the court; someone allowed by the court to express an opinion in a case even though not directly involved in the action.

**amicus humani generis** (Latin)    a friend of the human race.

**amicus usque ad aras** (Latin)    (lit., 'a friend even to the altars')  1. a friend who is always loyal.  2. a friend up to the point of conflict over religion. See also **usque ad aras.**

**ami(e) de coeur** (French)    a bosom friend; bosom buddy.

**ami(e) de cour** (French)    a false friend.

**ami(e) de table** (French)    a dinner companion.

**ami(e) du peuple** (French)    a friend of the people.

**ami(e) en voie** (French)    a friend at court.

**amigo,** *fem.* **amiga** (Spanish)    friend.

**amir** (Arabic)    (lit., 'commander')  1. a title for a Muslim lord or nobleman. Also **ameer; emir.**  2. a title for one of the descendants of Muhammad. Also **sherif.**  3. a title for certain Turkish officials.

**à moitié** (French)    halfway.

**à mon avis** (French)    in my opinion; to my way of thinking.

**Amontillado** (Spanish)    a pale, dry sherry from the Montilla district of Spain.

**amore** (Italian)    love.

**amore, con.**    See **con amore.**

**amoretto,** *pl.* **amoretti** (Italian)    (lit., 'little love')  1. *Fine Arts.* an infant cupid. Also **amorino.**  2. flirtation; casual love.

**amoricaine, à l'.**    See **à l'amoricaine.**

**amorino.**    See **amoretto, 1.**

**amor nummi** (Latin)    love of money.

**amoroso** (Italian)    *Music.* loving.

**amor patriae** (Latin)    love of one's country or homeland.

**amor proximi** (Latin)    love of one's neighbor.

**amor vincit omnia** (Latin)    love conquers all things.

**amour** (French)    love.

**amourette** (French)    1. a passing love affair.  2. *Cookery.*  marrow from the bones of a calf or lamb, used as a garnish.

**amour propre** (French)    self-esteem; vanity.

**amparo** (Spanish)    a shelter; help; support.

**amuse-gueules** (French)    cocktail snacks.

**anakoluthon** (Greek)    a change or shift of grammatical construction in mid-sentence; grammatical inconsistency.  Also **anacoluthon.**

**ananas** (French)    a pineapple.

**anathema sit** (Latin)    (lit., 'may he (*or* it) be anathema')  *Roman Catholicism.*  that thing is accursed (the formal declaration of excommunication or heresy).

**anchois** (French)    an anchovy.

**ancienne, à l'**.    See **à l'ancienne.**

**ancienne noblesse** (French)    the old nobility, as the 18th-century nobles of England and France.

**ancien régime** (French)    1. *French History.*  the government and social system in France before the Revolution of 1789.  2. any government or social system of time past.

**ancona** (Italian)    1. *Fine Arts.*  a group of paintings formally arranged, as for an altarpiece.   2. *Architecture.*  a framed recess where sculpture may be placed.

**ancora** (Italian)    still; yet.

**ancora una volta** (Italian)    *Music.*  one more time.

**Andacht, mit** (German)    *Music.*  with devotion.

**ándale** (Spanish)    hurry; hurry up.

**andaluza** (Spanish)    *Music.*  a general term applied to several different dances of southern Spain.

**andante** (Italian)    *Music.*  slow but moving along.

**andante cantabile** (Italian)    *Music.*  slow and melodic.

**andante maestoso** (Italian)    *Music.*  slow and majestic.

**andante ma non troppo** (Italian)    *Music.*  slow, but not excessively.

**andantino** (Italian)    *Music.*  a short and slow movement.

**andouille** (French)    a large pork sausage.

**andouillette** (French)    a small sausage made of chitlings.

**Anfang** (German)    beginning.

**Anfang, vom** (German)    *Music.*  from the beginning.

**Angangsritornell** (German)    *Music.*  prelude.

**Angelus** (Latin) *Roman Catholicism.* title and first word of a prayer traditionally recited at 6:00 a.m., noon, and 6:00 p.m., accompanied by the ringing of a bell.

**anginetti** (Italian) (lit., 'little angels') a variety of round, flaky cookies.

**anglais,** *fem.* **anglaise** (French) English.

**anglaise, à l'.** See à l'anglaise.

**Angleterre** (French) England.

**anglice** (Latin) in English.

**Angst** (German) anguish; alienation.

**anguilla,** *pl.* **anguille** (Italian) an eel.

**anguille** (French) an eel.

**anguille de mer** (French) a conger eel.

**anguis in herba.** See latet anguis in herba.

**Anhang** (German) 1. supplement; appendix. 2. *Music.* coda.

**an hua** (Chinese) a hidden mark on some Chinese porcelain that can only be seen when the piece is held up to the light.

**anima** (Latin) *Philosophy.* the soul.

**anima** (Italian) (lit., 'soul') *Music.* the sound-post of a violin or similar instrument.

**anima, con.** See con anima.

**anima mundi** (Latin) 1. spirit of the world; a creative energy that permeates the universe. 2. *Christianity.* the Holy Spirit.

**animato** (Italian) *Music.* animated; brisk.

**animé** (French) animated; lively.

**animelles** (French) animal testicles, for use in cooking.

**animis opibusque parati** (Latin) prepared in mind and resources.

**animoso** (Italian) *Music.* spirited; with boldness.

**animus** (Latin) 1. *Philosophy.* the mind; intention. 2. hostile feeling.

**animus furandi** (Latin) *Law.* intention to steal.

**animus testandi** (Latin) *Law.* intention to make a last will.

**ankh** (Egyptian) *Egyptian Art.* a cross with a loop at the top, a symbol of enduring life.

**Anklang** (German) *Music.* harmony; accord.

**ankus** (Hindi) an elephant goad.

**anno aetatis suae** (Latin) in the year of his (*or* her) age (usually with a specific number given; common on old gravestones as a means of indicating the age at which the person died). Also **aetatis suae, aetatis, aetate.** *Abbr.* **aet., aetat.**

**Anno Christi** (Latin) in the year of Christ. See also **Anno Domini.**

**Anno Domini** (Latin) in the year of the Lord (used to designate years in the Christian era). *Abbr.* **A.D.** (properly, used before the date).

**Anno Hebraico** (Latin)    in the Hebrew year, that is, reckoning from 3761 B.C. *Abbr.* **A.H.**

**Anno Hegirae** (Latin)    in the year of the Hegira, Muhammad's flight from Mecca in A.D. 622, the beginning of the Muslim era. *Abbr.* **A.H.**

**Anno Humanae Salutis** (Latin)    in the year of man's redemption (used as an equivalent of **Anno Domini**). *Abbr.* **A.H.S.** See also **Anno Domini**.

**Anno Lucis** (Latin)    in the year of light (used by Freemasons in reckoning the years elapsed since 4000 B.C.). *Abbr.* **A.L.**

**Anno Mundi** (Latin)    in the year of the world, that is, since God's creation of the world, often calculated as 4004 B.C. *Abbr.* **A.M.**

**Anno Regni** (Latin)    in the year of the reign (used with a specific number to designate the length of a monarch's rule). *Abbr.* **A.R.**

**anno urbis conditae** (Latin)    in the year of the founding of the city (referring to the founding of Rome in 753 B.C.). See also **ab urbe condita**.

**annuit coeptis** (Latin)    (lit., 'He (God) approves these beginnings') motto on the reverse of the Great Seal of the United States (adapted from Vergil, *Aeneid* IX.625). See also **novus ordo seclorum**.

**annulus et baculus** (Latin)    the ring and staff, symbols of a bishop.

**annus magnus** (Latin)    *Astronomy.* the great year or Platonic year, the period of time (about 26,000 years) that it takes for a complete revolution of the equinoxes.

**annus mirabilis** (Latin)    a year of wonders; frequently referring (as in the Dryden poem of that title) to the twelvemonth period in 1665 and 1666 in London, when the city experienced great devastation from both a plague and a fire.

**annus Platonicus.**    See **annus magnus**.

**Año Nuevo** (Spanish)    the New Year.

**Anschauung** (German)    *Philosophy.* direct perception via the senses, without mediation or interpretation by the mind.

**Anschluss** (German)    *Politics.* union, referring especially to the political union of Austria with Germany in 1938.

**ante bellum** (Latin)    before the war (in the U.S., used to mean before the Civil War). See also **post bellum**.

**ante Christum** (Latin)    before Christ, equivalent to B.C. *Abbr.* **A.C.**

**ante cibos** *or* **cibum** (Latin)    *Prescriptions.* before meals. *Abbr.* **a.c.**

**ante diem** (Latin)    before the day.

**ante lucem** (Latin)    before the dawn.

**ante meridiem** (Latin)    before midday; between midnight and noon. *Abbr.* **a.m., A.M.** See also **post meridiem**.

**antica, all'.**    See **all' antica**.

**antipasto** (Italian)    *Cookery.* an assortment of bite-size foods, such as ol-ives, artichoke hearts, anchovies, assorted meats, and cheeses, served as an appetizer or relish.

**à outrance.**   See **à l'outrance.**

**apaisé** (French)    appeased; pacified.

**aparejo** (Spanish)    a pack saddle.

**apartheid** (Afrikaans)    the policy of racial segregation as practiced in the Republic of South Africa.

**à peine** (French)    hardly; scarecly.

**aperçu** (French)    a quick overview; a summary.

**apéritif** (French)    wine or a strong alcoholic drink taken before a meal as a stimulant for the appetite.

**apertura** (Spanish)    (lit., 'opening') a relaxation of political and social re-pression.

**a piacere** (Italian)    *Music.* at the pleasure of the performer. Also **al piacere.**

**à pied** (French)    on foot.

**à pierre fendre** (French)    (lit., 'to split a stone') with great intensity or rigor.

**à plaisir** (French)    with pleasure.

**a poco a poco.**   See **poco a poco.**

**à point** (French)    to the point; direct. See also **cuit à point.**

**a posse ad esse** (Latin)    from possibility to realization.

**a posteriori** (Latin)    **1.** *Logic.* (lit., 'from the later (thing)') reasoning from effect(s) to cause by observation of evidence; inductive reasoning. See also **a priori. 2.** not in existence prior to experience, as any behavior based on learning.

**apparatchik** (Russian)    a loyal member of the Soviet bureaucracy.

**apparatus criticus** (Latin)    critical apparatus, that is, notes accompanying a page of text that cite critical emendations and variant readings of manu-scripts.

**appassionato,** *fem.* **appassionata** (Italian)    *Music.* with strong feeling.

**appel** (French)    a call, as a cry for help.

**appellation d'origine contrôlée** (French)    designating French wines pro-duced in a limited region according to regulated quality standards. *Abbr.* **A.O.C.**

**appliqué** (French)    (lit., 'applied') a decoration, as on fabric or in cabi-netry, made with pieces cut from another material and attached.

**appoggiato** (Italian)    (lit., 'leaned, propped') *Music.* a designation for a note that passes without a break to the succeeding one.

**appoggiatura** (Italian)    *Music.* an added note; a grace note.

**appui** (French)    *Architecture.* a separate constituent part, such as a window sill or the top element of a balustrade.

**appuyé,** *fem.* **appuyée** (French)    *Music.* supported; stressed.

**après** (French)    after.

**après coup** (French)    after the fact; too late.

**après-midi** (French)    afternoon.

**après moi le déluge** (French)    after me, the deluge (a statement attributed to Louis XV, anticipating the French Revolution).

**après-ski** (French)    after-ski, said of an activity or item of clothing.

**a prima vista** (Italian)    at first sight.

**a primo** (Latin)    from the first.

**a principio** (Latin)    from the beginning.

**a priori** (Latin)    (lit., 'from the prior (thing)')    1. *Logic.* reasoning from cause to effect(s) or from proposition to conclusion, without reliance on sensory evidence; pure reasoning; deductive reasoning.    2. existing prior to experience, as a faculty of mind or a character trait.    3. not based on prior study or knowledge. See also **a posteriori.**

**à propos** (French)    1. *adj.* appropriate; apt; opportune. 2. *prep.* regarding; concerning.  Also **à-propos; apropos; à propos de.**

**aqua ardens** (Latin)    (lit., 'burning water') *Alchemy.* alcohol.

**aqua benedicta** (Latin)    blessed water; holy water.

**aqua fortis** (Latin)    (lit., 'strong water') a designation for nitric acid.

**aqua pura** (Latin)    pure water.

**aquardiente.**    See **aguardiente.**

**aqua regia** (Latin)    (lit., 'royal water') *Chemistry.* a mixture of nitric and hydrochloric acids capable of dissolving gold and platinum.

**aquarelle** (French)    1. *Fine Arts.* a watercolor. 2. *Music.* said of a piece having the delicacy of a watercolor.

**Aquarius** (Latin)    the Water-bearer, a constellation and sign of the zodiac.

**à quatre mains** (French)    (lit., 'for four hands') *Music.* for two performers; for duet.

**a quattro** (Italian)    *Music.* for four voices or instruments.

**aquavit.**    See **akvavit.**

**aqua vitae** (Latin)    (lit., 'water of life') distilled spirits, especially brandy.

**aquí** (Spanish)    here; right here.

**aquila** (Latin)    1. eagle.    2. the standard of a Roman legion, which had the image of an eagle at the top.

**aquí se habla español** (Spanish)    Spanish is spoken here.  Also **se habla español.**

**a quo** (Latin)    from which (point), referring to a starting point in place or time. See also **terminus a quo.**

**à quoi bon?** (French)   to what purpose?; what's the good of it?

**arada** (Spanish)   *Music.* Spanish folk music thematically based on the activity of plowing.

**arado** (Spanish)   cultivated land; plowed field.

**aragonaise** (French)   *Music.* a style of dance that originated in Aragon, Spain.

**aragonesa** (Spanish)   *Music.* a Spanish dance from the region of Aragon.

**aragosta** (Italian)   a lobster.

**arancine** (Italian)   (lit., 'little oranges') fried rice balls.

**arba kanfoth** (Hebrew)   (lit., 'four corners') *Judaism.* a rectangular garment with fringes at each corner and a hole in the center for the head, worn under the clothes by Orthodox Jewish men.  Also **tallith katan.**

**arbiter bibendi** (Latin)   a toastmaster; master of the revels.  Also **magister bibendi; rex bibendi.**

**arbiter elegantiae** *or* **elegantiarum** (Latin)   a judge in matters of taste or elegance (from Tacitus' description of C. Petronius in *Annals* XVI.18).

**arbiter literarum** (Latin)   a judge of literature.

**arbor vitae** (Latin)   (lit., 'tree of life') *Anatomy.* a treelike structure of nerve tissue in the cerebellum.

**arcanum,** *pl.* **arcana** (Latin)   something known only by a privileged few.

**arcanum arcanorum** (Latin)   (lit., 'secret of secrets') a closely kept secret.

**arc-boutant** (French)   *Architecture.* a flying buttress.

**archebanc** (French)   *Furniture.* a high-backed bench with a chest beneath the seat.  Also **archbanc.**

**arco,** *pl.* **archi** (Italian)   *Music.* a bow, as for playing the violin.

**ardente** (Italian)   *Music.* fiery; ardent.

**ardentemente** (Italian)   *Music.* passionately.

**arditezza, con.**   See **con arditezza.**

**à rebours** (French)   against the grain; in a contrary way.

**à reculons** (French)   in reverse.

**Areopagus** (Greek)   *Greek history.* a political council of ancient Athens, named for the hill in the city on which it met.

**arête** (French)   1. a sharp mountain ridge.  2. the bony spine of a fish.

**argent** (French)   money.

**argentum** (Latin)   silver.  *Abbr.* Ag.

**argumenti causa** (Latin)   for the sake of argument.

**argumentum** (Latin)   1. argument.  2. exposition.

**argumentum ab auctoritate** (Latin)   an argument that relies on authority.

**argumentum ad absurdum** (Latin)   an argument carried to absurdity.

**argumentum ad baculum** (Latin)    (lit., 'argument to the rod') an argument based not on reason, but the threat of force. Also **argumentum baculinum**.

**argumentum ad cruminam** (Latin)    (lit., 'argument to the wallet') an appeal to material interest. Also spelled **argumentum ad crumenam**.

**argumentum ad hominem.**      See ad hominem.

**argumentum ad ignorantiam** (Latin)    (lit., 'argument to ignorance') an argument that attempts to take advantage of an audience's ignorance of facts.

**argumentum ad invidiam** (Latin)    (lit., 'argument to envy') an argument that appeals to an audience's envy, jealousy, or other base feeling.

**argumentum ad judicium** (Latin)    an argument appealing to common sense or judgment.

**argumentum ad misericordiam** (Latin)    an argument appealing for pity or mercy.

**argumentum ad populum** (Latin)    (lit., 'argument to the people') an appeal to the general public, especially to their passions.

**argumentum ad rem.**      See ad rem.

**argumentum ad verecundiam** (Latin)    (lit., 'argument to respect') an argument that alludes to a revered idea or personage, usually as a ploy to divert attention from the issue at hand.

**argumentum baculinum.**      See **argumentum ad baculum.**

**argumentum ex silentio** (Latin)    argument from silence, that is, one based on lack of information or the non-response of another party.

**aria** (Italian)    (lit., 'an air')   *Opera.* a vocal piece; song.

**aria aggiunta** (Italian)    (lit., 'added air')   *Opera.* a vocal piece added to a score to please the audience or performer.

**aria all'unisono** (Italian)    *Opera.* a vocal piece in which the accompaniment doubles the voice.

**aria buffa** (Italian)    *Opera.* a comic song.

**aria cantabile** (Italian)    *Opera.* a slow, smooth song which the singer may embellish.

**aria concertata** (Italian)    *Opera.* a vocal piece with full accompaniment.

**aria d'abilità** (Italian)    *Opera.* a vocal piece in which there is a display of difficult technical skill. Also **aria d'agilità; aria di bravura.**

**aria da capo** (Italian)    *Opera.* a vocal piece in which the first part is repeated.

**aria d'agilità.**      See aria d'abilità.

**aria d'entrata** (Italian)    *Opera.* a vocal piece with which an operatic performer makes his or her entrance.

**aria di bravura.**      See aria d'abilità.

**aria di mezzo carattere** (Italian)    *Opera.* a vocal piece having orchestral accompaniment and expressing strong emotion.

**aria d'imitazione** (Italian)    *Opera.* a vocal piece in which sounds are imitated, especially sounds from nature.

**aria di portamento** (Italian)    *Opera.* a vocal piece to be sung with smooth flow from one note to the next.

**aria fugata** (Italian)    *Opera.* a vocal piece with a fugal accompaniment.

**aria parlante** (Italian)    *Opera.* a declamatory song.

**Aries** (Latin)    the Ram, a constellation and sign of the zodiac.

**arietta** (Italian)    *Opera.* a short aria.

**ariette** (French)    *Music.* an aria lacking the characteristic middle section. See also **arietta.**

**arigato** (Japanese)    thank you.

**ariki** (Maori)    a Polynesian chieftain or king.

**arioso** (Italian)    *Opera.* 1. *adj.* in a cheerful manner.   —*n.* 2. a recitative similar to an **aria.**   3. a short air in an opera.

**a rivederci** (Italian)    till we meet again; goodbye. Also **arrivederci.** See also **arrivederla.**

**arma accipere** (Latin)    *Peerage.* to be made a knight.

**arma dare** (Latin)    *Peerage.* to grant knighthood.

**Armagnac** (French)    a brandy produced in southwestern France.

**arma virumque cano** (Latin)    (lit., 'I sing of arms and a man') the opening words of Vergil's *Aeneid.*

**armes, aux.**    See **aux armes.**

**armoire** (French)    a large wardrobe or cupboard.

**Aron Kodesh** (Hebrew)    *Judaism.* the Holy Ark, that is, the cabinet in a synagogue where the **Torah** scrolls are stored.

**arpeggio** (Italian)    *Music.* a chord in which the notes are played in rapid succession.

**arraché** (French)    *Music.* torn, referring to an intense form of **pizzicato.**

**arras** (French)    a woven fabric used for French tapestries in the 14th century.

**arrastra** (Spanish)    an early animal-powered device for processing ore. Also **arrastre.**

**arrectis auribus** (Latin)    (lit., 'with ears cocked') listening intently.

**arriba** (Spanish)    1. up; upward.   2. *Music.* faster.

**arricciato** (Italian)    *Fine Arts.* the wall to which rough plaster is applied in fresco painting.

**arricciatura** (Italian)    *Fine Arts.* the layer of rough plaster beneath the **intonaco** on which a fresco is painted.

**arrière, en.**    See **en arrière.**

**arrière-garde** (French) rear guard.

**arrière pensée** (French) mental reservation; ulterior motive; secret thought.

**arrivé** (French) a person who has newly acquired wealth or status.

**arrivederci.** See **a rivederci.**

**arrivederla** (Italian) till we meet again; goodbye (formal). See also **a rivederci.**

**arriviste** (French) a person who has gained wealth or status by unscrupulous practices.

**arroba** (Spanish) a unit of measurement approximately equivalent to twenty-five pounds or thirty-two pints.

**arrondi** (French) *Ballet.* round; rounded.

**arrondissement** (French) an administrative subdivision of the French government, such as the districts into which Paris is divided.

**arroyo** (Spanish) 1. a dry river bed. 2. small stream.

**arroz** (Spanish) rice.

**arroz con frijoles** (Spanish) *Cookery.* a dish of rice and beans.

**arroz con pollo** (Spanish) *Cookery.* a dish of chicken and rice.

**Ars Antiqua** (Latin) (lit., 'the old art') *Music.* a style characteristic of French music of the 14th and preceding centuries. See also **Ars Nova.**

**ars est celare artem** (Latin) art lies in concealing the artistry.

**ars gratia artis** (Latin) art for art's sake.

**ars longa, vita brevis** (Latin) (lit., 'art is long, life is short') art endures but life is transitory. Also **vita brevis, ars longa.**

**ars musica** (Latin) the art of music.

**Ars Nova** (Latin) (lit., 'the new art') *Music.* a style that developed in music during the 14th century in France and Italy and that represented a break with tradition. See also **Ars Antiqua.**

*Ars Poetica* (Latin) (lit., '*The Art of Poetry*') standard title for any treatise on poetry, taken from the traditional name given to the model work of Horace (*Epistles* II.3).

**art brut, l'.** See **l'art brut.**

**art de vivre, l'.** See **l'art de vivre.**

**artesanías** (Spanish) a marketplace where fine native crafts are displayed and sold.

**artesano** (Spanish) 1. *n.* an artisan. —*adj.* 2. *Wine.* made by hand in a small winery. 3. hand-crafted.

**artesonado** (Spanish) *Architecture.* 1. a wooden roof. 2. panelwork in a ceiling.

**artichaut** (French) an artichoke.

**articulé** (French) *Music.* well-articulated.

**artiste** (French)   an artist; a skilled performer.

**artiste maudit** (French)   (lit., 'cursed artist') the poet or artist seen as a suffering and unfortunate being. See also **poète maudit.**

**Artium Baccalaureus** (Latin)   the academic degree of Bachelor of Arts. *Abbr.* **A.B.**

**Artium Magister** (Latin)   the academic degree of Master of Arts. *Abbr.* **A.M.**

**art moderne** (French)   modern art.

**Art Nouveau** (French)   *Design.* New Art; a style of furnishings popular in the late 19th century and based on the curved lines in nature.

**art pour l'art, l'.**   See **l'art pour l'art.**

**arts d'agrément** (French)   accomplishments, such as music, painting, dancing, etc.

**asado** (Spanish)   1. *n., adj.* roast; roasted.   2. a meal of barbecued meat.

**a scelta** (Italian)   of your choice.

**asciutto** (Italian)   *Wine.* dry, the opposite of sweet.

**a secco** (Italian)   stranded; broke.

**asequia.**   See **acequia.**

**Ashkenazi,** *pl.* **Ashkenazim** (Hebrew)   the Jews of central and eastern Europe and their descendants, distinct from the **Sephardim** in customs and language.

**así** (Spanish)   like this; like that.

**asinus ad lyram** (Latin)   (lit., 'an ass at the lyre') a person with no musical ability.

**asperges** (French)   asparagus.

**aspergillum** (Latin)   a device used for sprinkling holy water.

**assemblage** (French)   *Fine Arts.* a technique in which various types of found objects are fastened together to form a unit; **collage.** See also **objet trouvé.**

**assemblé, pas.**   See **pas assemblé.**

**assez** (French)   enough.

**assiette** (French)   a plate.

**assiettes volantes** (French)   (lit., 'flying plates') extra dishes; small entrées.

**Assisi** (Italian)   an old form of cross-stitch embroidery, usually scarlet or blue on cream-colored linen, originating in the town of Assisi.

**assoluta** (Italian)   the chief female performer of an opera or ballet company. See also **prima ballerina; prima donna.**

**Asti Spumante** (Italian)   a sweet, sparkling white wine from the town of Asti in Piedmont.

**asturiano,** *fem.* **asturiana** (Spanish)   from the region of Asturias on the Cantabrian coast of Spain.

**Asymphonie** (German)   *Music.* dissonance.

**ataman** (Russian)   an elected chief of the Cossacks. Also **hetman.**

**à tatons** (French)   gropingly; by feeling one's way.

**atelier** (French)   a workshop, especially that of an artist or fashion designer.

**até logo** (Portuguese)   till we meet again; goodbye.

**a tempo** (Italian)   *Music.* in time; a return to the original tempo.

**a tempo giusto.**   See **tempo giusto.**

**a tempo primo** (Italian)   *Music.* in the first tempo given. See also **tempo primo.**

**a tempo rubato** (Italian)   *Music.* designating a passage played in an irregular tempo. See also **tempo rubato.**

**a tergo** (Latin)   from behind; from the rear. See also **vis a tergo.**

**à terre** (French)   (lit., 'on the ground') *Ballet.* 1. designating that the supporting foot or feet are flat on the floor. 2. a direction to assume a certain pose with the extended foot remaining on the floor instead of being lifted. Also **par terre.**

**Athenai** (Greek)   Athens.

**atman** (Sanskrit)   (lit., 'breath') *Hinduism.* 1. the principle of life. 2. (*cap.*) the World Soul, source of individual souls and goal to which they aspire.

**à toutes jambes** (French)   as fast as one's legs can go.

**à tout prix** (French)   at any price; at any cost.

**a tre** (Italian)   *Music.* for three instruments or voices.

**à trois** (French)   for three; of three.

**attacca** (Italian)   (lit., 'attack') *Music.* a direction to play the next part without pausing. See also **segue, 1.**

**attacca subito** (Italian)   (lit., 'attack immediately') *Music.* a direction to play immediately.

**attaché** (French)   a member of a diplomatic post.

**attaque** (French)   *Music.* an energetic beginning of a note or passage by vocal or instrumental artists.

**attentat** (French)   an assassination attempt.

**attitude** (French)   *Ballet.* a basic pose in which the dancer supports the body on one leg, raising the other leg behind with knee bent, and arching the arm corresponding to the raised leg.

**aubade** (French)   *Music.* a dawn serenade, as that of birds.

**auberge** (French)   an inn or tavern.

**aubergine** (French)   eggplant.

**aubergiste** (French)    an innkeeper.

**au besoin** (French)    in case of need; in a pinch.

**au beurre** (French)    *Cookery.* served with butter; buttered.

**au beurre fondu** (French)    *Cookery.* served with butter sauce or in melted butter.

**au beurre roux** (French)    *Cookery.* served with brown butter.

**au contraire** (French)    on the contrary.

**au courant** (French)    up-to-date; well-informed. See also **au fait**.

**auctor ignotus** (Latin)    (lit., 'unknown author') a talented but little-known author.

**audace** (French)    audacity; boldness; daring.

**au dessous** (French)    below; beneath.

**audi alteram partem** (Latin)    hear the other side.

**audiencia** (Spanish)    *Spanish history.* high courts or administrative bodies in the provinces or colonies of Spain.

**au fait** (French)    well-informed; conversant. See also **au courant**.

**Aufführung** (German)    *Music.* performance.

**Aufklärung** (German)    1. solution, enlightenment. 2. the Enlightenment.

**Auflage** (German)    an edition, as of a book.

**Auflösung** (German)    *Music.* resolution (of a discord).

**au fond** (French)    at the bottom; fundamentally.

**Aufschnitt** (German)    a slice; cut.

**Aufschwung, mit** (German)    with spirit.

**Auf Wiedersehen!** (German)    until we meet again!; goodbye!

**Aufzug** (German)    *Theater.* act.

**Augenblick** (German)    twinkling of an eye; a mere instant.

**au grand sérieux** (French)    in all seriousness.

**au gras** (French)    with fat.

**au gratin** (French)    *Cookery.* designating a dish, often a casserole, with a cheese sauce or topping.

**au jus** (French)    *Cookery.* with the natural juice of the meat.

**au lait.**    See **café au lait**.

**auld lang syne** (Scottish)    (lit., 'old long since') past times that are fondly remembered.

**au milieu** (French)    *Ballet.* designating exercises to be performed in the middle of the room, away from the **barre**.

**a una corda.**    See **una corda**.

**au naturel** (French)    1. in a natural state; naked. 2. *Cookery.* plainly cooked.

**au pair** (French)   (lit., 'at par')   a designation for a domestic employee, such as a governess, who receives room and board but no wages.

**au pied de la lettre** (French)   (lit., 'at the foot of the letter')   literally; exactly.

**au pis aller** (French)   if worse comes to worst.

**au point** (French)   1. to the point; precisely.   2. in focus.

**au premier** (French)   on the floor above the ground floor.

**au premier coup** (French)   (lit., 'at the first stroke')   *Fine Arts.* a method of painting in which the work is completed in the first session.

**aura popularis** (Latin)   (lit., 'the popular breeze') the favor of the people, regarded as fickle.

**aurea mediocritas** (Latin)   the golden mean.

**au revoir** (French)   goodbye; farewell.

**aurum** (Latin)   gold.   *Abbr.* **Au.**

**au sérieux** (French)   seriously; in earnest.

**Ausgabe** (German)   an issue or edition of a publication.

**Ausgleich** (German)   (lit., 'equalization') the political agreement between Austria and Hungary made in 1867, establishing the Dual Monarchy.

**Ausländer** (German)   foreigner.

**Auslese** (German)   1. a selection.   2. a German wine made from carefully selected grapes.

**au soleil** (French)   in the sun; by sunlight.

**aussi** (French)   too; also.

**Auszug** (German)   *Music.* an extract; arrangement.

**aut Caesar aut nihil** (Latin)   (lit., 'either Caesar or nothing') all or nothing.

**Autobahn** (German)   the German highway system allowing high-speed intercity travel.

**auto-da-fe.**   See **auto de fé.**

**auto de fé** (Spanish)   public punishment of prisoners under the Spanish Inquisition, especially by burning at the stake.   Also **auto-da-fe.**

**autore** (Italian)   an author.

**auto sacramental** (Spanish)   *Theater.* a dramatic representation of a biblical theme, often accompanied by music.

**autostrada,** *pl.* **autostrade** (Italian)   an Italian superhighway.

**autrefois** (French)   in the past; in bygone days.

**aux armes** (French)   to arms! (a battle cry).

**avant-coureur** (French)   forerunner; harbinger.

**avante** (Italian)   *Music.* before; preceding; forward.   Also **avanti.**

**avant, en.**   See **en avant.**

**avant-garde** (French)   the advance guard; pioneers or highly innovative individuals in a given field.

33

**avant la lettre** (French)    (lit., 'before the letter') before complete development; prematurely.

**avant propos** (French)    preliminary matter; preface. Also **avant-propos**.

**avant-scène** (French)    1. a proscenium.  2. a type of theater box on either side of the stage. See also **baignoire**.

**avatar** (Sanskrit)    *Hinduism.*  1. the incarnation of a god.  2. the concrete manifestation of a principle or view.

**ave atque vale** (Latin)    hail and farewell (from Catullus 101).

**Ave Caesar; morituri te salutamus** *or* **salutant** (Latin)    (lit., 'Hail Caesar; we (they) who are about to die salute you')  standard salutation used by Roman gladiators before combat.

**avec les pieds** (French)    *Music.*  with the feet, referring to the playing of an organ.

**Ave Maria** (Latin)    1. the Hail Mary, a common Christian prayer.  2. this prayer set to music.

**avenida** (Spanish)    avenue.

**a verbis ad verbera** (Latin)    from words to blows.

**a vinculo matrimonii** (Latin)    (free) from the bonds of marriage, in reference to a divorce.

**aviso** (Spanish)    advice; warning; notice.

**à voix forte** (French)    in full voice; in loud voice.

**à volonté** (French)    at will.

**a vostra salute.**    See **salute**.

**à votre santé** (French)    to your health; good health! (used as a toast).

**à vue** (French)    by sight.

**à vue d'oeil** (French)    before one's very eyes.

**a vuestra salud** (Spanish)    to your health.

**ayer** (Spanish)    yesterday.

**ayudante** (Spanish)    helper; assistant.

**ayuntamiento** (Spanish)    town council; municipal administrative body.

**azafrán** (Spanish)    saffron.

**azogue** (Spanish)    1. mercury.  2. restlessness.

**azote** (Spanish)    1. a lash; whip.  2. disaster; scourge.

**azotea** (Spanish)    *Architecture.*  a flat, platform-like roof, used as a patio.

**azúcar** (Spanish)    sugar.

**azul** (Spanish)    blue.

**azzurro** (Italian)    azure; sky blue.

# B

**baba au rhum** (French)   a rich rum cake; rum baba.

**babu** (Hindi)   1. a Hindu title of address, equivalent to *Mister* or *Sir*. 2. a disparaging term for an Indian whose knowledge of English is limited.

**babushka** (Russian)   (lit., 'grandmother') a woman's scarf worn over the head and tied under the chin.

**bacalao** (Spanish)   codfish.

**Baccalaureus Artium** (Latin)   the academic degree of Bachelor of Arts. *Abbr.* **B.A.**

**baccara(t)** (French)   a card game used for gambling.

**bacchanale** (French)   a wild party; a debauch.

**Bacchuslied** (German)   *Music.* Bacchanalian song.

**Backfisch** (German)   (silly) teenage girl.

**Bad** (German)   bath; spa.

**badia.**   See **abbadia.**

**badinage** (French)   1. banter; teasing; playfulness. 2. *Music.* a playful, lighthearted piece. Also **badinerie.**

**badinerie** (French)   1. silliness; jesting. 2. See **badinage, 2.**

**bagasse** (French)   1. crushed sugar cane with the juice extracted. 2. a kind of fiber paper.

**bagatelle** (French)   1. a trifle; something of small value. 2. *Music.* a short, light piece, commonly composed for piano.

**bagna cauda** (Italian)   *Cookery.* a hot dip for vegetables, flavored with anchovies.

**bagnio** (Italian)   1. a bath or bathhouse.   2. a brothel.

**baguette** (French)   1. a long, thin loaf of French bread. 2. *Architecture.* a small, semicircular molding. 3. *Music.* a drumstick; baton. 4. *Jewelry.* a rectangular cut of a precious gem, such as a diamond.

**bahadur** (Hindi)   an Indian title of respect, used after a name.

**Bahnhof** (German)   railroad station.

**baignoire** (French)　1. a bathtub.　2. a theater box on the same level as the stalls. See also **avant-scène**.

**baile** (Spanish)　a dance. Also **bayle**.

**baile flamenco** (Spanish)　gypsy dancing typical of southern Spain.

**bain de soleil** (French)　a sun bath.

**bain-marie** (French)　*Cookery.* a double boiler.

**Bairam** (Turkish)　*Islam.* either of two Islamic religious festivals observed in Turkey.

**bairn** (Scottish)　a child.

**bajo,** *fem.* **baja** (Spanish)　low; lower.

**baklava** (Turkish)　*Cookery.* a pastry made with paper-thin layers of dough filled with a mixture of ground nuts and honey or other ingredients.

**baksheesh** (Persian)　a tip or gratuity. Also **bakshish; buksheesh; bukshish**.

**balalaika** (Russian)　a Russian stringed instrument similar to a guitar, having a triangular body and usually three strings.

**balconet** (French).　See **bandeau, 2.**

**baldachino** (Italian)　*Architecture.* a canopy suspended over an altar, throne, or tomb.

**baliki** (Russian)　salted and smoked sturgeon.

**ballabile** (Italian)　*Music.* adaptable for dancing.

**ballerina,** *masc.* **ballerino** (Italian)　a ballet dancer.

**ballet blanc** (French)　a romantic form of ballet that originated in the 19th century and is commonly considered the pure, classical form.

**ballet chanté** (French)　(lit., 'sung ballet') a ballet in which the dancers also sing.

**ballet classique** (French)　1. a style of ballet that emphasizes traditional form and line and restricts emotional display.　2. a traditional ballet, as *Swan Lake.*

**ballet russe** (French)　the Russian style of ballet that developed in the 19th century, heavily influenced by French and Italian ballet masters.

**balletti** (Italian)　*Music.* dance airs.

**ballon d'essai** (French)　(lit., 'trial balloon') an action or project undertaken solely to test public reaction.

**ballonné** (French)　(lit., 'ball-like; bounced') *Ballet.* a bouncy step in which a dancer extends one leg and lands on the opposite foot.

**ballotine** (French)　*Cookery.* boned meat, fish, or poultry rolled around a stuffing and served sliced.

**ballotté** (French)　tossed or bounced around, as a leaf in the wind.

**bal masqué** (French)　a masked ball.

**bambino,** *pl.* **bambini** (Italian)　1. a child; infant.　2. *Fine Arts.* (*cap.*) the infant Jesus in sacred art.

**bámonos.**   See vámonos.

**bamos.**   See vamos.

**ban** (Serbo-Croatian)   a former title for the governor of certain Balkan states.

**banco** (Italian)   1. a seat; bench.   2. a bank.

**Band,** *pl.* **Bände** (German)   a volume, as one book of a set.

**bandeau** (French)   1. a narrow band or ribbon for the hair.   2. a strapless brassiere. Also **balconet.**

**banderilla** (Spanish)   *Bullfighting.* a colorfully decorated barbed wand thrust into the bull's shoulder.

**banderillero** (Spanish)   *Bullfighting.* a bullfighter who specializes in the use of the **banderilla.**

**bandido** (Spanish)   a bandit.

**bandola** (Spanish)   *Music.* a musical instrument similar to the lute.

**bandolero** (Spanish)   (lit., 'highwayman; robber') a belt worn diagonally over the shoulder to carry cartridges of ammunition.

**bandurria** (Spanish)   *Music.* a folk instrument of the guitar family.

**banzai** (Japanese)   (lit., 'ten thousand years') a Japanese battle cry wishing long life to the emperor.

**baquero.**   See vaquero.

**barba rossa** (Italian)   a red beard.

**barbeau** (French)   a cornflower pattern, especially on porcelain.

**barbotine** (French)   a thin, clay mixture used for making delicate ceramic decorations.

**barbouillage** (French)   1. a daub.   2. a scribble; scrawl.

**barcarola** (Italian)   *Music.* a song of the gondolier. Also **barcarula.**

**Bardolino** (Italian)   a light red wine produced near the village of Bardolino in northern Italy.

**barège** (French)   a gauze fabric used for making dresses and veils. Also **barege.**

**bargello** (Italian)   1. *Architecture.* a headquarters for army officers or civil police, so named after the 16th-century Florentine palace serving that purpose.   2. *Needlework.* a form of embroidery on canvas, also known as *flame stitch,* characterized by its zigzag patterns and rainbow-like effects.

**bar mitzvah** (Hebrew)   *Judaism.* a formal ceremony recognizing the admission into the adult Jewish community of a boy who has reached the age of 13 and completed prescribed studies. See also **bas mitzvah.**

**barocco** (Italian)   1. *Architecture.* baroque; a highly decorated style originating in the Renaissance, a reaction against classical forms.   2. *Music.* baroque, a popular style of the 17th and 18th centuries.

**barra** (Spanish)   1. a bar; rail.   2. a sand bar.

**barracón** (Spanish)   1. a barracks; long, low building.   2. slave quarters.

**barranca** (Spanish)   a deep ravine or gully. Also **barranco.**

**barre** (French)   *Ballet.* a waist-high bar used by dancers to support their bodies while practicing leg movements.

**barrera** (Spanish)   a barrier; barricade.

**barrio** (Spanish)   a Hispanic neighborhood, especially in a poor urban area.

**bas** (French)   low; inferior; subordinate.   See also **à bas . . . .**

**bas bleu** (French)   a woman with literary or intellectual interests; bluestocking.

**bas, de haut en.**   See **de haut en bas.**

**bas mitzvah** (Hebrew)   *Judaism.* a formal ceremony recognizing the admission into the adult Jewish community of a girl who has reached the age of 12 or 13. Also **bat(h) mitzvah.** See also **bar mitzvah.**

**bas-relief** (French)   *Fine Arts.* a type of relief sculpture that projects slightly from its background; low relief. Also **basso rilievo.**

**bassa ottava** (Italian)   *Music.* a direction to play a passage an octave lower than written. Also **basso al ottava.**

**basse cour** (French)   *Architecture.* a service court of a large villa.

**basse danse** (French)   a style of dance popular in the late Middle Ages, characterized by dignified walking instead of lively steps or jumping.

**basse-taille** (French)   designating an enameling technique in which a background in low relief is covered with transparent enamel.

**basso,** *fem.* **bassa** (Italian)   *Music.* low; bass.

**basso al ottava.**   See **bassa ottava.**

**basso buffo** (Italian)   *Music.* a bass singer who does comic roles.

**basso cantante** (Italian)   *Music.* a bass voice of singing or lyrical nature, above the **basso profondo.**

**basso concertante** (Italian)   *Music.* 1. the chief bass.   2. certain parts for the cello or bassoon.

**basso continuo** (Italian)   *Music.* figured bass, a shorthand method of indicating by numbers the bass chords.

**basso ostinato** (Italian)   *Music.* a ground bass; a short bass part repeated throughout a movement.

**basso profondo** (Italian)   *Music.* a bass of very low register. Also **basso profundo.**

**basso rilievo** (Italian)   *Fine Arts.* low-relief sculpture, in which the figures are cut so as to project only slightly from the background. Also **bas-relief; basso relievo, basso-rilievo.** See also **alto rilievo; cavo rilievo; mezzo rilievo; schiacciato rilievo; stiacciato.**

**basso ripieno** (Italian)   *Music.* a bass part that occurs solely in passages played by the full orchestra.

**basta** (Italian)    that's enough!

**bastide** (French)    *Architecture.* 1. a planned town of the Middle Ages. 2. a small farmhouse of Provence.

**bastinado** (Spanish)    a form of torture in which the soles of the feet are beaten with a stick.

**bata de cola** (Spanish)    *Dance.* a dress with a long ruffled train worn by female flamenco dancers.

**bateau mouche** (French)    a glass-bottomed sightseeing boat of Paris.

**bat(h) mitzvah.**    See **bas mitzvah.**

**batik** (Javanese)    1. a technique for dyeing fabric that uses wax to prevent the dye from coloring certain patterned portions. 2. a fabric dyed by this method.

**batiste** (French)    a type of fine, sheer fabric.

**battement** (French)    *Ballet.* a movement in which a dancer raises one leg, then returns it to the supporting leg.

**batterie de cuisine** (French)    *Cookery.* a set of kitchen utensils.

**battre les cartes** (French)    to shuffle the cards.

**battuta,** *pl.* **battute** (Italian)    *Music.* beat; measure.

**Bauer** (German)    peasant.

**Bauernlied** (German)    *Music.* peasant's song.

**Bauernsuppe** (German)    *Cookery.* peasant soup.

**Bauhaus** (German)    *Fine Arts.* renowned German school of design of the 1920s and 1930s founded by the architect Walter Gropius.

**bavardage** (French)    babbling; idle conversation.

**bayle.**    See **baile.**

**Bearbeitung** (German)    *Music.* arrangement.

**béarnaise** (French)    *Cookery.* a sauce that originated in the French province of Béarn, made with butter, egg yolks, vinegar, wine, shallots, and tarragon.

**beata** (Latin)    *Roman Catholicism.* designation for a woman or girl who has been beatified.

**beatae memoriae** (Latin)    of blessed memory; fondly remembered. Also **bonae memoriae.**

**Beata Virgo Maria** (Latin)    *Christianity.* the Blessed Virgin Mary.

**beati possidentes** (Latin)    happy are those who possess (implying the principle that possession is nine points of the law).

**beatus** (Latin)    *Roman Catholicism.* designation for a man or boy who has been beatified.

**beaucoup** (French)    a lot; much.

**beau geste** (French)    a gesture for effect.

**beau idéal** (French)    a conception of perfection; model of excellence.

**beau monde** (French)　the world of fashion; high society.

**Beaune** (French)　a variety of red Burgundy wine.

**beau parti** (French)　a good matrimonial catch.

**beauté du diable** (French)　(lit., 'beauty of the devil') the bloom of youth.

**beaux-arts** (French)　1. the fine arts. 2. (*cap.*) an ostentatious architectural style that originated in France.

**beaux esprits.**　See **bel esprit.**

**beaux quartiers** (French)　the elegant, upper-class sections of Paris.

**bébé** (French)　a baby.

**bécassine** (French)　a snipe.

**beccafico** (Italian)　*Cookery.* a dish made with song birds that have been nourished on figs and grapes. Also **becfigue** (French).

**becfigue.**　See **beccafico.**

**bec fin** (French)　the refined palate of a **gourmet.**

**béchamel** (French)　*Cookery.* a basic white sauce made of butter, flour, milk, and stock.

**bêche-de-mer** (French)　a sea slug or trepang.

**beffa** (Italian)　a jest.

**beignet** (French)　*Cookery.* 1. a light pastry that is fried and served sprinkled with sugar. 2. a fritter.

**Beispiel** (German)　example.　See also **zum Beispiel.**

**bel canto** (Italian)　*Music.* a style of singing characterized by purity of tone and brilliant vocal display.

**bel esprit,** *pl.* **beaux esprits** (French)　a person of great wit or intellect.

**bel étage** (French)　the main story of a building.

**bella figura** (Italian)　a good appearance.

**belle âme** (French)　(lit., 'a beautiful soul') a revered person.

**Belle Epoque, La.**　See **La Belle Epoque.**

**belle étoile, à la.**　See **à la belle étoile.**

**belle indifférence** (French)　(lit., 'beautiful indifference') *Psychology.* a neurotic attitude characterized by detachment from and indifference to reality.

**belle, ma.**　See **ma belle.**

**belle peinture** (French)　(lit., 'beautiful painting') *Fine Arts.* 1. naturalistic or realistic painting, as distinct from Impressionism. 2. painting associated with a sensuous intimacy between the artist and his or her materials.

**Belle Province, La.**　See **La Belle Province.**

**belles-lettres** (French)　literature considered as a fine art or aesthetic expression.

**bellissima figura** (Italian)　a brilliant impression or effect.

**bello flagrante** (Latin)　in the heat of battle; during a battle or war.

**bellum internecinum** (Latin)  internecine war; a very destructive conflict, especially a struggle within a group.

**bel paese** (Italian)  a semi-soft Italian cheese.

**ben** (Hebrew)  son of (used before the father's name in a personal name).

**bene** (Latin)  well; well done.

**bene** (Italian)  *Music.* well; much. Also **ben.**

**Benedicite** (Latin)  (lit., 'bless you')  first word and title of a canticle in the Anglican liturgy.

**Benedictus** (Latin)  *Christian liturgy.* the part of the liturgy of the Mass that follows the Sanctus.

**bene esse** (Latin)  (lit., 'to be well') a state of prosperity or well-being.

**beneficium clericale** (Latin)  benefit of clergy; exemption from secular authority, enjoyed by some churchmen in the Middle Ages.

**bene merenti** (Latin)  to one (who is) well-deserving.

**bene meritus** (Latin)  well-deserving. Also, *fem.,* **bene merita.**

**beneplacimento** (Italian)  *Music.* the will or pleasure of the performer. See also **a beneplacito.**

**ben marcato** (Italian)  (lit., 'well-marked') *Music.* designating something to be played decisively.

**bentsh** (Yiddish)  to bless.

**ben venuto** (Italian)  welcome.

**bergère** (French)  *Furniture.* a type of comfortable armchair with a rounded back, first made in France in the early 18th century.

**bergerie** (French)  (lit., 'sheepfold') *Literature.* a work with pastoral characters and setting.

**berretta** (Italian)  a stiff cap worn by Roman Catholic and Anglican priests. Also **biretta.**

**berrettina** (Italian)  the scarlet skullcap worn by Roman Catholic cardinals. Also **berrettino.**

**berro** (Spanish)  watercress.

**bersagliere,** *pl.* **bersaglieri** (Italian)  a rifleman in the elite corps of the Italian army.

**besant** (French)  *Architecture.* an ornamental circular disk used in Norman architecture.

**Bes Din.**  See **Beth Din.**

**beso** (Spanish)  a kiss.

**bestiarium** (Latin)  a bestiary or collection of animal fables.

**bête noire** (French)  (lit., 'black beast') an object of sharp, personal dislike or dread.

**beth** (Hebrew)  1. a house. 2. the name for the second letter of the Hebrew alphabet.

**Beth Din,** *pl.* **Batte Din** (Hebrew)    a Jewish court of law.  Also **Bes Din.**
**Betonung** (German)    accentuation.
**beurre** (French)    butter.
**beurre blanc** (French)    (lit., 'white butter')  *Cookery.* a sauce of butter, white wine, minced shallots, and cream.
**beurre fondu** (French)    *Cookery.* melted butter seasoned with lemon.
**beurre manié** (French)    (lit., 'kneaded butter')  *Cookery.* a thickening agent for sauces and soups made from butter kneaded with flour.
**beurre noisette** (French)    (lit., 'hazelnut butter')  *Cookery.* a lightly browned butter.
**bezugo** (Spanish)  *Texas and Southwestern U.S.*  buffalo fish.  Also **besugo.**
**bhakti** (Sanskrit)    *Hinduism.* selfless devotion.
**bhang** (Hindi)    Indian hemp, often used as a narcotic.
**Bharat** (Hindi)    the Hindi name for India.
**bheesty** (Urdu)    a water carrier.  Also **bheestie; bhisti.**
**bialy** (Yiddish)    a round, flat roll with a depression in the middle, frequently served sprinkled with onion.
**bianco** (Italian)    white.
**bianco sangiovanni** (Italian)    *Fine Arts.* a white pigment used in **fresco** painting.
**bianco sopra bianco** (Italian)    (lit., 'white over white') *Antiques.* a white pigment decoration used on a white or bluish-white glaze in early Italian **maiolica.**
**bibelot** (French)    a small ornament; a trinket.
**bidet** (French)    a small bath, of chair height, for personal hygiene; a sitzbath.
**Biedermeierstil** (German)    *Fine Arts.* a style of art and design developed in the early 19th century.
**bien** (French)    well; well done.
**Biennale** (Italian)    *Fine Arts.* a renowned Venice art show held every two years.
**biennium** (Latin)    a period of two years.
**bienséance** (French)    propriety; decorum.
**bientôt, à.**    See à bientôt.
**bienvenue** (French)    welcome.
**Bier** (German)    beer.
**Bierstube** (German)    tavern.
**bifteck** (French)    beefsteak.
**bijouterie** (French)    jewelry.
**Bildung** (German)    formation; education.

**Bildungsroman** (German)   *Literature.* a novel concerned with the education of its hero.   Also **Erziehungsroman.**

**billabong** (Australian)   a dead-end stream leading away from a river.

**billet doux,** *pl.* **billets doux** (French)   a love note.

**biltong** (Afrikaans)   strips of sun-dried meat.

**biretta.**   See **beretta.**

**birra** (Italian)   beer.

**biscottino,** *pl.* **biscottini** (Italian)   a little biscuit or cookie.

**biscotto,** *pl.* **biscotti** (Italian)   a biscuit; cookie.

**bis in die** (Latin)   *Prescriptions.* twice a day.   *Abbr.* **b.i.d.**

**bismillah** (Arabic)   in the name of **Allah.**

**bisnaga** (Spanish)   *Texas and Mexico.* a cactus whose spines are used as toothpicks.   Also **biznaga.**

**bistecca** (Italian)   a beefsteak.

**bistro** (French)   a small, simple cafe or restaurant.   Also **bistrot.**

**bitte** (German)   1.   please.   2.   don't mention it; you're welcome.

**blanc de blancs** (French)   (lit., 'white of whites') a very pale white wine, especially a champagne, made from white grapes.

**blanc fixe** (French)   (lit., 'fixed white') a white pigment for paint, made with barium sulfate.

**blanchailles** (French)   small white fish.

**blanc mange** (French)   *Cookery.* a white pudding made of milk, sugar, and cornstarch.

**blanco** (Spanish)   white, as a white wine.

**blanquette** (French)   *Cookery.* a stew of meat, especially veal, prepared with cream.

**blasé** (French)   indifferent or unconcerned in attitude.

**Blaue Reiter, der** (German)   *Fine Arts.* a German school of painting of the early 20th century.

**Blechinstrument** (German)   *Music.* brass instrument.

**blini** (Russian)   a Russian-style rolled pancake.

**blintz** (Yiddish)   *Cookery.* a thin pancake similar to a **crêpe** that is rolled around a filling of cheese or fruit, then fried or baked.   Also **blintze.**

**Blitzen** (German)   lightning.

**Blitzkrieg** (German)   (lit., 'lightning war(fare)') highly mechanized, rapid-moving assault tactics.

**blond de veau** (French)   *Cookery.* veal broth stock.

**blouson** (French)   a short jacket fitted at the waist, or the top of a dress or blouse in this style.

**Blut und Boden** (German)   (lit., 'blood and soil') term for a Nazi genetic theory.

**Blut und Eisen** (German) (lit., 'blood and iron') term for Bismarck's theory that political disputes can be settled through military force.

**Blutwurst** (German) sausage made with pork and pork blood; black pudding.

**B'nai B'rith** (Hebrew) (lit., 'sons of the covenant') an international Jewish organization that sponsors philanthropic, educational, and cultural activities to promote community welfare.

**bobèche** (French) a cupped ring placed on a candlestick to catch drippings from the candle.

**bobeleh.** See **bubeleh.**

**boca** (Spanish) mouth.

**bocage** (French) (lit., 'grove') *Fine Arts.* a decorative motif of foliage or the like.

**bocca chiusa** (Italian) (lit., 'closed mouth') *Music.* humming.

**bocca ridente** (Italian) *Music.* in singing, a smiling position of the mouth.

**bocce** (Italian) a variety of lawn bowling (from the plural of *boccia,* the ball used in the game). Also **bocci; boccie.**

**bocconcini** (Italian) (lit., 'tidbits') *Cookery.* small pieces of veal cooked in a sauce of white wine.

**Boche** (French) a derogatory term for a German, especially a German soldier.

**Bockbier** (German) bock beer.

**bodega** (Spanish) 1. a grocery store. 2. a wine store or wine cellar.

**boeuf** (French) beef.

**boeuf à la mode** (French) *Cookery.* larded and pot-roasted beef served with brown gravy.

**boeuf bourguignon** (French) *Cookery.* beef cubes simmered with onions, mushrooms, and red wine, in the style of Burgundy.

**bois** (French) a woods or park, as the Bois de Boulogne in Paris.

**bois brûlé** (French) (lit., 'burnt wood') *Canadian.* someone descended from an Indian and a white Canadian.

**bois de vache** (French) (lit., 'cow's wood') dried buffalo dung, used as a fuel by American pioneers.

**boisson** (French) a beverage.

**boîte** (French) a nightclub. Also **boîte de nuit.**

**boitelle, à la.** See **à la boitelle.**

**bok choy** (Chinese) Chinese cabbage. Also **pak choy.**

**bola** (Spanish) a South American hunting device consisting of thongs with heavy balls fastened to them that, when thrown, entangles the legs of the quarry. Also **bolas.**

**bolero** (Spanish)   *Music.*   1. a Spanish folk dance.   2. the music for this dance, used by various composers, notably Ravel.   3. a short jacket.

**bollito misto** (Italian)   *Cookery.*   a boiled mixture of meats served with a tomato or pepper sauce.

**bolognese.**   See **alla bolognese.**

**bombachas** (Spanish)   the long, loose-fitting trousers worn by gauchos.

**bomban-wa** (Japanese)   good evening (a salutation).

**bombe** (French)   *Cookery.*   a frozen dessert in a round mold made with ice cream and **mousse.**

**bombé** (French)   *Furniture.*   curved or bulging outward.

**bombilla** (Spanish)   a small tube with a strainer at the tip, used for drinking **mate.**

**bon,** *fem.* **bonne** (French)   good.

**bona** (Latin)   *Law.*   goods; possessions.

**bonae fidei emptor** (Latin)   *Law.*   a purchaser in good faith.

**bonae memoriae.**   See **beatae memoriae.**

**bona fide** (Latin)   (lit., 'in good faith')   honest; sincere; genuine.

**bona fides** (Latin)   good faith; honest intention.

**bon ami,** *fem.* **bonne amie**   (French)   a good friend; sweetheart.

**bona vacantia** (Latin)   *Law.*   property with no apparent owner.

**bonbon** (French)   a confection made with a **fondant,** fruit, or nut center and covered with chocolate.

**bonbonnière** (French)   1. a confectionary.   2. a box or dish for candy.

**bon chic, bon genre** (French)   affluent and elegant.

**bon compte, à.**   See **à bon compte.**

**bon droit, à.**   See **à bon droit.**

**bon genre** (French)   good taste or form.

**bon goût** (French)   good taste, as in culinary and aesthetic matters.

**bon gré, mal gré** (French)   (lit., 'good will, bad will')   willy nilly; arbitrarily.

**bonheur-du-jour** (French)   (lit., 'happiness of the day')   *Furniture.*   a small writing desk with a fall-front and slender legs.

**bonhomie** (French)   good-heartedness; a pleasant, good-natured manner.

**bonis avibus** (Latin)   under good auspices.

**bonito,** *fem.* **bonita** (Spanish)   handsome; pretty.

**bon jour** (French)   good day; hello. Also **bonjour.**

**bon marché** (French)   (lit., 'good buy')   1. a bargain.   2. a shop with low-priced items. See also **à bon marché.**

**bon marché, à.**   See **à bon marché.**

**bon mot** (French)   (lit., 'good word')   a particularly appropriate word; a clever saying.

**bonne** (French)   a maid or nanny. See also **bon.**

**bonne année** (French)   happy new year!

**bonne bouche, la.**   See **la bonne bonche.**

**bonne chance** (French)   good luck (usually said as an exclamation of good will).

**bonne chère** (French)   good living, especially referring to good food.

**bonne foi** (French)   (lit., 'good faith') sincerity.

**bonne heure, à la.**   See **à la bonne heure.**

**bonne nuit** (French)   good night.

**bonne raison, à.**   See **à bonne raison.**

**bonne santé** (French)   good health.

**bonnet de nuit** (French)   a nightcap.

**bonnet rouge** (French)   1. *French history.* the red cap of liberty worn by extremists during the French Revolution. 2. a political extremist; radical.

**bonsai** (Japanese)   a technique for cultivating dwarf trees and shrubs.

**bon soir** (French)   good evening. Also **bonsoir.**

**bon ton** (French)   1. elegant and socially correct form or style. 2. fashionable society.

**bonum commune** (Latin)   the common good.

**bon vivant** (French)   a person who lives in luxurious style.

**bon viveur** (French)   a person who lives a life of dissipation.

**bon voyage** (French)   (have a) pleasant trip.

**Bordeaux** (French)   the renowned wine region of southwest France.

**bordelaise, à la.**   See **à la bordelaise.**

**bordello** (Italian)   a house of prostitution.

**borinqueño,** *fem.* **borinqueña** (Spanish)   a Puerto Rican, from the Indian name for Puerto Rico, *Borinquen.*

**borracho** (Spanish)   1. *n.* drunkard.   2. *adj.* drunk.

**borscht** (Russian)   a type of soup made with beets and cabbage, originating in eastern Europe. Also **borshtsh.**

**bossa nova** (Portuguese)   a modern dance rhythm of Brazilian origin.

**botánica** (Spanish)   a store that sells herbs.

**botón** (Spanish)   (lit., 'button') a knot at the end of a rope.

**bouche bée** (French)   (lit., 'mouth open') *Music.* singing with the mouth open but without articulating words. Compare **bouche fermée.**

**bouchée** (French)   (lit., 'mouthful') *Cookery.* a small shell of puff pastry used for serving hot **hors d'oeuvres.**

**bouche fermée** (French)   (lit., 'mouth closed') *Music.* singing with the mouth closed; humming. Compare **bouche bée.**

**bouche ouverte, à.**   See **à bouche ouverte.**

**bouclé** (French)   a woven fabric with a nubby or rough appearance.

**boudin** (French)   *Cookery.* black pudding containing forcemeat and blood, commonly rolled into the shape of a sausage. Also **boudin noir; boudin ordinaire.**

**boudiné** (French)   shaped like a sausage.

**boudoir** (French)   a woman's bedroom.

**bouffant** (French)   puffed out, as a *bouffant hairdo.*

**bouffe.**   See **opera bouffe.**

**bouillabaisse** (French)   *Cookery.* a soup or stew made with various fish and shellfish.

**bouilli** (French)   *Cookery.* boiled or stewed meat.

**bouillie** (French)   baby food; pap.

**bouillon** (French)   *Cookery.* clear meat broth.

**boulangerie** (French)   a bakery.

**boulette** (French)   *Cookery.* a small ball of meat or dough.

**bouquet d'herbes.**   See **bouquet garni.**

**bouquet garni** (French)   *Cookery.* a small bunch of herbs tied in a cheese-cloth bag, used to season soups and stews and then removed. Also **bouquet d'herbes.**

**bourgeois,** *fem.* **bourgeoise** (French)   characteristic of the middle class; conventional and conservative in values and behavior.

**bourgeoise, à la.**   See **à la bourgeoise.**

**bourgeoisie** (French)   1. the middle class; **bourgeois** society. 2. *Marxism.* the social class opposed to the proletariat.

**Bourgogne** (French)   Burgundy.

**boustrophedon** (Greek)   (lit., 'like ox-turning,' that is, like plowing) a manner of ancient writing in which the letters are written in lines running alternately from left to right and from right to left. Also **boustrophēdon.**

**boutade** (French)   *Ballet.* an impromptu dance, whimsically performed.

**bouteille** (French)   a bottle.

**boutonniere** (French)   a flower or small bouquet worn on the lapel. Also **boutonnière.**

**bout-rimés** (French)   *Prosody.* words or word endings that form rhymes.

**bouzouki** (Greek)   a stringed instrument similar to a mandolin, characteristic of modern Greek music.

**bozzetto,** *pl.* **bozzetti** (Italian)   *Fine Arts.* a drawing or sketch; a model.

**bracero** (Spanish)   a legal Mexican migrant laborer working in the United States.

**braciola,** *pl.* **braciole** (Italian)   a cutlet or chop.

**braguero** (Spanish)   an extra girth on a saddle behind the stirrups.

**braisé** (French)   *Cookery.* braised.

**brandade** (French)   *Cookery.* a highly seasoned codfish stew.

**branle** (French)   *Music.* a lively round dance originating in 16th century France.  Also **bransle.**

**bras de lumière** (French)   (lit., 'arm of light') a wall light.

**brasero** (Spanish)   a brazier.

**bras ouverts, à.**   See **à bras ouverts.**

**bras, positions de.**   See **positions de bras.**

**brasserie** (French)   a restaurant specializing in simple, filling food.

**bratwurst** (German)   a variety of pork sausage.

**Bräu** (German)   brew; beer.

**Brauhaus** (German)   brewery.

**Brautlied** (German)   *Music.* bridal song.

**bravissimo,** *fem.* **bravissima** (Italian)   extremely well done!

**bravo,** *fem.* **brava** (Italian)   well done!

**bravura** (Italian)   1. a display of daring.   2. *Music.* a passage demanding great technical skill.  See also **di bravura.**   3. *Fine Arts.* a term used in criticism to refer to a painter's exceptional skill.

**bravura, aria di.**   See **aria d'abilità.**

**brea** (Spanish)   *Geology.* a thick, petroleum substance found in tar sands.

**breva conserva** (Spanish)   cigars that are bundled tightly together to create odd shapes.

**Brie** (French)   a soft-ripened cheese with a white rind.

**Brief** (German)   letter; correspondence.

**Briefmarke** (German)   postage stamp.

**brillante** (Italian)   *Music.* sparkling; in a brilliant fashion.

**brindis** (Spanish)   1. a toast.   2. *Bullfighting.* a bullfighter's short speech before killing the bull.

**brioche** (French)   *Cookery.* a light, sweet bun made with flour, butter, yeast, and eggs.

**brio, con.**   See **con brio.**

**brisé** (French)   *Ballet.* a step in which a dancer springs off one foot, beats both legs, then lands on both feet.

**brise-soleil** (French)   (lit., 'sun-break') *Architecture.* a sun shade on the exterior of a building.

**broché** (French)   woven with a pattern; brocaded.

**broche, à la.**   See **en brochette.**

**brochette** (French)   a skewer or spit.

**broderie à jour** (French)   openwork embroidery.

**brodetto** (Italian)   a fish soup.

**brodo** (Italian)   broth; stock.  Also **broda.**

**bronco** (Spanish)   a wild or treacherous horse.

**brouillé** (French)   scrambled; confused.

**Brucke, die** (German)   *Fine Arts.*  a group of Expressionist German painters of the early 20th century whose work resembled Fauvism.

**brujo,** *fem.* **bruja** (Spanish)   a sorcerer; magician; witch.

**brûlé** (French)   1. *Cookery.*  cooked or flavored with burnt sugar.  2.
*Pacific Northwest.*  an area of forest destroyed by fire.

**brûle-parfums** (French)   a small, decorative brasier used for burning in-
cense.

**Brunello** (Italian)   a variety of red wine produced in Tuscany.

**brut** (French)   *Wine.*  very dry, used especially of champagnes.

**brutti ma buoni** (Italian)   (lit., 'ugly but good') meringue cookies made
with ground almonds.

**brutum fulmen** (Latin)   (lit., 'insensitive thunderbolt') used in reference
to an idle threat or a show of force (from Pliny, *Nat. Hist.* II.117).

**brynza** (Rumanian)   a sharp cheese made from sheep's milk.  Also
**bryndza.**

**bubeleh** (Yiddish)   darling; dear one (a term of affection).  Also **bobeleh.**

**bucatini** (Italian)   a variety of **pasta** shaped like thick, hollow **spaghetti.**

**Buch** (German)   book.

**bûche de Noël** (French)   (lit., 'Christmas log') *Cookery.*  a rich chocolate
cake with mocha frosting, shaped like a log and served as a Christmas
specialty.

**Buchhandel** (German)   the book trade.

**Buchhandlung** (German)   a book shop.

**buena salud** (Spanish)   good health; greetings.

**buenas noches** (Spanish)   good night.

**buenas tardes** (Spanish)   good afternoon.

**buena suerte** (Spanish)   good luck.

**bueno** (Spanish)   good.

**buenos días** (Spanish)   good day; hello.

**Buen Retiro** (Spanish)   *Fine Arts.*  exceptionally fine 18th-century porce-
lains, named for the palace in Madrid.

**buen viaje** (Spanish)   have a good trip.

**buffa, opera.**   See **opera buffa.**

**buffo,** *fem.* **buffa** (Italian)   *Music.*  a singer who does comic roles in an
opera.

**Bühnenfestspiel** (German)   *Music.*  stage festival play.

**buksheesh.**   See **baksheesh.**

**bulerías** (Spanish)   *Music.*  the flamenco songs and dances of Jerez.

**Bund** (German)   union.

**Bundesrat** (German)   1.  the Federal Council in Germany (1871–
1919).  2.  the Upper House of the West German Federal Parliament.

**Bundesrepublik Deutschland** (German)  the German Federal Republic (West Germany).

**Bundestag** (German)  1.  the Federal Assembly of the German Diet (1815–1866).  2.  the Lower House of the West German Federal Parliament.

**buñuelitos** (Spanish)  *Cookery*. little fritters.

**buñuelos** (Spanish)  *Cookery*. sweet fried cakes; fritters.

**buona fortuna** (Italian)  good luck!

**buona notte** (Italian)  good night (said before retiring for the evening).

**buona sera** (Italian)  good evening.

**buon fresco** (Italian)  *Fine Arts*. painting done on damp plaster.  See also fresco.

**buon giorno** (Italian)  good day; good morning; good afternoon.

**buongustaio,** *pl.* **buongustai** (Italian)  one who appreciates fine food and drink.

**Buon Natale** (Italian)  Merry Christmas.

**buono** (Italian)  good (used as an exclamation).

**Burg** (German)  fortress; castle.

**Bürgermeister** (German)  mayor.

**burletta** (Italian)  *Music*. a variety of Italian comic opera popular during the 18th century.

**burrito** (Spanish)  (lit., 'little donkey')  *Cookery*. a flour tortilla rolled around a filling of beans, beef, or other ingredients.

**burro** (Italian)  butter.

**Burschenschaft** (German)  any of various German social fraternities of university students.

**bustier** (French)  a type of long, boned brassiere, worn inside a low-cut dress or as a top.

**butifarra** (Spanish)  a sausage common to certain regions of Spain.

**bwana** (Swahili)  boss; master.

# C

**cabala** (Hebrew)    1. an esoteric doctrine based on a mystical interpretation of Scripture, developed by rabbis in the Middle Ages. 2. any occult, esoteric, or secret doctrine or study. Also **cabbala; kabala; kabbala.**

**cabaletta** (Italian)    *Music.* a short, spirited melody ending an **aria** or duet, often with an accompaniment that recalls the galloping of a horse. Also **cabbaletta.**

**caballada** (Spanish)    fresh horses; remounts. Also **remonta; remuda.**

**caballero** (Spanish)    1. a horseman.    2. a Spanish gentleman.

**caballo** (Spanish)    a horse.

**cabaña, cabana** (Spanish)    1. a cabin; hut.    2. a small cabin used as a bathhouse.

**cabaret** (French)    1. a large restaurant that provides entertainment or floor shows as well as food and drink. 2. a floor show or the entertainment at a night club.

**cabbala.**    See **cabala.**

**Cabernet Sauvignon** (French)    a grape variety used in making red wine, originally produced in **Bordeaux.**

**cabestro** (Spanish)    a rope halter.

**cabeza** (Spanish)    head.

**cabillaud** (French)    codfish.

**cabinet d'aisance** (French)    (lit., 'closet of ease')    a rest room; toilet.

**cabochon** (French)    1. a polished but unfaceted precious stone that has an oval or convex form. 2. a decorative design that resembles an unfaceted gem, commonly used on 18th-century furniture.

**cabriole** (French)    1. *Furniture.* a tapering leg that curves outward at the top and inward toward the bottom, with the foot commonly designed to resemble an animal's paw. 2. *Ballet.* a leaping step in which one leg beats against the other without crossing.

**cabrito** (Spanish)    a milk-fed goat.

51

**caccia** (Italian)    1. the hunt; chase.    2. *Music.* a form in which two voices, often singing about the hunt, follow each other in rapid succession.

**cacciagione** (Italian)    wild game. Also **selvaggina.**

**cacciatore** (Italian)    (lit., 'hunter')    *Cookery.* designating a casserole dish prepared with olive oil, tomatoes, onion, and other seasonings.

**cachepot** (French)    a decorative covering or vase used to conceal a flower pot.

**cachet** (French)    1. an official seal or symbol, as that used on a letter or document.    2. a distinguishing mark or characteristic, especially one that confers prestige.

**cachucha** (Spanish)    *Music.* a Spanish folk dance similar to the **bolero.** Also **cachuca.**

**caciocavallo** (Italian)    a hard-ripened Italian cheese.

**cacique** (Spanish)    1. a chief of an Indian tribe.    2. a local political boss.

**cacoethes carpendi** (Latin)    a mania for faultfinding.

**cacoethes loquendi** (Latin)    a mania for talking.

**cacoethes scribendi** (Latin)    a mania for writing (from Juvenal, *Satires* 7.52).

**cacqueteuse.**    See **caquetoire.**

**cadenza** (Italian)    *Music.* an ornamental passage just before the end of a vocal piece or a movement that gives the performer a chance to display virtuosity.

**cadre** (French)    (lit., 'frame')    1. *Military.* an essential contingent of officers and enlisted personnel necessary to train a new unit.    2. a group of people qualified to train or lead an organization, such as a political party or business.

**caetera desunt.**    See **cetera desunt.**

**café** (French)    coffee.

**café au lait** (French)    1. hot coffee and scalded milk mixed together in equal amounts. Also **caffe latte** (Italian).    2. a light brown color.

**café brûlot** (French)    coffee with flaming brandy.

**café con leche** (Spanish)    a morning beverage consisting of equal parts of coffee and hot milk.

**café crème** (French)    coffee with cream. Also **café à la crème.**

**café filtre** (French)    strong, filtered coffee, commonly flavored with chicory and usually drunk black. Also **filtre.**

**café nature.**    See **café noir.**

**café noir** (French)    black coffee. Also **café nature.**

**Caffaggiolo** (Italian)    *Antiques.* a variety of **maiolica** produced near the Castle of Caffaggiolo.

**caffè espresso** (Italian)   a strong Italian-style coffee brewed by a pressurized method using finely ground, dark-roasted beans. Also **espresso.**

**caffè latte.**   See **café au lait.**

**cafone,** *pl.* **cafoni** (Italian)   a peasant; boor.

**cagnotte** (French)   *Gambling.* a money box used to hold the fees that a casino charges as a share of the stakes.

**cahier** (French)   (lit., 'notebook; journal')   **1.** *Bookbinding.* sheets of paper placed together for binding. **2.** an official report of an organization.

**caille** (French)   quail.

**"Ça Ira"** (French)   (lit., 'it will go on')   the title of a song popular during the French Revolution.

**calabozo** (Spanish)   a jail.

**calamaretti** (Italian)   small, baby squid.

**calamari** (Italian)   squid.

**calando** (Italian)   (lit., 'lowering')   *Music.* gradually decreasing in strength and speed.

**calcando** (Italian)   (lit., 'trampling')   *Music.* quickening gradually.

**caldo,** *fem.* **calda** (Italian)   warm; hot.

**caldo gallego** (Spanish)   *Cookery.* a Galician-style soup containing chick peas, sausage, pork, tomatoes, and potatoes.

**caliente** (Spanish)   hot; warm.

**calina** (Spanish)   a summertime haze that is common in Spain.

**caliph** (Arabic)   *Islam.* a title for a Muslim religious and civil leader. Also **kaliph.**

**calle** (Spanish)   street.

**calmato** (Italian)   *Music.* calmed.

**calore, con.**   See **con calore.**

**caloroso** (Italian)   (lit., 'warm')   *Music.* passionate.

**Calvados** (French)   a dry, apple brandy made in the Calvados region of Normandy.

**calzoni,** *sing.* **calzone** (Italian)   (lit., 'trousers')   *Cookery.* bread dough or dumplings stuffed with cheese, meat, or other fillings and baked.

**camarero** (Spanish)   a waiter; valet.

**camarón** (Spanish)   shrimp.

**cambio** (Spanish)   exchange rate.

**cambré** (French)   (lit., 'arched')   *Ballet.* a backward or sideways bending of the body from the waist.

**Camembert** (French)   a type of soft-ripened cheese made in small wheels.

**camera lucida** (Latin)   a device that can project an image from an optical instrument onto a sheet of paper, as for tracing.

**camera obscura** (Latin)   a device designed to receive a visual image through an aperture into a darkened area, once used for observation, exhibitions, etc.

**cameriera** (Italian)   a waitress; chambermaid.

**cameriere** (Italian)   a waiter.

**camino real** (Spanish)   (lit., 'royal road')   1. a highway.   2. the best way; the highest way. See also **El Camino Real.**

**Camorra** (Italian)   a Neapolitan secret society and criminal group of the 19th and early 20th centuries.

**camorrista,** *pl.* **camorristi** (Italian)   a member of the **Camorra.**

**campagnarde, à la.**   See **à la campagnarde.**

**campagne, à la.**   See **à la campagne.**

**Campari** (Italian)   a brand name for a red, bittersweet **aperitif.**

**campeador** (Spanish)   champion in battle, an epithet applied to El Cid.

**campesino,** *fem.* **campesina** (Spanish)   a peasant; a rural laborer.

**campo santo** (Spanish)   (lit., 'holy field') a cemetery. Also **camposanto.**

**cañada** (Spanish)   1. a valley.   2. a ravine.

**canapé** (French)   (lit., 'covering; canopy')   1. an appetizer consisting of a thin slice of bread or toast topped with cheese, **pâté,** etc.   2. *Furniture.* a style of 18th-century French sofa.   3. *Bridge.* a strategy of bidding short suits before long suits.

**canard** (French)   duck.

**Cancer** (Latin)   the Crab, a constellation and sign of the zodiac.

**cancionero** (Spanish)   *Literature.* a collection of songs and poems.

**candelia** (Spanish)   *Southwestern U.S. and Mexico.* severe weather that is damaging to agriculture.

**canestrelli** (Italian)   (lit., 'little baskets') a variety of Italian butter cookies.

**caneton** (French)   duckling.

**cannelé** (French)   fluted; grooved.

**cannellini** (Italian)   (lit., 'little tubes') white kidney beans.

**cannelloni** (Italian)   (lit., 'large tubes') *Cookery.* tube-shaped pieces of pasta containing a filling of meat or cheese and baked.

**cannelon** (French)   *Cookery.* 1. a fluted mold for ices and jellies.   2. a hollow tube of puff pastry.

**cannoli,** *sing.* **cannolo** (Italian)   (lit., 'tubes') *Cookery.* 1. a dessert specialty consisting of small tubes of fried pastry with sweet cheese- or cream-based filling.   2. short, cut lengths of macaroni.

**cañon** (Spanish)   a narrow, deep valley; canyon.

**cañoncito** (Spanish)   a small canyon.

**canso** (Provençal)   a Provençal lyric poem or love song. Also **cansó; canzo.**

**cantabile** (Italian)  *Music.* 1. designating a smooth, flowing style or passage.  2. in a song-like manner.

**Cantabrigiensis** (Latin)  pertaining to Cambridge, England, especially Cambridge University. *Abbr.* **Cantab.**

**cantando** (Italian)  *Music.* singing.

**cantante, basso.**  See **basso cantante.**

**cantata** (Italian)  *Music.* a composition, either religious or secular, with solos, choruses, and orchestral accompaniment, similar in style to an opera but without scenery. See also **oratorio.**

**cantatore** (Italian)  *Music.* a male singer.

**cantatrice** (Italian)  *Music.* a female singer.

**cante flamenco** (Spanish)  *Music.* a general term applied to the song typical of Spanish gypsies of Andalusia, unique in Western music for the minor tones it employs. See also **cante hondo.**

**cante hondo** (Spanish)  *Music.* a folk song of Spanish gypsies characterized by profound sadness in both theme and style; generally considered a subtype of **cante flamenco.**

**cantilena** (Italian)  *Music.* the melody of a composition; a songlike passage.

**cantillatio** (Latin)  *Church music.* chanting used for certain parts of the liturgy of the Mass.

**cantina** (Spanish)  a bar; a saloon.

**canto** (Italian)  1. a major division in a long poem.  2. *Music.* a song; melody.

**cantoris** (Latin)  (lit., 'of the singer')  *Church music.* indicating what is sung by the half of the choir sitting on the gospel side of the church, the same side as the choir director; opposed to **decani.** *Abbr.* **cant.**

**cantus** (Latin)  song; melody.

**cantus planus** (Latin)  *Church music.* plainsong; Gregorian chant.

**canzonetta** (Italian)  *Music.* a short form of the vocal **canzone;** any short song.

**canzone,** *pl.* **canzoni** (Italian)  1. *Literature.* a lyric verse form consisting of from five to seven stanzas and a final short stanza, with love, politics, or satire as the subject.  2. the musical settings of such poems. Also **canzona.**

**capa** (Spanish)  cape; cloak. See also **capote.**

**capataz** (Spanish)  boss; foreman.

**capeador** (Spanish)  *Bullfighting.* a bullfighter who teases the bull with his cape.

**capeando** (Spanish)  *Bullfighting.* working with the cape alone, said of the matador.

55

**capella.** See **a cappella.**

**capias** (Latin) *Law.* a writ ordering an arrest.

**capitán** (Spanish) 1. a military captain. 2. the leader of a group or tribe.

**capo,** *pl.* **capi** (Italian) (lit., 'head') 1. a leader of a branch of the **Mafia.** Also **caporegime.** See also **capo di tutti capi.** 2. *Music.* the beginning. See also **da capo.**

**capocollo** (Italian) a type of cold cut made from the neck of a pig.

**Capo-di-Monte** (Italian) 1. *Antiques.* a variety of high-quality soft-paste porcelain (named for an 18th-century factory near Naples where it was made). 2. Also **capodimonte.** porcelain pieces in this style.

**capo di tutti capi** (Italian) a Mafia leader who ranks above other leaders. See also **capo; Mafia.**

**caponata** (Italian) a relish made of eggplant and other vegetables.

**caporal** (Spanish) a foreman; boss.

**caporegime.** See **capo,** 1.

**capote** (Spanish) a cloak, especially one worn by a bullfighter. See also **capa.**

**cappella.** See **a cappella.**

**cappelletti,** *sing.* **cappelletto** (Italian) (lit., 'little hats') *Cookery.* a variety of stuffed **pasta,** usually served in soup.

**capperi** (Italian) capers.

**cappuccino** (Italian) (lit., 'a Capuchin monk,' in reference to the color of a Capuchin's robe) a mixture of espresso coffee and steamed milk. See also **caffè espresso; schiuma.**

**câpres** (French) capers.

**capriccio** (Italian) 1. whim; fancy. 2. *Music.* a composition in free form, often in quick tempo.

**capriccioso** (Italian) *Music.* in a free, imaginative style.

**Capricornus** (Latin) the Goat, a constellation and sign of the zodiac.

**Caput Mundi** (Latin) Head of the World, once used of Rome.

**caquetoire** (French) *Antiques.* a kind of narrow, upright chair with widely splayed arms, popular in 16th-century France. Also **cacqueteuse; caqueteuse.**

**cara** *or* **cara mia** (Italian) my dear; my beloved (used of a woman). See also **caro.**

**cara** (Spanish) face.

**carabinero** (Spanish) 1. a revenue guard. 2. a border guard.

**carabiniere,** *pl.* **carabinieri** (Italian) an Italian policeman; a military policeman; a rifleman.

**caracoles** (Spanish) (lit., 'snails') an exclamation of surprise.

**caractère.** See **danse de caractère.**

**caramba** (Spanish)   an exclamation of surprise.

**cara sposa** (Italian)   dear wife.

**carbonari,** *sing.* **carbonaro** (Italian)   members of the Carboneria, a secret political society of the 19th century sworn to establish a united, republican Italy.

**carillon à clavier** (French)   *Music.* an instrument consisting of an arrangement of keys and pedals that ring bells.

**carilloneur** (French)   a person who plays a carillon.

**Cariñena** (Spanish)   a variety of wine from Aragon in northeastern Spain that has an unusually high alcohol content.

**carísima** (Spanish)   dearest; loved one.

**carissima** (Italian)   dearest (one).

**carità** (Italian)   1. *Music.* tenderness; feeling.   2. *Fine Arts.* a portrayal of maternal love.

**caritas** (Latin)   *Christianity.* the virtue of charity, love of God and one's neighbor.

**carmagnole** (French)   1. a dance and song that were popular during the French Revolution. 2. a man's jacket with wide lapels and metal buttons, worn by the French revolutionaries.

**carmen,** *pl.* **carmina** (Latin)   poem; song; lyric.

**carne** (Italian, Spanish)   1. meat.   2. flesh.

**carne de vaca** (Spanish)   beef.

**carnero** (Spanish)   a ram.

**carnicería** (Spanish)   a meat shop; butcher shop.

**carnicero** (Spanish)   a butcher.

**caro** *or* **caro mio** (Italian)   my dear; my beloved (used of a man).   See also **cara.**

**carpaccio** (Italian)   *Cookery.* a dish of raw, thinly sliced beef dressed with vinegar and oil.

**carpe diem** (Latin)   (lit., 'seize the day') take advantage of present opportunity (from Horace, *Odes* I.11.8).

**carré** (French)   *Cookery.* a piece of lamb, pork, or veal cut from the loin.

**carré, en.**   See **en carré.**

**carrelet** (French)   a large European flounder; plaice.

**carretera** (Spanish)   a road; highway.

**carta** (Italian)   a menu.

**carte** (French)   a menu; bill of fare.   See also **à la carte.**

**carte, à la.**   See **à la carte.**

**carte blanche** (French)   (lit., 'blank card') 1. a sheet of paper that is blank except for a signature, given by the signer to another to write in anything he pleases. 2. full, unconditional authority granted to a person.

**carte de vins** (French)    a wine list.

**carte de visite** (French)    a calling card.

**carte du jour** (French)    the menu of the day.

**cartel** (Spanish)    (lit., 'poster')    *Bullfighting.* the reputation or prestige of a bullfighter.

**cartellino,** *pl.* **cartellini** (Italian)    (lit., 'label')    *Fine Arts.* the representation in a work of art of a small paper scroll with an inscription.

**Carthago delenda est** (Latin)    Carthage must be destroyed (unwavering opinion of Cato the Censor (234–149 B.C.), who urged the Roman Senate to all-out war on Rome's rival, Carthage).

**cartonnier** (French)    *Furniture.* an ornamental box for papers, usually placed on a desk.

**carton-pierre** (French)    a type of **papier-mâché** decorated to simulate carved stone or wood.

**casa** (Italian, Spanish)    a house.

**casa grande** (Spanish)    (lit., 'big house') the main house on a large estate or hacienda.

**casalinga, alla.**    See **alla casalinga.**

**Casa Rosada, la** (Spanish)    (lit., 'the pink house')    the presidential palace in Buenos Aires, from the balcony of which Evita Perón often made speeches.

**casa vinicola** (Italian)    a winery.

**Casbah.**    See **Kasbah.**

**cassata** (Italian)    *Cookery.* 1. a Sicilian cheesecake garnished with candied fruits.    2. a molded dessert dish with a filling of ice cream, whipped cream, and brandied fruits or nuts.

**casse-croûte** (French)    a snack; light lunch.

**cassis.**    See **crème de cassis.**

**cassoulet** (French)    *Cookery.* a stew of white beans simmered with meats such as preserved goose, lamb, pork, and sausage.

**castañeta** (Spanish)    a castanet.

**castellano,** *fem.* **castellana** (Spanish)    Castilian.

**Castelli** (Italian)    *Antiques.* a variety of **maiolica** produced in the Abruzzi region in the 16th century.

**castrato,** *pl.* **castrati** (Italian)    *Music.* a male singer with a falsetto voice (from the former practice of castrating boys before puberty to preserve their high voices). Also **evirato.**

**casus** (Latin)    an event; an occurrence.

**casus belli** (Latin)    an event that precipitates a war.

**catalán** (Spanish)    designating something from Catalonia in northeastern Spain.

**catalogue raisonné** (French)    a classified list of items, as books or paintings, with descriptions or annotations.

**caudillo** (Spanish)   1. a leader; chieftain; political boss.    2. See **El Caudillo**.

**causa** (Spanish)   a cause; a goal of political or social action.

**causa causans** (Latin)   *Philosophy.* the cause that causes all things; the First Cause or Supreme Being.

**causa sine qua non** (Latin)   a necessary precondition to an event. Also **conditio sine qua non.** See also **sine qua non.**

**cause célèbre** (French)   an event or incident that draws wide public attention, as a political debate or criminal trial.

**causerie** (French)   1. light conversation.   2. a literary essay.

**causeuse** (French)   *Furniture.* a settee for two.

**ça va** (French)   (lit., 'that goes') all right; fine.

**cava** (Spanish)   1. a Spanish sparkling wine from the area of Catalonia near Barcelona.   2. a winery that produces such wines.

**Cavandoli** (Italian)   a form of **macramé** (named for the Countess Valentina Cavandoli of Turin, who devised it as a pastime for orphans).

**ça va sans dire** (French)   that goes without saying.

**cavatelli** (Italian)   *Cookery.* pasta in the shape of small, fluted shells.

**cavatina** (Italian)   *Music.* a short **aria** noted for its simplicity.

**caveat actor** (Latin)   let the doer beware.

**caveat emptor** (Latin)   let the buyer beware; buy at your own risk.

**caveat lector** (Latin)   let the reader beware.

**caveat venditor** (Latin)   let the seller beware.

**caveat viator** (Latin)   let the traveler beware.

**cave canem** (Latin)   beware of the dog.

**cavetto** (Italian)   *Architecture.* a type of concave molding.

**cavolfiore** (Italian)   cauliflower.

**cavo rilievo** (Italian)   *Fine Arts.* relief carving in which no surface is higher than the plane of the surrounding border. Also **cavo-rilievo.**

**cazo** (Spanish)   a dipper.

**cazuela** (Spanish)   a semi-glazed earthenware pan used for **paella.**

**céad míle fáilte** (Gaelic)   (lit., 'a hundred thousand welcomes') a traditional Irish expression of welcome.

**ceci** (Italian)   chick peas.

**cedant arma togae** (Latin)   (lit., 'let arms yield to the toga') military authority should be subject to civil authority.

**celeramente** (Italian)   *Music.* speedily; with speed.

**celerità** (Italian)   *Music.* speed.

**cellarino.**   See **collarino.**

**cembalo.**    See **claricembalo.**

**cena** (Italian, Spanish)    supper.

**cencerro** (Spanish)    1. a large bell worn around the neck of a mule, horse, etc.    2. the lead animal in a large team that wears such a bell.

**cenci** (Italian)    (lit., 'rags')    *Cookery.* fried twists of dough, similar to doughnuts.

**censor deputatus** (Latin)    *Roman Catholicism.* an official charged with examining a work prior to publication to determine whether it is contrary to faith and morals.

**centavo** (Spanish)    one cent.

**centennium** (Latin)    a period of 100 years.

**centime** (French)    a French coin of small value, equal to one hundredth of a franc.

**centone.**    See **pasticcio, 2.**

**central** (Spanish)    *Caribbean.* a centrally located sugar-processing plant that serves the cane plantations of a given area.

**cequia.**    See **acequia.**

**certiorari** (Latin)    (lit., '(in order) to be informed')    *Law.* designating a writ issued by a superior court to a lower court requiring that records of a case be presented for review.

**cervelle** (French)    brains, such as calves' brains, prepared in various dishes.

**cerveza** (Spanish)    beer.

**cesta** (Spanish)    1. a basket.    2. *Jai alai.* a curved basket that fits over the hand, used for catching and throwing the ball. See also **fronton; jai alai.**

**c'est à dire** (French)    that is to say; in other words. Also **c'est-à-dire.**

**c'est autre chose** (French)    that's something else.

**c'est ça** (French)    that's it; that's right.

**c'est dommage** (French)    that's too bad; that's a shame.

**c'est la guerre** (French)    that's (the way of) war.

**c'est la vie** (French)    that's life (an expression of resignation).

**cetera desunt** (Latin)    the rest is missing. Also **caetera desunt; desunt c(a)etera.**

**ceteris paribus** (Latin)    with (all) other things being equal.

**cetro** (Spanish)    (lit., 'scepter')    a large cigar, usually about seven inches long.

**ceviche** (Spanish)    *Cookery.* an appetizer consisting of fish marinated in lime juice, onions, tomatoes, and olive oil.

**cha** (Chinese)    tea. Also **chah.**

**chacolí** (Spanish)    a young, acidic wine produced in the Basque country in northern Spain.

**chacun à son goût.**    See **à chacun son goût.**

**chaire,** *pl.* **chairete** (Greek)    welcome; farewell; hail (an exclamation expressing good will).

**chaise longue** (French)   *Furniture.* an easy chair or lounge chair with a long seat for the legs.

**challah** (Hebrew)   *Judaism.* leavened white bread made with eggs and a glaze of egg white, baked for Sabbath and holiday occasions. Also **challeh; challoth; hallah.**

**chamaco** (Spanish)   a young boy; kid.

**chambré** (French)   *Wine.* brought to room temperature.

**champignon** (French)   a mushroom.

**champlevé** (French)   *Fine Arts.* a type of enameling in which the enamel is put into cells incised in the metal ground. Also **taille d'épargne.**

**chanson** (French)   a song.

**chansonnier** (French)   1. a composer of songs, especially satirical ones. 2. a collection of troubador songs.

**chansons de geste** (French)   *Literature.* epic poems of medieval France, such as the *Chanson de Roland.*

**chansons de toile** (French)   medieval songs sung by women while spinning thread.

**chantage** (French)   blackmail.

**chantefable** (French)   *Literature.* a medieval tale in prose and verse, such as *Aucassin et Nicolette.*

**chanterelle** (French)   1. a type of mushroom. Also called **girolle.** 2. *Music.* the treble string of a violin.

**chanteuse** (French)   a female concert or nightclub singer.

**Chanukah.**    See **Hanukkah.**

**chapa** (Spanish)   1. a disk, usually silver, used as an ornament on a **sombrero.** 2. a metal plate.

**chaparejos** (Spanish)   *Southwestern U.S. and Mexico.* protective leather leggings worn by cowboys; chaps. See also **chivarras.**

**chapati** (Hindi)   unleavened bread in the form of a thin cake, baked on a griddle. Also **chapatti.**

**chapeau** (French)   a hat.

**chapeaux bas** (French)   hats off.

**chapel de fer** (French)   (lit., 'hat of iron') a wide-brimmed helmet intended to deflect blows from above.

**chapon** (French)   a capon.

**Charakterstück** (German)   1. *Music.* a character piece. 2. *Theater.* a character play.

**charango** (Spanish)   *Music.* a Latin American Indian instrument made from a tortoise shell.

**charbonnier** (French)   a charcoal burner.

**charcuterie** (French)   1. a pork butcher's shop. 2. dressed pork; cold cuts.

**charcutier** (French)   a pork butcher.

**chargé d'affaires** (French)   *Diplomacy.* an official assigned the duty of conducting business in the absence of an ambassador or minister. Also **chargé.**

**charnu** (French)   (lit., 'fleshy') *Wine.* full-bodied.

**charpoy** (Urdu)   a light bedstead used in India. Also **charpai.**

**charro** (Spanish)   1. *Mexico.* a skilled horseman. 2. the traditional dress of Mexican horsemen. 3. folk art and dress of Salamanca, Spain.

**Chartreuse** (French)   an aromatic, greenish **liqueur** made by Carthusian monks at Grenoble, France.

**Chasid.**   See **Hasid.**

**chasse** (French)   music that characterizes a hunt, especially music with galloping rhythms and horn playing.

**chassé** (French)   *Dance.* a gliding step in which one foot follows the other.

**chasse-café** (French)   a **liqueur** taken after coffee.

**chasse-cousins** (French)   anything inhospitable or impolite, usually calculated to discourage unwanted guests.

**chassé-croisé** (French)   1. *Dance.* a dance movement in which partners repeatedly change places. 2. any situation in which people repeatedly change places.

**chasseur** (French)   (lit., 'hunter') *Cookery.* a sauce made of shallots, white wine, and mushrooms.

**château,** *pl.* **châteaux** (French)   1. a castle or fortress of the Middle Ages. 2. an elegant rural estate resembling a French castle. 3. a private winery, especially of the **Bordeaux** region of France.

**Châteaubriand** (French)   *Cookery.* a large cut of beef tenderloin, broiled and served with **béarnaise** sauce.

**château d'eau** (French)   (lit., 'water castle') *Architecture.* a designed facade of a fountain or reservoir.

**Châteauneuf-du-Pape** (French)   a select variety of wine from the **Côtes du Rhone.**

**châtelaine** (French)   1. the mistress of a fashionable estate. 2. an ornamental waist chain to which small household items may be attached.

**chatoyant** (French)   shimmering; changeable in color or brilliance.

**chaudfroid** (French)   (lit., 'hot-cold') *Cookery.* a cooked dish of fowl or game, served cold with a jelly or sauce. Also **chaud-froid.**

**chaudière** (French)   1. a boiler.   2. a pot for cooking very large quantities of food.

**chaudron** (French)   a cauldron.

**chayote** (Spanish)   a mild squash of Mexico, often batter-dipped and fried.

**chef de cabinet** (French)   a chief private secretary to a government leader.

**chef de cuisine** (French)   the head cook; head chef.

**chef d'oeuvre** (French)   (lit., 'chief work') a masterpiece, especially in the arts.   Also **chef-d'oeuvre**.

**che guaio!** (Italian)   what a mess!; what a fix! (an expression of distress).

**che noia!** (Italian)   what a nuisance!; what a bore! (an expression of annoyance).

**cher** (French)   expensive.

**cherchez la femme** (French)   (lit., 'look for the woman') an expression implying that a woman or women are the cause of trouble or of a particular problem.

**chère amie** (French)   (lit., 'dear friend') a mistress.

**chéri,** *fem.* **chérie** (French)   sweetheart.

**che sarà sarà.**   See **que será será.**

**cheval** (French)   *Antiques.* a large mirror, commonly made to swivel or tilt, popular in the 18th century.

**cheval, à.**   See **à cheval.**

**cheval de bataille** (French)   1. a war horse; charger.   2. a hobby horse.

**cheval-de-frise** (French)   a military device, such as a piece of timber or a sawhorse, covered with spikes.

**chevalier** (French)   1. a member of a French order of merit, as the Legion of Honor.   2. the lowest ranking title in French nobility.

**chevet** (French)   *Architecture.* an apse of a Gothic cathedral.

**chèvre** (French)   (lit., 'goat') cheese made from goat's milk.

**chez** (French)   at or in the home of; with (used before a name).

**Chianti** (Italian)   a dry, full-bodied, red table wine produced in Tuscany, often put up in straw-covered bottles.   Also **chianti**.   See also **fiasco**.

**Chianti Classico** (Italian)   a select variety of **Chianti** made in a specified area between Florence and Siena.

**chiara.**   See **chiaro.**

**chiaramente** (Italian)   *Music.* distinctly.

**Chiaretto** (Italian)   a rosé wine produced in the region of Lake Garda.

**chiarezza** (Italian)   *Music.* clarity; distinctness.

**chiarina** (Italian)   *Music.* a clarion.

**chiaro,** *fem.* **chiara** (Italian)   clear; unconfused.

**chiaroscuro** (Italian) *Fine Arts.* 1. the effect of the use of light and shade, as in a painting. 2. a style of painting or drawing in which only light and shade are used, creating the effect of a third dimension.

**chibouk** (Turkish) an elongated Turkish pipe for smoking tobacco. Also **chibook; chibouque.**

**chicalote** (Spanish) a prickly poppy with white or yellow flowers.

**chicano,** *fem.* **chicana** (Spanish) 1. a Mexican worker living in the United States. 2. an American of Mexican descent.

**chico,** *fem.* **chica** (Spanish) 1. *n.* a small child. 2. *adj.* small.

**chicote** (Spanish) 1. the end of a length of rope. 2. a long whip.

**chiffonière** (French) *Antiques.* an 18th-century work table with shallow drawers.

**chiffré** (French) *Music.* figured.

**chile** (Spanish) *Cookery.* 1. a variety of pepper typical of Mexico, used in either green or dried form. Also **chili.** See also **chile con carne.**

**chile con carne** (Spanish) *Cookery.* a dish usually consisting of meat and beans in a sauce seasoned with **chile** pepper.

**chimichanga** (Spanish) *Cookery.* a **burrito** containing chicken, cheese, beans, and onions, served with sour cream and guacamole.

**chin-chin** (Chinese) (lit., 'please-please') an expression used as a toast and as a polite greeting or farewell.

**chinois** (French) a fine sieve.

**chinoise, à la.** See **à la chinoise.**

**chinoiserie** (French) decoration or design in a Chinese style or using Chinese motifs. Also **Chinoiserie.**

**chiquito,** *fem.* **chiquita** (Spanish) diminutive form of **chico,** used as a term of endearment.

**chivarras** (Spanish) *Southwestern U.S. and Mexico* leggings of goatskin with the hair left on; chaps. See also **chaparejos.**

**chlamys** (Greek) a short woolen mantle worn by men in ancient Greece.

**chocolatier** (French) a producer and retailer of fine chocolates.

**cholo,** *fem.* **chola** (Spanish) a Latin American of mixed Spanish and Indian blood; a half-breed.

**chorizo** (Spanish) *Cookery.* a sausage usually made with pork and flavored with paprika.

**chose jugée** (French) 1. *Law.* a case on which a decision has been reached. 2. any matter already decided.

**chosisme** (French) *Literature.* the emphasis placed on describing things rather than emotions in the **nouveau roman.**

**chou** (French) (lit., 'cabbage') a cabbage-shaped decoration, as a rosette.

**choucroute** (French) sauerkraut.

**choucroute garnie** (French) *Cookery.* sauerkraut baked with ham, bacon, and sausages.

**chou-fleur** (French) cauliflower.

**chou marin** (French) sea kale.

**chourice** (Portuguese) a variety of smoked pork sausage seasoned with hot chile pepper.

**choux** (French) cabbage.

**choux de Bruxelles** (French) Brussels sprouts.

**chow mein** (Chinese) *Cookery.* a Chinese dish of meat or shrimp and vegetables served on fried noodles.

**chronique scandaleuse** (French) a newspaper story, magazine article, or book that focuses on gossip or scandal.

**chuleta** (Spanish) a chop; cutlet.

**chulo** (Spanish) 1. *adj.* showy; flashy; attractive. 2. *n.* a smart aleck. 3. *n.* a pimp. 4. *Bullfighting.* a bullfighter's assistant.

**chuppah.** See huppah.

**churrasco** (Spanish) beef roasted over an open fire, typical of the Río de la Plata region of Argentina.

**churros** (Spanish) *Cookery.* long, ridged cylinders of fried batter, served hot with powdered sugar.

**chutzpa** (Yiddish) brazen impudence; unmitigated effrontery. Also **chutzpah.**

**ciao** (Italian) a greeting used on arrival or departure.

**cicerone,** *pl.* **ciceroni** (Italian) a guide; one who explains the features of a place (alluding to the Roman orator Cicero, noted for his loquaciousness).

**ciénega** (Spanish) a swamp; marshland; muddy area. Also **cienaga.**

**cigarrito** (Spanish) a cigarette. Also **segarrito.**

**cimborio** (Spanish) *Architecture.* a dome or lantern in a church, located above the intersection of the nave and transept.

**ciment fondu** (French) (lit., 'cast cement') an exceptionally strong cement used for structures that must support great weights and for castings of statues.

**cincho** (Spanish) a saddle girth. Also **cincha.**

**cinco** (Spanish) five.

**cinéaste** (French) 1. a film producer. 2. a technical assistant in film production. 3. an avid film lover.

**cinéma intimiste** (French) *Film.* a genre that deals with the daily life of ordinary people.

**cinéma vérité** (French) *Film.* a genre in which the filmmaker becomes a participant in the action, used especially in documentaries on social issues.

**cinq** (French) five.

**cinq positions des pieds.**   See pieds, cinq positions des.

**cinque** (Italian)   five.

**cinquecento** (Italian)   the 16th century or the 1500's, especially in reference to Italian fine arts or literature.

**cinquième position** (French)   *Ballet.* the fifth position, a basic position of the feet or arms, used in teaching.

**ciociara** (Italian)   *Music.* a Neapolitan costume dance with the theme of the unfaithful lover.

**cipolla,** *pl.* **cipolle** (Italian)   onion.

**cipollata** (Italian)   *Cookery.* a dish of onions and other vegetables.

**cipollino** (Italian)   a type of veined marble.

**circa** (Latin)   around; about (used especially of dates). *Abbr.* **c.** *or* **ca.**

**circulus in probando** (Latin)   (lit., 'a circle in the proof') *Logic.* circular reasoning, or using the conclusion as a premise in the argument. Also **circulus vitiosus.**

**circulus vitiosus.**   See **circulus in probando.**

**ciré** (French)   (lit., 'waxed') a highly glazed surface finish given to fabrics by treating them with wax.

**cire perdue** (French)   *Sculpture.* a technique used in casting in which a wax coating on a clay model enclosed in a mold is melted out and replaced with molten metal; the lost-wax process.

**cirque** (French)   *Geology.* a deep, circular hollow with steep sides, caused by erosion of snow and ice.

**ciseaux** (French)   (lit., 'scissors') *Ballet.* a scissorslike movement made by opening the legs to a wide position in the air.

**ciselé** (French)   (lit., 'chiselled') finely and painstakingly worked, as a delicate work of art or excellent piece of writing.

**cithara.**   See **kithara.**

**cito dispensetur!** (Latin)   *Prescriptions.* let it be dispensed quickly! *Abbr.* **cito disp!**

**citriolo,** *pl.* **citrioli** (Italian)   a cucumber.

**città** (Italian)   a city.

**ciudad** (Spanish)   a city.

**ci vediamo** (Italian)   I'll see you.

**civet** (French)   *Cookery.* a wine stew of venison or other game.

***Civitas Dei*** (Latin)   *City of God* (title of a work by St. Augustine).

**clafoutis** (French)   *Cookery.* a dessert consisting of fruit, such as cherries, baked in batter.

**clair de lune** (French)   (lit., 'light of moon') a pale shade of blue or green.

**clair-obscur.**   See **chiaroscuro.**

**clarete** (Spanish)   a rosé wine.

**claricembalo** (Italian)  *Music.* a harpsichord. Also **cembalo.**

**claro** (Spanish)  1. *n.* a light brown cigar.  2. *adj.* clear; light-colored.  3. *interj.* sure! of course!

**clausula** (Latin)  1. a phrase; clause.  2. *Rhetoric.* a short, sometimes rhythmical phrase that closes a periodic sentence.

**cliché** (French)  a very common expression or theme, considered trite because of overuse.

**Cloaca Maxima** (Latin)  (lit., 'the Greatest Sewer')  the central channel for waste drainage in ancient Rome.

**cloisonné** (French)  a technique of enamelwork in which colored areas are separated by thin metal strips fixed to the base.

**Cloisonnisme** (French)  *Fine Arts.* a style of painting that developed in the 19th century, characterized by bright colors, sharply delineated shapes, and the use of symbolism; Synthetism.

**clou** (French)  (lit., ' a nail')  a major point of focus or interest.

**cochifrito** (Spanish)  *Cookery.* a dish of lamb sauteed with garlic and spices. Also **cuchifrito.**

**cochon** (French)  a pig.

**cochon de lait** (French)  a suckling pig.

**cocido** (Spanish)  (lit., 'cooked')  *Cookery.* a long-simmered soup of meat and vegetables.

**cocotte** (French)  a long-handled earthenware casserole.

**coda** (Italian)  (lit., 'tail')  *Music.* a passage added at the end of a composition to make a distinct closing.  See also **da capo e poi la coda.**

**code civil** (French)  *Law.* the civil code of a country, as the **Code Napoléon.**

**Code Napoléon** (French)  the code of French civil law, first adopted in 1804 under Napoleon Bonaparte.

**codetta** (Italian)  *Music.* a short **coda.**

**codex,** *pl.* **codices** (Latin)  a manuscript volume of an ancient text, written on vellum.

**Codex Juris Canonici** (Latin)  *Roman Catholicism.* the code of canon laws that took effect in 1918, replacing the **Corpus Juris Canonici.**

**Codex Justinianus** (Latin)  the Justinian Code of Roman law.  See also **Corpus Juris Civilis.**

**coeur à la crème** (French)  *Cookery.* a dessert of molded cream cheese and heavy cream.

**coeur d'artichaut** (French)  an artichoke heart.

**coeur de lion** (French)  lionhearted; epithet of King Richard I of England.

**coeur ouvert, à.**  See **à coeur ouvert.**

**cogida** (Spanish)  *Bullfighting.* the goring of the bullfighter by the bull.

**cogito ergo sum** (Latin)    I think, therefore I am (Descartes' simple assertion of the existence of self).

**cognac** (French)    a type of brandy, properly referring to that produced in the area around the town of Cognac in France. Also **Cognac**.

**cognomen** (Latin)    1. surname.    2. nickname.    3. the third name in the Roman system for naming individuals, designating the immediate family name, as *Caesar* in *Gaius Julius Caesar*. See also **nomen**, 3; **praenomen**, 2.

**cognoscente,** *pl.* **cognoscenti** (Italian)    1. a connoisseur.    2. *(pl.)* an elite group that is thought to possess superior knowledge. Also **conoscente**.

**Cohen.**    See **Kohen**.

**coiffeur,** *fem.* **coiffeuse** (French)    1. a hairdresser or barber.    2. *(fem.)* a lady's dressing table.

**coiffure** (French)    a hairstyle; hairdo.

**Cointreau** (French)    a brand of colorless, orange-flavored **liqueur**.

**coitus interruptus** (Latin)    sexual intercourse broken off before climax.

**colazione** (Italian)    lunch.

**colazione, prima.**    See **prima colazione**.

**colla destra** (Italian)    *Music.* with the right hand.

**collage** (French)    *Fine Arts.* 1. a technique of composition in which various materials, as newspaper clippings, coins, and photographs, are pasted down together to make an artistic statement or create an aesthetic impression.    2. a work that is created by this technique. See also **assemblage**.

**colla parte.**    See **colla voce**.

**coll'arco** (Italian)    *Music.* with the bow, a direction following a **pizzicato**.

**collarino** (Italian)    *Architecture.* the neck molding of the Greek Doric, Roman Doric, and Tuscan capitals. Also **cellarino**.

**colla sinistra** (Italian)    *Music.* with the left hand.

**colla voce** (Italian)    (lit., 'with the voice') *Music.* a direction to the accompanist to follow the singer. Also **colla parte; secondando**.

**collé** (French)    (lit., 'glued') *Ballet.* designating that the legs of a dancer are held tightly together while in the air.

**collectanea** (Latin)    a book of passages selected from various sources; a miscellany.

**collegium musicum** (Latin)    a society of amateur musicians.

**colorado** (Spanish)    1. red.    2. brightly colored.    3. a medium-dark brown cigar.

**colorado claro** (Spanish)    a medium-brown cigar.

**coloratura** (Italian)    1. *Music.* singing that is embellished by runs and trills.    2. a soprano singer specializing in this style.    3. any sort of embellished display.

**comandante** (Spanish)    a commander, especially of a guerilla group.

**combien (d'argent)?** (French)    how much does it cost?

**comedia de capa y espada** (Spanish)    (lit., 'cloak and sword play') *Literature*.   Spanish plays, such as those by Calderón and Lope de Vega, with romantic plots concerning the upper middle classes and their problems.

**comédie de moeurs** (French)    *Theater*. a comedy of manners.

**Comédie Française** (French)    the national theater company of France, established by Louis XIV.  Also **La Maison de Molière; Théâtre-Français.**

**comédie humaine, la** (French)    the comedy of human existence; the general social spectrum.

**comédie larmoyante** (French)    (lit., 'tearful comedy') *Theater*. a sentimental comedy or comedy of domestic sentiment, popular in the 18th century.

**come prima** (Italian)    *Music*. as at first.

**come sopra** (Italian)    *Music*. as above.

**comida** (Spanish)    food; repast; a meal.

**comme ci, comme ça** (French)    (lit., 'like this, like that') so-so; neither good or bad.

**commedia dell'arte** (Italian)    *Theater*. an influential style of comedy, popular in Italy from the 16th through the 18th centuries, with stock characters and themes and a bare outline of plot.  See also **concetti; corago; lazzi; Pantalone; Pulcinella; Scaramouche; soggetto.**

**commedia è finita, la.**    See **la commedia è finita.**

**comme il faut** (French)    as it should be; proper; polite.

**comment allez-vous?** (French)    how are you? how's it going?

**comment ça va?** (French)    how's it going? how are things?

**communi consensu** (Latin)    by common consent.

**communiqué** (French)    an official notice or bulletin issued to the press or the public.

**cómo está?** (Spanish)    how are you?

**cómo le va?** (Spanish)    how is it going?

**compadre** (Spanish)    companion; good friend.

**compagnie** (French)    company.

**compagnon de voyage** (French)    a traveling companion.

**compañero** (Spanish)    **1.** companion.    **2.** fellow worker.    **3.** guerilla fighter.

**composé, pas.**    See **pas composé.**

**compos mentis** (Latin)    *Law*. sound-minded; fit to transact legal business.  See also **non compos mentis.**

**compos sui** (Latin)    in control of oneself.

**compote** (French)    1. *Cookery.* fruit that has been cooked in syrup, usually served as a dessert. 2. a glass or porcelain dish with a stem and lid, commonly used for serving confections or nuts. Also **compotier.**

**compotier.**    See **compote, 2.**

**compris** (French)    1. understood. 2. included.

**compte, à.**    See **à compte.**

**compte rendu** (French)    a report or critical review.

**comte** (French)    a count.

**comtesse** (French)    a countess.

**con abbandone** *or* **abbandono** (Italian)    *Music.* with abandon; in a passionate manner that does not heed strict tempo. See also **abbandono.**

**con affetto** (Italian)    *Music.* with affection; warmly.

**con amarezza** (Italian)    *Music.* with bitterness.

**con amore** (Italian)    *Music.* with love; tenderly.

**con anima** (Italian)    *Music.* with animation.

**con arditezza** (Italian)    *Music.* with boldness.

**con brio** (Italian)    *Music.* with spirit; with fire.

**con calore** (Italian)    *Music.* with passion.

**concentus** (Latin)    *Church music.* the part of the traditional liturgy of the Mass that is chanted by the congregation or choir. See also **accentus.**

**concertante** (Italian)    *Music.* a **concerto** in which two or more solo instruments or voices alternate or combine.

**concertata, aria.**    See **aria concertata.**

**concertato.** (Italian)    See **ripieno, 2.**

**concerto,** *pl.* **concerti** (Italian)    *Music.* a composition featuring the display of one or more instruments with orchestral accompaniment.

**concetti,** *sing.* **concetto** (Italian)    *Theater.* the premeditated speeches in **commedia dell'arte.** See also **lazzi.**

**concha** (Spanish)    (lit., 'shell') a decorative plate used on the clothes and gear of a cowboy.

**conchiglie** (Italian)    a fluted, shell-shaped **pasta.**

**conchiglietti** (Italian)    tiny **pasta** shells.

**concierge** (French)    1. a person who monitors the entrance to a building, as a porter or doorman. 2. in European hotels, a multilingual employee assigned to greet guests and arrange special events.

**conciergerie** (French)    1. a porter's lodge. 2. (*cap.*) a prison in Paris that held those condemned to the guillotine.

**concordia discors** (Latin)    discordant harmony; incongruous harmony (Horace, *Epodes* I.12.19).

**concours** (French)    a competition. See also **hors concours.**

**condition humaine, la.**    See **la condition humaine.**

conditio sine qua non.   See causa sine qua non.

con dolcezza (Italian)   *Music.* with sweetness.

con dolore (Italian)   *Music.* with sadness.

condottiere, *pl.* condottieri (Italian)   the captain of a band of mercenaries; a mercenary.

con espressione (Italian)   *Music.* with expression.

confer (Latin)   compare (used in cross references). *Abbr.* cf.

confiserie (French)   1. a pastry and sweet shop. 2. sweets.

confiseur (French)   a person who makes pastries and sweets; a confectioner.

confit (French)   *Cookery.* a morsel of meat that is preserved in its own fat.

Confiteor (Latin)   (lit., 'I confess') *Roman Catholicism.* title and first word of the liturgical profession of faith.

confitería (Spanish)   1. a confectioner's shop.   2. a coffee house.

confiture (French)   a confection or preserve, as a fruit jam.

confitures (French)   preserves.

con forza (Italian)   *Music.* with force.

confrere (French)   a fraternal or professional peer. Also confrère.

con fuoco (Italian)   *Music.* with passion.

con furia (Italian)   *Music.* with fury.

conga (Spanish)   1. a Cuban dance.   2. a type of drum with a long, slender barrel, played by beating with the hands.

congé (French)   departure; farewell; dismissal.

con grazia (Italian)   *Music.* with grace; gracefully.

con gusto (Italian)   *Music.* with taste; in a tasteful way.

con impeto (Italian)   *Music.* with force; impetuously.

con islancio (Italian)   *Music.* impulsively.

conjunctis viribus (Latin)   with united strength or force.

con molta passione (Italian)   *Music.* with great passion.

con moto (Italian)   *Music.* with motion; with animation.

connoisseur (French)   an expert in matters of taste and art.

conocedor (Spanish)   a connoisseur; a person who is especially knowledgeable in a given field, especially in the fine or culinary arts.

conoscente.   See cognoscente.

con permesso (Italian)   with your permission (used when making a polite request).

con prestezza (Italian)   *Music.* with swiftness.

conquistador (Spanish)   a Spanish conqueror of the New World.

71

**con scioltezza** (Italian) *Music.* 1. an indication, applied to long passages or entire movements, that the manner of the performance is according to individual taste. 2. an indication that a fugue is to be performed in free style.

**con semplicità** (Italian) *Music.* with simplicity.

**consensus facit legem** (Latin) general agreement makes law.

**consensus gentium** (Latin) agreement of people(s).

**consensus omnium** (Latin) the agreement of everyone.

**consigliere** (Italian) a trusted advisor to a **Mafia** chief.

**consommé** (French) *Cookery.* a clear soup made by slowly simmering meat and bones.

**con sordino** (Italian) *Music.* 1. in playing piano, an indication to play with the soft pedal down. See also **una corde.** 2. in playing a stringed instrument, an indication to play with the mute. See also **sordino.**

**con spirito** (Italian) *Music.* with spirit; in a lively way.

**consummatum est** (Latin) it is finished; in the Vulgate (John 19:30), the last words of Jesus on the cross.

**contadina, alla.** See **alla contadina.**

**contado** (Italian) a rural area around a city.

**conte** (Italian) a count.

**conte** (French) a tale, especially one about extraordinary events.

**conté** (French) a type of hard crayon in black, brown, or red.

**con tenerezza** (Italian) *Music.* tenderness.

**contessa** (Italian) a countess.

**conteur** (French) a storyteller; narrator.

**con timidezza** (Italian) *Music.* with timidity.

**continuato** (Italian) *Music.* continued; sustained.

**contorno** (Italian) *Cookery.* a side dish of vegetables or greens that accompanies a main dish of fish or meat.

**contra** (Spanish) (lit., 'against') a counter-revolutionary.

**contrabasso** (Italian) *Music.* a double bass. Also **contrabbasso.**

**contra bonos mores** (Latin) contrary to accepted behavior.

**contrada dei nobili** (Italian) the former designation for the section in Italian cities where the nobility lived.

**contradanza.** See **contredanse.**

**contrafagotto** (Italian) *Music.* a double bassoon. Also **contra-fagotto.**

**contralto** (Italian) *Music.* 1. the lowest female singing voice. 2. a singer with this voice.

**contra mundum** (Latin) (lit., 'against the world') used of an individual whose actions or innovations are contrary to widely accepted standards.

**contrapposto** (Italian)   *Fine Arts.* the opposing thrust between masses, as in figure painting.

**contrappunto** (Italian)   *Music.* counterpoint.

**contrapunctus** (Latin)   *Music.* counterpoint.

**contrattempo** (Italian)   *Music.* syncopation.

**contrebasse** (French)   a double-bass viol.

**contre coeur, à.**   See *à contre coeur.*

**contrecoup** (French)   *Medicine.* an injury to one part of the body that is the result of a blow at an opposite point.

**contredanse** (French)   a variety of country dance or square dance for couples; contradance.

**contretemps** (French)   1. an accident or misfortune that causes embarrassment. 2. *Ballet.* a compound step performed quickly, ahead of the beat of the music.

**con variazioni** (Italian)   *Music.* with variations.

**con velocità** (Italian)   *Music.* rapidly.

**convenance** (French)   1. appropriateness or suitability; propriety. 2. convenances, *pl.* social conventions.

**conversazione,** *pl.* **conversazioni** (Italian)   an informal gathering for the purpose of discussion, as a meeting of scholars to display and discuss their work.

**coq** (French)   a cock or rooster.

**coq au bruyère** (French)   a capercaillie or wood grouse.

**coq au vin** (French)   *Cookery.* chicken simmered in red wine sauce with mushrooms and other vegetables.

**coq de combat** (French)   a fighting cock; gamecock.

**coquetterie** (French)   coquetry; flirtatiousness.

**coquillage** (French)   a decorative shell motif.

**coquille** (French)   1. *Cookery.* a dish of meat or fish baked with a sauce and usually served in a shell. 2. the dish in which this is cooked, usually a shell or a shell-shaped casserole.

**coquille St. Jacques** (French)   *Cookery.* a dish of scallops cooked in a sauce with cream and mushrooms, served in a ramekin.

**corago** (Italian)   *Theater.* the manager or leader of a **commedia dell'arte** troupe.

**coram judice** (Latin)   *Law.* before a judge (who has jurisdiction).

**coram nobis** (Latin)   (lit., 'before us')   *Law.* designating a writ to reconsider a case in the same court that had ruled previously (issued, for example, when new facts come to light).

**coram non judice** (Latin)   *Law.* before one who does not have jurisdiction.

**coram populo** (Latin)    in public; before the people.

**corda,** *pl.* **corde** (Italian)    *Music.* a string. See also **una corda.**

**cordatura** (Italian)    *Music.* the scale or series of notes to which the strings of an instrument are tuned.

**cordillera** (Spanish)    a system of parallel mountain ranges.

**cordon bleu** (French)    (lit., 'blue ribbon')    *Cookery.* 1. a prize awarded for distinction as a chef. 2. a distinguished chef. 3. a preparation for chicken or veal combined with ham, melted cheese, and a white sauce.

**cordon militaire** (French)    a series of military installations formed to guard a specific area.

**cordon rouge** (French)    (lit., 'red ribbon') 1. a red sash worn by members of the French **Légion d'Honneur.** 2. a prize, as in culinary competitions, second to the **cordon bleu.**

**cordon sanitaire** (French)    (lit., 'sanitary line') 1. a guard or line of quarantine established to prevent the spread of a communicable disease. 2. a buffer zone between two hostile states.

**corista** (Italian)    *Music.* a device used for tuning, as a pitch-pipe or tuning fork.

**cornada** (Spanish)    *Bullfighting.* goring by the bull.

**cornichon** (French)    a small semi-sweet pickle; gherkin.

**corno** (Italian)    *Music.* a type of horn.

**corno a mano** (Italian)    *Music.* a horn played with the bell downward, as a French horn.

**corno da caccia** (Italian)    *Music.* a hunting horn.

**corno di bassetto** (Italian)    *Music.* a basset horn.

**corno inglese** (Italian)    *Music.* an English horn.

**cornuto** (Italian)    a cuckold.

**coro** (Italian)    *Music.* a choir; chorus.

**corona** (Spanish)    a medium-sized cigar, usually about five inches long.

**coronado** (Spanish)    1. crowned.    2. given an award.

**corps de ballet** (French)    the dancers in a ballet company that provide the choreographed support for soloists.

**corps diplomatique** (French)    official representatives of a foreign government, as an embassy staff.

**corps perdu, à.**    See **à corps perdu.**

**Corpus Christi** (Latin)    *Christianity.* the Body of Christ.

**corpus delicti** (Latin)    (lit., 'the body of a crime')    *Law.* the substantial facts necessary to show that a crime has been committed (used loosely to refer to the body of the victim in a murder case).

**corpus juris** (Latin)    *Law.* a code or collection of laws.

**Corpus Juris Canonici** (Latin)   *Roman Catholicism.* title for the body of canon law in force until 1918, replaced by the **Codex Juris Canonici.**

**Corpus Juris Civilis** (Latin)   the title of the entire body of Roman law collected by the emperor Justinian (483–565). Also called **Codex Justinianus.**

**corregidor** (Spanish)   a chief magistrate.

**corrida de toros** (Spanish)   (lit., 'running of the bulls') a bullfight. Also **corrida.**

**corridos** (Spanish)   songs of sadness and lament performed by the **mariachi** bands.

**corriente** (Spanish)   ordinary; common; run-of-the-mill.

**corrigendum,** *pl.* **corrigenda** (Latin)   something to be corrected; a correction.

**corso** (Italian)   a main street.

**cortège** (French)   1. a retinue of attendants. 2. a ceremonial procession, as in a state funeral.

**Cortes, las** (Spanish)   the representative assembly of Spain.

**coryphaeus** (Greek)   1. *Greek drama.* the leader of the chorus. 2. a leader of a group of singers.

**coryphée** (French)   *Ballet.* 1. a dancer who performs with a small group ranking above the **corps de ballet** but below the soloists.

**cosa** (Spanish)   thing.

**Cosa Nostra** (Italian)   (lit., 'Our Thing') a term said to be used by insiders for the criminal society generally called the **Mafia.** Also **La Cosa Nostra.**

**così così** (Italian)   so-so; neither bad nor good.

**così fan tutte** (Italian)   that is the way of women (*cap.,* title of a comic opera by Mozart).

**così fan tutti** (Italian)   that is the way of the world (an expression of resignation).

**cosmonaut** (Russian)   a Soviet space traveler.

**costoletta** (Italian)   a cutlet or chop.

**costumbrismo** (Spanish)   *Literature.* the use of local color, customs, and types by 19th-century Spanish writers as prime material for their works.

**costumier** (French)   a costumer, as for a ballet or theater company.

**cotechino** (Italian)   a highly spiced sausage made in Bologna.

**Côte d'Azur** (French)   (lit., 'the azure coast') the Mediterranean coast of France; the French Riviera.

**côte, de.**   See de côte.

**Côte d'Or** (French)   the Gold Coast, a **département** in southern France where a popular Burgundy wine is made.

**côtelette** (French)   a cutlet or chop.

75

côtes de boeuf (French)   ribs of beef.

Côtes du Rhone (French)   a renowned wine-producing region along the Rhone River in the south of France.

couchette (French)   a sleeping berth on a train.

cou-de-pied (French)   (lit., 'neck of the foot')   *Ballet.* the instep.

couleur de rose (French)   (lit., 'color of rose')   an optimistic view of life, as the impression of people who see life "through rose-colored glasses."

coulis (French)   *Cookery.*  1. juices, particularly meat juices that run out during cooking. 2. a thick soup made with puréed shellfish.

couloir (French)   a steep gorge on the side of a mountain.

coup (French)   1. a blow or sudden action. 2. a success, achievement, or clever maneuver.

coup d'archet (French)   *Music.* a stroke of the bow.

coup de bourse (French)   a profitable financial transaction.

coup d'éclat (French)   a brilliant accomplishment or bold move.

coup de dés (French)   a cast of dice.

coup de feu (French)   *Cookery.* the time devoted to preparation of a meal.

coup de foudre (French)   (lit., 'clap of thunder')   the moment of love at first sight.

coup de grâce (French)   (lit., 'blow of mercy')  1. a death blow, especially one delivered to end suffering. 2. any finishing blow.

coup de main (French)   (lit., 'blow from the hand')   a surprise attack; a sudden occurrence.

coup de maître (French)   a master stroke.

coup de plume (French)   (lit., 'stroke of the pen')   a literary attack; satire.

coup de poing (French)   (lit., 'blow from the fist')   a paleolithic stone tool with a striking edge.

coup de soleil (French)   sunstroke.

coup d'essai (French)   a first try.

coup d'état (French)   a sudden overthrow of a governing power by trickery or by force.

coup de tête (French)   (lit., 'a head blow')   a rash act; impetuous move.

coup de théâtre (French)   *Theater.*  1. a surprise development in a play. 2. any theatrical device used to create a sensational effect. 3. a smash hit.

coup de vin (French)   the amount of wine that can be taken in a single gulp.

coup d'oeil (French)   a quick glance.

coupé (French)   *Ballet.* a short cutting step. Also **pas coupé.**

coupure (French)   the cutting or deletion of a portion of a play or other piece of writing.

**courante** (French)   1. a 17th-century dance characterized by a fast, gliding step.  2. the music for this dance.

**cour d'honneur** (French)   (lit., 'court of honor')  the forecourt of a castle or palace.

**coureur de bois** (French)   (lit., 'runner of the woods') *Canadian history.* one of the French or French-Indian fur trappers who opened the Canadian wilderness.

**courgettes** (French)   zucchini squash.

**couronne** (French)   (lit., 'crown')  a crown roast.

**cours des miracles** (French)   (lit., 'courts of miracles')  dens of thieves, prostitutes, beggars, and criminals that flourished in medieval Paris.

**court-bouillon** (French)   *Cookery.* a wine broth in which fish or other seafood may be boiled.

**couscous** (Arabic)   *Cookery.* a North African dish of steamed **semolina**, often served with meat and vegetables.

**coûte que coûte** (French)   cost what it may; at whatever cost.

**couture** (French)   the craft of designing and making high-fashion clothing.

**couturier**, *fem.* **couturière** (French)   a person who designs and makes high-fashion clothing, especially for women.

**couvert, à.**   See **à couvert.**

**cozze** (Italian)   mussels.

**cracovienne** (French)   a spirited Polish folk dance that originated in Cracow; the krakowiak.

**cramignon** (French)   a street dance that originated in the Walloon sections of Belgium, usually performed by a large crowd of people.

**craquelé** (French)   crackled, as a glaze on china.

**craquelure** (French)   *Fine Arts.* a pattern of cracks on the surface of a painting.

**crécelle** (French)   *Music.* a rattle used in the percussion section of a band or orchestra.

**crèche** (French)   (lit., 'crib')  a reproduction of the Nativity of Jesus Christ, usually displayed during the Christmas season.

**crede Deo** (Latin)   trust in God.

**crede experto.**   See **experto cred(it)e.**

**credenda** (Latin)   things to be believed.

**credenza** (Italian)   *Furniture.* 1. a table or bench to hold church vessels. 2. a sideboard or buffet.

**credo** (Latin)   (lit., 'I believe')  1. a set of beliefs.  2. (*cap.*) *Church music.* that part of the Mass during which the Creed is pronounced, frequently set to music.

**crème** (French)   cream.

crème à la glace (French)    ice cream. Also crème glacée.

crème anglaise (French)    *Cookery.* a custard sauce.

crème brûlée (French)    *Cookery.* caramel custard or custard flavored with burnt sugar.

crème Chantilly (French)    whipped cream with powdered sugar. See also crème fouettée.

crème de cacao (French)    a chocolate-flavored liqueur.

crème de cassis (French)    a liqueur flavored with black currants.

crème de la crème (French)    the very best; the cream of the crop.

crème de menthe, creme de menthe (French)    a white or green liqueur flavored with mint.

crème fouettée (French)    whipped cream. See also crème Chantilly.

crème fraîche (French)    slightly soured, thick cream.

crème glacée.    See crème à la glace.

crème pâtissière (French)    pastry cream, used as an ingredient in sweet soufflés and tarts and as a filling for cakes and puff pastries.

créole, à la.    See à la créole.

crêpe (French)    *Cookery.* a thin, delicate pancake usually served with a filling. Also crepe.

crêpe de Chine (French)    Chinese silk crepe.

crêpe lisse (French)    a soft fabric that has the texture of gauze.

crêperie (French)    a stall or restaurant selling crêpes.

crêpe suzette (French)    *Cookery.* a thin dessert pancake prepared with orange-flavored liqueur, usually flambéed and served rolled or folded.

crépon (French)    a heavy, durable crepe fabric.

crescendo (Italian)    (lit., 'growing') a musical passage of gradually increasing force or loudness. See also decrescendo.

crescit eundo (Latin)    it grows as it goes.

crespolini (Italian)    *Cookery.* flour pancakes that are filled and baked in tomato sauce.

cresson (French)    cress; watercress.

crève-coeur (French)    heartbreak; a deep sorrow.

crevette (French)    a shrimp or prawn.

cri de guerre (French)    (lit., 'cry of war') *Heraldry.* a martial expression used as or in place of a motto.

cri du coeur (French)    (lit., 'cry of the heart') a cry of sorrow; lament.

crime d'état (French)    (lit., 'crime of the state) treason.

crimen falsi (Latin)    *Law.* a crime involving deceit, such as perjury or embezzlement.

crimen innominatum (Latin)    (lit., 'unnamed crime') *Law.* an act of sodomy.

**crimen laesae majestatis.** See **laesa majestas.**

**crime passionnel** (French)   a crime, especially murder, committed in the heat of passion.

**criollo,** *fem.* **criolla** (Spanish)   Creole.

**cristallo** (Italian)   *Antiques.* a clear, ductile glass produced in 16th-century Venice.

**croisé, croisée** (French)   (lit., 'crossed') *Ballet.* an attitude in which a dancer presents a three-quarter view of the body with the appearance of having one leg crossed over the other.

**croissant** (French)   *Cookery.* a crescent-shaped roll of light pastry.

**croix, en.** See **en croix.**

**croix botonée** (French)   a budding cross, that is, a cross that has budlike clumps at the end of each member.

**Croix de Feu** (French)   (lit., 'cross of fire') a former reactionary political party in France.

**Croix de Guerre** (French)   a French military decoration for valor in battle.

**croix fourchée** (French)   a forked cross.

**croix pattée** (French)   a cross that is narrower at its center than at the ends.

**croix pommée** (French)   (lit., 'rounded cross') a cross with knobs at the ends of its arms.

**croquante** (French)   *Cookery.* 1. a crisp pastry or tart. 2. an almond cake.

**croque-en-bouche, croquembouche** (French)   (lit., 'crunch in mouth') food coated with a crispy sugar glaze.

**croque-madame** (French)   *Cookery.* a grilled chicken and cheese sandwich, made with batter-dipped bread.

**croque-monsieur** (French)   *Cookery.* a grilled ham and cheese sandwich, made with batter-dipped bread.

**croquis** (French)   a sketch.

**crostini,** *sing.* **crostino** (Italian)   *Cookery.* 1. small slices of bread spread with cheese and other ingredients, then toasted.   2. rounds of bread fried in olive oil.

**croupier** (French)   a person who collects stakes and pays winners at a gambling table.

**croustade** (French)   *Cookery.* a shell of pastry, rice, or potatoes that is filled and baked or fried.

**croûte** (French)   *Cookery.* a pastry crust. See also **en croûte.**

**crouton** (French)   *Cookery.* a small cube of toasted bread, commonly used in soups and salads.

**cru** (French)   1. a French wine-producing vineyard. 2. a particular vintage of wine.

**cru classé** (French)    (lit., 'classified growth') a designation for a French chateau that has been recognized for the excellence of its wine.

**crudités** (French)    *Cookery.* raw vegetables, commonly served with a sauce as an appetizer.

**crux,** *pl.* **cruces** (Latin)    1. a cross.    2. a passage in a text that is difficult to interpret.    3. a difficulty or puzzlement.

**crux ansata** (Latin)    an ansate cross or **ankh,** a cross with a loop at the top.

**crux commissa** (Latin)    a T-shaped cross or tau cross; St. Anthony's cross.

**crux criticorum** (Latin)    a troubling point for critics.

**crux decussata** (Latin)    an X-shaped cross; St. Patrick's or St. Andrew's cross.

**crux interpretum** (Latin)    a phrase or passage that is difficult to translate.

**crux mathematicorum** (Latin)    a difficult mathematical problem.

**cruz** (Spanish)    a cross.

**cuadrilla** (Spanish)    *Bullfighting.* the group that assists the matador, including **banderilleros** and **picadores.**

**cuadro** (Spanish)    *Dance.* a group of **flamenco** musicians and dancers.

**cuarta** (Spanish)    a short whip or riding crop.

**cuatro** (Spanish)    1. four.    2. *Music.* quartet.

**Cuba Libre** (Spanish)    (lit., 'free Cuba') a cocktail made with rum and cola, named for the toasts made with it by Cuban revolutionaries.

**cucaracha** (Spanish)    a cockroach.

**cucina** (Italian)    1. kitchen.    2. cooking or cookery.

**cucina casalinga** (Italian)    simple, plain cooking. See also **alla casalinga.**

**cuesta** (Spanish)    a slope that rises gently to a crest then drops off sharply.

**cui bono(?)** (Latin)    1. for whose benefit? to whose advantage?    2. to what useful purpose?

**cuidado** (Spanish)    be careful; watch out.

**cui malo(?)** (Latin)    who will be harmed (by it)?

**cuir-boulli** (French)    (lit., 'boiled leather') leather that has been soaked or waxed, then molded to harden into a particular shape.

**cuisine** (French)    a style or manner of cooking.

**cuisine bourgeoise** (French)    plain or homestyle cooking.

**cuisine gourmande** (French)    fine cooking, incorporating rich ingredients and sauces.

**cuisine minceur** (French)    (lit., 'light cooking') food that is low in calories but attractively presented, as served in health and reducing spas. See also **nouvelle cuisine, la.**

**cuisinier** (French)    a cook or chef.

**cuisse** (French)    thigh; leg of fowl.

**cuissot** (French)    a haunch of meat, especially venison.

**cuit à point** (French)	*Cookery.* cooked to the very point of perfection. Also **à point.**

**cul-de-four** (French)	*Architecture.* a low spherical vault, as an oven vault.

**cul-de-lampe** (French)	a cone-shaped or pyramidal object or element of design.

**cul-de-sac** (French)	**1.** a cavity or tube that is open at one end. **2.** a street that is closed at one end; a blind alley or dead end. **3.** an impasse or problem for which there is no apparent solution.

**culebras** (Spanish)	(lit., 'snakes') three cigars twisted together into a spiral shape.

**culottes** (French)	**1.** floppy pants or breeches, as those once worn by the French army. **2.** women's short pants tailored to resemble a skirt. **3.** *Cookery.* (*sing.*) a rump of meat, as beef or lamb.

**culpa.**	See **mea culpa; mea maxima culpa.**

**cum dividendo** (Latin)	*Finance.* including the latest dividend. *Abbr.* **cum div.** See also **ex dividendo.**

**cum grano salis** (Latin)	with a grain of salt; said of something that is not to be literally believed.

**cum laude** (Latin)	with honor (the lowest level of distinction on academic degrees). See also **magna cum laude; maxima cum laude; summa cum laude.**

**cum notis variorum** (Latin)	including the notes of various commentators (seen on scholarly editions of texts). Also **editio cum notis variorum.** See also **variorum.**

**cum privilegio** (Latin)	(lit., 'with privilege (granted)') used to indicate that authority has been given to proceed with printing a book.

**cuprum** (Latin)	copper. *Abbr.* **Cu.**

**cura** (Spanish)	a priest.

**curé** (French)	a parish priest.

**curettage** (French)	*Surgery.* a procedure in which tissue is removed using a curette.

**curette** (French)	*Surgery.* a scoop-shaped instrument for scraping tissue.

**curia** (Latin)	the ancient Roman Senate chamber.

**curia domini** (Latin)	the court of a noble lord.

**curia regis** (Latin)	the king's court; used especially of the permanent council of officials consulted by Norman kings.

**curioso,** *pl.* **curiosi** (Italian)	a virtuoso performer.

**currente calamo** (Latin)	(lit., 'with a hurrying pen') in a relaxed or free style of writing.

**curriculum vitae** (Latin)	(lit., 'course of (one's) life') a list detailing the positions, offices, honors, and achievements in one's career. *Abbr.* **C.V.**

**cursus honorum** (Latin)   1. *Roman History.* the prescribed succession of elected and appointed positions that marked the progress of one's political career.   2. any such patterned succession of achievements used to gauge success.

**custos,** *pl.* **custodes** (Latin)   guardian; warden; inspector.

**custos morum** (Latin)   a guardian of morals.

**Custos Privati Sigilli** (Latin)   *English court.* the Keeper of the Privy Seal.

**Custos Rotulorum** (Latin)   an English county officer charged with keeping public records.

**cuvée** (French)   a blending of wines from several vintages or vineyards, done to assure consistent quality.

**cwm** (Welsh)   (lit., 'valley') a circular space in a hillside, formed by erosion, that serves as a natural amphitheater; a cirque.

**czar** (Russian)   1. title of the former emperor of Russia.   2. a supreme leader, often autocratic.   Also **tsar; tzar.**

**czardas** (Hungarian)   a Hungarian national dance with two movements, one slow and one fast.

**czarevitch** (Russian)   the son of a **czar,** especially the eldest son and heir. Also **tsarevitch.**

**czarevna** (Russian)   1. the daughter of a **czar.**   2. the wife of a **czarevitch.** Also **tsarevna.**

**czarina** (Russian)   the wife of a **czar;** the Russian empress.   Also **czaritza.** Also **tsarina.**

# D

**da** (Russian)   yes.

**da ballo** (Italian)   *Music.*  in dance style; like a dance.

**d'abord** (French)   at first.

**da camera** (Italian)   *Music.*  in chamber music style, that is, to be performed in a chamber instead of a large hall.

**da capo** (Italian)   *Music.*  a direction to go to the beginning and start again. Also **ritornello.**

**da capo al fine** (Italian)   *Music.*  a direction to go to the beginning and play to the end.  See also **fine.**

**da capo al segno** (Italian)   *Music.*  a direction to go to the beginning and play to the **segno.**

**da capo e poi la coda** (Italian)   *Music.*  a direction to go to the beginning and play to the **coda.**

**da cappello** (Italian)   *Music.*  in church or chapel style.  Also **da chiese.** See also **a cappella.**

**d'accord** (French)   in agreement; agreed.

**d'accordo** (Italian)   *Music.*  in tune; in harmony.

**dacha** (Russian)   a country house for vacations.

**da chiesa.**   See **da cappello.**

**dacquoise** (French)   *Cookery.*  baked meringue used as a layer in a fancy cake.

**daemon** (Greek)   a subordinate deity with spiritual power to influence a person or place.  Also **daimon.**

**dahabeah** (Arabic)   a large passenger boat used on the Nile.  Also **dahabeeyah; dahabiah; dahabi(y)eh; dahabiya(h).**

**daimio** (Japanese)   a Japanese nobleman, a vassal of the **mikado.**

**daimon.**   See **daemon.**

**dak** (Hindi)   relays of men or horses for transporting mail or cargo.  Also **dauk; dawk.**

**Dalai Lama** (Tibetan)   the chief monk of Tibet, thought to be reincarnated into a newborn at his death.

**dallage** (French)   *Architecture.* a floor or pavement of marble, stone, or tile.

**dal segno** (Italian)   *Music.* a direction to return to the **segno** and play from there to the end. Also **dal segno alla fine.**

**damnant quod non intelligunt** (Latin)   they condemn what they do not understand.

**damnosa hereditas** (Latin)   an accursed inheritance; one bringing more trouble than benefit.

**damnum absque injuria** (Latin)   *Law.* loss without cause for taking legal action.

**danke!** (German)   thank you!

**danke schön!** (German)   thanks very much!

**Danklied** (German)   thanksgiving song.

**danse** (French)   dance, especially ballet.

**danse comique** (French)   (lit., 'a comic dance') *Ballet.* a popular dance or dance of the people.

**danse de caractère** (French)   (lit., 'a dance of character') *Ballet.* 1. a dramatic dance based on a folk or national dance. 2. a dance based on the activities or movements associated with certain occupations or trades, as carpentry or sheepherding.

**danse d'école** (French)   *Ballet.* classical ballet as taught in academies and schools.

**danse de demi-caractère** (French)   (lit., 'semicharacter dancing') *Ballet.* a dance performed according to classical ballet technique, but depicting a special character or characteristic movement, as that employed by dancers depicting swans in the ballet *Swan Lake.*

**danse macabre** (French)   (lit., 'macabre dance') the Dance of Death, depicting Death, in the form of a skeleton, leading people to their graves.

**danse noble** (French)   (lit., 'noble dance') *Ballet.* the classical ballet style.

**danseur,** *fem.* **danseuse** (French)   a ballet dancer.

**danseur noble** (French)   *Ballet.* the leading male dancer.

**danza** (Italian)   a dance.

**danza española** (Spanish)   a Spanish dance.

**danza tedesca** (Italian)   (lit., 'German dance') a waltz.

**danzón** (Spanish)   a style of Cuban dance of African origin. Also **danzonetta.**

**da prima** (Italian)   at first; from the beginning.

**dariole** (French)   *Cookery.* a rich cream cake; duchess cake.

**Dasein** (German)   *Philosophy.* existence.

**daube** (French)  *Cookery.* a seasoned meat and vegetable stew.

**dauk.**  See **dak.**

**dauphin** (French)  former title for the eldest son and heir of the king of France.

**dauphine** (French)  the dauphiness, wife of the **dauphin.**

**dawk.**  See **dak.**

**dayan,** *pl.* **dayanim** (Hebrew)  a rabbinical judge in a Jewish religious court.

**de bene esse** (Latin)  (lit., 'according to well being') on certain specified terms.

**de bonis propriis** (Latin)  out of one's own goods or funds.

**de bono et malo** (Latin)  for better or worse; taking the bad with the good.

**déboulés.**  See **tours chaînés.**

**decani** (Latin)  (lit., 'of the dean') *Church music.* indicating what is sung by the half of the choir sitting on the epistle side of the church; opposed to **cantoris.** *Abbr.* **dec.**

**decennium** (Latin)  a period of ten years.

**deceptio visus** (Latin)  an optical illusion.

**décime** (French)  a tenth of a franc.

**deciso** (Italian)  *Music.* with decisiveness; firmly.

**déclassé,** *fem.* **déclassée** (French)  1. of an inferior social class. 2. out of social favor.

**décolletage** (French)  a low-cut neckline of a dress. Also **decolletage.**

**décolleté** (French)  1. having a low-cut neckline. 2. wearing a dress with a low-cut neckline.

**décor** (French)  1. a style of decoration, especially as applied to building interiors. 2. *Theater.* stage decoration; scenery. Also **decor.**

**de côte** (French)  *Ballet.* sideways, indicating that a dance step is to be performed to the right or left side.

**découpage** (French)  the technique of decorating with paper cutouts. Also **decoupage.**

**decrescendo** (Italian)  *Music.* becoming gradually softer. See also **crescendo.**

**de die in diem** (Latin)  from day to day; continuously.

**de droit** (French)  by legal right; rightfully. See also **de fait.**

**de face** (French)  (lit., 'in front') *Ballet.* designating a dancer facing the audience.

**de facto** (Latin)  1. in fact; actually.  2. *Law.* happening or being permitted in fact, even though in violation of a statute. Compare **de jure.**

**de fait** (French)  actually; in fact. See also **de droit.**

**défense de fumer** (French)  no smoking.

**Defensor Fidei** (Latin)    Defender of the Faith, a title used by British sovereigns.

**de fide** (Latin)    *Roman Catholicism.* (a matter) of faith; designating a dogma that may not be questioned.

**defitsitny** (Russian)    designating goods that are virtually unobtainable or in short supply in the Soviet Union.

**dégagé** (French)    (lit., 'disengaged') uncommitted; uninvolved.

**de gustibus (non est disputandum)** (Latin)    there is no (sense in) arguing about tastes.

**déhancement** (French)    *Fine Arts.* in statuary, a stance in which one hip is raised higher than the other.

**de haut en bas** (French)    (lit., 'from high to low') with a condescending or patronizing attitude.

**dehors** (French)    outside.

**Dei gratia** (Latin)    by the grace of God.

**de integro** (Latin)    from the beginning.

**déjà vu** (French)    (lit., 'already seen') 1. an impression that something encountered for the first time has been experienced previously. 2. *Criticism.* designating something trite or hackneyed, as an overused technique or type of scene in film.

**déjeuner** (French)    lunch.

**de jure** (Latin)    (lit., 'by law') 1. by right; rightfully. 2. *Law.* in accord with a specific statute. Compare **de facto**.

**delator temporis acti** (Latin)    an accuser or denouncer of the past. See also **laudator temporis acti**.

**dele** (Latin)    delete; erase (a proofreader's mark).

**delenda est Carthago.**    See **Carthago delenda est.**

**délicatesse** (French)    delicacy; a gentle touch.

**delicato** (Italian)    delicate.

**delineavit** (Latin)    he (*or* she) drew (this), used with the name of the artist.

**delirante** (Italian)    *Music.* frenzied.

**delirium tremens** (Latin)    (lit., 'trembling delirium') *Medicine.* a condition characterized by violent restlessness, trembling, and terrifying hallucinations, frequently a result of prolonged consumption of alcohol.

**delizioso** (Italian)    sweet; delicious.

**dell'adriatico** (Italian)    (lit., 'of the Adriatic') *Cookery.* marinated in oil and lemon juice, then grilled over a wood or charcoal fire.

**de luxe** (French)    of special quality or luxury. Also **deluxe**.

**démarche** (French)    (lit., 'step') 1. a plan or maneuver, as in diplomacy. 2. a change in tactics.

**démenti** (French)    a denial from an official source.

86

**dementia** (Latin)   *Medicine.* severe impairment of intellectual capacity.
**dementia praecox** (Latin)   (lit., 'precocious dementia') *Medicine.* schizo-
   phrenia.
**dementia senilis** (Latin)   *Medicine.* dementia of the aged; senility.
**demi, à.**   See **à demi.**
**demi-glace** (French)   *Cookery.* a sauce made from brown stock skimmed
   of fat and combined with other ingredients.
**demimondaine** (French)   a woman of the **demi-monde.**
**demi-monde** (French)   (lit., 'half-world') a class of women who have lost
   their social respectability owing to indiscreet behavior or promiscuity.
   Also **demimonde.**
**de minimis non curat lex** (Latin)   the law does not concern itself with
   trifles.
**demi-plié** (French)   (lit., 'half-bent') *Ballet.* a basic position in which the
   knees are slightly bent with toes turned outward.
**demi-tasse** (French)   (lit., 'half-cup') 1. a small cup used to serve after-
   dinner coffee. 2. the coffee served in such a cup. Also **demitasse.**
**démodé,** *fem.* **démodée** (French)   outmoded; out of fashion.
**demoiselle** (French)   1. an unmarried young girl or woman. 2. *Antiques.*
   a lady's wig stand of the 18th century.
**de mortuis nil nisi bonum** (Latin)   of the dead (say) nothing but good.
   Frequently shortened to **de mortuis.**
**dēmos** (Greek)   the general populace.
**de nada** (Spanish)   you're welcome; it's nothing.
**de natura rerum.**   See **De Rerum Natura.**
**de nihilo nihil.**   See **nihil ex nihilo (fit).**
**Denkschrift** (German)   memorial volume.
**denominaciones del origen** (Spanish) *Wine.* divisions of the wine-
   producing sections of Spain, administered by the government. *Abbr.* **D.O.**
**denominazione di origine controllata** (Italian)   a designation for Italian
   wine indicating that it meets certain standards of origin, grape variety, and
   quality. *Abbr.* **D.O.C.**
**de nos jours** (French)   nowadays; in this day and age.
**dénouement** (French)   (lit., 'untying') 1. *Literature.* the final outcome or
   resolution of the plot in a play or novel. 2. the resolution of an indecisive
   situation or dilemma. Also **denouement.**
**de nouveau** (French)   fresh or new, as in style.
**de novo** (Latin)   afresh; anew; from the beginning.
**Deo duce** (Latin)   with God as my leader.
**Deo duce, ferro comitante** (Latin)   with God as my leader and my sword
   as my companion.

**Deo ducente** (Latin)    under God's guidance.

**Deo favente** (Latin)    with God's favor.

**Deo gratias** (Latin)    thanks (be) to God.

**Deo juvante** (Latin)    with God's help (motto of Monaco).

**Deo Optimo Maximo** (Latin)    to God, the best and greatest. See also **Domino Optimo Maximo**.

**Deo volente** (Latin)    God willing. *Abbr.* **D.V.** Also **volente Deo.**

**département** (French)    one of the administrative subdivisions of France.

**de pied en cap** (French)    from head to foot.

**De Profundis** (Latin)    (lit., 'out of the depths (of despair)'), title of poems by Oscar Wilde and others (from Psalm 130:1).

**de proprio motu** (Latin)    out of its own motion; without outside agency.

**dépucellage** (French)    the loss of virginity.

**de race** (French)    pure; thoroughbred.

**der, die, das** (German)    forms of the German definite article.

**derecha** (Spanish)    right; right side.

**derecho** (Spanish)    a right; justice.

**de règle** (French)    required by rule or custom.

**De Rerum Natura** (Latin)    (lit., 'on the nature of things') **1.** title of Lucretius' work on Epicurean philosophy.    **2.** (*l.c.*) concerning the nature of the universe. Also **de natura rerum.**

**de rigueur** (French)    required by convention or the dictates of style; essential; indispensable.

**dernier cri** (French)    (lit., 'the last cry') **1.** the last word. **2.** the latest style or fashion.

**dernier ressort** (French)    the last resort.

**derrière** (French)    **1.** the buttocks. **2.** *Ballet.* behind or backward, applied to positions and steps in which a dancer moves the feet from a front to a back position.

**Deruta** (Italian)    *Antiques.* a type of **maiolica** from the village of Deruta.

**desaparecidos** (Spanish)    (lit., 'the vanished') children, students, or others who disappeared during the Argentine military regime (1976–1983).

**desayuno** (Spanish)    breakfast.

**descamisados** (Spanish)    (lit., 'the shirtless ones') the underclasses; the dissatisfied poor (used in Argentina especially during the Perón regime, 1946–55).

**déshabillé** (French)    carelessly or informally dressed. See also **en déshabillé.**

**desideratum,** *pl.* **desiderata** (Latin)    something desired or required.

**desipere in loco.**    See **dulce est desipere in loco.**

**dessein, à.**    See **à dessein.**

**dessin** (French)    a drawing design.

**dessous** (French)    (lit., 'under') *Ballet.* a term designating that the working foot of a dancer is to pass behind the supporting foot.

**dessous des cartes** (French)    (lit., 'the underside of the cards') secret information.

**dessus** (French)    (lit., 'over') *Ballet.* a term designating that the working
foot of a dancer is to pass in front of the supporting foot.

**dessus de table** (French)    (lit., 'top of the table') a decorative centerpiece
for a dinner table.

**De Stijl** (Dutch)    (lit., 'the Style,' the name of a Dutch art journal) *Fine
Arts.* an influential Dutch style of painting of the early 20th century.

**desto** (Italian)    *Music.* lively; sprightly.

**destra mano** (Italian)    *Music.* the right hand.

**destro,** *fem.* **destra** (Italian)    *Music.* **1.** right, referring to the hand.    **2.**
dextrous.

**de suite** (French)    *Ballet.* designating a step or movement that is to be
repeated several times without pausing.

**desunt c(a)etera.**    See **cetera desunt.**

**détaché** (French)    detached; unattached.

**détente** (French)    a relaxing, especially of international tensions.

**detinet** (Latin)    (lit., 'he detains') *Law.* a legal action to recover a debt or
specific property.

**détourné** (French)    (lit., 'turned') *Ballet.* a pivot turn of the body on both
feet.

**de trop** (French)    too much; too many; superfluous.

**deus ex machina** (Latin)    (lit., 'a god from a machine') **1.** *Greek drama.* a
god who resolves the plot by intervening late in the play.    **2.** any artificial
or improbable device for resolving difficulties.

**Deus Misereatur** (Latin)    May God Have Mercy (title of Psalm 67).

**Deus tecum** (Latin)    God (be) with you (singular).

**Deus vobiscum** (Latin)    God (be) with you (plural).

**Deus vult** (Latin)    God wills it (slogan of the First Crusade).

**deutsch** (German)    German; the German language.

**Deutsche Demokratische Republik** (German)    German Democratic Republic (East Germany).

**Deutsche Industrie-Norm** (German)    German manufacturing standards
used as bases for product comparison. *Abbr.* **DIN.**

**Deutschland über alles** (German)    'Germany above all,' title of the former
German national anthem.

**Deutschmark** (German)    basic currency of the German Federal Republic.    Also **Deutsche Mark.**

**deux** (French)   two.

**deux, à.**   See **à deux.**

**deuxième position** (French)   *Ballet.* the second position, a basic position of the feet or arms used in teaching.

**deux mains, à.**   See **à deux mains.**

**Devanagari** (Sanskrit)   the script used in writing Hindi, Sanskrit, and other languages of India.

**devant** (French)   *Ballet.* in front.

**de veras** (Spanish)   (as a question) you don't say?; (as an affirmation) for certain.

**devoir** (French)   1. an act of courtesy or respect. 2. a duty or responsibility.

**de volée** (French)   *Ballet.* designating a step that is to be performed with a flying or soaring movement. See also **volé.**

**devotissimo suo** (Italian)   yours truly.

**dharma** (Sanskrit)   *Hinduism.* 1. the essential spiritual character of something. 2. religious doctrine; religious obligation.

**dhobi** (Hindi)   a laundryboy.

**dhoti** (Hindi)   1. a loincloth worn by Hindu men. 2. the cotton fabric from which this garment is made.

**dhow** (Arabic)   an Arabian sailing ship with triangular sails.

**día** (Spanish)   day.

**diable** (French)   a devil.

**diable, à la.**   See **à la diable.**

**diablerie** (French)   devilish magic; sorcery; witchcraft.

**diablo** (Spanish)   the devil.

**dialogue des sourds** (French)   (lit., 'conversation of the deaf') the conversation of people who are not listening to each other.

**dialogue intérieur** (French)   (lit., 'interior dialogue') 1. a mental conversation with oneself. 2. a literary passage that relates a character's thoughts.

**diamanté** (French)   designating a fabric that sparkles from sequins or gemstones attached to it.

**dianoia** (Greek)   *Philosophy.* the intellect devoted to discursive reasoning.

**diario** (Spanish)   a daily newspaper.

**Diaspora** (Greek)   1. the scattering of the Jews from Palestine after the Babylonian captivity in 586 B.C. 2. any similar migration of people.

**diavola, diavolo.**   See **alla diavola; fra diavolo.**

**di bravura** (Italian)   *Music.* with brilliance; in a dazzling style. See also **aria d'abilità; bravura.**

**di buon'ora** (Italian)   early (in the morning).

**dichos** (Spanish)   sayings; proverbs.

90

**Dichtung** (German)  1.  literature; poetry.  2.  *Music.* poem.
**Dichtung und Wahrheit** (German)  fiction and fact; poetry and truth.
**dictum,** *pl.* **dicta** (Latin)  (lit., 'something said')  1. an authoritative pro-
nouncement.  2. a proverbial saying.
**dictum sapienti sat(is) est.**  See **verbum sapienti sat(is) est.**
**diebus alternis** (Latin)  *Prescriptions.* every other day.  *Abbr.* **dieb. alt.**
**diebus secundis** (Latin)  *Prescriptions.* every second day.  *Abbr.* **dieb. se-**
**cund.**
**dieci** (Italian)  ten.
**die geistige Welt.**  See **geistige Welt, die.**
**diem perdidi** (Latin)  (lit., 'I have lost a day')  said at the end of a day of
frustration.
**dies ater** (Latin)  (lit., 'a black day')  an ominous day.
**die schöne Welt.**  See **schöne Welt, die.**
**dies faustus** (Latin)  a favorable day.
**dies infaustus** (Latin)  a day of ill omen.
**Dies Irae** (Latin)  Day of Wrath, title of a hymn about the Day of Judgment.
**Dieu avec nous** (French)  God with us.
**Dieu et mon droit** (French)  God and my right (motto of English royalty).
**Dieu vous garde** (French)  God keep you.
**diez** (Spanish)  ten.
**diferencias** (Spanish)  *Music.* 16th-century variations composed for organ
or lute.
**differentia** (Latin)  factors which distinguish a thing from its general class.
**difficile** (French)  difficult.
**difficilior lectio potior** (Latin)  (lit., 'the more difficult reading is prefera-
ble')  *Textual criticism.* the presumption that an unusual reading (when
comparing manuscripts) is more likely to be the correct one.  Also **lectio**
**difficilior.**
**digestif** (French)  an after-dinner drink.
**di giorno** (Italian)  by day.
**dii penates** (Latin)  household gods.  See also **lares et penates.**
**dilettante,** *pl.* **dilettanti** (Italian)  1. one who pursues an activity or subject
merely as a hobby or for amusement; an amateur.  2. a lover of the fine
arts.
**diligencia** (Spanish)  a stagecoach.
**diligente** (Italian)  *Fine Arts.* a designation for a work produced through
effort rather than from inspiration.  See also **manieroso.**
**diluendo** (Italian)  *Music.* dying away.
**dilungando** (Italian)  *Music.* lengthening.

**di magro** (Italian)    meatless, referring to a sauce or antipasto.

**diminuendo** (Italian)    (lit., 'lessening') a musical passage of gradually decreasing force or loudness.

**di molto** (Italian)    (very) much.

**dîner** (French)    dinner.

**dinero** (Spanish)    money.

**Ding an sich** (German)    (lit., 'the thing by itself') the reality behind the outward appearance.

**di notte** (Italian)    by night.

**di nuovo** (Italian)    anew.

**Diós** (Spanish)    God.

**di più in più** (Italian)    more and more.

**Directoire** (French)    1. *French history.* the Directory, the executive board that ruled France from 1795 to 1799. 2. designating a French style of decoration that incorporated Greco-Roman and Egyptian motifs, especially popular during the Directory period.

**direttore** (Italian)    a director.

**direxit** (Latin)    he (*or* she) supervised (this work).

**dirigo** (Latin)    I direct (motto of Maine).

**dis aliter visum** (Latin)    the gods have deemed (it) otherwise (Vergil, *Aeneid* II.428).

**di salto** (Italian)    by leaps.

**discantus supra librum** (Latin)    (lit., 'descant on the book') *Music.* the improvisation of a counterpoint to the existing melody.

**discere docendo** (Latin)    to learn through teaching.

**discobolus** (Greek)    1. a discus thrower. 2. (*cap.*) a renowned classical statue of a discus thrower by the Greek sculptor Myron.

**discothèque** (French)    a night club featuring rock music for dancing and usually a decor with surrealistic lighting effects.

**discrétion, à.**    See à discrétion.

**disiecta** *or* **disjecta membra** (Latin)    disjointed or scattered (body) parts.

**distingué,** *fem.* **distinguée** (French)    distinguished; having an aristocratic demeanor.

**distrait,** *fem.* **distraite** (French)    distracted or absent-minded because of fear or anxiety; distraught.

**Distrito Federal** (Spanish)    the district of Mexico in which Mexico City is located. *Abbr.* **D.F.**

**dit** (French)    said.

**ditali** (Italian)    (lit., 'thimbles') tube-shaped pasta about an inch in length.

**ditalini** (Italian)    (lit., 'little thimbles') tube-shaped pasta, smaller than ditali, often served in soup.

**ditat Deus** (Latin)   God enriches (motto of Arizona).

**diva** (Italian)   *Music.* a renowned female opera singer. See also **prima donna.**

**divertimento** (Italian)   *Music.* 1. a light, melodic instrumental composition of several movements.   2. a fantasia based on airs from an opera, presented in an easy-going style.

**divertissement** (French)   1. an entertaining diversion. 2. See **divertimento.** 3. *Ballet.* a complete dance performed within a full-length ballet to display the special talents of various dancers.

**divide et impera** (Latin)   divide and rule.

**divisa** (Spanish)   *Bullfighting.* the brand or emblem of a ranch, consisting of a piece of cloth on a barb that is implanted in the bull's hump.

**divisi** (Italian)   (lit., 'divided')   *Music.* a direction indicating that the violinists are to divide into two groups to perform the double notes of the first violin part. *Abbr.* div.

**dix** (French)   ten.

**dixi** (Latin)   (lit., 'I have spoken')   said by one in authority whose words have just settled a matter. See also **ipse dixit.**

**djellabah** (Arabic)   a loose-fitting hooded cloak worn by Arab men, especially in North Africa. Also **djel(l)ab; jel(l)ab(a); jel(l)ib.**

**djibbah.**   See **jibba.**

**djin** *or* **djinn(i).**   See **jinn.**

**doble claro** (Spanish)   a pale, greenish-colored cigar.

**docendo discimus** *or* **discitur** (Latin)   we learn (*or* one learns) by teaching.

**Doctor Angelicus** (Latin)   the Angelic Doctor, epithet for Thomas Aquinas, 13th-century scholastic philosopher.

**Doctor Divinitatis** (Latin)   the academic degree of Doctor of Divinity. *Abbr.* **D.D.** Also **Divinitatis Doctor.**

**doctus cum libro** (Latin)   (lit., 'learned with a book')   designating someone having book-learning without practical experience.

**dojo** (Japanese)   a school for Oriental martial arts.

**dolce,** *pl.* **dolci** (Italian)   (lit., 'sweet')   1. a cake or pastry; a dessert.   2. *Music.* a soft musical passage.

**dolce far niente** (Italian)   (lit., 'sweet doing nothing')   pleasant idleness.

**dolcemente** (Italian)   *Music.* sweetly; softly.

**dolce stil nuovo** (Italian)   (lit., 'sweet new style')   *Literature.* a style of lyric poetry in the courtly love tradition, noted for its simplicity, sincerity, and the idealization of the beloved woman. See also **donna angelicata.**

**dolcezza** (Italian)   *Music.* sweetness; softness.

**dolcissimo** (Italian)   *Music.* sweetest; softest.

**dolente** (Italian)   *Music.* doleful; sorrowful.

93

**dolmade** (Greek)  *Cookery.* an appetizer made with pickled grape leaves stuffed with a rice mixture. Also **dolmathes.**

**doloroso** (Italian)  painful; full of sadness.

**domani** (Italian)  tomorrow.

**Domine, dirige nos** (Latin)  Lord, guide us (motto of London).

**domingo** (Spanish)  Sunday.

**Domino Optimo Maximo** (Latin)  to the Lord, Best and Greatest (motto of the Benedictine order). *Abbr.* **D.O.M.**

**Dominus illuminatio mea** (Latin)  the Lord is my light (motto of the University of Oxford).

**Dominus vobiscum** (Latin)  the Lord be with you.

**Domus Aurea** (Latin)  the Golden House, a palace built by the Roman emperor Nero.

**domus Dei** (Latin)  house of God.

**Domus Procerum** (Latin)  the House of Lords.

**don** (Italian)  1. a title of respect for a high **Mafia** leader.  2. a title of respect for a man regarded as a superior, as a priest or nobleman.

**Don,** *fem.* **Doña** (Spanish)  a title of respect used before a given name, e.g., *Don Pedro; Doña Inés.*

**doncel** (Spanish)  1. a royal page.  2. *Wine.* mild; mellow.

**donna** (Italian)  (lit., 'lady') a title of respect used with a lady's given name.

**donna angelicata** (Italian)  *Literature.* the idealized beloved woman in the lyric poetry of Dante and others. See also **dolce stil nuovo.**

**donna è mobile, la.**  See **la donna è mobile.**

**Donner** (German)  thunder.

**dopo** (Italian)  *Music.* after.

**Dopolavoro** (Italian)  (lit., 'after work') *Italian history.* an organization of the Mussolini era that provided cultural and recreational activities for workers.

**doppel** (German)  double.

**doppio** (Italian)  *Music.* double; twofold.

**doppio movimento** (Italian)  *Music.* a direction to double the preceding speed.

**doppio tempo** (Italian)  *Music.* double time.

**dorade** (French)  sea bream.

**dorado** (Spanish)  golden. See also **El Dorado.**

**dorsum** (Latin)  the back.

**dos** (Spanish)  two.

**dos à dos** (French)  *Ballet.* back-to-back. Also **dos-à-dos.**

**dos au public** (French) (lit., 'back to the public') *Ballet.* designating a step or maneuver done with the back of the dancer to the audience.

**dossier** (French) a file of documents containing detailed information on a particular person or subject.

**do svidanya** (Russian) till we meet again; goodbye.

**douane** (French) a European customs office.

**double** (French) *Ballet.* a step that is performed twice in quick sequence.

**doublé** (French) (lit., 'doubled') *Ballet.* designating certain compound steps.

**double entendre** (French) an expression that may be understood two ways, one of which is usually sexually suggestive.

**double entente** (French) an ambiguity or double meaning.

**doucement** (French) gently; softly.

**douceur** (French) 1. a gratuity; tip. 2. a bribe.

**do ut des** (Latin) (lit., 'I give that you may give') designation for a relationship in which someone gives or does something with the expectation that there will be reciprocation.

**doux** (French) *Wine.* sweet, said especially of a sweet champagne.

**doxa** (Greek) *Platonism.* opinion, as distinct from true knowledge. See also epistēmē.

**doyen,** *fem.* **doyenne** (French) the senior person in any group or profession.

**drachma** (Greek) the basic unit of currency in Greece.

**dramatis personae** (Latin) the characters in a play.

**dramma giocoso** (Italian) *Music.* a style of light opera popular during the 18th century. See also **opera buffa.**

**dramma lirico** (Italian) (lit., 'lyric drama') *Opera.* a term used to distinguish certain operatic works from the "music dramas" of Wagner. Also called **drame lyrique.**

**dramma per musica** (Italian) (lit., 'drama through music') *Music.* a term of the 17th and 18th centuries for opera.

**Drang nach Osten** (German) (lit., 'push toward the east') term for German eastward expansionism.

**drapeau tricolore** (French) the tricolored flag of France.

**Dreher** (German) *Music.* peasant dance.

**Drehleier** (German) *Music.* hurdy-gurdy.

**drei** (German) three.

**Dreibund** (German) *Politics.* Triple Alliance, used primarily in reference to the alliance of Germany, Austria-Hungary, and Italy in 1882.

**dressage** (French) the training of horses to obey commands and perform precise maneuvers. See also **haute école; manège.**

**droit** (French)    1. a legal right.   2. a set of rules or statutes that comprise the law.

**droit, de.**    See **de droit.**

**droit des gens** (French)    (lit., 'law of nations') international law.

**droit du seigneur.**    See **jus primae noctis.**

**droite, à.**    See **à droite.**

**Dubonnet** (French)    a brand of **apéritif** made with sweet red wine, quinine, and herbs.

**ducado** (Spanish)    a ducat, the former unit of currency of Spain.

**duce** (Italian)    leader; commander.  See also **Il Duce.**

**duces tecum** (Latin)    (lit., 'you shall bring with you')  *Law.* a subpoena ordering a person to bring evidence to court.

**duchesse** (French)    (lit., 'duchess')  1. a type of soft, heavy satin.  2. a type of lace.  3. *Cookery.* designating a preparation of mashed potatoes with eggs and cheese.  4. a type of couch or daybed assembled from several pieces that may be used separately.  See also **duchesse brisée.**

**duchesse brisée** (French)    a separate component of a **duchesse, 4.**

**ducit amor patriae** (Latin)    the love of country guides (me).

**due** (Italian)    two.

**duecento** (Italian)    the 13th century or the 1200's, especially in reference to Italian fine arts or literature.

**dueño,** *fem.* **dueña** (Spanish)  1. an owner.  2. a chaperone to a young woman.

**duetto** (Italian)    a duet.

**due volte** (Italian)    *Music.* two times; twice.

**du jour** (French)    of the day; today's (seen especially on restaurant menus).

**dulce** (Spanish)  1. *n.* sweetheart.  2. *n.* candy; confection.  3. *adj.* sweet.

**dulce est desipere in loco** (Latin)    it is pleasant to act foolishly on occasion (Horace, *Odes* IV.12.28).

**dulce et decorum est pro patria mori** (Latin)    sweet and fitting it is to die for one's country (Horace, *Odes* III.2.13).

**Duma** (Russian)    *Russian history.* a council, especially the elective assembly of Czar Nicholas II from 1905–1917.

**dumka** (Czech)    *Music.* a style of Slavic folk song that alternates in feeling between sadness and happiness.

**Dummkopf** (German)    *Derogatory.* a very stupid person.

**dum spiro, spero** (Latin)    while I breathe, I hope (from Vergil, *Aeneid* II.799).

**dum tacent, clamant** (Latin)   (lit., 'in their silence, they are crying out')
their silence is full of meaning (from Cicero, *Against Catiline* 1).

**dum vivimus, vivamus** (Latin)   while we live, let us live.

**dunkel** (German)   dark.

**duo concertante** (Italian)   *Music.* a duet in which each part alternates as
principal and subordinate.

**duomo,** *pl.* **duomi** (Italian)   (lit., 'dome') an Italian cathedral.

**dura lex sed lex** (Latin)   the law is harsh, but it is the law.

**dura mater** (Latin)   (lit., 'hard mother') *Anatomy.* the tough membrane
covering the brain and spinal cord.

**duramente** (Italian)   *Music.* with harshness; with sternness.

**durante bene placito** (Latin)   as long as the good graces (of authority) hold
out.

**durante vita** (Latin)   while life endures; during (one's) life.

**Durchführung** (German)   *Music.* development.

**duvet** (French)   a goose-down comforter.

**duxelles** (French)   *Cookery.* mushrooms, with various seasonings, sautéed
until all the moisture has evaporated.

**dux femina facti** (Latin)   a woman led the exploit (Vergil, *Aeneid* I.364).

# E

**eau de cologne** (French)    (lit., 'Cologne water') a less concentrated form of perfume.

**eau de parfum** (French)    a slightly diluted form of perfume. Also called **esprit de parfum.**

**eau de toilette** (French)    cologne; a diluted form of perfume.

**eau de vie** (French)    (lit., 'water of life') alcoholic spirits, especially brandy.

**eau forte** (French)    (lit., 'strong water') nitric acid.

**eau rougie** (French)    (lit., 'red water') a mixture of red wine and water.

**ébauche** (French)    a rough draft or outline; quick sketch.

**ébéniste** (French)    a cabinet maker especially proficient in the use of veneers and inlays.

**ébénisterie** (French)    cabinetwork produced by an **ébéniste.**

**écarté** (French)    (lit., 'discarded') a type of card game.

**ecce homo** (Latin)    (lit., 'behold the man') 1. the words with which Pilate presented Jesus to his accusers (John 19:5).    2. *Fine Arts.* (*cap.*) a representation of Jesus crowned with thorns.

**Eccellenza** (Italian)    a title of respect for certain officials and ecclesiastics, equivalent to *Your Excellency.*

**ecce signum** (Latin)    behold the sign; here is the proof.

**échalote** (French)    a scallion.

**échappé** (French)    (lit., 'escaped; escaping (position)') *Ballet.* a movement in which the dancer changes positions while jumping or raising the body. Also **temps échappé.**

**échappée de lumière** (French)    (lit., 'escape of light') *Fine Arts.* accidental light.

**échelle** (French)    (lit., 'ladder') 1. a vertical row of decoration or lacing on a garment in a ladderlike pattern. 2. *Music.* the scale.

**echt** (German)    genuine; authentic.

**éclair** (French)   (lit., 'lightning (flash)')   *Cookery.* a finger-shaped pastry filled with whipped cream or custard and usually covered with icing.

**éclaircissement** (French)   a clarification or explanation.

**éclat** (French)   1. a brilliant success meriting acclaim. 2. an elaborate or showy display.

**école** (French)   a school.

**école de dessin** (French)   an art school.

**école militaire** (French)   a military academy.

**école normale** (French)   a French teachers' training college.

**école polytechnique** (French)   a French college that specializes in engineering, scientific, and technical disciplines.

**e contra** (Latin)   on the other hand.

**e contrario** (Latin)   on the contrary.

**écorché** (French)   (lit., 'flayed') *Fine Arts.* an anatomical model or figure used to study muscles and blood vessels.

**écossaise** (French)   (lit., 'Scottish') *Music.* 1. an old folk dance in duple meter. 2. a lively piano composition in this style.

**écrasé** (French)   (lit., 'crushed') designating leather that has been crushed to produce a grained effect.

**écraseur** (French)   *Surgery.* an instrument used to clamp blood vessels and prevent hemorrhage.

**écrevisse** (French)   a crayfish.

**écru** (French)   designating a pale brown color, as raw silk or linen.

**écu** (French)   1. a type of shield used by French men-at-arms in the Middle Ages. 2. a former gold or silver coin of France which bore the image of a shield.

**écuelle** (French)   *Antiques.* a shallow bowl commonly having a high cover and two flat handles.

**Edelweiss** (German)   a white-flowered Alpine plant.

**editio cum notis variorum.**   See **cum notis variorum.**

**editio princeps** (Latin)   first edition.

**ef charisto** (Modern Greek)   thank you.

**effacé,** *fem.* **effacée** (French)   (lit., 'shaded') *Ballet.* a movement in which a dancer presents the audience with a three-quarter view of the body.

**effendi** (Turkish)   a title of respect for aristocrats and government officials.

**effleurage** (French)   a light, stroking motion used in massage.

**égalité** (French)   equality.

**eheu! fugaces labuntur anni** (Latin)   Alas! the fleeing years slip away (Horace, *Odes* II.14.1–2).

**eidolon,** *pl.* **eidola** (Greek)   a phantom; image; insubstantial form.

**eidos** (Greek) (lit., 'form') the basic concepts and approach to interpreting experience that are characteristic of a particular culture.

**ein** (German) one; a.

**Einleitung** (German) introduction; prelude.

**Einleitungspiel** (German) *Music.* overture; prelude. Also **Einleitung-satz.**

**Einstellung** (German) *Psychology.* a standard response to a problem.

**Eisen und Blut** (German) *Politics.* ⌐(lit., 'blood and iron') term for Bismarck's belief that political disputes can be settled through military force.

**eisteddfod** (Welsh) a meeting of Welsh bards and minstrels for performance and competition.

**eiusdem farinae** (Latin) (lit., 'of the same flour') of the same substance or origin.

**ejido** (Spanish) common grazing land.

**élan** (French) dash; fervor.

**élancé** (French) (lit., 'darted') *Ballet.* designating a quick, darting movement.

**élan vital** (French) (lit., 'vital force') a term from the philosophy of Bergson describing a creative or causative power in an organism.

**El Camino Real** (Spanish) the California coastal road during the time of Spanish settlement, called "the Route of the Missions." See also **camino real.**

**El Caudillo** (Spanish) the personal title of Francisco Franco, Spanish head of state from 1939–1975. See also **caudillo.**

**El Dorado** (Spanish) **1.** a mythical golden city sought by Spanish explorers of the New World. **2.** any place of great wealth. See also **dorado.**

**elegantemente** (Italian) *Music.* elegantly.

**elegantiae arbiter.** See **arbiter elegantiae.**

**élévation** (French) *Ballet.* the height of a dancer's jump.

**élévation, temps d'.** See **temps d'élévation.**

**élève** (French) a pupil.

**elixir vitae** (Latin) elixir of life.

**El Libertador** (Spanish) (lit., 'The Liberator') epithet given to Simón Bolívar, leader of South American independence movements.

**El Niño** (Spanish) (lit., 'The Child') a periodic oceanic phenomenon characterized by unusually warm tidal currents that cause widespread atmospheric disturbances and changing patterns of distribution in marine life.

**Elohim** (Hebrew) God.

**el todo** (Spanish) all, used with the name of a city to indicate participation by its citizens in some event or activity, as *el todo Madrid.*

101

**émail en plein** (French)     (lit., 'enamel in full') enamel made by the **basse-taille** technique.

**émaillerie à jour** (French)     a small **cloisonné** work that resembles stained glass, produced by removing the ground after transparent enamels have been applied.

**émail ombrant** (French)     (lit., 'shading enamel') a decorative technique in which a transparent enamel is laid over an **intaglio** design, creating the illusion of depth.

**embarcadero** (Spanish)     a quay; pier.

**embarras de choix** (French)     (lit., 'embarrassment of choice') the situation of having more options than one can deal with.

**embarras de richesse** (French)     (lit., 'embarrassment of riches') the situation of having so much wealth that one cannot keep track of all of it.

**emboîté** (French)     (lit., 'boxed-in (step)') *Ballet.* a kind of **jeté** executed without a brushing motion of the working foot. Also **pas emboîté; petit jeté; jeté passé.**

**embonpoint** (French)     portliness; stoutness.

**emeritus,** *fem.* **emerita** (Latin)     title given to a professor or minister who has retired after long and honorable service.

**émigré,** *fem.* **émigrée** (French)     a political refugee; emigrant.

**éminence grise** (French)     (lit., 'gray eminence') a person who has unofficial power, commonly exercised secretly and for personal gain (originally applied to Père Joseph, secretary and agent of Cardinal Richelieu).

**emir.**     See **amir, 1.**

**Emmenthaler** (German)     name for the original "Swiss cheese," from the Emmenthal valley in Switzerland.

**empanada** (Spanish)     *Cookery.*     1. a turnover containing meat, fish, or vegetables.     2. a sweet turnover filled with cherries.

**empanadilla** (Spanish)     *Cookery.* a small **empanada.**

**en arrière** (French)     *Ballet.* backward; behind.

**en avant** (French)     1. forward; in front; onward.     2. early; ahead of time.

**en bloc** (French)     as a unit; as a whole.

**en bordure** (French)     *Cookery.* served with a border, such as puréed vegetables.

**en brochette** (French)     *Cookery.* cooked on a skewer or spit. Also **à la broche.**

**en brosse** (French)     (lit., 'in (a) brush') designating a short hairstyle that is brushed to stand straight up.

**en cabochon.**     See **cabochon.**

**encabritado** (Spanish)     reared up, as a horse up on its hind legs.

**en carré** (French)  (lit., 'squared')  1. *Roulette.* designating a bet placed at a corner to cover four numbers at once.  2. *Ballet.* designating a step that is to be made in the shape of a squre.

**en casserole** (French)  *Cookery.* baked in a deep-dish pan or casserole.

**encastré** (French)  designating a kind of construction in which beams are fitted into masonry.

**enceinte** (French)  1. *adj.* pregnant.  2. *n.* a wall or enclosure of a fortified place.

**enchaînement** (French)  (lit., 'enchainment')  *Ballet.* a series of steps performed to a single musical phrase.

**enchanté** (French)  (lit., 'enchanted')  very pleased; delighted (commonly used as a polite remark when being introduced to another person).

**enchilada** (Spanish)  *Cookery.* a rolled **tortilla** filled with various ingredients in a sauce flavored with chile.

**encierro** (Spanish)  *Bullfighting.* a pen where bulls are kept before a bullfight. Also **toril.**

**en cocotte** (French)  *Cookery.* baked in a **cocotte.**

**encoignure** (French)  *Antiques.* a low, corner cabinet.

**encomendero** (Spanish)  *History.* a Spanish colonist who received a South American land grant. See also **encomienda.**

**encomienda** (Spanish)  *History.* a grant of land, often including Indian territory, made by Spanish kings to their colonists in South America. See also **encomendero, repartimiento.**

**en croix** (French)  (lit., 'crosswise')  *Ballet.* designating an exercise that is to be performed with the feet crossing from one position to another.

**en croûte** (French)  *Cookery.* cooked and served in a pastry crust.

**en cuirasse** (French)  (lit., 'in armor')  *Cookery.* enclosed in puff pastry, as a chop.

**encyclopédistes** (French)  *French history.* the writers who contributed to the 18th-century encyclopedia edited by Diderot and d'Alembert.

**en dernier ressort** (French)  at last resort.

**en déshabillé** (French)  partly dressed; not dressed. See also **déshabillé.**

**en effet** (French)  in effect; in reality.

**energicamente** (Italian)  *Music.* energetically.

**energico** (Italian)  *Music.* energetic.

**en face** (French)  1. opposite.  2. *Ballet.* facing; in front of; opposite.

**en fait** (French)  in fact.

**en famille** (French)  (lit., 'in the family')  intimate.

**enfant** (French)  a child.

**enfant prodigue** (French)  a prodigal son.

**enfants perdus** (French)    (lit., 'lost children')   soldiers assigned to a mission of certain death.

**enfant terrible** (French)    (lit., 'terrible child')   **1.** a problem child whose behavior is often wild and destructive. **2.** an eccentric adult whose behavior is embarrassing or indiscreet.

**enfant trouvé** (French)   a foundling; orphan.

**enfaticamente** (Italian)   *Music.* emphatically.

**en fête** (French)   in festive mood or attire.

**enfin** (French)   in conclusion; finally.

**engagé** (French)    (lit., 'engaged')   committed to or deeply involved in something.

**en garde** (French)   *Fencing.* a call to alert opponents in a match that the contest is about to begin.

**en gelée** (French)   *Cookery.* in aspic.

**engobe** (French)   *Applied Arts.* a white layer of ceramic used as a foundation for a transparent overlay.

**en grand** (French)   (lit., 'in grand style') *Fine Arts.* full-sized; at full length (in reference to a portrait).

**en grande tenue** (French)   (lit., 'in grand attire') in full military uniform.

**en grande toilette** (French)   in full dress.

**en grand seigneur** (French)   in grand style; like a great lord.

**en haut** (French)   (lit., 'on high') *Ballet.* designating a high position of the arms or legs.

**enjambement** (French)   *Poetry.* the running on of a thought from one line, couplet, or stanza to another.

**en l'air** (French)   *Ballet.* a motion of any part of a dancer's body made in the air above the supporting leg.

**enlèvement** (French)   *Ballet.* the lifting of the ballerina by her male partner.

**enluminure** (French)   *Applied Arts.* the technique of coloring or illuminating something, as a manuscript.

**en masse** (French)   all together; in a group.

**ennui** (French)   a feeling of weariness or disinterest.

**ennuyé,** *fem.* **ennuyée** (French)   experiencing **ennui.**

**en papillote** (French)   *Cookery.* **1.** designating meat cooked in a wrapping of paper or foil. **2.** designating cutlets with the ends decoratively wrapped in paper. **3.** *Hairdressing.* designating a hairstyle set in paper curlers.

**en parilla** (Spanish)   on the grill; grilled.

**en passant** (French)   **1.** by the way; in passing. **2.** *Chess.* a maneuver in which a pawn that has been moved two squares may be captured by an opposing pawn that passes it.

**en plein** (French)   **1.** *Roulette.* indicating that a bet has been placed on a single number rather than on a combination of numbers. **2.** *Applied Arts.* designating enamel work in which the ground, carved in **intaglio**, has its hollows filled with enamel.

**en plein air** (French)   in the open air (especially associated with the Impressionist painters, who characteristically painted outdoors and tried to capture the essence of nature). See also **plein-air.**

**en plein jour** (French)   in broad daylight.

**en prise** (French)   (lit., 'in prize') *Chess.* designating a piece that can be captured in the next move.

**en promenade** (French)   *Ballet.* slow turning in place while maintaining a pose.

**en rapport** (French)   in accord; in sympathy.

**en reculant** (French)   *Ballet.* a movement in which the working leg passes from front to back, with the dancer moving towards the back of the stage. See also **en remontant.**

**en règle** (French)   in order; in customary form.

**en remontant** (French)   *Ballet.* designating a movement of the working leg from front to back in which the dancer moves upstage. See also **en reculant.**

**en route** (French)   on the way.

**ens** (Latin)   *Philosophy.* being; thing; entity.

**ensalada** (Spanish)   a salad.

**en scène** (French)   on the stage.

**en seconde** (French)   *Ballet.* in the second position.

**ense et aratro** (Latin)   (lit., 'by sword and by plow') serving both in war and peace.

**ensemble** (French)   (lit., 'together') **1.** parts of a thing that, taken together, constitute a whole or create an aggregate effect. **2.** an entire outfit with all parts in harmony. **3.** *Performing Arts.* a company of entertainers or their performance.

**ens realissimum** (Latin)   (lit., 'the most real being') *Scholastic philosophy.* God conceived as the ultimate, perfect being.

**en suite** (French)   in succession; in a series.

**en surtout** (French)   (lit., 'above all') *Heraldry.* designating the position of a coat of arms at the top of a breastplate.

**entente** (French)   (lit., 'an understanding') an agreement of two or more governments to pursue a particular policy.

**entente cordiale** (French)   a friendly understanding or agreement, especially between two countries.

**en tête-à-tête** (French)   in a face-to-face meeting. See also **tête-à-tête.**

**en tire-bouchon** (French)   (lit., 'in a corkscrew') *Ballet.* a position in which the thigh of the working leg is in second position, and the point of the toe touches the knee of the supporting leg.

**entourage** (French)   1. attendants or followers, especially of high-ranking or famous persons. 2. physical surroundings.

**en tournant** (French)   *Ballet.* done while turning, referring to a step.

**en tout** (French)   in all; on the whole.

**en tout cas** (French)   in any case; in any event.

**en-tout-cas** (French)   1. an umbrella that also serves as a parasol. 2. an all-weather tennis court.

**entr'acte** (French)   1. *Performing Arts.* an interval or interlude between two acts of a performance. 2. a brief entertainment presented during this interval.

**entrada** (Spanish)   (lit., 'entrance; introduction') 1. an exploratory expedition.   2. *Music.* an introduction to a ballet.

**entrata** (Italian)   (lit., 'entrance') *Music.* an introduction or prelude. See also **aria d'entrata.**

**en travesti** (French)   (lit., 'in disguise') *Ballet.* designating a dancer wearing a costume of the opposite sex.

**entrechat** (French)   (lit., 'interweaving') *Ballet.* a jump in which a dancer crosses the legs several times while in the air.

**entrecôte** (French)   a cut of meat from between the ribs.

**entredeux** (French)   an insertion of lace or linen embroidery in a woman's dress.

**entrée** (French)   1. the act of entering or making an entrance. 2. the privilege of entering, as into an elite group. 3. (*especially U.S.*) a dish served as a main course. 4. *French cuisine.* a dish served as the third course in a full **menu**, prior to the main course. 5. *Ballet.* the opening segment of a performance.

**entrelacé** (French)   (lit., 'interlaced') *Ballet.* designating a scissorslike crossing of the legs used in various steps.

**entremés,** *pl.* **entremeses.**   See **tapa.**

**entremets** (French)   (lit., 'between courses') 1. a side dish or delicacy served between courses. 2. a dessert dish served after the cheese course.

**entre nous** (French)   between us; confidentially.

**entrepôt** (French)   a warehouse or commercial center where goods are received for reshipment.

**entrepreneur,** *fem.* **entrepreneuse** (French)   a person who owns and operates a commercial enterprise.

**entresol** (French)   (lit., 'floor between') a mezzanine level in a building.

**entubar** (Spanish)   to roll tobacco leaves in the process of hand-making cigars.

**en vérité** (French)   in truth.

**envidado.**   See envinado.

**envinado** (Spanish)   *Cookery.* designating a dish to which wine has been added. Also **envidado.**

**en voiture** (French)   (lit., 'in the car') all aboard!

**envuelto a mano** (Spanish)   packed by hand.

**eo ipso** (Latin)   by that very fact; by that fact alone.

**eo nomine** (Latin)   under *or* by that name.

**épater le bourgeois** (French)   to stun or shock middle-class values, as by a daring innovation or license in art.

**épaulement** (French)   (lit., 'shouldering') *Ballet.* artistic and dramatic use of the shoulders and upper body.

**épaulière** (French)   a piece of armor for the shoulder and upper arm.

**épée** (French)   *Fencing.* 1. a rapier with a three-sided blade and a guard over the tip. 2. the style of contest in which points are scored by touching any part of an opponent's body with the tip of the weapon.

**épinards** (French)   spinach.

**epistēmē** (Greek)   *Platonism.* true knowledge, as opposed to mere opinion. See also **doxa.**

**epistola,** *pl.* **epistolae** (Latin)   letter; epistle.

**epithalamion** (Greek)   a song or poem in honor of a wedding.

**e pluribus unum** (Latin)   out of many, one (motto of the United States).

**équilibre** (French)   *Ballet.* balancing of the body over the legs and feet.

**e re nata** (Latin)   (lit., 'arising from the thing') under the present circumstances; as matters stand. Also **ex re nata.**

**ergo** (Latin)   therefore.

**Erin go bragh** (Gaelic)   Ireland forever.

**Erlkönig** (German)   *Folklore.* the elf-king or erlking, said to work mischief on children.

**eroico,** *fem.* **eroica** (Italian)   *Music.* 1. heroic in style.   2. (*cap., fem.*) the name of Beethoven's Third Symphony.

**erotica,** *pl.* **erotice** (Italian)   *Music.* a song of carnal love.

**errare humanum est** (Latin)   to err is human. Also **errare est humanum; humanum est errare.**

**errata,** *sing.* **erratum** (Latin)   errors; list of errors in a book.

**ersatz** (German)   substitute.

**Erzähler** (German)   narrator.

**Erziehungsroman.**   See **Bildungsroman.**

**escabeche** (Spanish)   *Cookery.* a vinegar sauce used for preserving and marinating; a marinade.

**escalivado** (Spanish)   *Cookery.* roasted green and red peppers, eggplant, and tomatoes served as a vegetable or an appetizer.

**escalopes** (French)   *Cookery.* small, boneless pieces of meat or fish, fried in butter.

**escargots** (French)   *Cookery.* snails, usually cooked in garlic butter, considered a delicacy.

**escritoire** (French)   a writing desk.

**escuela** (Spanish)   a school.

**espada** (Spanish)   *Bullfighting.*  1. a sword.  2. (by extension) the matador himself.

**espagnole, à l'.**   See à l'espagnole.

**español,** *fem.* **española.** (Spanish)  1. the Spanish language.  2. Spanish.

**esperanza** (Spanish)   hope.

**espièglerie** (French)   a playful trick.

**espirando** (Italian)   *Music.* dying away; expiring.

**espontáneo** (Spanish)   (lit., 'the spontaneous one') *Bullfighting.* an attention seeker who leaps into the ring during the fight.

**espressione** (Italian)   *Music.* expression; feeling.

**espressivo** (Italian)   *Music.* expressive; with expression.

**espresso.**   See caffè espresso.

**esprit** (French)   liveliness of wit; cleverness.

**esprit de corps** (French)   a sense of unity and loyalty in a group of people with common goals.

**esprit de parfum.**   See eau de parfum.

**esprit d'escalier** (French)   (lit., 'stairway wit') a clever retort that is thought of too late, after an argument or conversation is finished.

**esprit de suite, l'.**   See l'esprit de suite.

**esprit gaulois** (French)   Gallic wit.

**esquisse** (French)   a preliminary sketch.

**esquisse-esquisse** (French)   *Architecture.* a rough sketch of a large project, showing only basic design elements.

**esse** (Latin)   *Philosophy.* essence; being.

**esse est percipi** (Latin)   *Philosophy.* to be is to be perceived, Berkeley's doctrine that the outside world exists only in the mind.

**esse quam videri** (Latin)   to be rather than to seem.

**está bién** (Spanish)   okay; that's fine.

**Estados Unidos, los** (Spanish)   the United States of America.

**estaminet** (French)   a small cafe.

**estancia** (Spanish)   a cattle ranch or estate of South America.  See also finca.

**estanciero** (Spanish)   a rancher; the owner of an **estancia**.

**estinguendo** (Italian)   *Music.* fading; dying away.

**est modus in rebus** (Latin)   there is a proper measure in all things (Horace, *Satires* I.1.106).

**estocada** (Spanish)   *Bullfighting.* the sword thrust.

**estofado** (Spanish)   *Cookery.* beef stew with tomatoes, onions, wine, and spices.

**esto perpetua** (Latin)   may she live forever! (motto of Idaho).

**estoque** (Spanish)   *Bullfighting.* a sword.

**estragon, à l'.**   See à l'estragon.

**estravaganza** (Italian)   *Music.* a composition of a very irregular kind.

**estufa** (Spanish)   (lit., 'stove')   *Architecture.* council chamber of an Indian village, located underground.

**es tut mir leid** (German)   I'm sorry.

**étagère** (French)   *Furniture.* an array of shelves that may stand on legs or be hung on a wall.

**et alii** *or* **aliae** (Latin)   and others.  *Abbr.* et al.

**étatisme** (French)   state control of industries and services.

**États Unis** (French)   the United States.

**et cetera** *or* **caetera** (Latin)   (lit., 'and the other things')   and so forth.  *Abbr.* etc.

**et cum spiritu tuo** (Latin)   and with your spirit (liturgical response to **Dominus vobiscum**).

**et ego in Arcadia** (Latin)   (lit., 'I, too, (have lived) in Arcadia')   I have delighted in the same ideals, too (alluding to Arcadia as the exemplar of pastoral bliss).

*Ethica* (Latin)   *Ethics,* title of works by Aristotle and others.

**et hoc genus omne** (Latin)   and all this sort of thing.  Also **et id genus omne.**

**et nunc et semper** (Latin)   both now and always.

**étoile** (French)   1. a star performer.  2. *Ballet.* a prima ballerina.

**étouffée.**   See étuvée.

**et passim.**   See passim.

**être de pied** (French)   (lit., 'to be of foot')   *Ballet.* designating that a dancer is in position to begin the next phase of the dance.

**et sequentia** *or* **sequentes** (Latin)   and what follows.  *Abbr.* et seq.; et seqq.; et sqq.

**et sic de similibus** (Latin)   and thus concerning similar things.

**et similia** (Latin)   and similar things.

**et tu, Brute** (Latin)    and you, Brutus! (alleged dying words of Julius Caesar when stabbed by his close associate, Brutus).

**étude,** *pl.* **études** (French)    1. *Music.* a composition, usually instrumental, intended mainly for practicing technique.    2. a study or concentrated focus on a theme or subject.

**étudiant** (French)    a student.

**étuvée** (French)    *Cookery.* designating a method of cooking by steaming in a covered pan. Also **étouffée.**

**étuvée, à l'.**    See **à l'étuvée.**

**et uxor** (Latin)    and (his) wife. *Abbr.* **et ux.**

**et vir** (Latin)    and (her) husband.

**évasé** (French)    widened or flaring at the top, as a vase.

**evirato.**    See **castrato.**

**ewige Jude, der** (German)    the wandering Jew.

**Ewigkeit** (German)    the unknown; eternity.

**Ewig-weibliche, das** (German)    the eternal feminine; the power of women as a spiritualizing cultural force.

**ex abundantia** (Latin)    out of the abundance.

**exactement** (French)    exactly; precisely.

**ex aequo et bono** (Latin)    *Law.* according to what is just and good.

**ex animo** (Latin)    from the heart; sincerely.

**ex ante** (Latin)    from what is to happen; based on anticipated performance. See also **ex post.**

**ex auctoritate mihi commissa** (Latin)    by virtue of the authority entrusted to me.

**ex capite** (Latin)    from the head; from memory.

**ex cathedra** (Latin)    (lit., 'from the official chair') said with official authority; by virtue of judicial or papal authority.

**excelsior** (Latin)    higher (motto of New York State).

**exceptio probat regulam (de rebus non exceptis)** (Latin)    the exception tests (*or* proves) the rule (concerning the things not excepted).

**exceptis excipiendis** (Latin)    with due exceptions having been made.

**excerpta** (Latin)    excerpts; selections.

**excudit** (Latin)    he (*or* she) printed or engraved (this); used with the name of the artisan. *Abbr.* **excud.**

**ex curia** (Latin)    *Law.* out of court.

**excursus** (Latin)    a digression; a detailed discussion on some tangential point.

**ex delicto** (Latin)    (lit., 'out of a wrong') *Law.* a cause for legal action arising out of a tort or wrong.

110

**ex dividendo** (Latin)   *Finance.* not including a declared dividend. *Abbr.* ex div. See also **cum dividendo.**

**ex dono** (Latin)   by the gift of; donated by (used on book plates, etc., with the name of the donor).

**exeat** (Latin)   (lit., 'let him go out') a permission for temporary absence.

**exegi monumentum aere perennius** (Latin)   I have built a monument more lasting than bronze; this achievement will stand the test of time (from Horace, *Odes* III.30.1).

**exempli causa** (Latin)   for the sake of example.

**exempli gratia** (Latin)   for example; for instance. *Abbr.* e.g.

**exemplum,** *pl.* **exempla** (Latin)   an example; an anecdote used to illustrate a moral point.

**exeunt** (Latin)   *Drama.* they leave the stage.

**exeunt omnes** (Latin)   *Drama.* they all leave the stage.

**ex facie** (Latin)   (lit., 'from the face') *Law.* (of a document) considered on the basis of its surface features; apparently.

**ex gratia** (Latin)   *Law.* by favor (not because of legal right).

**ex hypothesi** (Latin)   by hypothesis.

**exit** (Latin)   *Drama.* he (*or* she) leaves the stage.

**exitus acta probat** (Latin)   the end justifies the means; the result justifies the deeds (George Washington's family motto, from Ovid, *Heroides* II.85).

**ex lege** (Latin)   according to law.

**ex libris** (Latin)   from the books of (used on book plates, with the name of the owner).

**ex mero motu** (Latin)   purely out of impulse.

**ex more** (Latin)   according to custom.

**ex natura rei** (Latin)   out of the nature of things.

**ex necessitate rei** (Latin)   *Law.* arising from the necessity of the case.

**ex nihilo nihil fit.**   See **nihil ex nihilo (fit).**

**ex officio** (Latin)   by virtue of one's office or official position.

**exordium** (Latin)   the first part, especially the introductory part of a discourse.

**ex parte** (Latin)   (lit., 'from (one) side (only)') something done in the interest or to the benefit of one side in a controversy.

**ex pede Herculem** (Latin)   (lit., '(judge the size of) Hercules from his foot') from a part one can estimate the whole. See also **ex ungue leonem.**

**experientia docet (stultos)** (Latin)   experience teaches (fools).

**experto cred(it)e** (Latin)   trust the expert.

**explication de texte** (French)   *Literature.* a detailed analysis of a literary work or passage, concentrating on language and style.

**explicit** (Latin)   (lit., 'it is unfolded') formerly used to note the end of a manuscript scroll.  See also **incipit**.

**exposé** (French)     a revelation of a secret, especially something considered scandalous.

**ex post** (Latin)   from what has happened; based on an analysis of past performance.  See also **ex ante**.

**ex post facto** (Latin)   (lit., 'from a thing done afterward') after the fact; done subsequently.  Also **post facto**.

**expressis verbis** (Latin)   in express terms.

**expresso.**     See **espresso**.

**ex propriis** (Latin)   from one's own resources.

**ex relatione** (Latin)   (lit., 'by relation')  *Law.*  referring to a case reported or instituted not from personal knowledge but from a third or interested party.

**ex re nata.**     See **e re nata**.

**ex silentio.**     See **argumentum ex silentio**.

**ex tempore** (Latin)   (lit., 'out of the moment') said of something done, especially a speech given, without preparation.

**extérieur, à l'.**     See **à l'extérieur**.

**extra muros** (Latin)     beyond the walls; outside of an institution.

**extrémité, à l'.**     See **à l'extrémité**.

**ex ungue leonem** (Latin)   (discern the presence of) the lion from its claw, that is, one can perceive the whole from a part.  See also **ex pede Herculem**.

**ex uno disce omnes** (Latin)   from one (example) learn all.

**ex voluntate** (Latin)   voluntarily.

**ex voto** (Latin)   in accordance with (one's) vow or prayer.

# F

**fabada** (Spanish)  *Cookery.*  a stew of the Asturian region of Spain, containing dried white beans, sausages, and meat.

**fabliau**, *pl.* **fabliaux** (French)  *Literature.*  a short metrical tale, often ribald, popular with medieval French poets.

**fabula** (Latin)  story; dramatic piece.

**fabula palliata** (Latin)  Roman comic drama in which the characters wore the pallium, a Greek garment.

**fabula praetexta** (Latin)  Roman tragic drama in which the characters wore the bordered **toga praetexta**.

**fabula togata** (Latin)  Roman drama in which the characters wore the Roman toga.

**fac** (Latin)  make (it); do (it).

**façade** (French)  1. *Architecture.*  the front of a structure, especially a decorative facing.  2. a false or artificial appearance. Also **facade**.

**face, de.**  See **de face**.

**face, en.**  See **en face**.

**facetiae** (Latin)  jokes; humorous writings.

**facile** (Italian)  *Music.*  easy; fluent.

**facile** (French)  easy.

**facile princeps** (Latin)  easily the leader.

**facilis descensus Averni** (Latin)  the descent to Avernus (hell) is easy (Vergil, *Aeneid* VI.126).

**facilità** (Italian)  *Music.*  ease; fluency.

**façon de parler** (French)  a way or manner of speaking.

**façonné** (French)  a kind of fabric that is woven with a distinct figured pattern or design.

**facta non verba** (Latin)  deeds, not words.

**factum est** (Latin)  it is done.

**factura** (Spanish)  a bill; invoice.

**fade** (French)  dull; tastelesss.

113

**fado** (Portuguese)   a type of Portuguese popular song, typically played on guitar.

**faex populi,** *pl.* **faeces populi** (Latin)   the dregs of society; the rabble.

**fagioli** (Italian)   beans. See also **pasta e fagioli**.

**fagotto** (Italian)   a bassoon.

**faïence** (French)   *Antiques.* glazed and highly decorated earthenware pottery of fine quality. Also **faience**.

**faille** (French)   a lightweight fabric, as of silk or rayon, with a ribbed pattern.

**faire le salon** (French)   *Fine Arts.* to review an art show.

**faisan,** *fem.* **faisane** (French)   pheasant.

**fait, de.**   See **de fait**.

**fait accompli,** *pl.* **faits accomplis** (French)   an accomplished fact; something already completed.

**faites vos jeux** (French)   *Gambling.* place your bets.

**faja** (Spanish)   a sash worn around the waist.

**fajitas** (Spanish)   *Cookery.* tortillas filled with strips of meat, avocado, and a sauce made of **chiles**.

**fakir** (Arabic)   a Muslim or Hindu mendicant or ascetic.

**falangista** (Spanish)   a member of the Spanish fascist party.

**Falerno** (Italian)   a dry red or white wine produced near Naples.

**falla** (Spanish)   *Geology.* fault; break.

**falsetto** (Italian)   *Music.* artificially high-pitched singing, especially in a male voice.

**fama volat** (Latin)   the report (*or* rumor) flies.

**fanático** (Spanish)   a fanatic.

**fandango** (Spanish)   a lively Spanish folk dance in triple time, usually performed with castanets.

**fantasia** (Italian)   (lit., 'fantasy') *Music.* 1. any composition in which form is secondary to the imagination of the composer.   2. melodies taken from an opera or other work. See also **divertimento, 2.**

**Fantasiestück** (German)   *Music.* fantasia.

**fantastisch** (German)   fantastic; capricious.

**fantoccino,** *pl.* **fantoccini** (Italian)   1. a puppet; marionette.   2. a puppet play.

**farandole** (French)   1. a lively group dance originating in the Provence region of France.   2. a display of assorted desserts in a restaurant.

**Farbeton.**   See **Tonfarbe**.

**farceur,** *fem.* **farceuse** (French)   1. a person who writes or plays in farces.   2. a wag; jokester.

**farci** (French)   *Cookery.* stuffed, as poultry or fish.

114

**far niente** (Italian)    the state of doing nothing. See also **dolce far niente**.

**fas** (Latin)    right and proper. See also **nefas**.

**fasces** (Latin)    (lit., 'bundles') a bundle of rods with an axhead projecting from it; a symbol of official authority.

**Fascisti** (Italian)    members of the Fascist party, especially the regime of Mussolini that ruled Italy from 1922 to 1943.

**fasti** (Latin)    *Roman history.* days on which conduct of business was permitted. See also **nefasti dies**.

**fata morgana** (Italian)    1. a mirage in which distant objects are reflected in the sea or in a sort of aerial screen above the sea.    2. a female sorceress. 3. *(cap.) Literature.* Morgan le Fay of the Arthurian legends.

**fata obstant** (Latin)    the fates oppose; it is impossible (Vergil, *Aeneid* IV.440).

**fatiha** (Arabic)    (lit., 'beginning') *Islam.* the opening chapter of the **Koran**. Also **Fatihah**.

**fatrasie** (French)    *Literature.* a medieval genre consisting of a series of satirical plays.

**fausse tortue** (French)    *Cookery.* mock turtle.

**faute de mieux** (French)    for lack of something better.

**fauteuil** (French)    1. *Antiques.* an upholstered armchair, usually with open sides. 2. a theater stall or box.

**Fauve** (French)    (lit., 'wild beast') *Fine Arts.* a term applied to Henri Matisse and individuals of his school, whose style is known as *Fauvism.*

**faux,** *fem.* **fausse** (French)    mock; false; imitation.

**faux ami** (French)    1. a false friend. 2. **faux amis** *(pl.) Language.* a pair of words from two different languages that have the same or very similar spellings but quite different meanings.

**faux-bois** (French)    imitation wood.

**fauxbourbon** (French)    *Music.* a particular technique of harmonization involving the blending of three voices.

**faux-croco** (French)    imitation alligator, used in shoes and handbags.

**faux-marbre** (French)    imitation marble.

**faux pas** (French)    (lit., 'false step') a mistake in manners or social conduct; a social blunder.

**fé** (Spanish)    faith. See also **auto de fé**.

**fecit** (Latin)    he (*or* she) made it (written with the artist's name on a work of art). *Abbr.* **fec.**

**fegato** (Italian)    liver.

**felix culpa** (Latin)    O fortunate fault! (St. Augustine's allusion to the original sin as leading to man's redemption in Christ).

**Feliz Navidad** (Spanish)    Merry Christmas.

115

**fellah,** *pl.* **fellahin** (Arabic)    a peasant or laborer.

**femme** (French)    a woman.

**femme de chambre** (French)    1. a lady's maid. 2. a chambermaid. Also **fille de chambre.**

**femme fatale** (French)    (lit., 'fatal woman')    an irresistibly seductive woman, particularly one whose charms lead men into danger.

**fenouil** (French)    fennel.

**feria** (Spanish)    a fair; festival; holy day.

**fermata** (Italian)    *Music.* 1. a pause.    2. the pause mark in a **concerto** that shows the point where the **cadenza** starts.

**fermé, fermée** (French)    (lit., 'closed')    *Ballet.* designating that the feet of a dancer are in the closed position.

**ferme ornée** (French)    (lit., 'decorated farm')    a country residence with a picturesque architectural design.

**Fernet Branca** (Italian)    a type of wine with herbs, used as a digestive.

**ferragosto** (Italian)    the Italian vacation period that begins with the Feast of the Assumption on August 15.

**ferri, ai.**    See **ai ferri.**

**ferrum** (Latin)    iron. *Abbr.* **Fe.**

**Fest** (German)    festival.

**festa** (Italian)    a festival.

**festa teatrale** (Italian)    *Opera.* a production on a grand scale, designed to honor a public occasion such as a victory or a royal marriage.

**festina lente** (Latin)    make haste slowly.

**festivamente** (Italian)    *Music.* in a festive manner.

**Festschrift** (German)    a commemorative volume, especially a collection of articles compiled by colleagues and former students to honor a scholar who is retiring.

**Festspiel** (German)    1. festival. 2. festival performance.

**Festung Europa** (German)    (lit., 'Fortress of Europe')    a term for Nazi-occupied Europe, claimed to be invulnerable.

**feta** (Greek)    a mild, white Greek cheese made of goat's milk.

**fête** (French)    a festival; religious feast day.

**fête champêtre** (French)    an outdoor festival or garden party.

**fettucini** (Italian)    1. a variety of **pasta** made with eggs and cut into long, narrow strips.    2. *Cookery.* a designation for dishes that use this variety of **pasta** with various sauces.

**feu de joie** (French)    (lit., 'fire of joy')    the firing of guns or a bonfire in celebration of a joyous occasion.

**feuilletée.**    See **pâté feuilletée.**

**feuilleton** (French)   1. a special section of a newspaper, usually at the bottom of a page, devoted to light literature, criticism, etc. 2. material appearing in such a section, as serialized fiction.

**fianchetto** (Italian)   *Chess.* the movement of the bishop to the second square of the knight to control the long diagonal.

**fiaschetteria** (Italian)   a wine shop, occasionally combined with a restaurant, selling wine by the bottle or glass.

**fiasco,** *pl.* **fiaschi** (Italian)   a round-bottomed glass bottle with a straw covering, used especially for **Chianti.**

**fiat** (Latin)   (lit., 'let it be done') an authoritative decree.

**fiat justitiam pereat mundus** (Latin)   let justice be done even though the world perish.

**fiat justitiam ruat caelum** (Latin)   let justice be done even though the heavens fall.

**fiat lux** (Latin)   let there be light (Genesis 1:3).

**fiat voluntas tua** (Latin)   thy will be done (from the Lord's Prayer, Matthew 6:10).

**ficelles** (French)   tricks of a trade; fakeries.

**Fidei Defensor.**   See **Defensor Fidei.**

**Fidelismo** (Spanish)   the political doctrine of Fidel Castro. See also **Fidelista.**

**Fidelista** (Spanish)   one who subscribes to the policies and doctrines of Fidel Castro. See also **Fidelismo.**

**fideliter** (Latin)   faithfully.

**fides Punica** (Latin)   Punic (i.e., Carthaginian) faith; treachery.

**fidus Achates** (Latin)   faithful Achates; a devoted friend or follower (alluding to the companion of Aeneas in Vergil's *Aeneid*).

**fieramente** (Italian)   *Music.* ferociously; scornfully.

**fierezza** (Italian)   1. *Music.* fierceness; boldness.   2. *Fine Arts.* boldness of touch.

**fieri facias** (Latin)   (lit., 'cause it to be done') a writ commanding a sheriff to use a debtor's property to satisfy a claim.

**fiesta** (Spanish)   1. a party; celebration.   2. a holiday.

**figurant,** *fem.* **figurante** (French)   1. *Ballet.* a ballet dancer who dances only with a group.   2. *Theater.* an extra; supernumerary.

**figurante** (Italian)   *Music.* a ballet dancer who plays an independent part in a piece such as an opera.

**figurato** (Italian)   (lit., 'figured') *Music.* embellished or adorned, as with accompaniments.

**figure** (French)   (lit., 'figure') *Dance.* a pattern described by dancers in performing a series of steps, a key factor in choreography.

117

**filar il suono** (Italian)   *Music.* to extend a tone, usually with gradually increasing and decreasing force. Also **filar la voce.**

**filar il tuono** (Italian)   *Music.* to sing a tone with an unchanging amount of volume and expression.

**filar la voce.**   See **filar il suono.**

**filet** (French)   a boneless strip of fish or meat, as the tenderloin.

**filet mignon** (French)   (lit., 'dainty filet') a small, very tender steak cut from tenderloin of beef.

**fileto di pomodoro** (Italian)   *Cookery.* a sauce made from tomatoes with herbs and olive oil.

**filetto** (Italian)   filet; tenderloin.

**filius nullius** (Latin)   (lit., 'a son of nobody') an illegitimate son. Also **nullius filius.**

**fille de chambre.**   See **femme de chambre.**

**fille de joie** (French)   a woman of pleasure; courtesan.

**film d'auteur** (French)   *Cinema.* a film that is considered the personal statement of its director.

**film noir** (French)   a term used by French critics to describe dark, suspenseful movies.

**filo.**   See **phyllo.**

**fils** (French)   1. son. 2. sons.

**filtre.**   See **café filtre.**

**fin** (French)   end; finish.

**fin** (Italian)   *Music.* as far as. Also **fino.**

**fin, à la.**   See **à la fin.**

**finale** (Italian)   1. the closing segment of any extended performance or display.   2. *Music.* the last movement or closing passages of a **sonata,** symphony, opera, or similar cyclic work.

**financière** (French)   *Cookery.* 1. designating a preparation for meat or poultry garnished with cockscombs, **quenelles,** sweetbreads, truffles, and olives. 2. a sauce made with Madeira wine and truffles.

**finca** (Spanish)   a plantation; farm; ranch. Also **estancia.**

**fin de siècle** (French)   (lit., 'end of the century') a term designating the end of the 19th century, especially in reference to the changes in social and moral conventions characteristic of the period.

**fine** (French)   a common, unexceptional French brandy.

**fine** (Italian)   *Music.* the end of a piece.

**fine bouche** (French)   a refined palate. Also **la fine bouche.**

**Fine Champagne** (French)   a high quality French brandy distilled from grapes grown in the Champagne region.

**fines herbes** (French)    *Cookery.* a mixture of chopped herbs used for seasoning soups, sauces, etc.

**fin gourmet** (French)    a renowned connoisseur of fine food.  See also gourmand; gourmet.

**finis** (Latin)    the end; conclusion.

**finis coronat opus** (Latin)    the end crowns the work.

**fin mot** (French)    (lit., 'the fine word') the main point or inner meaning of an issue.

**fino.    See fin.**

**fino** (Spanish)    *Wine.* a type of delicate sherry, somewhat heavier than amontillado.

**finocchio** (Italian)    fennel.

**finocchiona** (Italian)    a type of salami with fennel seeds, made in Tuscany.

**fioco** (Italian)    *Music.* hoarse; faint.

**fioreggiante** (Italian)    (lit., 'flowering') *Music.* in a florid style.

**fiorentina, alla.    See alla fiorentina.**

**fiorette.    See fioritura.**

**fiorito** (Italian)    *Music.* flowery; florid.

**fioritura,** *pl.* **fioriture** (Italian)    *Music.* melodic ornaments interpolated by singers and violinists.  Also **fiorette** (*pl.* **fioretti**); **ornamenti.**

**fjeld** (Norwegian)    a rocky plateau of the Scandianavian peninsula.

**fjord** (Norwegian)    a narrow inlet of the sea bordered by steep cliffs, typical of the coast of Norway.

**flacon** (French)    a small bottle or flask.

**flacon d'odeur** (French)    a perfume bottle.

**flagrante bello** (Latin)    while the war is raging.

**flagrante delicto.    See in flagrante delicto.**

**flambé,** *fem.* **flambée** (French)    (lit., 'flamed') **1.** *Cookery.* designating food served in flaming liquor, especially brandy.  **2.** *Ceramics.* designating a thick glaze that is streaked with colors.

**flamenco** (Spanish)    designating something in the style of Spanish gypsies, especially referring to music and dance.  See also **baile flamenco; cante flamenco.**

**flan** (Spanish)    *Cookery.* caramel custard.

**flânerie** (French)    idleness; laziness.

**flâneur** (French)    an idler; loafer.

**flauta** (Spanish)    (lit., 'flute') *Cookery.* a large corn **tortilla** containing marinated chicken, served with sour cream.

**flebile** (Italian)    *Music.* mournful.

**flebilmente** (Italian)    *Music.* mournfully.

flèche (French)  (lit., 'arrow') 1. *Architecture*. a steeple or spire, especially one of Gothic style. 2. *Fencing*. a technique of rapid attack towards an opponent.

flèches d'amour (French)  (lit., 'arrows of love') thread-like crystals of rutile embedded in quartz.

fléchette (French)  a steel dart thrown from an airplane, used as a personnel weapon in World War I.

fleur-de-lis, *pl.* fleurs-de-lis (French)  (lit., 'flower of lily') a symbol or design consisting of three lily petals tied together, the emblem of French royalty. Also fleur-de-lys.

floración (Spanish)  (lit., 'flowering') *Geology*. an outcropping of rocks.

florida, *masc.* florido (Spanish)  flowery; flowered. See also pascua florida.

florilegium (Latin)  a literary anthology.

floruit (Latin)  he (*or* she) flourished (used with dates to designate the productive years of an individual). *Abbr.* fl. *or* flor.

foco.  See fuoco.

focosamente (Italian)  *Music*. in a fiery way.

focoso (Italian)  *Music*. fiery.

Föhn (German)  a warm, dry wind that descends the leeward side of a mountain ridge. Also Foehn.

foie (French)  liver.

foie gras (French)  *Cookery*. the liver of geese or ducks specially fattened by force-feeding, used to make delicacies such as pâté de foie gras.

folie à deux (French)  a delusion shared by two people.

folie de grandeur (French)  delusion of grandeur; megalomania.

folio verso (Latin)  on the other side (of the page). *Abbr.* f.v.

fond, à.  See à fond.

fonda (Spanish)  an inn; wayside restaurant.

fondant (French)  *Cookery*. a thick sugar paste used to make candies.

fondo d'oro (Italian)  *Fine Arts*. the gilded background used to set off figures in medieval illumination and in primitive painting.

fondu (French)  (lit., 'melted') *Ballet*. a gradual bending of the supporting leg.

fondue (French)  (lit., 'melted') *Cookery*. 1. a dish of Swiss origin in which pieces of bread are dipped in a sauce of hot melted cheese and seasonings. 2. any similar dish in which food is dipped in a hot mixture before eating. 3. a preparation for vegetables in which they are cooked very long until reduced to a pulp.

fons et origo (Latin)  the source and origin.

fons malorum (Latin)  the source of evils.

**fonte émaillée** (French)   enameled cast iron, as certain cookware.
**fontina** (Italian)   a mild, soft, white cheese.
**force de frappe** (French)   *Military.* a swift and devastating striking force.
**force majeure** (French)   (lit., 'superior force') *Law.* an unexpected event so disruptive that it may excuse a party from a contract.
**forestière, à la.**   See **à la forestière.**
**formaggio** (Italian)   cheese.
**formes libres** (French)   (lit., 'free forms') *Fine Arts.* designating works that defy traditional standards or objective interpretation, primarily reflecting the fantasy of an artist.
**forno, al.**   See **al forno.**
**forte** (Italian)   *Music.* loud. *Abbr.* **f.**
**forte forte** (Italian)   *Music.* very loud. *Abbr.* **ff.** Also **fortissimo.**
**forte-piano** (Italian)   *Music.* loud and then soft. *Abbr.* **fp.**
**forte possible** (Italian)   *Music.* as loud as possible.
**fortissimo** (Italian)   *Music.* very loud. Also **forte forte.**
**fortiter in re, suaviter in modo** (Latin)   (be) bold in action, gentle in manner.
**fortunae filius** (Latin)   a son of fortune; a lucky man.
**fortuna fortes juvat** (Latin)   fortune favors the brave.
**fortuna sequatur** (Latin)   let fortune follow.
**forza, con.**   See **con forza.**
**forzando** (Italian)   (lit., 'forcing') *Music.* putting emphasis upon a single note. *Abbr.* **fz.**
**fouetté** (French)   (lit., 'whipped') *Ballet.* a whiplike movement of the body or leg.
**fourché** (French)   forked or divided at the end. Also **fourchée.**
**fourchette** (French)   a fork.
**fourgon** (French)   a long, covered wagon for baggage, supplies, etc.
**fourragère** (French)   a decorative braid worn on the shoulder of a uniform.
**foyer** (French)   (lit., 'home') **1.** the lobby of a hotel or theater. **2.** an entrance area of a residence.
**fra** (Italian)   a shortening of *frate* ('brother; friar') used as a title.
**fra diavolo** (Italian)   (lit., 'brother devil') *Cookery.* lobster or other seafood prepared with a spicy tomato sauce. See also **alla diavola.**
**fragola,** *pl.* **fragole** (Italian)   a strawberry.
**fraise** (French)   a strawberry.
**Fraktur** (German)   *Printing.* Gothic-style lettering; black letter.
**framboise** (French)   a raspberry.
**franc** (French)   the basic monetary unit of France and other countries.

**français,** *fem.* **française** (French)    French.

**française, à la.**    See **à la française.**

**franchezza** (Italian)    (lit., 'frankness; openness')    *Music.* freedom of spirit; boldness.

**frangipane** (French)    *Cookery.* a kind of sweet cake filled with cream and nuts.

**frappé** (French)    (lit., 'beaten')    **1.** designating a drink poured over finely chopped ice.    **2.** *Ballet.* a maneuver in which a dancer beats the toes of the working foot against the ankle of the supporting foot.

**frater** (Latin)    brother.

**Frau** (German)    woman; wife; Mrs.

**Frauenchor** (German)    *Music.* women's choir.

**Fräulein** (German)    young lady; Miss.

**freddamente** (Italian)    *Music.* with coldness.

**freddo** (Italian)    **1.** *Music.* cold; indifferent.    **2.** *Cookery.* served cold.

**fregiatura,** *pl.* **fregiature** (Italian)    *Music.* embellishment. See also **fioritura.**

**Freiherr** (German)    title of German nobility, equivalent to English baron.

**frère** (French)    brother.

**frescamente** (Italian)    *Music.* freshly; vigorously.

**fresco** (Italian)    **1.** *Fine Arts.* mural painting done with water-based paints on a surface of plaster (**intonaco**), either damp while the painting is done (**buon fresco**), or dry (**fresco secco**). See also **arricciato; arricciatura; gesso; gesso grosso; gesso sottile; in secco; intonaco; rinzafatto; sinopia.**

**fresco, al.**    See **al fresco.**

**fresco secco.**    See **fresco.**

**fresser** (Yiddish)    a glutton.

**frijoles** (Spanish)    *Cookery.* kidney beans and other varieties of beans used as a staple ingredient.

**frijoles refritos** (Spanish)    *Cookery.* boiled kidney beans, mashed and fried in lard or bacon fat; refried beans.

**frisch** (German)    **1.** fresh.    **2.** brisk; lively.

**frisson** (French)    a shiver produced by fear or excitement.

**frito** (Spanish)    *Cookery.* fried.

**frittata** (Italian)    *Cookery.* a flat omelet that may contain diced vegetables, cheese, ham, or herbs.

**frittelle** (Italian)    *Cookery.* fritters made with cheese, ham, and cooked vegetables.

**fritto misto** (Italian)    *Cookery.* a mixture of deep-fried food, usually seafood.

**frittoria** (Italian)    a street vendor that sells deep-fried vegetables.

**frittura** (Italian)    *Cookery.* the method of cooking by frying.

**friture** (French)    1. *Cookery.* frying; fried food.    2. a snack bar specializing in fried potatoes and kebabs.

**frizzante** (Italian)    a wine that is slightly sparkling because of minor secondary fermentation in the bottle.

**fromage** (French)    cheese.

**fronton, frontón** (Spanish)    1. a jai alai arena.    2. the wall against which the ball is played. See also **cesta; jai alai.**

**frottage** (French)    *Applied Arts.* 1. a technique for recording an image from a surface in relief by rubbing lead, charcoal, or chalk on paper stretched over the surface.    2. a rubbing produced by this technique.

**frottola,** *pl.* **frottole** (Italian)    (lit., 'fib; lie'; *pl.* 'nonsense')  *Music.* a late medieval choral form similar to the madrigal, for the unaccompanied singing of humorous or sentimental words.

**frou-frou** (French)    1. a rustling sound, as of a silk dress.    2. excessive ornamentation of ribbons, lace, etc.

**fruits de mer** (French)    shellfish.

**frutta** (Italian)    fruit.

**frutti di mare** (Italian)    *Cookery.* seafood, especially a plate of various seafoods served either raw or cooked.

**fueros** (Spanish)    a body of rights and privileges traditionally granted by Spanish monarchs to each of various culturally distinct regions of the country, especially to the Basque Provinces.

**fuga** (Italian)    (lit., 'flight')  *Music.* a fugue, that is, a composition in which one or more themes are introduced and repeated according to the rules of counterpoint.

**fugata, aria.    See aria fugata.**

**fugato** (Italian)    *Music.* a passage in fugal style appearing in a non-fugal composition, such as an opera.

**fughetta** (Italian)    *Music.* a short fugue.

**fugit hora** (Latin)    the hour flies; time flies.

**fugu** (Japanese)    a type of puffer fish eaten as a delicacy in Japan after the removal of highly poisonous internal organs.

**Führer, der** (German)    (lit., 'the leader')    1. title used by Adolf Hitler as dictatorial leader of Germany (1933–1945).    2. a dictatorial person.

**fuma** (Spanish)    a cigar roughly fashioned by hand from leftover cuttings.

**fumet** (French)    *Cookery.* a liquid obtained by boiling poultry, fish, or vegetables, used to flavor stocks and sauces.

**Fundador** (Spanish)    a variety of Spanish wine.

**funebre, marcia.    See marcia funebre.**

**fünf** (German)    five.

**funghi,** *sing.* **fungo** (Italian)    mushrooms.

**fuoco** (Italian)    (lit., 'fire')   *Music.* passion; force. Also **foco.** See also **con fuoco.**

**fuorusciti** (Italian)    the political exiles who left Italy in opposition to Mussolini.

**furia, con.**    See **con furia.**

**furiosamente** (Italian)    *Music.* passionately; impetuously.

**furioso** (Italian)    *Music.* furious; passionate.

**furore** (Italian)    *Music.* fury; enthusiasm.

**furor loquendi** (Latin)   a frenzy for speaking.

**furor poeticus** (Latin)   poetic frenzy.

**furor scribendi** (Latin)   a frenzy for writing.

**fusain** (French)    *Fine Arts.* 1. a fine charcoal used for drawing. 2. a drawing or sketch made with this charcoal.

**fusilli** (Italian)    a spiral-shaped **pasta.**

**fusuma** (Japanese)    a sliding door separating rooms in a Japanese house.

# G

**gaiamente** (Italian)   *Music.* gaily; merrily.  Also **gajamente.**

**galantemente** (Italian)   *Music.* gallantly; pleasingly; with grace.

**Galanter Stil** (German)   *Music.* gallant style, an instrumental style of the early 18th century.

**galantine** (French)   *Cookery.* a form of boned meat or poultry, stuffed, pressed into a shape, and simmered in broth.

**galbe** (French)   *Fine Arts.* an outline or profile of a form, especially the human body.

**gallego,** *fem.* **gallega** (Spanish)   Galician; designating something from the Spanish province of Galicia.

**galleta** (Spanish)   a small cake; cookie.

**Galliano** (Italian)   a brand of Italian liqueur that is anise-flavored and yellow in color.

**gallina** (Spanish)   a hen.

**gallo** (Spanish)   1. a fighting cock; rooster.   2. a cockfight.

**galoubet** (French)   *Music.* a wind instrument with three holes that can be played with one hand, popular in the 16th and 17th centuries.

**gamba** (Italian)   (lit., 'knee')  *Music.* designating instruments of the viola family that are held downwards between the knees or legs.  See also **viola da gamba.**

**gamba** (Spanish)   a large shrimp; prawn.

**gamberetti** (Italian)   shrimp.

**gambero,** *pl.* **gamberi** (Italian)   crayfish.

**gambusino** (Spanish)   a prospector.

**gamin** (French)   a boy left free to wander the streets.

**gamine** (French)   1. a tomboy.   2. a small, playful girl.

**ganadería** (Spanish)   a ranch where bulls or cattle are raised.

**gancho** (Spanish)   a curved branding iron.

**ganef.**   See **gonif.**

**ganiff.**   See **gonif.**

125

**ganja** (Hindi)    marijuana, smoked as a sacrament in certain religious cults.

**Gaon,** *pl.* **Geonim** (Hebrew)    (lit., 'majesty') *Judaism.* 1. the title of one of the heads of the Talmudic academies in Babylonia, in use from the 6th to the 11th century. 2. an honorary title for an eminent Talmudic scholar. See also **Talmud.**

**garbanzos** (Spanish)    chick peas.

**garbo** (Italian)    *Music.* manners; grace.

**garçon** (French)    a waiter in a restaurant.

**garde à cheval** (French)    a mounted guard.

**garde de corps** (French)    a bodyguard.

**garde-feu** (French)    a fire screen.

**garde-manger** (French)    1. a cool room or storage area used for certain foods, as cold buffet. 2. a chef who prepares cold dishes.

**gardez la foi** (French)    keep the faith.

**gargouillade** (French)    *Ballet.* a step in which a dancer springs into the air from one foot and moves the other foot in a circular motion.

**garni** (French)    *Cookery.* garnished.

**garniture de cheminée** (French)    *Antiques.* a set of five porcelain vases used as a mantlepiece decoration.

**garrocha** (Spanish)    *Bullfighting.* the lance used by the **picador** to enrage the bull.

**garum** (Latin)    a rich sauce or condiment made from fish, popular in Roman times.

**Gastarbeiter** (German)    foreign (migratory) worker.

**Gasthaus** (German)    (lit., 'guest house') a small German inn.

**Gasthof** (German)    hotel.

**gastronome** (French)    a **gourmet**; epicure.

**gâteau,** *pl.* **gâteaux** (French)    *Cookery.* a cake, especially a sweet dessert cake.

**gâte-sauce** (French)    (lit., 'spoil-sauce') a bad cook.

**Gattinara.**    See **Spanna.**

**gauche** (French)    (lit., 'left; awkward') socially repulsive; in bad taste (said of a person or action).

**gauche, à.**    See **à gauche.**

**gaucherie** (French)    1. awkwardness; lack of etiquette or social grace. 2. a boorish or tactless act.

**gauchiste** (French)    a French leftist.

**gaucho** (Spanish)    a cowboy, especially of the **pampas** of Argentina.

**Gaudeamus Igitur** (Latin)    therefore let us rejoice (first words of a well-known song of youth).

**gaudioso** (Italian)    *Music.* exulting; gay.

**gaufrette** (French)   (lit., 'little waffle') *Cookery.* a biscuit; a sugar wafer.

**Gauleiter** (German)   1. a leader appointed by the Nazis to control a small political district.   2. any petty dictator.

**Gauloise** (French)   a brand of French cigarettes.

**gavage** (French)   forced feeding, as that done to fatten poultry or livestock.

**Gavi** (Italian)   a variety of dry white wine produced in Piedmont.

**gavotta** (Italian)   *Music.* a dance of the 17th and 18th centuries, in two- or four-in-a-measure time, often performed after a minuet.

**gavotte** (French)   an old French dance in quadruple time.

**gazpacho** (Spanish)   *Cookery.* a soup made of tomatoes and other vegetables, served cold.

**Gebrauchsmusik** (German)   *Music.* (lit., 'functional music') music written in a simple style.

**Gedicht** (German)   a poem.

**gefilte fish** (Yiddish)   *Cookery.* fish cakes made from forcemeat of boneless white fish, **matzoh** meal, eggs, and seasonings. Also **gefülte fish; gefulte fish.**

**Gefühl** (German)   feeling.

**geisha** (Japanese)   a Japanese woman trained as a professional companion and entertainer for men.

**Geist** (German)   intellect; spirit.

**Geistesgeschichte** (German)   history of ideas or cultural history.

**geistige Welt, die** (German)   the intelligentsia.   See also **schöne Welt, die.**

**gelateria** (Italian)   an ice cream parlor.

**gelato** (Italian)   an Italian-style ice cream or sherbet.

**Geld** (German)   money.

**gelée** (French)   *Cookery.* jelly.

**gelée, en.**   See en gelée.

**gelsomino** (Italian)   jasmine.

**gelt** (Yiddish)   money.

**Gemara** (Hebrew)   *Judaism.* the latter of the two parts of the **Talmud,** consisting of commentaries appended to the **Mishnah.**

**Gemeinschaft** (German)   an association based on love or kinship.

**Gemini** (Latin)   the Twins, a sign of the zodiac; the constellation of Castor and Pollux.

**gemütlich** (German)   congenial, friendly.

**Gemütlichkeit** (German)   coziness; congeniality.

**gendarme** (French)   a French policeman.

**gendarmerie** (French)   a unit of **gendarmes.**

**génépi** (French)    a sweet absinthe, made from alpine wormwood.

**generalísimo** (Spanish)    a supreme military commander.

**generalissimo** (Italian)    a title used of a commander in chief.

**género chico** (Spanish)    (lit., 'little style') *Theater.* short plays often telling of lower class life and including songs and dances.

**generoso** (Italian)    *Music.* lofty in style.

**genius loci** (Latin)    the presiding deity of a place.

**genovese, alla.**    See **alla genovese.**

**genre** (French)    1. genus; kind; style.    2. *Art.* a particular category or style of creative work.

**genro** (Japanese)    an elder statesmen of Japan.

**gens de bien** (French)    benevolent people; philanthropists.

**gens de condition** (French)    people of social rank.

**gens d'église** (French)    churchmen; ecclesiastics.

**gens de guerre** (French)    military personnel.

**gens de lettres** (French)    literary people; authors.

**gens de loi** (French)    lawyers.

**gens de peu** (French)    people of lower social rank.

**gens de robe** (French)    people associated with the law or the courts, as lawyers and judges.

**gens du monde** (French)    worldly people; fashionable people.

**gentil,** *fem.* **gentille** (French)    kindly; gentle; noble.

**gentile** (Italian)    *Music.* delicate; tender.

**gentilhomme** (French)    a gentleman; a kind man.

**genus homo** (Latin)    the human race.

**Gesamtausgabe** (German)    complete edition; complete works.

**Geschmack** (German)    taste.

**Gesellschaft** (German)    a society; a commercial company.

**Gesellschaft mit beschränkter Haftung** (German)    private limited liability company. *Abbr.* **GmbH.**

**gesso** (Italian)    1. *Fine Arts.* a surface prepared with plaster of Paris as a ground for **fresco** painting. See also **gesso grosso; gesso sottile.**    2. *Architecture.* Also **gesso duro.** a hard plaster or stucco, frequently used in Italy for sculptural decoration.

**gesso duro.**    See **gesso,** 2.

**gesso grosso** (Italian)    *Fine Arts.* a layer of coarse plaster used in preparing a surface for **fresco** painting.

**gesso sottile** (Italian)    *Fine Arts.* a layer of fine plaster, placed over an underlying layer of **gesso grosso,** in preparing a surface for **fresco** painting.

**Gestalt** (German)    *Psychology.* a unified configuration having properties that cannot be derived from the sum of its parts.

**Gestapo** (German)   acronym for *Geheime Staatspolizei*, the German secret police under the Nazis.

**Gesundheit!** (German)   health!; said after someone sneezes.

**get** (Hebrew)   *Judaism.* a divorce granted in accord with Jewish law.

**gettone** (Italian)   a token used in public phones in Italy.

**ghee** (Hindi)   a sort of liquid butter made from cow or buffalo milk. Also **ghi**.

**ghiribizzoso** (Italian)   *Music.* capricious; whimsical.

**gi** (Japanese)   a **karate** uniform, usually white.

**giallo antico** (Italian)   (lit., 'ancient yellow') a rich yellow marble found in use at some ancient sites in Italy.

**gibier** (French)   wild game.

**gibier à plume** (French)   feathered game.

**giglio** (Italian)   (lit., 'lily') an ornamental form similar to the **fleur-de-lis,** often associated with Florence.

**ginete** (Spanish)   a horseman, especially one who breaks untrained animals.

**giochevole** (Italian)   *Music.* lively; playful; gleeful.

**Gioconda, La.**   See **La Gioconda.**

**giocondo** (Italian)   *Music.* playful; joyous. Also **giocondoso.**

**giocoso** (Italian)   *Music.* sportive; merry.

**giovanotto** (Italian)   a robust young man.

**gioviale** (Italian)   *Music.* jovial.

**giro** (Spanish)   a draft; money order.

**girolle.**   See **chanterelle, 1.**

**gitano,** *fem.* **gitana** (Spanish)   a gypsy.

**giustamente** (Italian)   *Music.* with precision.

**giustezza** (Italian)   *Music.* precision.

**giusto,** *fem.* **giusta** (Italian)   (lit., 'just') *Music.* **1.** in strict time.   **2.** in suitable time.

**glace** (French)   **1.** ice. **2.** ice cream.

**glacé** (French)   **1.** frozen. **2.** iced or frosted, as a cake. **3.** candied, as fruits. **4.** having a glossy finish, as fabric.

**glasnost** (Russian)   openness in Soviet society, allowing for disclosure and public discussion of formerly restricted subjects.

**glendi** (Greek)   a large party with music and dancing.

**glissade** (French)   a sliding or gliding movement, as in dancing or skiing.

**glissando** (Italian)   *Music.* **1.** *n.* the drawing of the finger quickly down or up a series of adjacent keys on a piano or strings on a harp.   **2.** *adv.* in a gliding manner, said of violin playing.

**glissé** (French)   *Ballet.* designating a step or movement to be performed with a **glissade.**

129

**Gloria** (Latin)  *Christian liturgy.*  a prayer in the liturgy of the Mass, frequently set to music.

**Gloria in Excelsis Deo** (Latin)  Glory (be) to God on high (Luke 2:14).

**Gloria Patri** (Latin)  Glory (be) to the Father.

**gnocchi,** *sing.* **gnocco** (Italian)  *Cookery.*  small dumplings made of flour or potatoes, either poached or baked and served with various sauces.

**gnōthi seauton** (Greek)  know thyself.

**go** (Japanese)  a board game for two played with black and white pieces or counters, the object being to gain control of the board by blocking and capturing the opponent's pieces.

**gobang** (Japanese)  a game played on a go board in which players attempt to be the first to place five counters in a row. Also **gomoku.**

**gogo, à.**  See **à gogo.**

**gomokuzogan** (Japanese)  a form of metalwork decoration consisting of fine copper or brass wire inlaid in iron. See also **guri bori.**

**gomoku.**  See **gobang.**

**gondola** (Italian)  a light boat with high, pointed ends, propelled by a single oar at the stern, used in the canals of Venice.

**gondoliera** (Italian)  *Music.* a rhythmical style with six- or twelve-beats-in-a-measure, associated with the movement of a **gondola.**

**gongorismo** (Spanish)  *Literature.* ornate writing in the style of Luís de Góngora and other 17th-century poets.

**gonif** (Yiddish)  1. a dishonest person; thief. 2. a clever or ingenious person. Also **ganef; ganiff.**

**gopak** (Russian)  a Ukrainian folk dance. Also **hopak.**

**gorge de pigeon** (French)  (lit., 'throat of pigeon') iridescent; displaying a rainbow of colors. Also **gorge-de-pigeon.**

**gorgheggio** (Italian)  *Music.* any long, swift passage in which one vowel is sung with many notes.

**Gorgonzola** (Italian)  a semi-soft, blue-veined cheese produced in the area of Gorgonzola in Lombardy.

**gorilka** (Ukrainian)  vodka flavored with pepper.

**Götterdämmerung** (German)  *Mythology.* twilight of the gods; the final battle of the gods versus evil, in which all things are destroyed.

**Gott mit uns** (German)  (lit., 'God is with us') motto of the kings of Prussia.

**gouache** (French)  *Fine Arts.* a painting technique using opaque watercolors prepared with gum.

**gourmand,** *fem.* **gourmande** (French)  1. a person with a keen interest in fine food. 2. a glutton.

**gourmandise** (French)  excessive eating.

**gourmet** (French)  a connoisseur of fine food; an epicure.

**goût** (French)    taste; style; preference.  See also **chacun à son goût.**

**goûter** (French)    a light snack.

**goût raffiné** (French)    refined taste.

**goutte** (French)    *Heraldry.* a pear-shaped or drop-shaped figure.

**goutte à goutte** (French)    drop by drop.

**governo** (Italian)    *Wine.* a method of vinification used in the **Chianti** area that causes a secondary fermentation to take place.

**goy,** *pl.* **goyim** (Yiddish)    a Gentile; non-Jew.

**graciano** (Spanish)    a variety of grape valued for the bouquet and freshness it gives to wine.

**gracias** (Spanish)    thank you.

**gracioso** (Spanish)    (lit., 'graceful') *Literature.* a comic role in Spanish drama.

**gradatim** (Latin)    step by step; gradually.

**gradin** (French)    a series of steps or seats, one positioned above another.  Also **gradine.**

**graduale** (Latin)    *Church music.* 1. a responsorial chant, part of the Mass.  2. a book containing all the words and music of the liturgy to be sung by the choir.

**gradus ad Parnassum** (Latin)    (lit., 'steps to Parnassus') title of a manual for writing Latin verse.

**Graf** (German)    title of nobility equivalent to English *earl.*

**graffiti,** *sing.* **griffito** (Italian)    (lit., 'little writings')  1. writings, often irreverent or obscene, scribbled in restrooms and other public places.  2. *Architecture.* Also **sgraffito.** decoration made on plaster surfaces by marking a pattern while the surface is soft.  3. *Fine Arts.* Also **sgraffito; stecco.** pottery decorations that are inscribed through the coating of an unfired piece, revealing a different color underneath.

**grama** (Spanish)    grass, especially a type of grass used for animal forage.

**gran.**    See **grande.**

**grand choeur, à.**    See **à grand choeur.**

**grand cru** (French)    (lit., 'great vintage') a French wine of renown from a particular vineyard.

**grand diplôme** (French)    the diploma granted by the Cordon Bleu Cookery School of Paris.

**grande** (Italian, Spanish)    big; great. Also **gran.**

**grande dame** (French)    (lit., 'great lady') a respected or dignified woman.

**grande de España, un** (Spanish)    a Spanish nobleman.

**grande parure.**    See **parure.**

**grande passion** (French)    an intense sexual attraction.

**Grande Voleuse, La.**  See **La Grande Voleuse.**

**grandezza** (Italian)   *Music.* loftiness; dignity.

**grand feu** (French)   *Ceramics.* a firing at high temperature. See also **petit feu.**

**Grand Guignol** (French)   a drama of sensationalistic horror.

**grandioso** (Italian)   *Music.* majestic; stately.

**gran-disegno** (Italian)   *Fine Arts.* 1. a design that is great in concept.   2. a drawing of a monument.

**grandisonante** (Italian)   *Music.* rich and full sounding.

**grand mal** (French)   *Pathology.* an acute form of epilepsy characterized by severe seizures. See also **petit mal.**

**Grand Marnier** (French)   a brand of orange-flavored **liqueur** made from cognac.

**Grand Monarque, Le.**   See **Le Grand Monarque.**

**grand monde** (French)   (lit., 'the great world') the upper class; high society. Also **haut monde; le haut monde.**

**grand orchestre, à.**   See **à grand orchestre.**

**Grand Prix** (French)   (lit., 'grand prize') a variety of international auto racing run over winding road courses.

**grand seigneur** (French)   a highly respected older man. See also **en grand seigneur.**

**grands frais, à.**   See **à grand frais.**

**Grand Siècle, Le.**   See **Le Grand Siècle.**

**gran gusto** (Italian)   *Music.* great tastefulness.

**granita** (Italian)   sherbet.

**granité** (French)   *Cookery.* a slightly sweetened sherbet.

**gran turismo** (Italian)   a car suitable for extended trips because of its superior performance, room, and comfort. *Abbr.* **GT.**

**grappa** (Italian)   a strong Italian brandy distilled from the pomace of a wine press.

**grasseyé** (French)   *Language.* pronounced gutturally, as the Parisian *r*-sound.

**gratias agere** *or* **agimus** (Latin)   to give (*or* we give) thanks.

**gratinée** (French)   *Cookery.* topped with grated cheese or bread crumbs. See also **au gratin.**

**gratis** (Latin)   free; without charge.

**grave** (Italian)   *Music.* 1. solemn and slow in expression.   2. low in pitch.

**gravemente** (Italian)   *Music.* solemnly.

**Graves** (French)   a district in the **Bordeaux** wine region of France, noted particularly for white wines.

**gravitas** (Latin)   seriousness of purpose in one's overall demeanor.

**grazia, con.**   See con grazia.

**grazie** (Italian)   thanks!

**graziosamente** (Italian)   *Music.* with grace.

**grazioso** (Italian)   *Music.* graceful.

**grecque, à la.**   See à la grecque.

**grenouille** (French)   frog.

**griffe** (French)   a designer label lending prestige to mass-produced fashions.

**griglia, alla.**   See alla griglia.

**grillade** (French)   *Cookery.* a dish of grilled meat.

**grillé** (French)   *Cookery.* grilled; broiled.

**gringo,** *fem.* **gringa** (Spanish)   a derogatory term usually applied to North Americans.

**grisaille** (French)   *Fine Arts.* a monochromatic painting or other work of art done in shades of gray.

**grissini** (Italian)   breadsticks.

**gros poisson** (French)   (lit., 'a big fish') a prestigious or important person.

**gros rouge** (French)   a hearty, full-flavored red wine.

**Grosses Orchester** (German)   *Music.* full orchestra.

**grosso,** *pl.* **grossi** (Italian)   (lit., 'grand; full; deep') *Music.* designating a concerto in which a group of solo instruments alternates with the strings of the orchestra or with the orchestra as a whole.

**grottesca,** *pl.* **grottesche** (Italian)   *Fine Arts.* a decorative style in which human and animal figures, flowers, and foliage are intermingled in designs of fantasy.

**Grundthema** (German)   *Music.* leading motif.

**Gruyère** (French)   a hard cheese with a sweet, pungent, nutty flavor, similar to Swiss cheese.

**guacamole** (Spanish)   *Cookery.* a dip or garnish made of ripe avocado mashed with onions, lemon juice, and spices.

**guajira** (Spanish)   1. *Music.* a Cuban peasant dance.   2. a white Cuban peasant woman.

**guano** (Spanish)   seabird manure, found in vast accumulations off or along the coasts of Peru and Chile, gathered and used as fertilizer.

**guapo,** *fem.* **guapa** (Spanish)   handsome; pretty; brave.

**guaracha** (Spanish)   1. a lively Cuban dance characterized by an air of light suggestiveness.   2. the music for this dance.

**guarnacha** (Spanish)   a variety of grape used to make wine with a high alcohol content.

**guarpo** (Spanish)   an alcoholic beverage made from sugar cane juice.

**guazzo** (Italian)   *Fine Arts.* a method of watercolor painting.

**guéridon** (French)   *Antiques.* a small table used to hold small objects, as a candelabrum.

**guerre à mort** (French)   war to the death.

**guerre à outrance** (French)   all-out war.

**guía** (Spanish)   (lit., 'guide') a safe-conduct pass.

**guichet** (French)   a ticket office window; box office.

**Guide Michelin** (French)   a tourist's handbook noted for its star system of rating restaurants. Also **Guide Vert.**

**guinguette** (French)   a French inn or tea garden.

**guipure** (French)   a heavy, decorative lace.

**gulag** (Russian)   1. a Soviet prison camp. 2. the Soviet penal system.

**guri bori** (Japanese)   a form of decorative carving in Japanese metalwork. See also **gomokuzogan.**

**guru** (Hindi)   1. *Hinduism; Buddhism.* a personal religious instructor. 2. a personal teacher in any special subject.

**gusla** (Slavic)   a primitive stringed instrument played with a bow, used by a guslar.

**guslar** (Slavic)   one of a former class of Yugoslavian bards who recited lengthy epics from memory while accompanying themselves on a gusla.

**gusto** (Italian)   *Music.* tastefulness as to pace, force, phrasing, and other elements of performance. See also **con gusto; gran gusto.**

**gustosamente** (Italian)   *Music.* tastefully.

**gustoso** (Italian)   *Music.* tasteful; agreeable.

**gut** (German)   1. good. 2. well.

**guten Abend** (German)   good evening!

**gute Nacht** (German)   good night!

**guten Morgen** (German)   good morning!

**guten Tag** (German)   good day!

**Gut Shabbes** (Yiddish)   *Judaism.* good Sabbath (a Sabbath greeting).

**Gymnasium** (German)   a German secondary school preparatory to a university.

**gyro** (Greek)   a sort of sandwich made with slices of roast lamb, sauce, and other ingredients served in **pita** bread.

# H

haba (Spanish)   a large bean; lima bean.

habañera (Spanish)   1. *adj.* designating something from Havana.   2. a style of Cuban dance with a slow tempo.   3. the music for this dance.

habano (Spanish)   a Cuban cigar.

Habdalah (Hebrew)   *Judaism.* a ceremony marking the end of the Sabbath celebration. Also Havdalah.

habeas corpus (Latin)   (lit., 'you may have the body') *Law.* a writ requiring that a person be freed from detainment and formally charged.

habeat sua fata libelli (Latin)   books have their own destiny.

habichuela (Spanish)   a green bean; string bean.

habitant (French)   1. a French settler of Canada or Louisiana.   2. someone descended from such a settler.

habitué (French)   1. a person who frequents a place.   2. a customer.

habla usted el español? (Spanish)   do you speak Spanish?

haboob (Arabic)   a violent sandstorm on the deserts of North Africa or Arabia. Also habub.

habub.   See haboob.

habutai (Japanese)   a sheer silk used in Japanese garments.

haček (Czech)   a diacritical mark placed over a consonant to indicate a palatalized pronunciation.

hacendado (Spanish)   a wealthy man; a land owner.

hachis (French)   chopped meat; hash.

hacienda (Spanish)   a large estate; a ranch or plantation. See also casa grande.

Hadassah (Hebrew)   a Zionist organization for women, founded in New York City.

hadith (Arabic)   *Islam.* the collection of traditional sayings and accounts of Muhammad and his companions.

hadj.   See hajj.

hadji.   See hajji.

135

**Haftarah** (Hebrew)    *Judaism.* a chapter from the book of the Prophets chanted or read in the synagogue on Sabbaths and holy days.

**Haggadah** (Hebrew)    *Judaism.* a book containing the liturgy of the **Seder** service. Also **Haggada.** See also **Aggadah.**

**hagia** (Greek)    (lit., 'holy things') *Eastern Christian Church.* a designation for the Eucharistic elements.

**Hagiographa** (Greek)    (lit., 'sacred writings') *Judaism.* the third of the three traditional divisions of the books of Jewish Scripture. Also **Ketubim.** See also **Nebiim; Tanach; Torah.**

**Haiduk** (Hungarian)    a mercenary soldier of 16th-century Hungary.

**haik** (Arabic)    an oblong cloth used as an outer garment in Arab countries.

**haikai** (Japanese)    a Japanese form of linked verse.

**haiku** (Japanese)    a form of Japanese verse written in three lines containing a total of 17 syllables.

**hajj** (Arabic)    *Islam.* the pilgramage to Mecca, which all Muslims aspire to make once in their lives. Also **hadj.**

**hajji** (Arabic)    *Islam.* a Muslim who has completed a pilgrimage to Mecca. Also **hadji.**

**Hakenkreuz** (German)    (lit., 'hooked cross') term for the Nazi swastika.

**hakim**[1] (Arabic)    1. a wise or learned man. 2. a physician. Also **hakeem.**

**hakim**[2] (Arabic)    a governor; ruler; judge.

**Halakah** (Hebrew)    *Judaism.* the entire body of Jewish law and tradition as contained in Scripture, the **Talmud,** and later legal codes. See also **Aggadah.**

**halavah.**    See **halvah.**

**Halbenote** (German)    *Music.* half note.    Also **Halbe; Halbetaktnote.**

**hallah.**    See **challah.**

**Halt** (German)    1. stop!  2. *Music.* pause.

**halvah** (Yiddish)    a confection of Turkish origin made from honey and ground sesame seeds. Also **halavah; halva.**

**hamartia** (Greek)    *Greek drama.* the tragic flaw of the protagonist that precipitates the tragedy.

**hamza** (Arabic)    1. the Arabic glottal stop. 2. the diacritical mark used in written Arabic to indicate the glottal stop.

**Handbuch** (German)    compendium; comprehensive reference book.

**Hanukkah** (Hebrew)    *Judaism.* the eight-day Jewish festival commemorating the victory of the Maccabees. Also **Chanukah.** See also **menorah.**

**haole** (Hawaiian)    a non-Polynesian.

**haori** (Japanese)    a loose-fitting, knee-length Japanese coat.

**hapax legomenon** (Greek)    (lit., 'once read') a word or expression that is found only once in a designated body of literature. Also **hapax.**

**hara** (Japanese)    the area just below the navel, believed in Oriental schools of discipline and martial arts to be the center of the body and source of its power.

**hara-kiri** (Japanese)    1. a ritual suicide, as carried out by disgraced Japanese warriors. 2. an act of self-destruction. Also **hari-kiri; seppuku.**

**Haram** (Arabic)    *Islam.* the Great Mosque at Mecca. See also **Kaaba.**

**hareng** (French)    herring.

**haricot** (French)    a bean.

**haricot de mouton** (French)    *Cookery.* lamb stew.

**haricots verts** (French)    green string beans.

**hari-kiri.**    See **hara-kiri.**

**Harmoniemusik** (German)    *Music.* 1. music for wind instruments. 2. a musical band of wood, brass, and percussion.

**Hasenpfeffer** (German)    *Cookery.* stew of hare in pepper and vinegar sauce.

**Hasid,** *pl.* **Hasidim** (Hebrew)    *Judaism.* a member of a sect that emphasizes simple, zealous faith and mysticism as opposed to rabbinical formal learning. Also **Chasid.**

**Haskalah** (Hebrew)    *Judaism.* the Jewish movement of secular enlightenment during the 18th and 19th centuries, begun in Germany by Moses Mendelssohn (1729–1786).

**hasta la vista** (Spanish)    I'll see you later; goodbye.

**hasta luego** (Spanish)    (lit., 'until then') goodbye.

**hasta mañana** (Spanish)    I'll see you tomorrow.

**Hatikvah** (Hebrew)    the national anthem of Israel.

**haud ignota loquor** (Latin)    I speak of things scarcely unknown.

**haud** (*or* non) **passibus aequis** (Latin)    with unequal steps.

**Hauptmann** (German)    a captain in the German armed forces.

**Hauptthema** (German)    principal theme.

**Hausfrau** (German)    housewife.

**hautbois** (French)    *Music.* a type of oboe; hautboy.

**haute bourgeoisie** (French)    the upper middle class; gentry.

**haute coiffure** (French)    high-fashion hairdressing.

**haute couture** (French)    1. the world of high-fashion women's dressmaking and designing. 2. the fashions created by leading designers.

**haute cuisine** (French)    *Cookery.* gourmet cooking, especially the techniques and dishes characteristic of classic French cooking.

**haute école** (French)    *Manege.* difficult feats or maneuvers.

**haute époque** (French)    the period during the reigns of Louis XIV, Louis XV, and Louis XVI of France, especially with reference to art, furniture, and architecture.

**haut en bas, de.**    See de haut en bas.

**haute politique** (French)    high-level politics.

**hauteur** (French)    haughtiness.

**haute voix, à.**    See à haute voix.

**haut goût** (French)    *Cookery.* strong flavor; heavy seasoning.

**Haut-Médoc** (French)    a district in the **Bordeaux** wine region of France, home to some of the most famous French vintages.

**haut monde** (French)    fashionable society.

**haut-relief** (French)    *Fine Arts.* sculpture in high relief. See also **bas-relief**.

**haut ton** (French)    1. high fashion. 2. high social standing.

**Havdalah.**    See **Habdalah**.

**havelina.**    See **javalina**.

**hecho a mano** (Spanish)    made by hand.

**Heft** (German)    volume of a series; issue of a periodical.

**Hegira** (Arabic)    1. *Islam.* the flight of Muhammad from Mecca to Medina in 622, marking the beginning of the Muslim era. 2. (*l.c.*) any journey to a more desirable place. Also **Hejira; Hijra; Hijrah**.

**hegumen(os)** (Greek)    the head of a monastery of an Eastern Christian rite.

**Heil!** (German)    hail!

**Heiligenschein** (German)    (lit., 'saint's shining light') a halo surrounding the shadow of a person's head, caused by diffraction in certain atmospheric conditions.

**heimish** (Yiddish)    homey; unpretentious.

**Hejira.**    See **Hegira**.

**helados** (Spanish)    ices; ice cream.

**hell** (German)    pale; light in color.

**Herr** (German)    gentleman; sir; Mr.; lord.

**Herrenvolk** (German)    (lit., 'master race') term for the Nazi concept that the Germans were racially superior and therefore justified in ruling others.

**hetaira,** *pl.* **hetairae** (Greek)    1. a female prostitute of ancient Greece. 2. a woman who uses her charms to advance her social position.

**hetman** (Polish)    an elected chief of the Cossacks. Also **ataman**.

**hibachi** (Japanese)    a small charcoal grill or stove.

**hibakusha** (Japanese)    persons who survived but were affected by the atomic blasts at Hiroshima or Nagasaki.

**hic et ubique** (Latin)    here and everywhere.

**hic iacet (sepultus)** (Latin)    here lies (buried); used on gravestones with the name of the deceased.

**hidalgo** (Spanish)    a man of high social standing or political prominence.

**hidalguía** (Spanish)   gentlemanliness; nobility of character.

**hierba mate.**   See **yerba mate.**

**hier wird deutsch gesprochen** (German)   German is spoken here.   Also, (hier) **man spricht deutsch.**

**hijo** (*fem.* **hija**) **natural** (Spanish)   an illegitimate son or daughter of a Spanish king or nobleman.

**Hijra.**   See **Hegira.**

**hiragana** (Japanese)   one of the two Japanese syllabaries, more widely used and cursive in style.   See also **katakana.**

**hoc age** (Latin)   do this; get on with it.

**Hochdeutsch** (German)   High German, the dialect recognized as standard in Germany.   See also **Plattdeutsch.**

**hodie non cras** (Latin)   today, not tomorrow.

**hogan** (Navaho)   a Navaho dwelling constructed of branches covered with mud and sod.

**hoi polloi** (Greek)   (lit., 'the many') the common people; the masses (often said with an attitude of superiority).

**hokku** (Japanese)   the opening verse of a **haiku** poem.

**Holi** (Hindi)   the Hindu spring festival.

**hollandaise, à la.**   See **à la hollandaise.**

**homard** (French)   lobster.

**hombre** (Spanish)   a man.

**homme d'affaires** (French)   an agent; a businessman.

**homme de bien** (French)   a good man; an honorable man.

**homme de guerre** (French)   a military man; a warrior.

**homme de lettres** (French)   a literary man.

**homme de paille** (French)   (lit., 'man of straw') a man who is set up to take blame or censure; a gullible man.

**homme d'épée** (French)   a swordsman; fencer.

**homme d'esprit** (French)   a brilliant or witty man.

**homme d'état** (French)   a statesman.

**homme de théâtre** (French)   a man associated with the theater or stage.

**homme du monde** (French)   a worldly man.

**homme du peuple** (French)   a man of the people.

**homo faber** (Latin)   man the maker.

**homo ludens** (Latin)   playful or joking man.

**homo ridens** (Latin)   laughing man.

**homo sapiens** (Latin)   (lit., 'wise man') modern man; the human species.

**honda** (Spanish)   a loop at the end of a rope used to form a lariat.

**honi soit qui mal y pense** (French)   (lit., 'woe to him who thinks evil of it') motto of the Order of the Garter.

**honnête homme** (French)    a gentleman; well-bred man.

**honoris causa** (Latin)    for the sake of honor (describing an honorary degree).

**hookah** (Arabic)    a pipe for smoking in which the smoke is drawn through water and thus cooled.

**hopak.**    See **gopak.**

**hora** (Hebrew)    a traditional round dance of Romania and Israel. Also **horah.**

**hora somni** (Latin)    *Prescriptions.* before going to sleep; at bedtime. *Abbr.* **h.s.**

**horribile dictu** (Latin)    horrible to relate.

**horribile visu** (Latin)    horrible to be seen.

**hors concours** (French)    out of the running; ineligible for competition. *Abbr.* **h.c.**

**hors concours** (French)    designating someone or something not entered in competition.

**hors d'affaire** (French)    out of danger.

**hors de combat** (French)    out of the fight; disabled; unable to compete.

**hors de commerce** (French)    designating something that is not available commercially.

**hors de propos** (French)    badly timed; irrelevant.

**hors de saison** (French)    out of season.

**hors d'oeuvre,** *pl.* **hors d'oeuvres** (French)    (lit., 'out of the work') *Cookery.* **1.** an appetizer served before the start of a meal. **2.** bite-size tidbits of food served as a snack.

**hors la loi** (French)    forbidden by law; outlawed.

**Horst Wessel Lied** (German)    a Nazi anthem commemorating an early hero of the movement.

**hortus conclusus** (Latin)    an enclosed garden; a private retreat.

**hostería** (Spanish)    hostelry; inn.

**hôtel de ville** (French)    a French city hall.

**hôtel garni** (French)    a boardinghouse; rooming house. Also called **hôtel meublé.**

**hôtelier** (French)    an innkeeper; hotel manager. Also **hotelier.**

**hôtel meublé.**    See **hôtel garni.**

**howdah** (Hindi)    a seat for riding on the back of an elephant. Also **houdah.**

**hoya** (Spanish)    a valley or depression in a mountainous area.

**huarache** (Spanish)    a type of sandal made from woven strips of leather.

**hubris** (Greek)    1. a transgression of the ancient Greek moral order occurring when a mortal tries to equal or surpass the gods.    2. excessive pride; arrogance.    Also **hybris**.

**huerta** (Spanish)    1. a kitchen garden.    2. an irrigated region, such as Valencia on the Mediterranean coast.

**huésped,** *fem.* **huéspeda** (Spanish)    1. a guest; lodger.    2. a host or hostess; landlord.

**huevo** (Spanish)    an egg.

**huevos rancheros** (Spanish)    *Cookery.*    fried eggs served on **tortillas** and topped with **ranchero** sauce.

**huile** (French)    oil.

**huile, à l'.**    See **à l'huile**.

**huis clos, à.**    See **à huis clos**.

**huit** (French)    eight.

**huitain** (French)    *Literature.*    eight lines of verse; an eight-line poem.

**huître** (French)    oyster.

**hula** (Hawaiian)    a traditional Polynesian dance performed with swaying motion and graceful arm movements that relate a story.    Also **hula-hula**.

**humanum est errare.**    See **errare humanum est**.

**huppah** (Hebrew)    *Judaism.*    the canopy used in a Jewish marriage ceremony.    Also **chuppah**.

**hybris.**    See **hubris**.

**hydrargyrum** (Latin)    mercury.    *Abbr.* **Hg**.

**hysteron proteron** (Greek)    (lit., 'last first')    1. *Logic.*    a fallacious proof in which the thing to be proved is used as a premise; begging the question.    2. *Rhetoric.*    a reversal of normal word order.

# I

**iacta alea est.** See **jacta alea est.**

**ibidem** (Latin)   in the same place or source. *Abbr.* **ibid.**

**Ich dien** (German)   (lit., 'I serve') motto of the Prince of Wales.

**ichthus** *or* **ichthys** (Greek)   (lit., 'fish') a word used as a symbolic reference to Jesus Christ (the Greek spelling being taken as an acronym for *Iesous Christos Theou huios Soter,* 'Jesus Christ, son of God, Savior').

**ici** (French)   here; in this place.

**ici on parle français** (French)   French is spoken here.

**id** (Latin)   (lit., 'it') *Psychoanalysis.* that part of the psyche that is the source of instinctive energy and of the libido.

**idée fixe,** *pl.* **idées fixes** (French)   (lit., 'fixed idea') a persistent or obsessive notion that deludes the person in whom it occurs.

**idée maîtresse** (French)   a main theme.

**idée mère** (French)   (lit., 'mother idea') original concept; basic idea.

**idées reçues** (French)   common beliefs; accepted teachings.

**idem** (Latin)   the same (as given previously). *Abbr.* **id.**

**id est** (Latin)   that is. *Abbr.* **i.e.**

**id genus omne** (Latin)   all that sort.

**idiot savant** (French)   a person of generally low mental ability who has a highly developed special aptitude.

**Iesus Hominum Salvator** (Latin)   Jesus, Savior of Mankind. *Abbr.* **I.H.S.**

**Iesus Nazarenus Rex Iudaeorum** (Latin)   Jesus of Nazareth, King of the Jews. *Abbr.* **I.N.R.I.**

**ignis fatuus** (Latin)   (lit., 'foolish fire') a flitting, phosphorescent light sometimes seen over marshy ground; a will o' the wisp.

**ignorantia legis neminem excusat** (Latin)   ignorance of the law excuses no one.

**ignoratio elenchi** (Latin)   (lit., 'ignorance of the argument') *Logic.* the fallacy of arguing about a point that is not under discussion; an irrelevant argument.

143

**ikebana** (Japanese)    the Japanese art of flower arrangement.

**Il Duce** (Italian)    (lit., 'the leader') a title used by Benito Mussolini, Fascist premier of Italy (1922–43).

**illuminati** (Latin)    enlightened ones; persons or groups claiming special enlightenment.

**illuminato,** *pl.* **illuminati** (Italian)    1. a person who professes to have special knowledge or enlightenment.    2. *pl.* (*cap.*) members of a short-lived secret society of republican free thought founded in Bavaria in 1776.    3. Also **Alumbrados.** the name given to adherents of a 16-century heretical Spanish sect.    4. the Rosicrucians.

**il Magnifico** (Italian)    a fruity red wine produced in Tuscany.

**il n'y a pas de quoi** (French)    you're welcome; it doesn't matter; don't mention it.

**ils ne passeront pas** (French)    they shall not pass, the rallying cry of French soldiers at Verdun in 1916.

**il tocco** (Italian)    one o'clock, the hour for lunch.

**il y a** (French)    there is; there are.

**imago** (Latin)    (lit., 'a copy') a typical example of some concept or thing.

**imam** (Arabic)    *Islam.* a title for a Muslim spiritual leader.

**imboccatura** (Italian)    *Music.* the shaping of the lips to the mouthpiece of a wind instrument in order to produce the desired tones.

**imbottigliato all'origine** (Italian)    an estate-bottled wine.

**imbottito, panino.**    See **panino imbottito.**

**imbottitura** (Italian)    *Cookery.* stuffing.

**imbroglio** (Italian)    (lit., 'tangle') 1. confusion; complication.    2. *Music.* a musical passage of several parts that create confusion by being played simultaneously.

**imitazione, aria d'.**    See **aria d'imitazione.**

**immer schlimmer** (German)    worse and worse.

**Immortel,** *pl.* **Immortels** (French)    a member of the French Academy.

**imo pectore.**    See **ab imo pectore.**

**impasto** (Italian)    *Fine Arts.* 1. the technique of applying paint thickly on the surface of a canvas.    2. a painting done with this technique. Also **pastose.**

**impazientemente** (Italian)    *Music.* impatiently.

**impedimenta** (Latin)    encumbrances; baggage.

**imperator** (Latin)    emperor; commander. *Abbr.* **imp.**

**imperioso** (Italian)    *Music.* imperious.

**imperium in imperio** (Latin)    an empire within an empire.

**impeto** (Italian)    *Music.* impetus; driving force. See also **con impeto.**

**impetuoso** (Italian)    *Music.* impetuous.

**impitoyable** (French)    a large-capacity glass designed for tasting wines.

**impos animi** (Latin)    of weak mind.

**impresa** (Italian)    (lit., 'enterprise') a heraldic device; personal motto.

**impresario** (Italian)    the organizer, manager, or head of a performing group such as an opera or ballet.

**imprimatur** (Latin)    (lit., 'let it be printed') 1. *Roman Catholicism.* permission to print a work on a subject regarding faith and morals, granted by a bishop after the *nihil obstat.* See also **nihil obstat.**    2. approval; sanction.

**imprimatura** (Italian)    *Fine Arts.* a colored wash applied to a panel or canvas before or after the making of the preliminary drawing.

**imprimé** (French)    a printed dress fabric commonly of cotton or linen.

**imprimis** (Latin)    (lit., 'among the first') in the first place; first in a sequence.

**impromptu, à l'.**    See **à l'impromptu.**

**improvisatore.**    See **improvvisatore.**

**improviste, à l'.**    See **à l'improviste.**

**improvvisata** (Italian)    *Music.* an improvisation or impromptu composition.

**improvvisatore,** *pl.* **improvvisatori** (Italian)    *Music.* a performer skilled at improvisation. Also **improvisatore.**

**in absentia** (Latin)    in absence (indicating that the person in question is not present).

**in actu** (Latin)    in actuality.

**in aeternum** (Latin)    forever.

**in altissimo** (Italian)    *Music.* in the register above F **in alto.**

**in alto** (Italian)    *Music.* in the octave above the treble staff. Also **in alt.**

**in articulo mortis** (Latin)    at the moment of death.

**in bianco** (Italian)    *Fine Arts.* in blank; in white.

**incalcando** (Italian)    (lit., 'trampling down') *Music.* becoming faster and louder.

**incalzando** (Italian)    *Music.* pressing forward; hastening.

**in camera** (Latin)    (lit., 'in (the judge's) chambers') privately; not in open court.

**incipit** (Latin)    (lit., '(here) begins') the first word in manuscripts of many Latin works, preceding the title and the author's name. See also **explicit.**

**incliné,** *fem.* **inclinée** (French)    *Ballet.* a term designating that a dancer holds the head inclined to the side.

**incognito** (Italian)    a designation for someone who is living or traveling in disguise or with concealed identity.

**incomunicado** (Spanish)   confined without opportunity for outside contact.

**inconnu,** *fem.* **inconnue** (French)   someone unknown; a stranger.

**incordamento** (Italian)   *Music.* the tension of the strings of an instrument.

**incubus** (Latin)   **1.** a male demon believed to have sexual intercourse with women while they sleep. See also **succubus.**   **2.** a nightmare.

**incunabula** (Latin)   (lit., 'swaddling clothes'; 'cradle') early printed books, usually referring to those printed before 1500.

**in curia** (Latin)   *Law.* in open court.

**indebolendo** (Italian)   *Music.* becoming weak.

**Index Expurgatorius** (Latin)   *Roman Catholicism.* a list of books not to be read by the faithful unless certain passages were deleted or altered.

**Index Librorum Prohibitorum** (Latin)   (lit., 'Index of Prohibited Books') *Roman Catholicism.* an official listing of books not to be read without special dispensation.

**index locorum** (Latin)   an index of places.

**index nominum** (Latin)   an index of names.

**index rerum** (Latin)   an index of things or subjects.

**index verborum** (Latin)   an index of words.

**indicato** (Italian)   *Music.* indicated; emphasized.

**indivia** (Italian)   endive.

**in dubio** (Latin)   in doubt; in case of doubt.

**in esse** (Latin)   in being; actually, as contrasted with **in posse.**

**in excelsis** (Latin)   in the highest (degree).

**in extenso** (Latin)   at full length; in its entirety.

**in extremis** (Latin)   (lit., 'at the farthest points') in the last agonies; at death's door.

**in facie curiae** (Latin)   *Law.* in the presence of the court.

**infanta** (Spanish)   **1.** a daughter of the king of Spain.   **2.** the wife of the infante.

**infante** (Spanish)   a son of the king of Spain not in line for succession.

**in fieri** (Latin)   in (the state of) coming to be. See also **in esse, in posse.**

**in flagrante delicto** (Latin)   (lit., 'in blazing crime') in the very act of committing the offense.

**in foro conscientiae** (Latin)   in the court of conscience.

**infra** (Latin)   below; further on in the page or book.

**infra dignitatem** (Latin)   beneath one's dignity. *Abbr.* **infra dig.**

**in fretta** (Italian)   *Music.* hastily.

**in futuro** (Latin)   in the future; for the future.

**inganno** (Italian)   a trick; deception.

**ingénue** (French)   1. an innocent young girl.  2. an actress who plays this role.

**inglese** (Italian)   English, or in the English style.

**in hoc signo vinces** (Latin)   by this sign you shall conquer (words inscribed on a cross seen in a vision by the Emperor Constantine and taken as his motto).

**in infinitum.**   See **ad infinitum.**

**in initio** (Latin)   in the beginning.

**in jure** (Latin)   according to law.

**in loco** (Latin)   in the place; on the spot.

**in loco citato.**   See **loco citato.**

**in loco parentis** (Latin)   in the place of a parent; as if with parental authority.

**in malam partem** (Latin)   in a bad sense.

**in medias res** (Latin)   (lit., 'into the middle of things') said of a narrative that begins in the middle of the action (from Horace, *Ars Poetica* 148).

**in mediis rebus** (Latin)   in the middle of things.

**in memoriam** (Latin)   in memory (of).

**in modo di** (Italian)   *Music.* in the manner of.

**innamorato,** *fem.* **innamorata** (Italian)   1. *n.* a beloved; lover.  2. *adj.* in love.

**in nomine Domini** (Latin)   in the name of the Lord.

**in nubibus** (Latin)   (lit., 'in the clouds') vague.

**in nuce** (Latin)   in a nutshell.

**in ovo** (Latin)   (lit.. 'in the egg') undeveloped; immature.

**in pace** (Latin)   in peace.

**in pari delicto** (Latin)   *Law.* in equal fault; equally culpable.

**in partibus infidelium** (Latin)   (lit., 'in the lands of the unbelievers') *Roman Catholicism.* said of the see of a bishop whose jurisdiction is an area under the religious control of another group.

**in perpetuam rei memoriam** (Latin)   in everlasting memory of the event.

**in perpetuum** (Latin)   in perpetuity. Also **in perpetuo.**

**in personam** (Latin)   (lit., 'against the person') *Law.* an action involving a person, as contrasted with one relating to property. See also **in rem.**

**in pleno** (Latin)   in full.

**in pleno lumine** (Latin)   (lit., 'in full light') in the light of day; in the open; in public.

**in posse** (Latin)   in possibility; possibly, as contrasted with **in esse.**

**in potentia** (Latin)   in potentiality; potentially.

**in praesenti** (Latin)   at the present time; now.

**in principio** (Latin)   in the beginning. *Abbr.* **in pr.**

**in propria persona** (Latin)   in one's own person or character.

**in puris naturalibus** (Latin)   (lit., 'in pure, natural (conditions)') stark naked.

**in re** (Latin)   (lit., 'in the matter') *Law.* in the case of; concerning. Also **re.**

**in rem** (Latin)   (lit., 'against a thing') *Law.* designating a case initiated against property rather than against a person. See also **in personam.**

**in rerum natura** (Latin)   in the nature of things.

**in saecula saeculorum** (Latin)   (lit., 'into ages of ages') for ever and ever.

**insalata** (Italian)   a salad.

**in se** (Latin)   in itself.

**in secco** (Italian)   *Fine Arts.* a designation for the process of touching up a fresco when the plaster is dry.

**insensibilmente** (Italian)   *Music.* gradually; imperceptibly.

**in situ** (Latin)   in place; undisturbed from its original position.

**in solidum** *or* **solido** (Latin)   (lit., 'for the whole') *Law.* indicating joint and several responsibility for a debt.

**insouciance** (French)   indifference; lack of care or concern.

**insouciant** (French)   carefree; indifferent.

**in specie** (Latin)   in kind; in the same form.

**in statu quo** (Latin)   (lit., 'in the state in which') in the condition found at a particular time. See also **status quo.**

**insurrectos** (Spanish)   participants in a political rebellion.

**intaglio** (Italian)   1. *Applied Arts.* the art of engraving a design into a surface, creating a sunken relief.   2. a gem or stone engraved in this way. 3. *Printing.* a die cut to produce a design in relief. Also **intaglio rilevato.**

**intarsia** (Italian)   1. *Antiques.* the technique of inlaying pieces of ivory upon wood to form pictorial scenes or geometric patterns.   2. *Needlework.* a knitting or weaving technique in which a surface design is created without threads being carried across the back of the pattern. Also **tarsia.**

**intavolatura** (Italian)   *Music.* tablature, the system of instrumental notation used in the 15th through 18th centuries.

**integer vitae** (Latin)   (one who is) blameless in life (opening words of Horace, *Odes* I.22).

**in tenebris** (Latin)   in darkness; in a state of doubt.

**inter alia** (Latin)   among other things.

**inter alios** (Latin)   between *or* among other persons.

**inter cibos** (Latin)   *Prescriptions.* between meals. *Abbr.* **i.c.**

**intérieur, à l'.**   See **à l'intérieur.**

**intermedio.**   See **intermezzo.**

**intermezzo,** *pl.* **intermezzi** (Italian)    *Music.*   1. a short movement joining two parts of a longer composition such as a **sonata** or symphony.    2. *Opera.* a musical passage performed with the curtain raised to indicate the passage of time.    3. formerly, a light entertainment, such as a comic drama or ballet, between the acts of a play or opera. Also **intermedio.**

**Internationale** (French)    a song of the French Revolution, now an anthem of radical and communist workers.

**inter nos** (Latin)    between *or* among ourselves.

**inter pares** (Latin)    between *or* among equals.

**inter pocula** (Latin)    (lit., 'between cups') 1. while having several drinks. 2. under the influence of alcohol.

**inter se** (Latin)    between *or* among themselves.

**inter vivos** (Latin)    (lit., 'among the living') *Law.* designating a gift made while the donor is alive rather than as a bequest.

**intime** (French)    intimate; cozy.

**intonaco** (Italian)    (lit., 'plaster') *Fine Arts.* in **fresco** painting, the final or ground layer of plaster.

**in toto** (Latin)    on the whole; in entirety.

**intra muros** (Latin)    within the walls (of a city or institution); relating to internal matters.

**in transitu** (Latin)    in transit; on the way.

**intra vires** (Latin)    within one's powers or authority.

**Introit** (Latin)    (lit., 'he goes in') *Christian liturgy.* the beginning portion of the Mass.

**in usum Delphini** (Latin)    for the use of the Dauphin; bowdlerized (alluding to the books expurgated for the eldest son of Louis XIV of France).

**in utero** (Latin)    in the womb; unborn.

**in vacuo** (Latin)    in a vacuum; in isolation; in the abstract.

**invictus** (Latin)    unconquered.

**in vino veritas** (Latin)    in wine there is truth; truth is told under the influence of alcohol.

**invita Minerva** (Latin)    (lit., 'with Minerva unwilling') without benefit of inspiration (alluding to Minerva as the Roman goddess of wisdom and the arts).

**in vitro** (Latin)    *Medicine.* in glass, as in a test tube; under laboratory conditions, as contrasted with **in vivo.**

**in vivo** (Latin)    *Medicine.* in the living organism, as of reactions occurring in the living body, contrasted with **in vitro.**

**involtini,** *sing.* **involtino** (Italian)    *Cookery.* a dish made with thin slices of meat that are stuffed and braised in butter and oil.

**ipse dixit** (Latin)  (lit., 'he himself said it') a dogmatic or authoritative statement. See also **dixi**.

**ipsissima verba** (Latin)  the very words themselves, used of a verbatim quotation or to refer to an original or special document.

**ipsissimis verbis** (Latin)  1. in these very words; verbatim.  2. with or by these very words.

**ipso facto** (Latin)  by the very fact alone; by virtue of a certain act.

**ipso jure** (Latin)  *Law.* by the law itself; by the actual operation of the law.

**ira furor brevis est** (Latin)  anger is a brief madness (Horace, *Epistles* I.2.62).

**irato** (Italian)  *Music.* irate.

**irlandaise, à l'.**  See **à l'irlandaise**.

**ironicamente** (Italian)  *Music.* ironically.

**irresoluto** (Italian)  *Music.* undecided in style.

**isba** (Russian)  a Russian log hut. Also **izba**.

**ishime** (Japanese)  a roughened, irregular surface on Japanese metalwork.

**islancio, con.**  See **con islancio**.

**ispravnik** (Russian)  a Russian local police chief.

**Issei** (Japanese)  a Japanese immigrant to the United States. See also **Kibei; Nisei; Sansei**.

**istesso.**  See **stesso**.

**istoriato** (Italian)  *Antiques.* painting on ceramics as done by Italian maiolica painters of the 16th century, the subjects being historical or legendary.

**ita est** (Latin)  it is so.

**Italianità** (Italian)  the sense of ethnic heritage among Italians living in the southern part of Switzerland.

**italienne, à l'.**  See **à l'italienne**.

**item** (Latin)  (lit., 'likewise') formerly used to introduce individual articles in a list.

**Ite, missa est** (Latin)  (lit., 'go; (the congregation) is dismissed') *Roman Catholicism.* the final words in the liturgy of the Latin Mass.

**iter** (Latin)  a journey.

**iterum** (Latin)  anew; over again.

**ius.**  See entries at **jus**.

**izba.**  See **isba**.

**izquierda** (Spanish)  1. the left; left side.  2. the political left.

**Izvestia** (Russian)  (lit., 'news') the official Soviet government newspaper.

**izzat** (Hindi)  personal dignity; personal prestige.

# J

**ja** (German)   yes.

**jabot** (French)   an ornamental neck frill, such as that worn by men in the 18th century.

**jacal** (Spanish)   a shack; hut.

**jacquard** (French)   fabric woven on a Jacquard loom.

**Jacquerie** (French)   a peasant revolt, especially the revolt of French peasants in 1358.

**Jacques Bonhomme** (French)   the symbolic personification of France, equivalent to *Uncle Sam* personifying the United States.

**jacta** *or* **iacta alea est** (Latin)   (lit., 'the die is cast') there is no turning back now, the matter is in the hands of fortune (in Suetonius, *Julius Caesar* 32, the comment of Caesar upon leading his forces across the Rubicon into Italy, an act signifying civil war).

**j'adoube** (French)   *Chess.* I adjust, a phrase indicating that a player does not intend to move a piece, but merely straighten it.

**Jahrhundert** (German)   a century.

**jai alai** (Spanish)   a ball game of Basque origin played by up to six participants on a large, indoor court, the object being to keep the ball in play by catching and hurling it against the front wall of the court. See also **cesta; fronton; pelota.**

**jalapeños** (Spanish)   small, green, hot Mexican **chile** peppers, used as a condiment.

**jambalaya** (Louisiana French)   *Cookery.* a Creole dish made of rice, herbs, vegetables, hot peppers, and meat or fish, usually ham or shrimp.

**jambon** (French)   ham.

**jamón** (Spanish)   ham.

**januis clausis** (Latin)   behind closed doors; in private.

**japonaiseries** (French)   Japanese art objects.

**jarabe** (Spanish)   1. *Music.* a 19th-century Spanish dance and musical style. **2.** *Cookery.* a syrup.

151

**jarabe tapatío** (Spanish)    the Mexican hat dance.

**jardin anglais** (French)    a landscape garden in the English manner.

**jardin chinois** (French)    a garden in the Chinese manner.

**jardinière.**    See à la jardinière.

**jardinière, à la.**    See à la jardinière.

**javalina** (Spanish)    *Texas, Mexico.* a peccary; wild hog.

**jawohl** (German)    yes; certainly.

**jefe** (Spanish)    boss; chief.

**jefe político** (Spanish)    a local law-enforcement official.

**jellaba.**    See djellabah.

**je m'en fiche.**    See je m'en fous.

**je m'en fous** (French)    I don't care; I don't give a damn. Also **je m'en fiche.**

**je ne sais quoi, je-ne-sais-quoi** (French)    (lit., 'I don't know what') an expression applied to something that defies description or explanation.

**je suis prêt,** *fem.* **prête** (French)    I am ready.

**Jesus.**    See entries at **Iesus.**

**jet d'eau** (French)    a jet of water, as in a fountain.

**jeté** (French)    (lit., 'thrown') *Ballet.* any of several movements in which a dancer jumps from one foot to the other with a throwing movement of a leg.

**jeu de hasard** (French)    a game of chance.

**jeu de mots** (French)    a play on words; a pun.

**jeu d'esprit** (French)    (lit., 'play of spirit') 1. a witticism. 2. a literary work marked by keen use of wit.

**jeu de théâtre** (French)    a stage trick.

**jeune fille** (French)    a young, unmarried girl.

**jeune premier,** *fem.* **jeune première** (French)    *Theater.* the juvenile lead in a play.

**jeunesse** (French)    youth; young people.

**jeunesse dorée** (French)    (lit., 'gilded youth') stylish and sophisticated children of the wealthy.

**jibba** (Arabic)    a long-sleeved, collarless coat worn by Muslims. Also **djibbah; jibbah.**

**jihad** (Arabic)    1. *Islam.* a holy war undertaken as a sacred duty. 2. a bitter conflict over principles.

**jingu** (Japanese)    *Shintoism.* a major shrine.

**jinja** (Japanese)    *Shintoism.* 1. a shrine. 2. (*cap.*) the branch of Shinto recognized as the official religion of Japan. Also **Kokka.**

**jinn** (Arabic)    *Islam.* one of a class of spirits below the angels that appear on earth and influence mankind. Also **jin; jinni; djin; djinn(i).**

**jinriksha** (Japanese)   a small, two-wheeled passenger vehicle pulled by a man.  Also **jinricksha; jinrickshaw; jinrikisha; ricksha; rickshaw; rikisha; rikshaw.**

**jiujitsu.**   See **jujitsu.**

**jiva** (Sanskrit)   *Hinduism; Jainism.* the individual soul.  Also **jivatma.**

**Jodel** (German)   *Music.* in Alpine folksongs, vocalization with frequent changes from chest tones to falsetto.  Also **Yodel.**

**joie de vivre** (French)   (lit., 'joy of living') strong enthusiasm and delight in being alive; a sparkling, vigorous optimism.

**joli,** *fem.* **jolie** (French)   attractive; pretty.

**jolie-laide** (French)   (lit., 'pretty-ugly') a woman who is attractive in an unconventional way.

**jongleur** (French)   a wandering medieval minstrel or entertainer, especially in France and Norman England.

**jornada** (Spanish)   1. a day's journey in the desert without stopping for water.   2. a military expedition.

**joropo** (Spanish)   a Venezuelan ballroom dance in triple time.

**jota** (Spanish)   1. a Spanish folk dance in triple time, performed with castanets and rhythmic tapping of the heels.   2. the music for this dance.   3. the letter *j*.

**jour, à.**   See **à jour.**

**jour de fête** (French)   a festival; holiday.

**jour gras** (French)   (lit., 'fat day') a day of feasting.

**jour maigre** (French)   (lit., 'lean day') a day of partial or total fasting or abstinence from meat, as prescribed by some churches.  See also **repas maigre.**

**journal intime** (French)   a personal diary.

**jours, de nos.**   See **de nos jours.**

**joyería** (Spanish)   a jewelry store.

**Joyeux Noël** (French)   Merry Christmas.

**judo** (Japanese)   a method of self-defense without weapons that resembles jujitsu but stresses the athletic benefits.

**judoka** (Japanese)   an expert or participant in **judo.**

**juerga** (Spanish)   a gypsy celebration at which **flamenco** is danced.

**Jugendstil** (German)   *Fine Arts.* in German-speaking countries, a movement associated with Art Nouveau.

**jujitsu** (Japanese)   a method of self-defense without weapons that takes advantage of an opponent's momentum to disable him.  Also **jiujitsu.**  See also **judo; karate.**

**julienne** (French)   *Cookery.* designating something cut into very thin strips, as vegetables.

**Jungfrau** (German)   virgin.

**Junggrammatiker, der** (German)   (lit., 'the young grammarians') a group of 19th-century linguists who proposed universal laws of phonetics.

**Junker** (German)   member of a class of Prussian nobility noted for militarism and arrogance.

**Junkerei** (German)   aristocratic arrogance.

**junta** (Spanish)   1. a small group exercising political control following a coup d'état.   2. a council or administrative body.  See also **junto.**

**junto** (Spanish)   (lit., 'together') a self-appointed committee with political aspirations.  See also **junta.**

**Jup(p)iter Fluvius** (Latin)   Jupiter the Rainmaker; a reference to rainy weather.

**Jup(p)iter Optimus Maximus** (Latin)   Jupiter the Best and Greatest.

**Jup(p)iter Tonans** (Latin)   Jupiter the Thunderer.

**jure** (Latin)   by right; by law.  See also entries at **jus.**

**jure belli** (Latin)   by the law or rules of war.

**jure divino** (Latin)   by divine right.

**jure gentium** (Latin)   by the law of nations.

**jure humano** (Latin)   by human law; by the will of the people.

**jure uxoris** (Latin)   by the right of a wife.

**Juris Doctor** (Latin)   the academic degree of Doctor of Law, the standard degree of a lawyer. *Abbr.* **J.D.**

**Juris Utriusque Doctor** (Latin)   Doctor of Both (canon and civil) Laws. *Abbr.* **J.U.D.**

**jus** (Latin)   law; legal right.

**jus** (French)   *Cookery.* juice, especially natural juices of roasted beef.

**jus ad rem** (Latin)   (lit., 'right to a thing') *Law.* legal right to something without possession of it.

**jus belli** (Latin)   law of war.

**jus canonicum** (Latin)   canon law.

**jus civile** (Latin)   civil law.

**jus commune** (Latin)   a common right; common law.

**jus divinum** (Latin)   divine law.

**jus et norma loquendi** (Latin)   the rule and norms of speaking; common usage.

**jus gentium** (Latin)   the law of nations.

**jus gladii** (Latin)   (lit., 'the right of the sword') the power or prerogative to exact punishment.

**jus hereditatis** (Latin)   the right of inheritance.

**jus in re** (Latin)   (lit., 'a right in something') *Law.* absolute right of ownership over a thing.

154

**jus mariti** (Latin)   *Law.* the right of a husband to his wife's movable estate.

**jus militare** (Latin)   martial law; the law of the military.

**jus naturae** (Latin)   the law of nature.

**jus naturale** (Latin)   natural law.

**jus possessionis** (Latin)   *Law.* the right of possession.

**jus primae noctis** (Latin)   (lit., 'law of the first night') the supposed right of a feudal lord to deflower his tenant's bride on the wedding night.  Also **droit du seigneur** (French).

**jus proprietatis** (Latin)   *Law.* the right of property.

**jus relictae** (Latin)   the right of the widow to her husband's property.

**jus sanguinis** (Latin)   (lit., 'the right of blood') the principle that a person's citizenship is determined by that of his parents.

**jus soli** (Latin)   (lit., 'the law of the soil') the principle that a person's citizenship is determined by his place of birth.

**juste milieu, juste-milieu.**   See le juste milieu.

**justitia omnibus** (Latin)   justice to all (motto of the District of Columbia).

**juzgado** (Spanish)   1. a court of law; court house.   2. *South America.* a jail.  Also **jusgado.**

**j'y suis, j'y reste** (French)   here I am, here I am staying (statement by Count de MacMahon when advised to withdraw from the Malakoff fortifications during the Crimean War).

# K

**ka** (Egyptian)   *Egyptian religion.* a spiritual life force; immortal soul.

**Kaaba** (Arabic)   *Islam.* a cubical building near the Great Mosque at Mecca that contains a sacred black stone; the focal point of the **hajj**. See also **kiblah**.

**Kab(b)ala.**   See **cabala.**

**Kabinettwein** (German)   cabinet wine; premium German wine.

**kabob** (Arabic)   *Cookery.* small pieces of meat cooked on a skewer with various vegetables. Also **kebab; kebob; kabab.** See also **shish kebab.**

**kabuki** (Japanese)   the popular dramatic genre of Japan with elaborate costuming and stylized acting performed by an all-male company. See also **Nō.**

**Kaffeeklatsch** (German)   an informal meeting for relaxed conversation, usually with coffee served.

**kaffiyeh** (Arabic)   the characteristic Arab headdress consisting of a length of cloth folded and wrapped around the head and held in place by a cord, the **agal.** Also **keffiyeh; kuf(f)i(y)eh.**

**kafir** (Arabic)   an infidel; non-Muslim. Also **kaffir.**

**kahuna** (Hawaiian)   a native medicine man.

**kairon gnōthi** (Greek)   know the opportunity.

**Kaiser** (German)   former title of the German or Austrian imperial monarch.

**kai su, teknon** (Greek)   even you, child? (alleged dying words of Julius Caesar to Brutus; Latinized as **et tu, Brute**).

**kai ta loipa** (Greek)   and the rest; equivalent to **et cetera.** *Abbr.* **ktl.**

**kakemono** (Japanese)   a scroll decorated with a text or a painting, hung vertically on a wall and unrolled for display.

**kaliph.**   See **caliph.**

**kamaina** (Hawaiian)   a long-time resident of Hawaii.

**kambal** (Hindi)   a coarse woolen blanket or shawl.

**kamikaze** (Japanese)     (lit., 'divine wind') **1.** *n.* a member of an elite corps of the Japanese air force who would crash their explosive-laden planes into enemy targets. **2.** *adj.* characteristic of a kamikaze; suicidal.

**Kammermusik** (German)    *Music.* chamber music.

**Kampf** (German)    battle; struggle; conflict.

**kampong** (Malay)    a Malay-speaking village or community.

**kana** (Japanese)    the system for writing Japanese using a syllabic script, either the **hiragana** or **katakana**. See also **kanji**.

**Kanaka** (Hawaiian)    **1.** a native Hawaiian. **2.** a native of the South Sea islands.

**kana-majiri** (Japanese)    the standard system for writing modern Japanese, using **kanji** for root concepts, supplemented by **kana**.

**kanji** (Japanese)    the system of writing Japanese using Chinese-derived ideographs. See also **kana**.

**kantele** (Finnish)    *Music.* an ancient Finnish instrument resembling a psaltery.

**kanzu** (Swahili)    a long, white, man's robe common to central Africa.

**Kapelle** (German)    **1.** chapel. **2.** *Music.* musical band.

**Kapellmeister** (German)    *Music.* conductor. Also **Capellmeister**.

**Kapellmeistermusik** (German)    *Music. Derogatory.* technically correct but uninspired music.

**kapote** (Yiddish)    a long coat worn by Jewish men of eastern Europe.

**kapusta** (Polish)    cabbage.

**kaputt** (German)    *Colloquial.* broken; finished; ruined; lost.

**karate** (Japanese)    (lit., 'empty hands') a method of self-defense without weapons that emphasizes striking and disabling the opponent with the hands, elbows, knees, or feet. See also **gi; makiwara; shuto; tameshiwara**.

**karma** (Sanskrit)    (lit., 'work; deed; fate') **1.** *Hinduism; Buddhism.* personal action that brings on inevitable good or bad results, either in this life or in a reincarnation. **2.** personal destiny.

**karmadharaya** (Sanskrit)    *Linguistics.* a compound made up of two words, the first an adjective and the second a substantive, as *redcoats, grandfather*, etc.

**Kasbah** (Arabic)    the Arab quarter of a North African city, especially the older, native quarter of Algiers. Also **Casbah**.

**Käse** (German)    cheese.

**kasha** (Russian)    *Cookery.* a dish made of boiled grain, usually buckwheat, that has been hulled and crushed.

**katakana** (Japanese)    one of the two Japanese syllabaries, less used and more angular in style. See also **hiragana**.

**katana** (Japanese)    the long, curved sword used by the **samurai**.

**kat'exochen** (Greek)  pre-eminently; **par excellence.**

**kazachok** (Russian)  a lively Slavic folk dance performed by men, featuring the **prisiadka.** Also **kazatsky.**

**kazatsky.**  See **kazachok.**

**kebab** *or* **kebob.**  See **kabob.**

**keffiyeh.**  See **kaffiyeh.**

**kefir** (Russian)  fermented cow's milk, drunk as a beverage.

**ken** (Japanese)  a straight, double-edged Japanese sword. Also **tsurugi.**

**kendo** (Japanese)  a form of combat using bamboo staves.

**kepi** (French)  a French military cap with a round, flat top and a short brim in front. Also **képi.**

**kermis** (Dutch)  1. an annual village festival of the Benelux countries. 2. a similar event held for charity. Also **kermess(e)**; **kirmess.**

**ketubah** (Hebrew)  *Judaism.* a formal contract between the husband and wife in a Jewish marriage.

**Ketubim.**  See **Hagiographa.**

**khamsin** (Arabic)  (lit., 'fifty') a hot, southerly wind of Egypt that blows for about fifty days in the spring.

**khan** (Turkish)  1. a hereditary leader of an Altaic-speaking tribe. 2. the ruler of the Tatars and emperor of China during the Middle Ages, descended from Genghis Khan. 3. a title of respect used in central Asian countries.

**kibbutz** *pl.* **kibbutzim** (Hebrew)  an Israeli agricultural commune.

**kibbutznik** (Hebrew)  a member of a **kibbutz.**

**Kibei** (Japanese)  a person of Japanese descent who was born in the United States but educated in Japan. See also **Issei; Nisei; Sansei.**

**kiblah** (Arabic)  *Islam.* the point towards which Muslims face to pray, in the direction of Mecca and particularly the **Kaaba.**

**kielbasa** (Polish)  a Polish-style sausage, smoked and flavored with garlic.

**kilij** (Turkish)  a crescent-shaped Turkish sword.

**kilim** (Turkish)  a small, rectangular Oriental rug.

**kimchi** (Korean)  *Cookery.* a pickled and seasoned mixture of cabbage, onions, and fish, the Korean national dish. Also **kimchee.**

**kimono** (Japanese)  a loose-fitting robe with wide sleeves and a wide sash at the waist. See also **obi**[1].

**Kind,** *pl.* **Kinder** (German)  child.

**Kinder, Kirche, Küche** (German)  (lit., 'children, church, kitchen') slogan for a traditional view of priorities for women.

**kino** (German)  a movie theater (especially in Europe).

**kir** (French)  a drink of white wine with a jigger of **cassis.**

**Kirche** (German)  church.

**kirmess.** See **kermis.**

**Kirschwasser** (German)  a cherry-flavored liqueur.

**kishka** (Yiddish)  *Cookery.* a sausagelike preparation consisting of a seasoned filling of flour, meat, etc., stuffed into intestine casing and baked. Also **kishke.**

**kithara** (Greek)  an ancient Greek stringed musical instrument. Also **cithara.**

**Kitsch** (German)  (lit., 'trash') term applied to gaudy or tasteless art or design that is intended to appeal to popular taste.

**kittel** (Yiddish)  *Judaism.* a white ceremonial robe.

**Klavier** (German)  *Music.* piano. Also **Clavier.**

**Klaviertiger** (German)  (lit., 'keyboard tiger') a virtuoso pianist with an aggressive style of playing.

**klong** (Thai)  a canal, as in Bangkok.

**klösse** (German)  dumplings.

**knaidel,** *pl.* **knaidlach** (Yiddish)  *Cookery.* a dumpling made with **matzoh** meal, often served in soup. Also **knaydl.**

**knäkebröd** (Swedish)  a type of flat, unleavened rye bread.

**Knesset** (Hebrew)  the Israeli parliament.

**knish** (Yiddish)  *Cookery.* a fried or baked roll of dough with a filling, as meat or potato.

**Kohen,** *pl.* **Kohanim** (Hebrew)  a member of the Jewish priestly caste. Also **Cohen.**

**Koine** (Greek)  the vernacular dialect of ancient Greek common during the Hellenistic and Roman periods; the language of the New Testament. Also **Koinē.**

**Kokka.** See **jinja, 2.**

**kolkhoz** (Russian)  a Soviet agricultural collective.

**kölnisch(es) Wasser** (German)  cologne.

**komatik** (Eskimo)  an Eskimo sled.

**Komponist** (German)  composer.

**Komsomol** (Russian)  a Communist youth organization in the Soviet Union.

**Konditorei** (German)  pastry shop.

**König und Kaiser** (German)  (lit., 'king and emperor') formal title of German imperial monarchs.

**konnichi-wa** (Japanese)  good day (a salutation).

**kopeck** (Russian)  a Russian coin of small value; 100th of a **ruble.** Also **kopek.**

**kopje** (Afrikaans)  a small hill.

**Koran** (Arabic)    *Islam.* the sacred text of the Islamic religion, said to have been dictated to Muhammad by Gabriel. Also **Quran.**

**korē** (Greek)    (lit., 'girl') an ancient Greek sculptural representation of a girl or young woman. See also **kouros.**

**kosher** (Yiddish)    1. *Judaism.* in accord with Jewish dietary or ceremonial laws. 2. genuine; legitimate; trustworthy.

**koto** (Japanese)    a Japanese stringed musical instrument.

**koumis(s).**    See **kumiss.**

**kouros** (Greek)    (lit., 'boy') an ancient Greek sculptural representation of a boy or young man. See also **korē.**

**kraken** (Norwegian)    a legendary Norwegian sea monster said to cause whirlpools.

**Kreis** (German)    circle; cycle.

**kreplach** (Yiddish)    *Cookery.* filled pockets of noodle dough, usually served in soup. Also **kreplech.**

**Krieg** (German)    war.

**Kriegspiel** (German)    (lit., 'war game') 1. *Chess.* form of play in which each opponent, while seeing only his own pieces on the board, must envision the moves of opposing pieces from reports of a referee. 2. enactment of tactical maneuvers on a large map with movable pieces that represent military forces.

**kris** (Malay)    a heavy Malayan dagger with a wavy blade; creese.

**ktēma es aiei** (Greek)    a possession forever (Thucydides I.22).

**Küche** (German)    cooking; cuisine.

**Kuchen** (German)    cake; pastry; tart.

**kuf(f)i(y)eh.**    See **kaffiyeh.**

**kugel** (Yiddish)    *Cookery.* a casserole dish of noodles or potatoes.

**kukri** (Hindi)    a large curved knife used by Gurkhas for hunting and combat.

**kulak** (Russian)    a prosperous Russian peasant, often with others working for him, stereotypically a miser.

**Kultur** (German)    culture viewed as an influential principle in a society.

**Kulturkampf** (German)    *German history.* conflict between the imperial government and the Roman Catholic Church over control of educational and ecclesiastical appointments (1872–86).

**Kulturkreis** (German)    basic cultural traits that form the nucleus for subsequent cultures.

**kumiss** (Russian)    a beverage of fermented milk drunk especially by Asian nomads. Also **koumis(s).**

**kümmel** (German)    (lit., 'caraway seed') 1. a clear **liqueur** flavored with caraway seeds. 2. a Leyden cheese containing caraway seeds.

**kung fu** (Chinese)    a Chinese ascetic discipline noted for its rigorous physical training in martial arts.

**Kunst** (German)    art.

**Künstler** (German)    artist.

**Künstlerroman** (German)   *Literature.* a novel about an artist.

**Kunstlied** (German)    an art song, as distinct from a folk song.

**Kursaal** (German)    meeting hall at a health resort.

**kurta** (Hindi)    a collarless shirt worn by men in India.

**kvass** (Russian)    a Russian beer made with rye. Also **quass**.

**kvetch** (Yiddish)    to fret or complain excessively.

**Kyrie eleison** (Greek)    (lit., 'Lord, have mercy') *Christianity.* a refrain used in certain services, often set to music.

# L

**laager** (Afrikaans)    an encampment, usually within a circle of wagons. Also **lager.**

**La Belle Epoque** (French)    the period between the Franco-Prussian War and World War I (1871–1914), characterized by peace in Western Europe and a productive surge in the arts and sciences.

**La Belle Province** (French)    (lit., 'the beautiful province') a name for Quebec.

**la bonne bouche** (French)    (lit., 'the good mouth') **1.** a delicious tidbit that one delays eating until the end of the meal. **2.** any desirable thing that is saved for the end.

**labor omnia vincit** (Latin)    work conquers all things.

**Lachryma Christi** (Latin)    (lit., 'tear of Christ') an Italian white wine.

**la commedia è finita** (Italian)    (lit., 'the comedy is ended') *Music.* a phrase used, frequently with overtones of melancholy, to indicate awareness that an absolute end has been reached (the final words of Leoncavallo's opera, *I Pagliacci*).

**la condition humaine** (French)    the human condition; the state of mankind.

**La Cosa Nostra.**    See **Cosa Nostra.**

**lacrimae rerum.**    See **sunt lacrimae rerum.**

**lacrimoso** (Italian)    *Music.* tearful. Also **lagrimoso.**

**lacuna,** *pl.* **lacunae** (Latin)    a gap in a book or manuscript.

**ladino** (Spanish)    **1.** *adj.* crafty; tricky.    **2.** *Central America and Mexico. n.* a white man; a person of Spanish, not Indian descent.    **3.** *(cap.)* the language of the Sephardic Jews, a mixture of Spanish and Hebrew.

**la dolce vita** (Italian)    (lit., 'the sweet life') a self-indulgent and hedonistic lifestyle.

**la donna è mobile** (Italian)    the woman is fickle (the first words of an **aria** in Verdi's *Rigoletto*).

**ladrón** (Spanish)    a thief.

**laesa majestas** (Latin)   (lit., 'injured greatness') **1.** an offense against a ruler's dignity or power; lese majesty; high treason.   **2.** an attack upon a revered practice or institution.   Also **laesae majestatis.**

**la fine bouche.**   See **fine bouche.**

**lager.**   See **laager.**

**La Gioconda** (Italian)   a title for Leonardo da Vinci's *Mona Lisa.*

**lagniappe** (French)   *Louisiana and southwest Texas.* a term used to describe something extra given to a customer as a token of appreciation. See also **pilón.**

**La Grande Voleuse** (French)   (lit., 'The Great Robber') a derogatory expression for England.

**Lágrima** (Spanish)   the smooth, amber-colored wine of Malaga, made with no mechanical pressing.

**lagrimoso.**   See **lacrimoso.**

**laguna** (Spanish)   a small pond or lake.

**lai** (French)   *Literature.* **1.** a French medieval narrative poem of adventure and romance. **2.** a lyric poem, especially a love poem, composed to be sung as a popular ballad.

**laisser-aller, laissez-aller** (French)   (lit., 'allow to go') unchecked freedom or license.

**laisser faire, laissez faire** (French)   (lit., 'allow to act') *n.* **1.** a policy of noninterference by government in private economic affairs and interests. **2.** a general policy of noninterference in the affairs of others.   *—adj.* **3.** **laisser-faire, laissez-faire.** designating any policy of noninterference.

**laissez passer** (French)   (lit., 'allow to pass') a permit to travel, especially one issued in lieu of a passport.

**lait** (French)   milk.

**laitue** (French)   lettuce.

**lama** (Tibetan)   a priest or monk in Tibetan Buddhism.

**La Mancha** (Spanish)   **1.** a large wine-growing region in the southern half of Spain's central plateau.   **2.** *Literature.* the home of Don Quixote.

**la Manche** (French)   the English Channel.

**Lambrusco** (Italian)   a slightly sparkling, semi-sweet red wine produced in northern Italy.

**lamé** (French)   a shiny, decorative fabric interwoven with metallic threads.

**lamentabile** (Italian)   *Music.* in lamenting style; mournful. Also **lamentando, lamentevole, lamentoso.**

**lamentando.**   See **lamentabile.**

**lamentevole.**   See **lamentabile.**

**lamentoso.**   See **lamentabile.**

**la nation boutiquière** (French)    (lit., 'a nation of shopkeepers') Napoleon Bonaparte's description of England.

**la nausée** (French)    nausea; existentialist disgust.

**landsman** (Yiddish)    a person from the same town or region in Europe as another.

**Landtag** (German)    *German history.* a local state parliament.

**langlauf** (German)    cross-country skiing.

**langosta** (Spanish)    lobster.

**langouste** (French)    rock lobster; spiny lobster.

**langoustine** (French)    a large prawn; baby crawfish.

**langue de boeuf** (French)    beef tongue; ox tongue.

**langue-de-chat** (French)    (lit., 'cat's tongue') *Cookery.* a type of long, thin biscuit served with desserts.

**langue d'oc** (French)    the medieval dialect of southern France, characterized by the use of *oc* as the affirmative.

**langue d'oïl** (French)    the medieval dialect of northern France, characterized by the use of *oïl* as the affirmative.

**langue maternelle** (French)    native tongue.

**languendo** (Italian)    *Music.* languishing. Also **languente.**

**languente.**    See **languendo.**

**languidamente** (Italian)    *Music.* languidly.

**la nouvelle cuisine.**    See **nouvelle cuisine, la.**

**la petite bourgeoisie.**    See **petite bougeoisie.**

**lapin** (French)    rabbit.

**lapis lazuli** (Latin)    a deep-blue mineral stone.

**La Pittura Colta** (Italian)    *Fine Arts.* cultivated painting, a late modernist style dominated by classical allegory.

**lapsus calami** (Latin)    a slip of the pen.

**lapsus linguae** (Latin)    a slip of the tongue.

**lapsus memoriae** (Latin)    a lapse of memory.

**lapsus pennae** (Latin)    a slip of the pen.

**lardons** (French)    *Cookery.* small pieces of salt pork used in various preparations, such as **pâté.**

**la règle du jeu** (French)    (lit., 'the rule of the game') an expression indicating that accepted rules must be followed in an endeavor.

**lares et penates** (Latin)    1. *Ancient Rome.* household gods, privately worshiped and thought to protect the home.    2. cherished possessions.

**La Résistance** (French)    1. the French underground movement during World War II that fought against the German occupation. 2. any such underground movement in an occupied country.

**largamente** (Italian)    (lit., 'broadly') *Music.* in a full, broad style.

**larghetto** (Italian)   *Music.* slow and dignified, but to a lesser degree than largo.

**larghissimo** (Italian)   *Music.* very slow.

**largo** (Italian)   (lit., 'broad, wide')   *Music.* slow and dignified.

**largo** (Spanish)   (lit. 'long') a strap on a Western saddle used to secure the cinch.   Also **látigo.**

**larigo** (Spanish)   a ring on a Western saddle through which the **largo** is passed.

**la ringrazio** (Italian)   thank you (formal).

**l'art brut** (French)   (lit., 'raw art')   *Fine Arts.* the artistic creations of the insane, the unschooled, and clairvoyants, characterized by crudity, raw detail, and a certain directness.

**l'art de vivre** (French)   (lit., 'the art of living') zest for life; a capacity for getting the most out of life.

**l'art pour l'art** (French)   art for art's sake.

**lasagna,** *pl.* **lasagne** (Italian)   **1.** a variety of **pasta** that is wide and flat, often with curly edges.   **2.** *Cookery.* a dish consisting of layers of this **pasta** combined with tomato-meat sauce and cheese, then baked.

**La Scala** (Italian)   the renowned opera house of Milan.

**Lasciate ogni speranza** (Italian)   (lit., 'Abandon all hope') the words written above the gates of hell in Dante's *Inferno.*

**La Section d'Or** (French)   *Fine Arts.* the name for a group of Cubist painters who exhibited together in 1912.

**La Serenissima** (Italian)   (lit., 'the most serene') a name given to Venice at the height of its power in the late 15th century.

**latet anguis in herba** (Latin)   a snake hides in the grass (often shortened to *anguis in herba* 'snake in the grass,' that is, a disloyal friend; from Vergil, *Eclogues* III.93).

**látigo.**   See **largo.**

**latine** (Latin)   in Latin.

**latke** (Yiddish)   a potato pancake.

**latte** (Italian)   milk.

**latticinio** (Italian)   (lit., 'dairy foods')   *Antiques.* a Venetian technique for making ornamental glass stems of a milky appearance.   Also **latticino.**

**laudator temporis acti** (Latin)   (lit., 'praiser of time past') one who venerates "the good old days" (from Horace, *Ars Poetica* 173).   See also **delator temporis acti.**

**lau lau** (Hawaiian)   *Cookery.* a meat and fish mixture that is wrapped in leaves and steamed.

**laus Deo** (Latin)   praise (be) to God.

**laveche.**   See **leveche.**

**lavoro di commesso** (Italian)    *Fine Arts.* an inlay or mosaic of bone, ivory, or semi-precious stones.

**lazo** (Spanish)   a rope used by cowboys; lasso.

**lazzi** (Italian)   *Theater.* the improvised bits of comedy inserted in the fixed scenarios of the **commedia dell'arte.**

**l'chaim** (Hebrew)   to life; to your health (often used as a toast). Also **lechayim.**

**le beau monde.**   See **beau monde.**

**Lebensabend** (German)   evening of life; old age.

**Leben Sie wohl!** (German)   farewell!

**Lebensraum** (German)   *Politics.* living space (for an expanding population); slogan of the Nazis.

**le bon genre.**   See **bon genre.**

**lechayim.**   See **l'chaim.**

**leche** (Spanish)   milk.

**leche frita** (Spanish)   (lit., 'fried milk')  *Cookery.* custard squares dipped in egg and bread crumbs and fried.

**lechón** (Spanish)   suckling pig.

**lectio difficilior.**   See **difficilior lectio potior.**

**le demi-monde.**   See **demi-monde.**

**Lederhosen** (German)   Alpine-style shorts made of leather and worn with suspenders.

**le dernier cri.**   See **dernier cri.**

**le dessous des cartes.**   See **dessous des cartes.**

**le droit des gens.**   See **droit des gens.**

**le fin mot.**   See **fin mot.**

**legabile.**   See **legato.**

**legalis homo** (Latin)   (lit., 'a lawful man')  *Law.* one having full legal rights.

**legando.**   See **legato.**

**legatissimo** (Italian)   *Music.* extremely smooth.

**legato** (Italian)   *Music.* smooth; performed so that the notes are smoothly connected. Also **legabile; legando.**

**legatura** (Italian)   (lit., 'bond, binding')  *Music.* a slur, indicated by a curved line above or below a group of notes to show that they are to be played smoothly.

**legatus a latere** (Latin)   (lit., 'a legate from the side (of the pope)')  *Roman Catholicism.* a special papal legate.

**leggero.**   See **leggiero.**

**leggieramente** (Italian)   *Music.* lightly.

**leggiero** (Italian)   *Music.* light. Also **leggero.**

**legibus solutus** (Latin)    not subject to obedience to the law, used of later Roman emperors and absolute monarchs.

**Légion d'Honneur** (French)    the Legion of Honor, a French order of distinction awarded to individuals who perform acts of exceptional civic or military merit.

**Le Grand Monarque** (French)    (lit., 'The Great Monarch') epithet used of French King Louis XIV of France (1643–1715).

**le grand monde.**    See **grand monde.**

**Le Grand Siècle** (French)    (lit., 'the great century') epithet used for the reign of Louis XIV of France (1643–1715), a high point in French culture.

**legua** (Spanish)  *Texas, Mexico, Phillipines.*    **1.** a measure of distance approximately equal to two-and-one-half miles.    **2.** a measure of area approximately equal to four-and-one-half acres.

**legumi** (Italian)    vegetables.

**le haut monde.**    See **grand monde.**

**Lehnwort** (German)    loanword.

**lei** (Hawaiian)    a floral wreath, usually worn around the neck.

**leitmotif** (German)    leading theme or motif in a musical composition or other work of art, often associated with a certain character, idea, or situation.    Also **leitmotiv.**

**le juste milieu** (French)    the golden mean; the happy medium.

**Le Métro** (French)    the Paris subway.

**le monde** (French)    the world; society in general.

**le monde savant** (French)    (lit., 'the learned world') the academic community.

**le mot juste.**    See **mot juste, le.**

**Le Moyen Âge.**    See **Moyen Âge, Le.**

**lene** (Italian)  *Music.* gentle.    Also **leno.**

**leno.**    See **lene.**

**lentamente** (Italian)  *Music.* slowly.

**lentando** (Italian)  *Music.* becoming slower.

**lentejas** (Spanish)    lentils.

**lenticchie** (Italian)    lentils.

**lentille** (French)    lentil.

**lento** (Italian)  *Music.* slow.

**lento assai** *or* **molto** (Italian)  *Music.* very slow.

**Leo** (Latin)    the Lion, a constellation and sign of the zodiac.

**Le Penseur** (French)    the Thinker (title of a famous sculpture by Rodin).

**le petit caporal** (French)    (lit., 'the little corporal') an epithet used of Napoleon Bonaparte.

**le petit monde.**    See **petit monde.**

**le premier pas** (French)    the first step.

**le premier venu,** *fem.* **la première venue** (French)    (lit., 'the first to come') the first person encountered on any occasion.

**le roi le veut** (French)    the king wills it (used to indicate royal assent).

**le roi s'avisera** (French)    the king will consider it (used to indicate royal consideration of an issue, especially preliminary to royal veto).

**Le Roi Soleil** (French)    the Sun King, an epithet for Louis XIV of France.

**le Salon.**    See **salon, 3.**

**les convenances.**    See **convenance.**

**lèse majesté, lèse-majesté** (French)    (lit., 'injured greatness') **1.** a crime against a sovereign power; treason. **2.** an attack against a sacred custom or institution. See also **laesa majestas.**

**les jeux sont faits** (French)    (lit., 'the plays are made') *Roulette.* an expression used by a **croupier** to alert players that wagers are placed and the wheel is about to be spun.

**l'esprit de suite** (French)    team spirit or mutual dedication to a cause.

**lessatura** (Italian)    poaching; boiling.

**les savants** (French)    the learned people; **literati.**

**les scènes à faire.**    See **scène à faire.**

**lesso** (Italian)    **1.** *n.* boiled meat. **2.** *adj.* boiled.

**lesto** (Italian)    *Music.* quick.

**le style, c'est l'homme** (French)    the style is the man himself, an apothegm of Buffon.

**Les Vingt.**    See **Société des Vingt.**

**l'état, c'est moi!** (French)    (lit., 'the state, it is I!') an expression attributed to Louis XIV of France indicating his view of absolute monarchy.

**le tout ensemble** (French)    the whole matter taken together.

**lettre de cachet** (French)    a sealed letter, especially a letter of a sovereign ordering the imprisonment of the bearer.

**lettre de change** (French)    a bill of exchange.

**lettre de créance** (French)    **1.** a letter of credit. **2.** *Diplomacy.* credentials.

**lettre de recréance** (French)    *Diplomacy.* a letter of recall, presented by a diplomat at departure from an assignment.

**levari facias** (Latin)    (lit., 'you may cause (it) to be levied') *Law.* a writ directing an officer to seize a debtor's property in order to satisfy the debt.

**leveche** (Spanish)    a warm southern wind or **sirocco** that blows onto the southeastern coast of Spain. Also **laveche.**

**lex,** *pl.* **leges** (Latin)    law.

**lex loci** (Latin)    (lit., 'the law of the place') local laws and customs.

**lex mercatoria** *or* **mercatorum** (Latin)    mercantile law.

**lex non scripta** (Latin)    the unwritten law; common law.

**lex scripta** (Latin)    written law; statute law.

**lex talionis** (Latin)    (lit., 'law of talion') the law of retaliation; "an eye for an eye."

**lex terrae** (Latin)    the law of the land.

**liberamente** (Italian)    *Music.* freely as to tempo and rhythm.

**libertà** (Italian)    *Music.* freedom as to tempo and rhythm. Also **licenza**.

**Libertador, El.**    See **El Libertador**.

**libertas** (Latin)    liberty; freedom.

**liberté, égalité, fraternité** (French)    (lit., 'liberty, equality, fraternity') the slogan of the French Revolution.

**libitum.**    See **ad libitum**.

**Libra** (Latin)    the Scales, a constellation and sign of the zodiac.

**librairie** (French)    a bookstore.

**libretto,** *pl.* **libretti** (Italian)    (lit., 'little book') *Music.* 1. the text or words of an opera or other musical composition.    2. a book containing this text.

**libris clausis** (Latin)    with closed books, said of an academic examination.

**licentia vatum** (Latin)    poetic license.

**licenza.**    See **libertà**.

**licet** (Latin)    (lit., 'it is allowed') *Law.* permissible; legal.

**lidia** (Spanish)    *Bullfighting.* a general term for the bullfight and its attendant ceremonies.

**lidiador de toros** (Spanish)    *Bullfighting.* a general term for a bullfighter.

**Liebchen** (German)    beloved; sweetheart.

**Liebfraumilch** (German)    a semisweet German white wine.

**Lied,** *pl.* **Lieder** (German)    song; poem; ballad.

**lièvre** (French)    hare.

**ligne** (French)    1. *Ballet.* the graceful and harmonious form taken by a dancer, creating a visually appealing effect. 2. a fine measurement used in watchmaking to gauge the thickness of a movement,  equal to 0.0888 inches or 2.2558 millimeters.

**lignum vitae** (Latin)    (lit., 'the wood of life') a type of tropical tree with extremely hard, heavy wood.

**limae labor** (Latin)    (lit., 'the work of the file') close, careful revision of a literary work (Horace, *Ars Poetica* 291).

**lingua Adamica** (Latin)    the language of Adam, the original language of mankind.

**lingua franca** (Italian)    1. a language used as a medium of communication between people who speak different native languages.    2. the Italian-Provençal jargon formerly used for communication in eastern Mediterranean ports.

**lingua volgare** (Italian)    the common language of Italy, as opposed to the regional dialects.

**linguica** (Portuguese)    a variety of spicy, smoked pork sausage.

**linguini** (Italian)    (lit., 'little tongues')  a variety of **pasta** made in long, very thin strips.

**liquet** (Latin)    it is clear.

**liqueur** (French)    a flavored, usually sweet, alcoholic liquor, commonly served after dinner; a cordial.

**liquoroso** (Italian)    a sweet wine that has been fortified with alcohol.

**lira,** *pl.* **lire** (Italian)    the basic unit of Italian currency.

**lis litem generat** (Latin)    1. litigation breeds litigation.  2. strife begets strife.

**lis pendens** (Latin)    *Law.*  a pending suit.

**lis sub judice** (Latin)    *Law.*  a suit awaiting the decision of the court.

**lit d'alcôve** (French)    *Antiques.*  a bed set in an alcove, popular in the 18th century.

**lit de justice** (French)    (lit., 'bed of justice') the cushioned seat on which the king of France sat when at sessions of parliament.

**lite pendente** (Latin)    *Law.*  while the suit is pending.

**literae humaniores** (Latin)    (lit., 'the more humane letters') the humanities, especially Latin, Greek, philosophy, logic, ethics, etc.

**literati** (Latin)    the class of well-educated and widely read people.

**literatim** (Latin)    literally.

**Litterarum Doctor** (Latin)    the honorary academic degree of Doctor of Letters. Abbr. **Litt. D.**

**littérateur,** *fem.* **littératrice** (French)    1. an author of a literary work.  2. a person with literary interests.

**liutaio** (Italian)    *Music.*  a maker of stringed instruments.

**livre** (French)    a former French unit of currency that was discontinued in the late 18th century.

**livre à clef.**    See **roman à clef.**

**livre d'heures** (French)    a book of hours; a richly decorated medieval book containing prayers for the canonical hours, used in monasteries and convents.

**Lladró** (Spanish)    *Applied Arts.*  a type of porcelain figurine created by the contemporary Spanish ceramist of the same name.

**llanero,** *fem.* **llanera** (Spanish)    a resident of the **llanos** of South America.

**llanos** (Spanish)    an extensive area of flat, grassy plains in South America, especially in Argentina.

**lobo** (Spanish)    a wolf.

**loch** (Scots Gaelic)    a lake.

**loco** (Italian)   (lit., 'place') _Music._ an indication for a return to the normal pitch after going an octave higher or lower. Also **luogo.**

**loco,** _fem._ **loca** (Spanish)   crazy.

**loco citato** (Latin)   in the place (already) cited. Also **in loco citato.** _Abbr._ **loc. cit.**

**loco parentis.**   See **in loco parentis.**

**locum tenens** (Latin)   (lit., 'holding the place') one who temporarily performs the duties of another (used especially of a physician or clergyman).

**locus,** _pl._ **loci** (Latin)   1. a place.   2. a passage, as in writing.

**locus classicus** (Latin)   (lit., 'the classic source') a passage cited frequently to illustrate a particular idea.

**locus communis** (Latin)   a commonplace; a passage commonly cited in a particular context.

**locus criminis** (Latin)   the scene of the crime.

**locus delicti** (Latin)   the scene of the crime.

**locus in quo** (Latin)   (lit., 'the place in which') the particular place where something under discussion may be found or was done.

**locus poenitentiae** (Latin)   (lit., 'a place for repentance') _Law._ an opportunity to withdraw consent before being contractually obligated.

**locus sigilli** (Latin)   (lit., 'the place of the seal') _Law._ the place on a document for a signature or personal seal. _Abbr._ **L.S.**

**locus standi** (Latin)   (lit., 'a place to stand') 1. _Law._ the right to appear in court.   2. a recognized attitude with regard to participation in some activity.

**loggia** (Italian)   1. a colonnaded gallery or passage projecting from a building.   2. paintings used to decorate such a structure.

**logion,** _pl._ **logia** (Greek)   1. a saying or maxim of a religious teacher, especially one attributed to Jesus but not found in the Gospels.   2. (_pl._) a collection of sayings attributed to Jesus.

**logos** (Greek)   (lit., 'word; account; reason') 1. _Christianity._ (_cap._) the divine Word, incarnated in Christ.   2. _Philosophy._ the rational principle governing the universe.

**loi de guerre** (French)   the law of war.

**loisir, à.**   See **à loisir.**

**loma** (Spanish)   a broad-topped ridge or hill.

**lomita** (Spanish)   a small **loma.**

**lomo de cerdo** (Spanish)   pork loin.

**lomo fino** (Spanish)   the tenderloin of beef.

**longueur** (French)   _Literature._ a long and boring passage.

**lonja** (Spanish)   1. _Architecture._ a slightly raised atrium or portico.   2. a market; commodity exchange.

**loquitur** (Latin)  *Drama.* (he *or* she) speaks, used in stage directions along with the name of a character. *Abbr.* **loq.**

**louis d'or** (French)  a former gold coin of France; pistole.

**Louis Quatorze** (French)  (lit., 'Louis the Fourteenth') designating the style of architecture and furnishings characteristic of France in the late 17th century, noted for its classical elements.

**Louis Quinze** (French)  (lit., 'Louis the Fifteenth') designating the rococo style of architecture and furnishings characteristic of France in the early and mid-18th century.

**Louis Seize** (French)  (lit., 'Louis the Sixteenth') designating the style of architecture and furnishings characteristic of France in the late 18th century, with a re-emphasis on classical models.

**Louis Treize** (French)  (lit., 'Louis the Thirteenth') designating the style of architecture and furnishings characteristic of France in the early 17th century, a transition period from Renaissance designs to the **Louis Quatorze** period.

**loukoum** (Turkish)  fig paste, used in making sweets.

**loup-garou** (French)  a werewolf.

**lox** (Yiddish)  smoked salmon, often eaten on a bagel with cream cheese.

**luau** (Hawaiian)  a traditional Hawaiian feast with food and entertainment.

**luce di sotto** (Italian)  *Fine Arts.* light coming from below, a device used in painting to create a dramatic effect.

**lucri causa** (Latin)  for the sake of material gain.

**lucus a non lucendo** (Latin)  (lit., 'a grove, from not giving light') an absurd etymology or explanation (the Latin phrase is a classic false etymology adopted from Quintilian).

**lues venerea** (Latin)  venereal disease; syphilis.

**Luftwaffe** (German)  the German air force.

**lumache** (Italian)  snails.

**lumachine** (Italian)  (lit., 'little snails') a small, snail-shaped pasta.

**lumen fidei** (Latin)  (lit., 'the light of faith') divine revelation.

**Lumpenproletariat** (German)  *Marxism.* the social class below the proletariat, consisting of people indifferent to the cause of revolution.

**luogo.**  See **loco.**

**lupara** (Italian)  a large, heavy shotgun, frequently used in Sicily.

**lupus in fabula** (Latin)  (lit., 'the wolf in the story') one who appears just when he has been mentioned, equivalent to *speak of the devil* . . . .

**l'usage du monde** (French)  the way of the world.

**lusingando** (Italian)  (lit., 'flattering') *Music.* a direction to play in a coaxing, personal way.

**lustrum** (Latin)   **1.** *Ancient Rome.* a ritual purification, performed by the censors every five years.   **2.** a period of five years.

**lusus naturae** (Latin)   a freak of nature.

**luttuosamente** (Italian)   *Music.* mournfully; sadly.

**luttuoso** (Italian)   *Music.* mournful; sorrowful.

**lux et veritas** (Latin)   light and truth (motto of Yale University).

**lux in tenebris** (Latin)   light in the darkness.

**lycée** (French)   a state-operated French secondary school.

**lyonnais,** *fem.* **lyonnaise** (French)   (lit., 'of Lyon')   *Cookery.* prepared with onions.

# M

**ma belle** (French)  my beautiful one (a term of endearment).

**macchia** (Italian)  *Fine Arts.* a sketch giving the bare outline of a scene; the underpainting of a completed work.

**macédoine** (French)  *Cookery.* a mixture of fruit or vegetables served as a salad.

**macellaio** (Italian)  a butcher.

**ma chère,** *fem.* **ma chérie** (French)  my dear; my darling (a term of endearment used of a woman). See also **mon cher.**

**machete** (Spanish)  a long knife with a broad blade, designed for cutting sugar cane or vegetation, also used as a weapon.

**machismo** (Spanish)  strong masculine characteristics or image; virility.

**macho** (Spanish)  (lit., 'male') characterized by overt masculine characteristics.

**Machtpolitik** (German)  power politics.

**Mâcon** (French)  a variety of wine from southern Burgundy.

**macte animo** (Latin)  (lit., 'be increased in spirit') courage!

**macte virtute** (Latin)  (lit., 'be increased in virtue') well done! bravo!

**macushla.**  See **acushla.**

**Mädchen** (German)  a girl.

**madeleine** (French)  *Cookery.* a small, rich cake that is baked in a special mold.

**mademoiselle** (French)  a formal mode of address used for a young girl or unmarried woman.

**Madonna** (Italian)  My Lady, referring to the Virgin Mary.

**madre** (Italian, Spanish)  mother.

**madrileña** (Spanish)  1. from Madrid.  2. a type of Spanish dance.

**madrilène** (French)  *Cookery.* a cold soup flavored with tomato.

**madrina** (Spanish)  godmother.

**madroño** (Spanish)  a variety of small evergreen with edible berries. Also **madroña, manzanita.**

175

**maduro** (Spanish)    (lit., 'mature; ripe') a very dark brown cigar.

**maestà** (Italian)    *Music.* majesty; dignity. Also **maestade.**

**maestade.**    See **maestà.**

**maestosamente** (Italian)    *Music.* with majesty; with dignity.

**maestoso** (Italian)    *Music.* majestic.

**maestro,** *pl.* **maestri** (Italian)    (lit., 'master') 1. *Music.* a conductor; eminent composer.    2. an individual accomplished in a particular field of activity who is regarded as a model for others.

**maestro di cappella** (Italian)    *Music.* the conductor of a church choir or orchestra.

**Mafia** (Italian)    a secret criminal society that originated in Sicily and is linked to a wide-ranging network of organized crime. Also **Maffia.** See also **capo; capo di tutti capi; Cosa Nostra; consigliere; don; mafioso; omertà.**

**mafioso,** *pl.* **mafiosi** (Italian)    (*often cap.*) a member of the **Mafia.**

**Magen David.**    See **Mogen David.**

**maggiore** (Italian)    *Music.* major, referring to a key.

**Magi.**    See **magus.**

**magister** (Latin)    master; learned teacher.

**Magister Artium** (Latin)    the academic degree of Master of Arts. *Abbr.* **M.A.**

**magister bibendi** (Latin)    a toastmaster; master of the revels. Also **arbiter bibendi; rex bibendi.**

**magister dixit** (Latin)    the master said (so), used by medieval scholastics in referring to an idea from Aristotle.

**magisterium** (Latin)    *Roman Catholicism.* the authority to teach that resides with the Church hierarchy.

**Magister Ludi** (Latin)    the master of the game (title of a novel by Herman Hesse).

**Magna C(h)arta** (Latin)    1. *English history.* the Great Charter, the bill of liberties signed by King John at Runnymede in 1215.    2. any document stating basic rights.

**magna cum laude** (Latin)    with great honor (the second level of distinction on academic degrees). See also **cum laude; maxima cum laude; summa cum laude.**

**Magnificat** (Latin)    first word and title of a Christian prayer, taken from the words of Mary to Elizabeth in the Vulgate Bible (Luke 1:46–55).

**magnífico** (Spanish)    magnificent; wonderful.

**magnifico** (Italian)    1. *adj.* magnificent. 2. *n.* a great man.

**Magnifico, il.**    See **il Magnifico.**

**magnifique** (French)    magnificent; wonderful.

**magnum bonum** (Latin)   a great good.

**magnum in parvo** (Latin)   a great deal in a small space. See also **multum in parvo.**

**magnum opus** (Latin)   (lit., 'a great work') a masterpiece.

**magro, di.**   See **di magro.**

**maguey** (Spanish)   a plant common to the southwestern U.S., Mexico, and Central America, used in the manufacture of rope as well as of **tequila** and **pulque.**

**magus,** *pl.* **magi** (Latin)   **1.** wizard; sorcerer.   **2.** (*cap.*) *Christianity.* one of the Magi, the Three Wise Men who came to visit the infant Jesus.

**maharaja** (Hindi)   a ruling prince of an Indian state. Also **maharajah.**

**maharani** (Hindi)   **1.** the wife of a **maharaja. 2.** a ruling princess of an Indian state. Also **maharanee.**

**maharishi** (Hindi)   a Hindu sage or spiritual teacher.

**mahatma** (Sanskrit)   a person held in high esteem for his wisdom.

**Mahdi** (Arabic)   *Islam.* the Muslim messiah, expected to establish a spiritual and temporal reign of righteousness.

**mahjong** (Chinese)   a game of Chinese origin played with small dominolike tiles. Also **mah-jongg.**

**mahout** (Hindi)   an elephant driver.

**maiale** (Italian)   pork.

**Maigelein** (German)   *Antiques.* a type of German drinking glass.

**maigre** (French)   designating food allowed by the rules of religious abstinence, generally non-meat items. See also **jour maigre; repas maigre.**

**maillot** (French)   *Ballet.* dancer's tights.

**maillot jaune** (French)   the yellow jersey worn by the leader of the Tour de France bicycle race.

**main armée, à.**   See **à main armée.**

**maiolica** (Italian)   *Antiques.* earthenware covered with a tin-enamel glaze and painted in bright colors, made in Italy from the 15th through the 18th centuries. See also **istoriato.**

**maison, à la.**   See **à la maison.**

**maison de jeu** (French)   casino; gambling house.

**Maison de Molière, La** (French)   epithet for the **Comédie Française.**

**maison de santé** (French)   (lit., 'house of health') a private sanitarium.

**maison de société** (French)   a house of prostitution.

**maison meublée** (French)   a furnished house.

**maître chef** (French)   a master cook; head chef.

**maître d'.**   See **maître d'hôtel.**

**maître de ballet,** *fem.* **maîtresse de ballet** (French)   *Ballet.* the master or mistress of the company, responsible for training the dancers.

**maître de danse** (French)    dance master.

**maître d'hôtel** (French)    (lit., 'master of (the) hotel') **1.** (*usually shortened to* **maître d'**) the host at a restaurant, who greets diners and takes them to their tables. **2.** the owner or manager of a hotel.

**maître d'hôtel, à la.**    See **à la maître d'hôtel.**

**maître fromager** (French)    a master cheese maker.

**maíz** (Spanish)    dried corn.

**majolica** (Italian)    *Antiques.* pottery with relief decorations beneath a colored glaze, produced in 19th-century England.

**majordomo.**    See **mayordomo.**

**makimono** (Japanese)    a scroll containing text or a painting, unrolled vertically in the hands.

**makiwara** (Japanese)    a punching post used in practicing **karate.**

**mal** *or* **maladie du siècle** (French)    (lit., 'sickness of the age') a term for the period of moral decadence that followed the fall of Napoleon Bonaparte.

**maladie d'amour** (French)    lovesickness.

**maladie du pays** (French)    homesickness; emotional depression caused by separation from one's native country. Also called **mal de pays.**

**mala fide** (Latin)    in bad faith; dishonestly.

**mala fides** (Latin)    bad faith; intent to deceive.

**malagueña** (Spanish)    **1.** from Malaga in southern Spain.    **2.** a Spanish dance in 3/4 time, similar to the **fandango.**

**malahini** (Hawaiian)    a newcomer to Hawaii.

**mal de mer** (French)    seasickness.

**mal de pays.**    See **maladie du pays.**

**malentendu** (French)    (lit., 'misunderstood') a misunderstanding.

**malgré lui** (French)    in spite of himself.

**malgré moi** (French)    in spite of myself.

**malgré nous** (French)    in spite of ourselves.

**malgré soi** (French)    in spite of oneself.

**malgré tout** (French)    in spite of everything.

**mali exempli** (Latin)    of bad example.

**malo animo** (Latin)    with evil intent.

**malocchio** (Italian)    the evil eye.

**malpais, malpaís** (Spanish)    (lit., 'bad country') a desert area, usually one covered with volcanic detritus.

**malum in se,** *pl.* **mala in se** (Latin)    something evil in itself or by its very essence.

**malum prohibitum** (Latin)    (lit., 'a prohibited wrong') *Law.* an act prohibited by law but not necessarily wrong or immoral.

**mal vu** (French)   (lit., 'seen badly') viewed with disapproval.

**mama-loshen** (Yiddish)   (lit., 'mother tongue') the Yiddish language.

**mamma mia** (Italian)   an expression of surprise or wonder, equivalent to *my goodness!*

**mamzer.**   See **momzer.**

**mana** (Polynesian)   *Anthropology.* a supernatural power that is thought to be concentrated in people or things.

**manada** (Spanish)   a flock; herd.

**mañana** (Spanish)   1. tomorrow.   2. morning.

**mancando** (Italian)   *Music.* dying away. Also **mancante.**

**mancante.**   See **mancando.**

**manchega** (Spanish)   1. designating something from La Mancha in Central Spain.   2. a dance from this region, similar to the **seguidilla.**

**Manche, la.**   See **la Manche.**

**mancia** (Italian)   money given in thanks for service; a tip.

**mandala** (Sanskrit)   *Oriental Art.* a schematic depiction of the universe and its deities.

**mandamus** (Latin)   (lit., 'we order') *Law.* a writ requiring the performance of a specified action.

**mandorla** (Italian)   (lit., 'almond') *Fine Arts.* an almond-shaped or pointed oval design often found around depictions of Christ and the saints in early Christian art.

**mane** (Latin)   *Prescriptions.* in the morning. *Abbr.* m.

**manège** (French)   the art of training and riding horses.

**manet** (Latin)   *Drama.* (he or she) remains (used in stage directions along with the name of the character).

**mangana** (Spanish)   a loop thrown to catch an animal by its forelegs.

**mangia** (Italian)   eat!

**mangiamo** (Italian)   let's eat!

**mangiapreti** (Italian)   one who is opposed to the policies of the Vatican.

**mangiare** (Italian)   to eat.

**manica.**   See **posizione.**

**manicotti** (Italian)   (lit., 'little muffs') *Cookery.* a dish made of large rectangles of **pasta** that are stuffed and baked.

**manieroso** (Italian)   *Fine Arts.* a designation for a work that gives evidence of inspiration. See also **diligente.**

**mano** (Spanish)   hand.

**mano a mano** (Spanish)   1. hand-to-hand.   2. *Bullfighting.* a duel in the ring between rival bullfighters to determine who can kill the first three bulls more quickly.

**mano destra** (Italian)   *Music.* the right hand. *Abbr.* m.d.

**manque** (French)    *Roulette.* a term for the numbers 1 to 18.

**manqué** (French)    (lit., 'lacking') failed or unsuccessful, usually in reference to an artist.

**man spricht deutsch** (German)    German is spoken here.   Also, **hier wird deutsch gesprochen.**

**manteca** (Spanish)   lard.

**mantequilla** (Spanish)   butter.

**mantilla** (Spanish)   a woman's lace shawl worn over the hair and reaching to the shoulders.

**mantra** (Sanskrit)    *Hinduism; Buddhism.* a word or phrase to be repeated during meditation.   See also **Om.**

**manu forti** (Latin)    (lit., 'with a strong hand') by force.

**manu propria** (Latin)    (done) by one's own hand.

**manzanilla** (Spanish)    a dry, pale sherry.

**manzanita.**    See **madroño.**

**manzo** (Italian)   beef.

**mao tai** (Chinese)    a type of Chinese brandy.

**maquereau** (French)    a mackerel.

**maquiladoras** (Spanish)    Mexican factories that process materials from the U.S. and send them back as finished products.

**maraca** (Spanish)    a dried gourd containing seeds or pebbles, used as a rhythm instrument.

**marasca** (Italian)    a wild cherry, used in making **maraschino.**

**maraschino** (Italian)    **1.** *n.* a strong, sweet **liqueur** distilled from **marasca** cherries.   **2.** a designation for cherries preserved in sweet syrup, used in drinks and desserts.

**marc** (French)    a brandy distilled from fermented grape pressings.

**marcato** (Italian)    *Music.* with each note emphasized.

**marchand de vin** (French)    (lit., 'wine merchant') *Cookery.* a brown sauce of butter and red wine.

**marché aux fleurs** (French)    a flower market.

**marché aux puces** (French)    a flea market.

**märchen** (German)    folklore; fairy tales.

**marchese** (Italian)    a marquis.

**marcia funebre** (Italian)    *Music.* a funeral march.

**Mardi Gras** (French)    (lit., 'Fat Tuesday') a festive holiday celebrated on the day before Ash Wednesday (the beginning of Lent), notably in New Orleans and Rio de Janeiro.

**mare clausum** (Latin)    (lit., 'a closed sea') *International Law.* waters within the jurisdiction of a particular country.

**mare liberum** (Latin) (lit., 'a free sea') *International Law.* waters not controlled by a particular country, hence open to all.

**marengo, à la.** See **à la marengo.**

**mare nostrum** (Latin) (lit., 'our sea') Roman term for the Mediterranean.

**marginalia** (Latin) marginal notes.

**mariachi** (Spanish) 1. a roving street musician of Mexico. 2. a popular song sung by a mariachi musician. Also spelled **mariache.**

**mariage de conscience** (French) (lit., 'marriage of conscience') a marriage ceremony performed to affirm the legality of a possibly invalid marital bond.

**mariage de convenance** (French) (lit., 'marriage of convenience') a marriage arranged solely to gain some advantage, as wealth or power.

**mariage de la main gauche** (French) (lit., 'marriage of the left hand') a morganatic marriage.

**mariage de politique** (French) a marriage arranged for political reasons.

**mariage d'inclination** (French) a marriage in which the partners are ideally suited; a love match.

**marimba** (Spanish) a musical instrument popular in Central and South America with an array of resonant wooden bars that are played with mallets.

**marinara.** See **alla marinara.**

**mariné,** *fem.* **marinée** (French) *Cookery.* marinated; pickled.

**mariscos** (Spanish) shellfish; seafood.

**marrano** (Spanish) a pejorative name given to Spanish and Portuguese Jews of the late Middle Ages who had converted to Christianity but still practiced their Jewish faith.

**marron glacé** (French) a candied chestnut.

**Marsala** (Italian) 1. a dark-brown, sweet-tasting, fortified wine used in sauces and as a dessert wine. See also **mosto cotto.** 2. *Cookery.* Also **al Marsala.** a designation for a dish made with this wine.

**Marsala all'uovo.** See **zabaglione.**

**Marseillaise** (French) the French national anthem.

**martellato** (Italian) (lit., 'hammered') *Music.* designating a note played strongly and decisively on a bowed instrument.

**marziale** (Italian) *Music.* in a martial style.

**mas** (French) a large Provençal farmhouse.

**masa** (Spanish) 1. *Cookery.* dough; batter. 2. mortar.

**mascarpone** (Italian) a soft, smooth cheese made with fresh cream, used in the preparation of desserts.

**mascherone** (Italian) 1. *Architecture.* a grotesque sculptured head or face, used as a decorative ornament. 2. a painted or carved mask.

**masjid** (Arabic)    *Islam.* a mosque. Also **musjid.**

**massé** (French)    (lit., 'hammered') *Billiards.* a shot made with the cue stick held in a nearly vertical position.

**massé** (French)    (lit., 'hammered') *Billiards.* a shot made with the cue stick held almost vertically.

**masseur,** *fem.* **masseuse** (French)    a person skilled in administering body massage.

**massimo,** *fem.* **massima** (Italian)    *Music.* greatest; utmost.

**matador** (Spanish)    *Bullfighting.* the principal bullfighter.

**matelassé** (French)    an embossed or quilted fabric woven on a loom.

**matelote** (French)    *Cookery.* a fish stew made with wine.

**mate, maté** (Spanish)    a beverage popular in the **pampas** and the Río de la Plata region of Argentina, made from the leaves of a type of holly bush, yerba mate.

**mater** (Latin)    mother.

**Mater Dolorosa** (Latin)    (lit., 'grieving mother') *Fine Arts.* a representation of the Virgin Mary in sorrow for the death of Jesus.

**materfamilias** (Latin)    matriarch of a family or household.

**materia medica** (Latin)    (lit., 'medicinal materials') the class of medicinal drugs prescribed by physicians and the study of them.

**matière** (French)    *Fine Arts.* the physical elements of a painting, as canvas, paint, brushes, etc.

**mattinata** (Italian)    *Music.* a morning song.

**matzo** (Yiddish)    *Judaism.* unleavened bread baked in thin, flat pieces, used especially at Passover. Also **matzoh; matzah.**

**mauresco.**    See **morisco.**

**mauvaise honte** (French)    false shame.

**mauvais goût** (French)    bad taste, especially in regard to aesthetic matters.

**mauvais sujet** (French)    a rogue; bad character; black sheep.

**mavin** (Yiddish)    an expert; knowledgeable person. Also **maven.**

**maxima cum laude** (Latin)    with greatest honor, a high level of academic distinction. See also **cum laude; magna cum laude; summa cum laude.**

**maya** (Sanskrit)    *Hinduism.* the illusory world experienced by the senses, masking the world of reality.

**mayordomo** (Spanish)    a foreman; overseer of a large ranch or **hacienda.**

**mazel tov** (Hebrew)    (lit., 'good luck') *Judaism.* best wishes; congratulations.

**mazuelo** (Spanish)    a variety of grape, high in tannin, that contributes to the acidity of wine.

**mazuma** (Yiddish)    money.

**mazzocchio** (Italian)    a supporting structure for ornamental headdresses, used in Florence in the 15th century.

**mea culpa** (Latin)    through my fault; the error is mine. See also **mea maxima culpa.**

**mea maxima culpa** (Latin)    through my own very great fault; the error is mine (taken from the **Confiteor,** a Latin prayer of repentance).

**medaglia d'oro** (Italian)    a gold medal.

**mēden agan** (Greek)    nothing to excess; observe the golden mean.

**medesimo tempo** (Italian)    *Music.* at the same tempo.

**Medicinae Doctor** (Latin)    the academic degree of Doctor of Medicine. *Abbr.* **M.D.**

**Médoc** (French)    a district in the **Bordeaux** wine region of France. See also **Haut-Médoc.**

**Meerschaum** (German)    a white, claylike mineral from which pipe bowls are carved.

**megillah** (Hebrew)    (lit., 'scroll,' referring to a book of Scripture, especially Esther) a long, complicated story.

**mein Gott** (German)    my God!

**mein Herr** (German)    a formal mode of address, equivalent to *Sir.*

**Meistersinger** (German)    member of a medieval guild established for the cultivation of music and poetry.

**me iudice** *or* **judice** (Latin)    (lit., 'with me as judge') in my opinion.

**melamed** (Hebrew)    a teacher in a Jewish school, especially one who teaches elementary Hebrew.

**mélange** (French)    2. a mixture; medley. 2. a confused mixture.

**melanzana** (Italian)    eggplant.

**melisma,** *pl.* **melismata** (Greek)    *Music.* a single syllable sung or chanted over several notes.

**melone** (Italian)    a melon.

**membretto** (Italian)    *Architecture.* a minor wing of a building.

**membrum virile** (Latin)    the male member; penis.

**memento mori** (Latin)    (lit., 'remember (that you must) die') an object (such as a skull) serving as a reminder of the inevitability of death.

**memoriter** (Latin)    known by heart; recalled from memory.

**memsahib** (Hindi)    an Indian term of respect for a European woman.

**ménage** (French)    1. a household. 2. household management; housekeeping.

**ménage à trois** (French)    a domestic arrangement of three people living together, as a married couple and a lover of the husband or wife.

**mench.**    See **mensh.**

**Mendoza** (Spanish)    a large wine- and fruit-producing city in Argentina.

**meninas** (Spanish)    1. handmaidens (of a queen).    2. (*cap.*) title of a painting by Velásquez.

**meno mosso** (Italian)    *Music.* less quick.

**menorah** (Hebrew)    *Judaism.* the nine-branched candelabrum used during the celebration of Hanukkah.

**mensa et t(h)oro.**    See **separatio mensa et t(h)oro.**

**Mensch** (German)    man; human being.

**mensh** (Yiddish)    (lit., 'human being') a decent, honorable person. Also **mench.**

**mens legis** (Latin)    the spirit or intention of the law.

**mens rea** (Latin)    (lit., 'a guilty mind') *Law.* criminal intent.

**mens sana in corpore sano** (Latin)    a sound mind in a sound body (Juvenal, *Satires* 10.356).

**menthe** (French)    mint. See also **crème de menthe.**

**Mentrida** (Spanish)    a wine district near Toledo in central Spain.

**menu** (French)    *Cookery.* a list of the dishes and wines to be served as courses in a formal meal.

**menu gibier** (French)    small game.

**meo periculo** (Latin)    at my own risk.

**meo voto** (Latin)    by my wish.

**mercado** (Spanish)    a market; marketplace.

**merci** (French)    thanks.

**merci beaucoup** (French)    thanks very much.

**merienda** (Spanish)    an afternoon snack, necessitated by the late dinner hour of Spain and South America.

**merum sal** (Latin)    (lit., 'pure salt') Attic wit; incisive wit. See also **sal Atticum.**

**merveille, à.**    See **à merveille.**

**merveilleux,** *fem.* **merveilleuse** (French)    marvelous; miraculous.

**mesa** (Spanish)    (lit., 'table') a plateau; tableland.

**mescal.**    See **mezcal.**

**meshuga** (Yiddish)    *Slang.* crazy. Also **meshugga; meshug(g)e.**

**meshugana** (Yiddish)    *Slang.* a crazy person. Also **meshuggana; meshug-(g)ene(h).**

**mesilla** (Spanish)    *Southwestern U.S.* a small **mesa.**

**mesón** (Spanish)    a roadhouse; inn.

**mesquite** (Spanish)    a bush native to Mexico and the southwestern U.S. which bears pods that are used as fodder, and whose wood is used for cooking. Also **mesquit; musqueto; musquit; musquito.**

**messa di voce** (Italian)  (lit., 'placing of the voice') *Music.* a singing technique in which a note is held and gradually increased and decreased in loudness.

**mestizo,** *fem.* **mestiza** (Spanish)  a person of racially mixed parentage, usually part American Indian.

**mesto** (Italian)  *Music.* mournful; sad.

**metate** (Spanish)  *Mexico and Southwestern U.S.* a sort of stone mortar used to grind corn. Also **matet, matete.**

**méthode champenoise** (French)  the technique of fermenting champagne in the bottle.

**métier** (French)  1. a person's trade or profession. 2. an area in which a person has special ability or training. 3. *Fine Arts.* an artist's special subject interest.

**métis,** *fem.* **métisse** (French)  1. a person of mixed ancestry. 2. *French Canada.* a person whose parentage is half-white and half-Indian.

**Métro, Le.**  See **Le Métro.**

**metteur en scène** (French)  *Theater.* a director or manager of a production.

**meubles** (French)  furniture.

**meubles d'occasion** (French)  second-hand furniture.

**meum et tuum** (Latin)  mine and yours.

**mezcal** (Spanish)  an alcoholic beverage distilled from the juice of certain types of agave. Also **mescal, muscal.**

**mezuzah** (Hebrew)  *Judaism.* a small case attached to the doorpost at the entrance to a Jewish home, containing a small scroll with several verses of Scripture on it. Also **mezuza; mezzuza.**

**mezzadria** (Italian)  an Italian feudal system in which a landowner provided housing and land for peasants who farmed the land and divided half of their produce with him.

**mezza maiolica** (Italian)  (lit., 'half-maiolica') *Antiques.* lead-glazed earthenware imitative of **maiolica** and decorated with **sgraffito.**

**mezza voce** (Italian)  *Music.* using half the power of the voice. Also a **mezza di voce; mezza-voce.**

**mezzo carattere, aria di.**  See **aria di mezzo carattere.**

**mezzo forte** (Italian)  *Music.* moderately loud. Also **mezzo-forte.** *Abbr.* **mf.**

**mezzogiorno** (Italian)  (lit., 'noon') a term used of the southern part of Italy.

**mezzo mezzo** (Italian)  so-so; neither good nor bad.

**mezzo piano** (Italian)  *Music.* moderately soft. Also **mezzo-piano.** *Abbr.* **mp.**

**mezzo rilievo** (Italian)    *Fine Arts.* relief sculpture in which the figures are cut so as to project moderately from the background. Also **mezzo relievo; mezzo-rilievo.** See also **alto rilievo; basso rilievo.**

**mezzo soprano** (Italian)    *Music.* 1. a voice in between **soprano** and contralto.    2. a woman having such a voice.

**mezzotermine** (Italian)    a middle course; a compromise.

**midrash** (Hebrew)    *Judaism.* a commentary on biblical text.

**mignard** (French)    affected; mannered; dainty.

**mignardise** (French)    affectation or ornateness of style or manners.

**Migra, la** (Spanish)    the nickname for the U.S. Immigration Service stationed along the Mexican-U.S. border.

**mikado** (Japanese)    a title of the emperor of Japan, especially in the feudal era of Japanese history.

**mikvah** (Hebrew)    *Judaism.* a bath or bathhouse for ritual cleansing. Also **mikva; mikveh.**

**milanese, alla.**    See **alla milanese.**

**miles gloriosus** (Latin)    the braggart soldier, a stock comic character (from a comedy by Plautus).

**milieu** (French)    1. environment; surroundings.    2. intellectual or artistic atmosphere.

**milieu, au.**    See **au milieu.**

**militaire, à la.**    See **à la militaire.**

**millefiori** (Italian)    (lit., 'a thousand flowers') *Antiques.* ornamental glass mosaic first produced in Roman times and revived by 16th century Venetian glassmakers. See also **millefleurs.**

**millefleur** (French)    (lit., 'a thousand flowers') 1. *Design.* designating a background depicting many flowers.    2. **millefleurs.** a perfume whose fragrance is based on many different kinds of flowers.

**millier** (French)    a metric ton; 1000 kilograms. Also **tonneau.**

**milpa** (Spanish)    a small cornfield; cultivated plot of land.

**minaccevolmente** (Italian)    *Music.* threateningly. Also **minacciando.**

**minacciando.**    See **minaccevolmente.**

**minchia** (Italian)    a vulgar expression of strong surprise or disgust, roughly equivalent to *damn.*

**minestra** (Italian)    soup.

**minestrina** (Italian)    a thin, clear broth.

**minestrone** (Italian)    *Cookery.* a hearty soup containing pieces of vegetables, usually with noodles, rice, or barley added.

**Minnesinger** (German)    a medieval knightly lyric poet.

**minutiae** (Latin)    trivial details; trifles.

**minyan** (Hebrew) *Judaism.* the minimum number required to conduct a Jewish service, being ten adult males.

**mirabile dictu** (Latin) wonderful to relate.

**mirabile visu** (Latin) wonderful to behold.

**mirabilia** (Latin) wonders; astonishing things.

**miroton** (French) *Cookery.* a type of meat stew flavored with onions.

**mise en scène** (French) 1. *Theater.* the aspects that make up the staging of a play or scene. 2. the setting of a play or story. 3. the surroundings or setting of an event.

**miserabile dictu** (Latin) sad to tell.

**miserabile vulgus** (Latin) the wretched crowd; the rabble.

**miserere** (Latin) (lit., 'have pity') 1. (*cap.*) first word and title given to the 51st Psalm (50th in Douay Bible). 2. a prayer or appeal for mercy.

**miserere nobis** (Latin) have pity on us.

**misericordia** (Latin) mercy.

**Mishnah** (Hebrew) *Judaism.* the earlier of the two parts of the **Talmud,** containing the codified oral laws. See also **Gemara.**

**Missa** (Latin) *Roman Catholicism.* the Mass.

**Missa bassa** (Latin) *Roman Catholicism.* low Mass, in which the celebrant is not assisted during the ceremony. See also **Missa solemnis.**

**Missa cantata** (Latin) *Roman Catholicism.* sung Mass.

**Missa catechumenorum** (Latin) *Roman Catholicism.* the Mass of the Catechumens, the early part of the liturgy to the Offertory.

**Missa fidelium** (Latin) *Roman Catholicism.* the Mass of the Faithful, the latter part of the liturgy including the Communion.

**Missa solemnis** (Latin) (lit., 'solemn Mass') *Roman Catholicism.* high Mass, in which the celebrant is assisted during the ceremony, as on certain holy days and special occasions. See also **Missa bassa.**

**misterioso** (Italian) *Music.* mysterious.

**misura** (Italian) *Music.* the length of duration of sound.

**misurato** (Italian) *Music.* measured; in strict time.

**Mittagessen** (German) lunch. Also **Mittagsessen.**

**Mitteleuropa** (German) *Politics.* central Europe.

**mittimus** (Latin) (lit., 'we send') *Law.* 1. an order for an officer to convey a person to prison and for the jailer to receive him. 2. transcript of the minutes of a conviction and sentence.

**mitzvah,** *pl.* **mitzvoth** (Hebrew) *Judaism.* 1. one of the 613 commandments in or derived from Scripture. 2. a meritorious deed conforming to the spirit of one of these commandments. Also **mitzva.**

**mobile perpetuum.** See **perpetuum mobile.**

**mobile vulgus** (Latin)    the fickle crowd (English *mob* is a shortening of this phrase).

**mochila** (Spanish)    1. a mailpouch.    2. a knapsack.

**mocho** (Spanish)    short; squat; sawed-off.

**mode, à la.**    See **à la mode.**

**modello** (Italian)    *Fine Arts.* a small sketch or drawing of a work that will later be done on a larger scale.

**mode nouvelle** (French)    a new fashion or style.

**moderado** (Spanish)    1. moderate.    2. soft-spoken.

**moderato** (Italian)    *Music.* moderate in regard to speed. *Abbr.* **mod.**

**moderato cantabile** (Italian)    *Music.* with the melody moderately smooth or flowing.

**modernismo** (Spanish)    *Literature.* a movement of the late 19th century originating in South America, characterized by unusual imagery and verse forms.

**mode stricte** (French)    a conservative fashion or style.

**modiste** (French)    a dressmaker or milliner.

**modus loquendi** (Latin)    manner of speaking; style of speech or rhetoric.

**modus operandi** (Latin)    method of doing things; procedure. *Abbr.* **m.o.**

**modus vivendi** (Latin)    (lit., 'manner of living') a temporary arrangement for working or getting along pending settlement of differences.

**moelle de boeuf** (French)    beef marrow.

**moeurs** (French)    manners; social customs.

**moeurs de province** (French)    provincial habits or manners.

**Mogen David** (Hebrew)    *Judaism.* the Star of David, the six-pointed star that is the symbol of Israel. Also **Magen David.**

**moi** (French)    me; myself.

**moiré** (French)    a watery or wavelike effect on a fabric.

**moitié, à.**    See **à moitié.**

**mole** (Spanish)    *Cookery.* a dark-colored sauce flavored with **chile** and served most often with chicken.

**mole poblano** (Spanish)    the national dish of Mexico, made with turkey or chicken in a **mole** sauce flavored with chocolate.

**mole verde** (Spanish)    a spicy green sauce made with green **chiles.**

**molino de viento** (Spanish)    a windmill.

**moll** (German)    *Music.* minor.

**mollah.**    See **mullah.**

**mollemente** (Italian)    *Music.* gently.

**molta passione, con.**    See **con molta passione.**

**molto** (Italian)    much; very.

**molto allegro** (Italian)    *Music.* very quick.

**momentito** (Spanish)   (wait) just a minute. Also **momentico.**

**momzer** (Hebrew)   (lit., 'bastard') a detestable person. Also **mamzer.**

**mon ami** (French)   my friend (used in addressing a close friend).

**mon avis, à.**   See **à mon avis.**

**mon cher** (French)   my dear; my darling (a term of endearment used of a man). See also **ma chère.**

**mondain,** *fem.* **mondaine** (French)   1. *adj.* designating something characteristic of fashionable society. 2. a fashionable or worldly person.

**monde** (French)   (lit., 'world') 1. one's social environment. 2. the world of fashion.

**monde, le.**   See **le monde.**

**monde savant, le.**   See **le monde savant.**

**Mon Dieu** (French)   my God! (an exclamation of great surprise).

**monologue intérieur** (French)   *Literature.* 1. a passage in which a character's thoughts are presented. 2. the stream-of-consciousness technique.

**Monopole** (French)   a designation for a French wine that is blended and bottled by the shipper.

**monosabio** (Spanish)   (lit., 'wise monkey') *Bullfighting.* the assistant to a picador.

**monseigneur** (French)   a title and form of address for princes and bishops.

**monsieur** (French)   the French form of address for a man, equivalent to *Sir* or *Mister.*

**monsignore,** *pl.* **monsignori** (Italian)   monsignor, a title of certain Roman Catholic officials, lower in rank than bishops.

**monstre sacré** (French)   (lit., 'sacred monster') a public idol or celebrity with eccentric ways.

**mons Veneris** (Latin)   (lit., 'mount of Venus') *Anatomy.* the pubic symphysis of the human female.

**montage** (French)   a combination into one composition of elements drawn from various disparate sources, as in photography. See also **collage.**

**montani semper liberi** (Latin)   mountaineers are always free (motto of West Virginia).

**montera** (Spanish)   *Bullfighting.* a bullfighter's hat.

**Montilla** (Spanish)   a sherry-like Spanish wine produced south of Cordoba.

**monumentum aere perennius.**   See **exegi monumentum . . . .**

**moonshee.**   See **munshi.**

**mora** (Latin)   (lit., 'delay') *Prosody.* in quantitative meter, the unit of time equivalent to the duration of pronouncing a short syllable.

**morbidezza** (Italian)   1. *Music.* softness; gentleness. 2. *Fine Arts.* delicacy in reproducing flesh tints. 3. *Literature.* sensitivity of treatment.

morceau, *pl.* morceaux (French)    (lit. 'morsel') an excerpt from a longer passage, as of music or poetry.

morcilla (Spanish)    blood sausage.

more (Latin)    in the way or manner (of).

more anglico (Latin)    in English style.

more dictu (Latin)    *Prescriptions.* in the manner directed. *Abbr.* more dict.; mor. dict.

more hibernico (Latin)    in Irish style.

more maiorum *or* majorum (Latin)    according to the custom of the ancestors. See also mos maiorum.

more meo (Latin)    in my own style.

morendo (Italian)    *Music.* dying away.

mores (Latin)    customs; unwritten laws. See also o tempora! o mores!

more Socratico (Latin)    in the Socratic manner, as using questions to elicit an idea.

more solito (Latin)    in the customary manner.

more suo (Latin)    in his usual way; in his own style.

Morgen (German)    morning.

Morgenlied (German)    *Music.* morning song.

morgue anglaise (French)    supercilious behavior characteristic of the English.

morilles (French)    morels.

morisco, *fem.* morisca (Spanish)    1. *adj.* Moorish.    2. a dance of Moorish origin.

morituri te salutamus *or* salutant.    See Ave Caesar . . . .

mormorando (Italian)    *Music.* murmuring. Also mormorante; mormorevole; mormoroso; murmurando.

morra (Italian)    a game in which two people each bring one hand quickly from behind the back while one tries to guess the total number of fingers that will be extended.

morral (Spanish)    *Texas.* a feed bag.

mors tua, vita mea (Latin)    (lit., 'your death, my life') you must die so I may live.

mortadella (Italian)    a sausage meat made from pork.

mortis causa (Latin)    by reason of death; in anticipation of death.

mortuus sine prole (Latin)    dead without offspring. *Abbr.* m.s.p. See also obiit sine prole.

Moscato (Italian)    designating a variety of different wines made from the Muscat family of grapes.

mos maiorum *or* majorum (Latin)    the custom of the ancestors; long-practiced traditions.

**mosso** (Italian)   *Music.* with movement; rapid.

**mostaccioli** (Italian)   a hollow, tube-shaped pasta that is cut diagonally.

**mosto cotto** (Italian)   *Wine.* an extremely sweet, concentrated grape juice used to fortify **Marsala.**

**mot** (French)   (lit., 'word') a witty remark. See also **bon mot.**

**mot à mot** (French)   word for word. Also **mot pour mot.**

**mot de guet** (French)   a watchword; password. Also **mot d'ordre; mot de passe.** See also **mot de ralliement.**

**mot de l'enigme** (French)   the answer to the riddle; the key to solving the mystery.

**mot de passe.**   See **mot de guet.**

**mot de ralliement** (French)   the countersign to the password. See also **mot de guet.**

**mot d'ordre.**   See **mot de guet.**

**mot d'usage** (French)   a word in common use.

**Motiv** (German)   motif.

**motivaguida** (Italian)   *Music.* the leading motif. Also **tema fondamentale.**

**mot juste, le** (French)   the word that is exactly right or appropriate for a situation.

**moto, con.**   See **con moto.**

**mot pour mot.**   See **mot à mot.**

**mot pour rire** (French)   a joke; a witticism.

**mot propre** (French)   the proper designation or term for a thing.

**motu proprio** (Latin)   (lit., 'of one's own accord') *Roman Catholicism.* a personal rescript from the pope, made without counsel.

**mouche** (French)   a beauty mark.

**mouchoir** (French)   a handkerchief.

**moue** (French)   a pouting expression.

**mouillé** (French)   *Phonetics.* a designation for combinations of letters pronounced with a *y*-sound, as *ll* or *ñ* in Spanish.

**moulin** (French)   a vertical shaft through glacial ice formed by water flowing down through a crack.

**Moulin Rouge** (French)   a renowned music hall in Paris.

**moussaka** (Greek)   *Cookery.* a casserole dish of slices of sautéed eggplant layered with a filling of ground lamb or beef and topped with white sauce and cheese.

**mousse** (French)   *Cookery.* a light, fluffy mixture with a base of whipped cream, flavored with various ingredients.

**mousseline** (French)   muslin.

**mousseline de laine** (French)   a thin, worsted fabric used in dressmaking.

**mousseline de soie** (French)    a thin fabric of silk or rayon, similar to chiffon.

**mousseux** (French)    frothy or sparkling, as wine.

**moutarde** (French)    mustard.

**mouton** (French)    mutton.

**Moyen Âge, Le** (French)    the Middle Ages.

**mozo** (Spanish)  1. a youth; young man.  2. a servant; waiter.

**mozzarella** (Italian)    a type of mild-flavored, soft, white cheese.

**mozzarella in carozza** (Italian)    (lit., 'mozzarella in a carriage')  *Cookery.* mozzarella cheese that is breaded and deep-fried.

**mozzetta** (Italian)    *Roman Catholic Church.* a short cloak that covers the shoulders and is buttoned in front, worn by the pope and other ecclesiastics.

**muchacha** (Spanish)    a girl.

**muchacho** (Spanish)    a boy.

**mudejar** (Spanish)  1. a Moor who remained in Spain after the Spanish reconquest of the country.  2. *Architecture.* a style of the Early Spanish Renaissance, influenced by Moorish art and craftsmanship.

**muezzin** (Arabic)    *Islam.* the crier who calls people to daily prayer from a minaret or mosque.

**mufti** (Arabic)  1. *Islam.* an adviser in religious law.  2. civilian dress worn by someone who normally wears a uniform.

**mujer** (Spanish)    a woman.

**mukluk** (Eskimo)    a soft, fur-lined boot of sealskin or deerskin.

**mulada** (Spanish)    a herd of mules.

**mulato** (Spanish)    a person of racially mixed parentage.

**muleta** (Spanish)    *Bullfighting.* a red cloth attached to a rod, used by the matador in the final phase of the bullfight.

**mullah** (Persian)    *Islam.* a title for a Muslim religious teacher.  Also **mulla; mollah.**

**multum in parvo** (Latin)    (lit., 'much in little') a great deal within a limited space or scope. See also **magnum in parvo.**

**München** (German)    the city of Munich, capital of Bavaria, in SW West Germany.

**munshi** (Hindi)  1. a native Indian interpreter or language teacher.  2. a native Indian secretary.  Also **moonshee.**

**mura** (Japanese)    a Japanese village or hamlet.

**murciana** (Spanish)  1. designating something from Murcia in southeastern Spain.  2. a dance originating in Murcia, a type of **fandango.**

**murmurando.**    See **mormorando.**

**muscae volitantes** (Latin)    (lit., 'flying flies') specks before the eyes.

**muscal.** See mezcal.

**muscoli** (Italian)   mussels.

**musica di camera** (Italian)   *Music.* chamber music.

**musica falsa** *or* **ficta** (Latin)   (lit., 'false *or* made-up music') alterations (of certain notes) made to improve harmonic progressions.

**musica reservata** (Latin)   (lit., 'music reserved (for)') 16th-century designation for music suited for connoisseurs and private occasions.

**musjid.**   See masjid.

**must** (Urdu)   a state of frenzy periodically affecting male elephants. Also **musth.**

**mustizo.**   See mestizo.

**mutatis mutandis** (Latin)   (lit., 'with things changed that must be changed') after the necessary or appropriate changes have been made.

**mutato nomine** (Latin)   with the name changed (the story applies to you); Horace, *Satires* I.1.69.

**Mütterchen** (German)   mamma; mother dear.

**muumuu** (Hawaiian)   a long, brightly colored dress worn by Hawaiian women.

**muy bien** (Spanish)   very well; okay.

**muy bueno** (Spanish)   very good.

**muzhik** (Russian)   (lit., 'little man') a Russian peasant.

**Mynheer** (Dutch)   a title of respect, equivalent to *Sir* or *Mister.*

**mythos** (Greek)   mythology; myth, as distinct from folktale.

# N

nabob. See nawab, 1.

nachalstvo (Russian) the authorities; the elite leadership of the Soviet Union.

nachos (Spanish) *Cookery.* tortillas fried in oil until crisp and covered with melted cheese.

Nachspiel (German) *Music.* postlude.

Nacht (German) night.

Nachtmusik (German) *Music.* serenade.

nada (Spanish) nothing; not at all. See also de nada.

naïveté (French) a state of mind characterized by lack of sophistication, experience, or information.

nanook (Eskimo) a polar bear.

napoléon (French) a pastry consisting of thin layers of puff pastry filled with custard. See also mille-feuille.

napolitaine, à la. See à la napolitaine.

napolitana, alla. See alla napolitana.

naranja (Spanish) orange.

narod (Russian) the masses; the people.

nation boutiquière, la. See la nation boutiquière.

natrium (Latin) sodium. *Abbr.* Na.

natura abhorret vacuum (Latin) nature abhors a vacuum.

natura morta. See nature morte.

nature morte (French) *Fine Arts.* still life.

natürlich (German) 1. natural. 2. naturally; of course.

Naturtöne (German) *Music.* natural notes; primary tones.

nausée, la. See la nausée.

navarin (French) *Cookery.* a stew of lamb with turnips and potatoes.

navet (French) turnip.

Navidad. See Feliz Navidad.

**nawab** (Urdu)    1. a deputy governor of the Mogul empire. Also **nabob. 2.** a Muslim title of distinction used in India and Pakistan.

**nebbech.**    See **nebbish.**

**Nebbiolo** (Italian)    1. a noted grape variety.    2. the red wine made from these grapes, sometimes sparkling.

**nebbish** (Yiddish)    an ineffectual, hapless person; insignificant person. Also **neb(b)ech; nebish.**

**Nebiim** (Hebrew)    *Judaism.* the books of the Prophets, the second of the three traditional divisions of the books of Jewish Scripture. See also **Hagiographa; Tanach; Torah.**

**nécessaire** (French)    a box or case for toiletries.

**née** (French)    (lit., 'born') a designation used before a woman's surname to indicate that it was her name at birth, that is, the maiden name of a married woman.

**nefas** (Latin)    something offensive; an impropriety or sacrilege. See also **fas.**

**nefasti dies** (Latin)    (lit., 'unlucky days') *Roman history.* days on which official business was not permitted; holidays. See also **fasti.**

**negligee, négligé** (French)    (lit., 'undress') 1. a woman's nightgown or robe. 2. any loose, flowing clothing to be worn in the **boudoir.**

**negligente** (Italian)    *Music.* negligently. Also **negligentemente.**

**négociant en vin** (French)    a wine merchant or wholesaler. Also **négociant.**

**negritas** (Spanish)    (lit., 'little black ones') *Cookery.* chocolate mousse served in individual dishes.

**nein** (German)    no.

**nekulturny** (Russian)    coarse; uncultured; socially unacceptable.

**nemine contradicente** (Latin)    (lit., 'with no one dissenting') *Law.* with unanimous consent. *Abbr.* **nem. con.**

**nemine dissentiente** (Latin)    with no one dissenting. *Abbr.* **nem. diss.**

**nemo me impune lacessit** (Latin)    no one assails me with impunity (motto of Scotland).

**ne nimium** (Latin)    (lit., 'not too much') avoid excess. See also **mēden agan.**

**ne plus ultra** (Latin)    (lit., 'no more beyond') the uttermost point; the acme of perfection.

**ne quid nimis** (Latin)    (lit., 'nothing too much') avoid excess. See also **mēden agan.**

**nero antico** (Italian)    (lit., 'ancient black') a type of black marble found in use at some Roman sites.

**nessun maggior dolor** (Italian)　　(lit., 'no greater sorrow')　the words of Francesca da Rimini in Dante's *Inferno*, referring to remembrance of happiness past.

**n'est-ce pas** (French)　isn't it so? (used at the end of a question expecting an affirmative answer).

**netsuke** (Japanese)　a small carved or ceramic figure, originally used as a decorative button or fastener.

**neuf** (French)　nine.

**neun** (German)　nine.

**névé** (French)　hardened snow on high mountains that compacts into glacial ice.

**nicht** (German)　not.

**nicht wahr?** (German)　isn't that right?

**niellatori** (Italian)　artisans of **niello.**

**niello** (Italian)　*Applied Arts.* a technique of decorating metal with inlaid black enamel.

**niente** (Italian)　nothing.

**nihil** (Latin)　nothing. Also **nil.**

**nihil ad rem** (Latin)　(lit., 'nothing to the point')　irrelevant.

**nihil dicit** (Latin)　(lit., 'he says nothing')　*Law.* a judgment made in the absence of a plea.

**nihil ex nihilo (fit)** (Latin)　nothing (comes) from nothing. Also **de nihilo nihil; ex nihilo nihil.**

**nihil obstat** (Latin)　(lit., 'nothing stands in the way')　*Roman Catholicism.* the official declaration, after an authoritative review, that a work does not violate Church doctrine regarding faith and morals. See also **imprimatur.**

**nihil sub sole novi** (Latin)　(there is) nothing new under the sun.

**Nihon.**　See **Nippon.**

**Nihongo** (Japanese)　the Japanese language.

**nil** (Latin)　nothing. Also **nihil.**

**nil admirari** (Latin)　(lit., 'not to be astonished')　do not be surprised or excited by anything; keep perfect equanimity (Horace, *Epistles* I.6.1).

**nil debet** (Latin)　(lit., 'he owes nothing')　a plea denying a debt.

**nil desperandum** (Latin)　(lit., 'nothing must be despaired of')　never despair (Horace, *Odes* I.7.27).

**nil nisi bonum.**　See **de mortuis . . . .**

**nil sine Deo** (Latin)　nothing without God.

**nil sine numine** (Latin)　nothing without providence (motto of Colorado).

**n'importe** (French)　it doesn't matter; it isn't important.

**ninja** (Japanese)　a warrior who is highly trained in various martial arts disciplines.

197

**niño,** *fem.* **niña** (Spanish)    1. a child; little boy; little girl.    2. See **El Niño.**

**Nippon** (Japanese)    a Japanese name for Japan. Also **Nihon.**

**nirvana** (Sanskrit)    1. *Buddhism.* the attainment of freedom from repeated reincarnations and hence from the sufferings of life.    2. a state of obliviousness to pain and suffering.

**Nisei** (Japanese)    a person of Japanese descent who was born and educated in the United States. See also **Issei; Kibei; Sansei.**

**nisi** (Latin)    (lit., 'unless')   *Law.* designating a decree that is operational unless or until cause against it is shown.

**nisi prius** (Latin)    (lit., 'unless before')   *Law.* referring to a court which tries cases before a judge and jury. (Originally, in English law, a writ beginning with these words directed a sheriff to summon a jury to Westminster "unless before" that day a judge of assizes came to the county.)

**nitor in adversum** (Latin)    I strive in the face of opposition.

**Nō** (Japanese)    the classic dramatic genre of Japan with highly formalized conventions and themes. See also **kabuki.**

**nobile** (Italian)    *Music.* noble.

**noblesse** (French)    1. nobility; high social rank.    2. the noble class.

**noblesse de robe** (French)    (lit., 'nobility of the gown') the respected social position accorded judges and lawyers.

**noblesse oblige** (French)    the obligations incumbent on those of superior social rank.

**noblezza** (Italian)    *Music.* nobility.

**nocciole,** *sing.* **nocciola** (Italian)    hazelnuts.

**noche** (Spanish)    night.

**Nochebuena, la** (Spanish)    Christmas Eve.

**Noche Triste** (Spanish)    (lit., 'sad night') the night of July 1, 1520, when Cortés's soldiers suffered heavy losses at the hands of Aztec forces.

**noci,** *sing.* **noce** (Italian)    walnuts.

**nocte** (Latin)    *Prescriptions.* at night. *Abbr.* **noct.**

**nocte et mane** (Latin)    *Prescriptions.* at night and in the morning. *Abbr.* **n. et m.**

**nocturne** (French)    a work of art, as a musical piece, that evokes the feeling of nighttime or has dreamlike qualities.

**Noël** (French)    1. Christmas.    2. a Christmas carol.

**nogada** (Spanish)    Mexican-style praline candy.

**noia** (Italian)    boredom; ennui.

**noir** (French)    *Roulette.* any one of the black areas on which one may wager. See also **rouge.**

**noisette** (French)    1. a hazelnut.    2. a small, usually round portion of meat, especially a cut from the filet.

**noix de muscade** (French)    nutmeg.

**noix de veau** (French)    the fleshy underpart of a calf's thigh.

**nolens volens** (Latin)    (lit., 'unwilling, willing') willy-nilly; whether willing or not.

**noli me tangere** (Latin)    1. touch me not (Jesus's admonition to Mary Magdalene after his resurrection; John 20:17).    2. *Fine Arts.* a picture depicting the scene.    3. a flower, the touch-me-not.

**nolle prosequi** (Latin)    (lit., 'to be unwilling to prosecute') *Law.* a discontinuance or cancellation of criminal proceedings. *Abbr.* **nol. pros.**

**nolo contendere** (Latin)    (lit., 'I do not wish to contest') *Law.* a plea made with the consent of the court by which the defendant neither admits nor denies the charges, but is subject to a fine or sentence.

**nolo episcopari** (Latin)    (lit., 'I do not wish to serve as bishop') a formal refusal of an office or honor.

**nom de guerre** (French)    (lit., 'war name') a pseudonym; assumed name.

**nom de plume** (French)    a pen name; assumed name.

**nom de théâtre** (French)    a stage name.

**nom emprunté** (French)    a borrowed name.

**nomen,** *pl.* **nomina** (Latin)    1. name; designation.    2. noun.    3. the second name in the Roman system for naming individuals, designating the *gens* or clan, as *Julius* in *Gaius Julius Caesar.* See also **cognomen, 3; praenomen, 2.**

**nomen est omen** (Latin)    (lit., 'the name is an omen') expression of the superstition that to speak of something will make it happen.

**nomenklatura** (Russian)    a designation for jobs in the Soviet system that are under the direct control of the Communist party.

**nomen nudum** (Latin)    *Biology.* the mere name of an organism, without a scientific description.

**non aequis passibus.**    See **haud passibus aequis.**

**non assumpsit** (Latin)    (lit., 'he did not undertake') *Law.* a plea by which the defendant denies that he made an alleged promise.

**non c'è male** (Italian)    not bad (response to a query about one's health).

**non compos mentis** (Latin)    *Law.* not of sound mind; not legally competent to manage one's own affairs.    See also **compos mentis.**

**non constat** (Latin)    (lit., 'it is not established') a conclusion that does not necessarily follow from appearances.

**non culpabilis** (Latin)    *Law.* not guilty. *Abbr.* **non cul.**

**non ens** (Latin)    nonentity.

**non esse** (Latin)    nonexistence.

**non est** (Latin)    1. it is not; it is nonexistent.    2. See **non est inventus.**

**non est inventus** (Latin)    (lit., 'he has not been found') *Law.* a report by a sheriff that a person under summons to appear in court has not been found. Also **non est.**

**nonetto** (Italian)    *Music.* a composition written for nine instruments, usually a string quartet or quintet and woodwinds.

**non libet** (Latin)    it does not please (me).

**non licet** (Latin)    it is not permitted.

**non liquet** (Latin)    it is not clear. *Abbr.* **n.l.**

**non mi ricordo** (Italian)    I don't remember.

**nonna** (Italian)    grandmother.

**nonno** (Italian)    grandfather.

**non obstante** (Latin)    notwithstanding.

**non obstante veredicto** (Latin)    (lit., 'notwithstanding the verdict') *Law.* a judgment rendered by order of the court that goes against the verdict.

**non olet.**    See **pecunia non olet.**

**non omnis moriar** (Latin)    I shall not wholly die (Horace, *Odes* III.30.6).

**non passibus aequis.**    See **haud passibus aequis.**

**non placet** (Latin)    (lit., 'it does not please (me)') a negative vote.

**non possumus** (Latin)    (lit., 'we cannot') a statement refusing a request, used especially of papal denials.

**non prosequitur** (Latin)    (lit., 'he does not follow up') *Law.* a judgment dismissing an action when a plaintiff fails to prosecute. *Abbr.* **non pros.**

**non repetatur** (Latin)    *Prescriptions.* do not repeat. *Abbr.* **non rep.**

**non sequitur** (Latin)    (lit., 'it does not follow') an illogical inference or a conclusion that does not follow from the premises. *Abbr.* **non seq.**

**non sibi sed aliis** (Latin)    not for ourselves but for others.

**non tanto allegro** (Italian)    *Music.* not so quick; not too lively.

**non tratto** (Italian)    *Music.* not dragged; not slow.

**non troppo** (Italian)    *Music.* not too much; moderately.

**non troppo presto** (Italian)    *Music.* not too fast.

**nopales** (Spanish)    *Cookery.* cactus pads, steamed or sauteed in oil or butter and used as an accompaniment to egg dishes, or as a salad or dip ingredient. Also called **nopalitos.**

**noques** (French)    *Cookery.* dumplings boiled in soup.

**noria** (Spanish)    a device, powered by a draft animal, designed to raise water from a well.

**Normalton** (German)    *Music.* normal tone; the note A, to which instruments are tuned in an orchestra.

**norte, el** (Spanish)    1. north.    2. the north wind.

**norteños** (Spanish)    (lit., 'northerners') traditional Mexican folk songs.

**nosce te ipsum** *or* **teipsum** (Latin)    know thyself. See also **gnōthi seauton.**

**nosh** (Yiddish)    1. *v.* to eat a snack or tidbit between meals.    2. *n.* a small snack or tidbit.

**nosher** (Yiddish)    a person who often eats small snacks between meals.

**nostrano** (Italian)    (lit., 'ours')  1. *Cookery.* local, as of a method of preparation.    2. homegrown, as of produce.    3. *n.* the wine produced in Italian Switzerland.

**nota** (Italian)    *Music.* a note.

**nota bene** (Latin)    note well. *Abbr.* n.b.; N.B.

**nota buona** (Italian)    *Music.* an accented note.

**nota cattiva** (Italian)    *Music.* an unaccented note.

**nota sensibile** (Italian)    *Music.* the leading note.

**nota sostenuta** (Italian)    *Music.* a sustained note.

**notturno** (Italian)    *Music.* 1. any composition that evokes a feeling of the night; nocturne.    2. a type of slow piano piece associated with the Romantic period in music.

**nouilles** (French)    noodles.

**noumenon,** *pl.* **noumena** (Greek)    *Philosophy.* an object perceived with the mind or intellect, not with the senses.

**nous** (Greek)    *Philosophy.* the mind or intellect.

**nouveau, de.**    See de nouveau.

**nouveau riche,** *pl.* **nouveaux riches** (French)    1. a social class with acquired wealth but lacking in taste and culture.    2. See also **parvenu.** An individual in this class.

**nouveau roman** (French)    *Literature.* a type of novel that discards conventional plot and structure, concentrating on the description of events and objects to reveal the consciousness seeing or experiencing them. See also **nouveau théâtre; nouvelle vague.**

**nouveauté** (French)    novelty.

**nouveau théâtre** (French)    *Theater.* drama in which the main emphasis is on the consciousness of the characters as they react to outside stimuli. See also **nouveau roman; nouvelle vague.**

**nouvelle** (French)    a short story.

**nouvelle cuisine, la** (French)    (lit., the 'new (manner of) cooking') a modern style of cooking that features lean meats and fish, fresh vegetables and fruits, prepared without rich sauces and dressings. See also **cuisine minceur.**

**nouvelle vague** (French)    (lit., 'new wave') *Film.* a style of cinema concentrating on events as they are perceived or remembered by an individual character. See also **nouveau roman; nouveau théâtre.**

**nove** (Italian)    nine.

**novecento** (Italian)    the 20th century or the 1900's, especially in reference to Italian fine arts or literature.

**novela picaresca** (Spanish)    a picaresque novel; a genre of 16th- and 17th-century Spanish narratives which related the adventures of a rogue hero, the **picaro.**

**novella** (Italian)    _Literature._ **1.** a short novel.    **2.** a brief prose narrative of the medieval or Renaissance period, such as the stories of Boccaccio's _Decameron._

**novia** (Spanish)    **1.** a girlfriend; fiancée.    **2.** a bride.

**novillada** (Spanish)    _Bullfighting._ a bullfight in which overage or underage bulls are fought by lesser skilled bullfighters.

**novillero** (Spanish)    _Bullfighting._ the bullfighter of the **novillada.**

**novio** (Spanish)    **1.** a boyfriend; fiancé.    **2.** a bridegroom.

**novissima verba** (Latin)    last words; dying words.

**novus homo** (Latin)    (lit., 'a new man')    an upstart; one who has risen to prominence from humble origins.

**novus ordo seclorum** (Latin)    a new order of the ages (motto on the Great Seal of the United States; adapted from Vergil, _Eclogues_ IV.5).    See also **annuit coeptis.**

**nu** (Yiddish)    well; so (frequent interjection and interrogative element, with a range of connotations).

**nuance** (French)    **1.** a subtle shade or variation of expression or color.    **2.** _Fine Arts._ delicate shading or gradation.    **3.** _Music._ variations in expression; subtle tone coloring.

**nuda veritas** (Latin)    the naked truth.

**nudis verbis** (Latin)    in plain words.

**nudnik** (Yiddish)    an obnoxious or very stupid person.

**nudum pactum** (Latin)    (lit., 'a bare pact')    _Law._ an agreement made on good will alone, without a consideration to bind it.

**nudzh** (Yiddish)    to poke at; pester; nag.    Also **nudj.**

**nudzhik** (Yiddish)    a person who pesters or nags.

**nuée ardente** (French)    a swiftly moving, sometimes incandescent volcanic cloud containing ash in its lower part.

**nueve** (Spanish)    nine.

**nugae** (Latin)    trifles; trivialities.

**nugae literariae** (Latin)    literary trifles.

**nulli secundus** (Latin)    second to none.

**nullius filius.**    See **filius nullius.**

**nullius juris** (Latin)    _Law._ of no legal force.

**numerus clausus** (Latin)    (lit., 'closed number')    designating any group or institution to which admission is strictly limited.

**nunc dimittis** (Latin)   (lit., 'now you may send (him) away')   permission to depart (from the first words of the canticle of Simeon, Luke 2:29–32).

**nunc est bibendum** (Latin)   now is the time for drinking (Horace, *Odes* I.37.1).

**nuncio** (Italian)   a diplomatic representative of the pope. Also **nunzio**.

**nunc pro tunc** (Latin)   (lit., 'now for then')   *Law.* an action having a retroactive effect.

**nuoc nam** (Vietnamese)   *Cookery.* a type of fish sauce.

**nuove musiche** (Italian)   (lit., 'new musics')   *Music.* a name given in the 16th century to the practice of combining drama and harmonic music, the precursor of opera.

**nuovo, di.**   See di nuovo.

**nutrendo** (Italian)   *Music.* sustaining.

**nutrito** (Italian)   *Music.* sustained.

**nyet** (Russian)   no.

# O

**obbligato** (Italian)   *Music.* 1. *adj.* essential, referring to the parts of a composition that cannot be left out.   2. *n.* an instrumental accompaniment to a vocal piece.

**obeah.**   See obi².

**Oberst** (German)   a colonel in the German armed forces.

**obiit** (Latin)   he (*or* she) died. *Abbr.* **ob.**

**obiit sine prole** (Latin)   he (*or* she) died without offspring. *Abbr.* **o.s.p.** See also **mortuus sine prole.**

**obiter dictum,** *pl.* **obiter dicta** (Latin)   (lit., 'said incidentally') 1. *Law.* a supplementary opinion given by a judge but not part of the decision.   2. (*pl.*) remarks made in passing.

**obiter scriptum,** *pl.* **obiter scripta** (Latin)   (lit., 'written on the way') an incidental composition; something written hastily.

**obi¹** (Japanese)   a broad sash worn at the waist over a **kimomo.**

**obi²** (West African)   1. magic or sorcery practiced in parts of Africa and the West Indies.   2. a charm used in these practices. Also **obeah.**

**objet d'art,** *pl.* **objets d'art** (French)   an item of artistic value, usually of small size.

**objet de piété** (French)   an object used in religious devotion, such as a crucifix or rosary beads.

**objet de vertu,** *pl.* **objets de vertu** (French)   (lit., 'object of virtue') an object of art or curio of exceptional merit.

**objet d'occasion** (French)   a secondhand item.

**objet trouvé,** *pl.* **objets trouvés** (French)   (lit., 'found object') a natural or common object presented as if it is a work of art. See also **assemblage.**

**oblast** (Russian)   an administrative province of the Soviet Union.

**obscurum per obscurius** (Latin)   (explaining) an obscurity by something more obscure.

**observandum,** *pl.* **observanda** (Latin)   a thing to be observed.

**ocho** (Spanish)   eight.

**odi et amo** (Latin)   I hate and I love (Catullus 85).

**odi profanum vulgus** (Latin)   I hate the impious rabble (Horace, *Odes* III.1.1).

**odium aestheticum** (Latin)   bitter rivalry over aesthetic principles.

**odium generis humani** (Latin)   hatred of the human race.

**odium literarium** (Latin)   bitter rivalry among writers.

**odium medicum** (Latin)   bitter rivalry among physicians.

**odium musicum** (Latin)   bitter rivalry among musicians.

**odium scholasticum** (Latin)   bitter rivalry among scholars; academic quibbling.

**odium theologicum** (Latin)   bitter disputation among theologians.

**odor lucri** (Latin)   (lit., 'the smell of wealth')   expectation of profit.

**oeil-de-boeuf** (French)   *Architecture.* a round or oval window in the frieze or roof of a building; oxeye.

**oeuf** (French)   egg.

**oeufs à la coque** (French)   boiled eggs.

**oeufs à la neige** (French)   *Cookery.* a dessert consisting of meringue floating on custard.

**oeufs à la russe** (French)   *Cookery.* hard-boiled eggs with mayonnaise sauce.

**oeufs à l'indienne** (French)   *Cookery.* curried eggs.

**oeufs au miroir** (French)   *Cookery.* eggs fried sunnyside up.

**oeufs brouillés** (French)   *Cookery.* scrambled eggs.

**oeufs frais** (French)   freshly laid eggs.

**oeufs pochés** (French)   *Cookery.* poached eggs.

**oeufs sur le plat** (French)   *Cookery.* fried eggs served with the yolk up.

**oeuvre,** *pl.* **oeuvres** (French)   1. the work of an artist, writer, or composer, considered as a whole. 2. a single work of an artist, writer, or composer.

**oeuvres complètes** (French)   *Literature.* the complete works of an author.

**oidor** (Spanish)   (lit., 'listener') *Spanish history.* a justice in the audiencias.

**ojo** (Spanish)   (lit., 'eye') a spring-fed pool.

**Oktoberfest** (German)   harvest-time beer festival.

**olé** (Spanish)   *Bullfighting.* an expression of approval shouted by the spectators at a bullfight.

**olet lucernam** (Latin)   (lit., 'it smells of the lamp')   said of a thing, such as a literary work, that shows signs of laborious revision.   Also **redolet lucernam.**

**olio** (Italian)   oil.

**olio** (Spanish)   1. a stew.   2. a mixture; medley.

**olio d'oliva** (Italian)   olive oil.

**olive ripiene** (Italian)    *Cookery.* olives stuffed with chopped ham and chicken and then fried.

**olla** (Spanish)    a large pot.

**olla podrida** (Spanish)    (lit., 'rotten pot')  1. *Cookery.* a dish consisting of stewed meats and vegetables.    2. an incongruous mixture; a hodgepodge.

**oloroso** (Spanish)    a rich, dark-colored sherry.

**Om** (Sanskrit)    *Hinduism.* a mystical syllable used in **mantras.**

**ombré** (French)    designating a fabric woven so as to have a shaded effect.

**ombres chinoises** (French)    (lit., 'Chinese shadows') a form of pantomime in which shadows of cut-out characters are projected onto a translucent screen.

**omen faustum** (Latin)    a favorable omen.

**omertà** (Italian)    the Sicilian code of silence, under which information regarding a crime is never given to authorities.

**omne vivum ex vivo** (Latin)    everything alive comes from a living thing.

**omnia ad Dei gloriam** (Latin)    all for the glory of God.

**omnia bona bonis** (Latin)    to the good, all things are good.

**omnia mors aequat** (Latin)    death makes all things equal.

**omnia opera.**    See **opera omnia.**

**omnia vincit amor** (Latin)    love conquers all things (Vergil, *Eclogues* X.69).

**omnia vincit labor** (Latin)    labor overcomes all things.

**omni hora** (Latin)    *Prescriptions.* at every hour. *Abbr.* **omn. hor.**

**omni mane** (Latin)    *Prescriptions.* every morning. *Abbr.* **omn. man.**

**omnium-gatherum** (pseudo-Latin)    a heterogeneous collection.

**ondé** (French)    designating a fabric which has a wavy pattern.

**ondeggiamento** (Italian)    *Music.* an undulating effect, as **tremolo** or **vibrato.** See also **ondeggiando.**

**ondeggiando** (Italian)    *Music.* undulating. Also **ondeggiante.**

**on dit** (French)    they say; it is said.

**on-dit** (French)    a rumor; a bit of gossip.

**on parle français.**    See **ici on parle français.**

**onus probandi** (Latin)    the burden of proof.

**opera.**    See **opus.**

**opéra bouffe** (French)    *Music.* comic or light opera. Also **opéra-bouffe.**

**opera buffa** (Italian)    *Music.* comic or light opera that may have spoken dialogue or, as in the Italian practice, be entirely set to music. See also **dramma giocoso; opera seria.**

**opéra comique** (French)    *Music.* light opera that includes spoken dialogue. Also **opéra-comique.**

**opera del duomo** (Italian)    *Architecture.* a section in an Italian cathedral serving as a vestry room or museum.

**opera omnia** (Latin)    the complete works (of an author or composer).

**opera seria** (Italian)    *Music.* serious opera, as opposed to **opera buffa.**

**opere citato** (Latin)    in the work quoted. *Abbr.* **op. cit.**

**operetta** (Italian)    *Music.* 1. a light opera with spoken dialogue; a musical comedy.    2. a short opera.

**opposition** (French)    *Ballet.* the relationship of the arm or of the head and shoulders to the working leg.

**optimates** (Latin)    the aristocracy.

**opus,** *pl.* **opera** (Latin)    a work; a composition.

**opus anglicanum** (Latin)    (lit., 'English work') medieval English embroidery.

**opusculum** (Latin)    a little work; a small book.

**opus Dei** (Latin)    (lit., 'the work of God') *Roman Catholicism.* 1. daily monastic duties.    2. (*cap.*) the name of a politico-religious society.

**opus incertum** (Latin)    irregular masonry work.

**opus isodomum** (Latin)    masonry work with courses of equal height.

**opus postumum** (Latin)    a posthumous work.

**opus pseudoisodomum** (Latin)    masonry work with even courses of varying heights.

**opus reticulatum** (Latin)    masonry work having some pieces set obliquely.

**opus spicatum** (Latin)    masonry work laid in a herringbone pattern.

**ora et labora** (Latin)    pray and work.

**ora pro nobis** (Latin)    pray for us.

**orate fratres** (Latin)    pray, brethren.

**oratio obliqua** (Latin)    1. *Rhetoric.* indirect discourse.    2. hearsay.

**oratio recta** (Latin)    *Rhetoric.* direct quotation.

**oratorio** (Italian)    *Music.* a musical drama on a religious theme, similar to opera but intended for concert or church peformance.

**orbis terrarum** (Latin)    the whole world.

**ordinaire, à l'.**    See **à l'ordinaire.**

**ordonnance** (French)    the arrangement and composition of an artistic work, as a painting, building, or literary work.

**ordre du jour** (French)    agenda.

**orejones** (Spanish)    (lit., 'big ears') a dried pear or apricot cut in strips.

**oremus** (Latin)    let us pray.

**ore rotundo** (Latin)    with full, round voice; with polished speech (Horace, *Ars Poetica* 323).

**ore tenus** (Latin)    by word of mouth; verbally.

**orge** (French)    barley.

**orgue de barbarie** (French)    a portable organ operated by turning a handle.

**orgue de salon** (French)    a harmonium.

**oriflamme** (French)    the red silk standard used by ancient kings of France.

**origami** (Japanese)    the Japanese technique of folding paper into decorative shapes.

**origine contrôlée.**    See **appellation d'origine contrôlée.**

**orihon** (Japanese)    a Japanese manuscript scroll or book.

**ornamenti.**    See **fioritura.**

**ornatamente** (Italian)    *Music.* with melodic decoration; in a flowery style.

**orné,** *fem.* **ornée** (French)    adorned; ornamented.

**oro** (Spanish)    gold.

**ortaggi** (Italian)    greens; vegetables.

**Orvieto** (Italian)    a light white wine from Umbria, either dry or sweet.

**oscuro** (Spanish)    (lit., 'dark') a black cigar.

**oseille** (French)    sorrel.

**osso buco** (Italian)    *Cookery.* a designation for various preparations of stewed or braised veal shank.

**osteria** (Italian)    an inn; tavern.

**ostinato** (Italian)    *Music.* obstinate; unceasing.

**Ostpolitik** (German)    German post-war policy to establish better relations with eastern European countries.

**o tempora! o mores!** (Latin)    (lit., 'Oh, the times! Oh, the morals!') a lament over the growing degeneracy of an era (Cicero, *Against Catiline* 1).

**otium cum dignitate** (Latin)    leisure with dignity; honorable retirement (Cicero, *Pro Sestio* 14).

**ottava** (Italian)    *Music.* an octave; an eighth.

**ottava alta** (Italian)    *Music.* the octave above; an octave higher.

**ottava bassa** (Italian)    *Music.* the octave below; an octave lower.

**ottava rima** (Italian)    *Prosody.* a stanza of eight lines with three rimes, a form that originated in 14th-century Italy.

**otto** (Italian)    eight.

**ottocento** (Italian)    the 19th century or the 1800's, especially in reference to Italian fine arts or literature.

**oubliette** (French)    a secret dungeon entered through a trapdoor, as in old castles.

**outrance** (French)    the furthest extremity; extravagance.    See also **à l'outrance.**

**outré** (French)    outrageous; beyond the limits of propriety.

**outremer** (French)    **1.** overseas (from the perspective of France, usually in reference to French territories). **2.** the color ultramarine.

**ouvert,** *fem.* **ouverte** (French)    *Ballet; Music.* open; opened.

**ouverture à la gauche** (French)    (lit., 'overture to the left') a French political movement favoring improved relations with Eastern European countries.

**ouvrage** (French)    the work of a skilled craftsman.

**ouzo** (Greek)    a Greek **liqueur** flavored with anise.

**ovolo** (Italian)    *Antiques.* a quarter-round molding.

**Oxoniensis** (Latin)    pertaining to Oxford, England; designating degrees granted by the University of Oxford. *Abbr.* **Oxon.**

**oy** (Yiddish)    an exclamation of surprise, pain, disappointment, etc.

**oy vey** (Yiddish)    an exclamation expressing disappointment or grief.

# P

**pacatamente** (Italian) *Music.* placidly.

**pacato** (Italian) *Music.* placid.

**pace** (Latin) (lit., 'in peace,' 'by favor of') notwithstanding; in spite of (used, sometimes ironically, to express polite disagreement with a respected opinion).

**pace et bello** (Latin) in peace and in war.

**pace in terra** (Italian) peace on earth.

**pace tua** (Latin) by your leave.

**padre,** *pl.* **padri** (Italian) 1. a priest. 2. father.

**padre** (Spanish) 1. father. 2. a priest.

**padrino** (Spanish) 1. godfather. 2. a protector; patron.

**padrona** (Italian) a mistress; landlady; owner.

**padrone** (Italian) a boss; employer; master.

**padron mio** (Italian) my master (spoken by a subordinate as an expression of deference).

**paella** (Spanish) *Cookery.* a dish originating in Valencia, in eastern Spain, made with seafood or meat combined with rice and seasoned with saffron.

**paesan(o),** *pl.* **paesani** (Italian) a fellow countryman, especially a fellow Italian.

**paglia e fieno** (Italian) (lit., 'straw and hay') *Cookery.* green and white noodles served together.

**paillard** (French) *Cookery.* a thin slice of meat or poultry, sauteed or grilled.

**pailles de parmesan** (French) cheese straws.

**paillette** (French) 1. a spangle or sparkling ornament on a woman's dress. 2. *Fine Arts.* a decorative piece of foil used in enamel painting.

**pain** (French) bread.

**pain de campagne** (French) (lit., 'country bread') a round loaf of coarse-textured bread.

**pair** (French) *Roulette.* an even number.

**pak choy.**   See **bok choy.**

**pakka.**   See **pukka.**

**palazzo,** *pl.* **palazzi** (Italian)   1. a very large, elaborate residence.   2. a palace.

**palcoscenico** (Italian)   *Music.* a stage.

**Palestrina** (Italian)   a type of stitch used in embroidery and canvaswork.

**pallida mors** (Latin)   pale death (Horace, *Odes* I.4.13).

**palma** (Spanish)   a medium-sized cigar, usually about six inches long.

**Palme d'Or** (French)   the Golden Palm, the highest award of the Cannes Film Festival.

**palmeral** (Spanish)   a date grove.

**paloma** (Spanish)   a dove.

**Palomino Fino** (Spanish)   a white grape grown in the wine-producing area around Jerez in Spain.

**pampas** (Spanish)   the vast grassy plains of Argentina, used for raising beef cattle.

**pampre** (French)   *Architecture.* ornamental fruit clusters or vine leaves used to decorate the hollow circumvolutions of columns carved with a twisted pattern.

**panaché** (French)   1. plumed; striped.   2. mixed, referring to multi-flavored ice cream or to a medley of vegetables or herbs.

**panade** (French)   *Cookery.* a soup made with French bread simmered with water, butter, and milk. Also **panata** (Italian).

**panadería** (Spanish)   a bakery.

**panais** (French)   parsnip.

**panata.**   See **panade.**

**panatella** (Italian)   a dish for invalids consisting of boiled bread with flavoring added.

**pan di Spagna** (Italian)   *Cookery.* sponge cake, often used as a base for desserts.

**pane** (Italian)   bread.

**pané** (French)   breaded; made with breadcrumbs.

**panem et circenses** (Latin)   (lit., 'bread and circuses') food and entertainment given out to placate the masses (Juvenal, *Satires* X.81).

**panettone** (Italian)   *Cookery.* a dome-shaped sweet bread or coffee cake with raisins and candied fruits.

**panforte** (Italian)   *Cookery.* a flat, hard fruit cake with almonds and citron, originally made in Siena.

**Pange, lingua** (Latin)   (lit., 'Sing, (O my) tongue') opening words of two Latin hymns.

**panificio** (Italian)   a bakery.

**panino imbottito** (Italian)   (lit., 'stuffed roll') *Cookery.* a sort of sandwich consisting of a roll cut in half and filled with cold cuts.

**panne** (French)   velvet or plush material.

**Pantalone** (Italian)   *Theater.* the stock character of the stupid old man in the **commedia dell'arte.**

**panta rhei** (Greek)   everything flows; the world is in a constant state of flux (the principle of the ancient Greek philosopher Heraclitus).

**pañuelo** (Spanish)   a kerchief worn around the neck or over the head.

**panure** (French)   *Cookery.* fine crumbs sprinkled over meats and fish or used as a topping for casseroles.

**paon** (French)   peacock.

**paparazzo,** *pl.* **paparazzi** (Italian)   a photographer who specializes in the comings and goings of celebrities.

**papier collé** (French)   (lit., 'glued paper') *Fine Arts.* a form of design consisting of various objects and materials glued on a flat surface. Also **papiers collés.**

**papier mâché, papier-mâché** (French)   **1.** *n.* a material made of paper pulp or layers of paper and glue that can be shaped while damp and becomes hard and strong when dry.  *—adj.* **2.** anything made from this material. **3.** flimsy; illusory; easily destroyed.

**papiers déchireés** (French)   *Fine Arts.* a technique, developed by Picasso from **origami,** in which torn paper is affixed to a background.

**papiers découpés** (French)   *Fine Arts.* a design created from paper cut into patterns and affixed to a background.

**papillon** (French)   butterfly.

**papillote** (French)   *Cookery.* **1.** oiled or buttered paper used to wrap meat or fish before grilling. **2.** a paper frill used in food decoration. See also **en papillote.**

**paprikash** (Hungarian)   *Cookery.* designating a dish in which paprika is the principal seasoning.

**paradiso** (Italian)   heaven; paradise.

**parador** (Spanish)   **1.** an inn; roadhouse.   **2.** state-owned lodgings in Spain, Portugal, and Puerto Rico, located in reconstructed castles, monasteries, or mansions.

**par avance** (French)   in advance; in expectation (of).

**par avion** (French)   (lit., 'by plane') a designation for air mail.

**Parcae** (Latin)   *Roman mythology.* the three Fates, dispensers of one's destiny.

**pardonnez-moi** (French)   pardon me; excuse me.

**pareve** (Yiddish)   *Judaism.* dietetically neutral, containing neither animal nor dairy products. Also **pareveh; parve.**

**par excellence** (French)    to the highest degree; eminent.

**par exemple** (French)    for instance; for example.

**parfum** (French)    perfume; fragrance.

**parfum atomiseur** (French)    spray perfume.

**pari passu** (Latin)    **1.** at an equal step or rate; proceeding together.    **2.** equably; fairly.

**pari ratione** (Latin)    by a similar line of reasoning; for a like reason.

**parisienne, à la.**    See **à la parisienne.**

**parlando** *or* **parlante** (Italian)    *Music.* in a speaking or declamatory style.

**parlato** (Italian)    *Music.* spoken.

**parmentier** (French)    *Cookery.* **1.** *adj.* containing potatoes.   —*n.* **2.** a creamy potato soup. **3.** a hash of mashed potatoes and ground meat.

**parmigiana, alla.**    See **alla parmigiana.**

**parmigiano** (Italian)    parmesan, an aged cheese made of goat's milk, originally produced near Parma. Also **parmigiano-reggiano.**

**parole d'honneur** (French)    word of honor.

**pars pro toto** (Latin)    a part for the whole.

**par terre.**    See **à terre.**

**parti** (French)    *Architecture.* the overall scheme of a design, especially in its planning stage.

**particeps criminis** (Latin)    (lit., 'sharer of the crime') *Law.* accomplice.

**partida** (Spanish)    a group of people; gang; squad; party.

**partie** (French)    *Music.* **1.** a suite. **2.** an air with variations. **3.** one of the groups singing its own line of notes in part song.

**partim** (Latin)    in part. *Abbr.* **p.**

**parti pris** (French)    a preconceived position or opinion; bias; prejudice.

**parure** (French)    **1.** a matching set of jewelry. **2.** fancy attire.   Also **grande parure.**

**parve.**    See **pareve.**

**parvenu,** *fem.* **parvenue** (French)    a person of undistinguished background who has acquired wealth or importance but lacks style or sophistication. See also **nouveau riche.**

**pas** (French)    *Ballet.* **1.** a step or series of steps. **2.** a dance.

**pas assemblé** (French)    *Ballet.* a step in which the dancer springs upward and brings the feet together while in the air.

**pas battus** (French)    *Ballet.* steps embellished with a beat.

**pas composé** (French)    (lit., 'composed step') *Ballet.* a compound step that includes elements of several other steps or movements.

**pas coupé.**    See **coupé.**

**pas couru** (French)    *Ballet.* a movement of three running steps serving as a lead-in to a leap.

**pascua florida** (Spanish)   1. Easter.  Also called **las pascuas.**   2. the name given by Ponce de León to Florida when he discovered it around Easter in 1513.

**pas d'action** (French)     *Ballet.* a dance or scene intended to express an emotion or depict an action.

**pas d'âne** (French)     a ring-shaped guard for the forefinger on the hilt of a sword.

**pas de basque** (French)     *Ballet.* a leaping step adapted from Basque folk-dancing.

**pas de bourrée** (French)     *Ballet.* a short running step with numerous variations.

**pas de chat** (French)     (lit., 'cat step') *Ballet.* a type of cat-like, springing step.

**pas de cheval** (French)     (lit., 'horse step') *Ballet.* a step in which the dancer paws the ground with one foot.

**pas de ciseaux** (French)     *Ballet.* a scissors step.

**pas de côté** (French)     (lit., 'sideways step') *Dressage.* a maneuver in which the horse moves sideways or at an oblique angle.

**pas de deux** (French)     *Ballet.* a dance for two people.

**pas de deux grand** (French)     *Ballet.* a classical dance performed by the **prima ballerina** and the **danseur noble.**

**pas d'élévation.**   See **temps d'élévation.**

**pas de poisson** (French)     (lit., 'fish step') *Ballet.* a form of **soubresaut** performed with the back curved and the legs held together.  Also **sissonne sobresaut; temps de poisson.**

**pas de quatre** (French)     *Ballet.* a dance for four people.

**pas des écharpes** (French)     *Ballet.* a scarf dance.

**pas-de-souris** (French)     (lit., 'mouse steps') steps leading from a moat to an entrance into a castle.

**pas de trois** (French)     *Ballet.* a dance for three people.

**pas de valse** (French)     *Ballet.* a waltz step.

**pas du tout** (French)     not at all; you're welcome.

**pas emboîté.**   See **emboîté.**

**paseo** (Spanish)   1. a walk.   2. a ride on horseback for pleasure.

**paseo de las cuadrillas** (Spanish)   *Bullfighting.* a parade of bullfighters and their entourages.

**pas glissant** (French)     (lit., 'a slippery step') a delicate situation.

**pas glissé** (French)     *Ballet.* a gliding step.

**pasha** (Turkish)     a title of high-ranking Turkish officials, placed after a name.

**pas marché** (French)     *Ballet.* a stately walking step.

**paso doble** (Spanish) *Music.* 1. a type of lively march often played at bullfights. 2. a dance done to this type of music.

**passatelli** (Italian) *Cookery.* a fresh **pasta** made of eggs, breadcrumbs, and parmesan cheese.

**passe** (French) *Roulette.* any one of the numbers from 19 through 36.

**passé,** *fem.* **passée** (French) 1. past; outdated; aged. 2. faded, in reference to beauty. 3. *Ballet.* designating a movement in which the dancer goes from one position to another.

**passeggiata** (Italian) an afternoon stroll, usually in the main street of a town, to look at and be looked at by others.

**passe-partout** (French) 1. a master key. 2. a universal passport. 3. a mounting for a photograph or drawing. 4. a picture frame made of glass and cardboard held together by gummed paper.

**passepied** (French) a lively French dance in triple meter.

**passe-pied** (French) *Ballet.* a small **jeté** with alternation of foot position.

**passerelle** (French) a footbridge.

**pas seul** (French) *Ballet.* a dance for a single performer.

**passim** (Latin) here and there; in many different places (said of passages or references scattered throughout a book). Also **et passim.**

**passionatamente** (Italian) *Music.* passionately.

**passionato** (Italian) *Music.* passionate.

**passione, con molta.** See **con molta passione.**

**pas sissonne.** See **sissonne.**

**passito** (Italian) a sweet wine made from sun-dried grapes.

**pasta** (Italian) (lit., 'paste') *Cookery.* noodles and similar products made from a dough of **semolina** flour, water, and sometimes eggs, then rolled and shaped for use.

**pasta asciutta** (Italian) (lit., 'dry pasta') *Cookery.* any kind of cooked **pasta** served with a sauce.

**pasta e fagioli** (Italian) *Cookery.* a dish consisting of navy beans and **pasta** mixed together with onion, garlic, and olive oil.

**pasta in brodo** (Italian) *Cookery.* cooked **pasta** served in soup or broth.

**pasta puttanesca** (Italian) (lit., 'prostitute's pasta') *Cookery.* a dish consisting of shell-shaped pasta in a sauce of olive oil, garlic, capers, and anchovies.

**pastel** (Spanish) 1. a pie; pastry. 2. a cake.

**pastèque** (French) watermelon.

**pasticceria** (Italian) 1. a shop selling fancy pastries, cookies, and cakes. 2. a pastry.

**pasticcio** (Italian)   1. a work of music, literature, or art made up of elements from various sources; **pastiche.**   2. a hodge-podge, a confused mixture.   3. *Music.* an operatic medley. Also **centone.**   4. *Cookery.* a dish consisting of layers of pasta, meat sauce, and cheese that is covered with a cream sauce and baked.

**pastiche** (French)   1. a work of art, music, or architecture incorporating elements of other works.   2. an imitation of a work of art.   3. a confusing mixture.

**pasticheur** (French)   *Fine Arts.* an artist who imitates the works of others rather than creating true originals.

**pastille** (French)   1. a small round candy.   2. a medicinal lozenge.

**pastina** (Italian)   *Cookery.* pasta cut into tiny patterns and cooked and served in broth.

**pastis** (French)   an anise-flavored **liqueur** of Provence.

**pas tombé** (French)   *Ballet.* a movement in which the weight of the dancer falls on one foot.

**pastorale** (Italian)   *Music.* 1. a piece that evokes a pastoral or rustic feeling.   2. a genre of stage presentation of the 15th through the 18th centuries, a precursor of opera, that combined music and ballet, often with a rustic theme.   3. an instrumental composition suggestive of bagpipe music.

**pastorelle** (French)   *Literature.* a genre of medieval lyric poetry with rustic characters and settings.

**pastose.**   See **impasto.**

**pastoso** (Italian)   (lit., 'sticky; soft')   *Music.* mellow, said of a performance.

**pastrami** (Yiddish)   seasoned, smoked or pickled beef, served as a cold cut.

**patchouli** (Tamil)   an East Indian fragrance derived from a certain plant oil.

**pâte** (French)   porcelain paste used in making ceramics.

**pâté** (French)   *Cookery.* 1. liver or other meat and seasonings ground or chopped into a paste and baked.   2. a pie or patty.

**pâte à chou** (French)   *Cookery.* cream puff paste, a pastry dough used to make éclairs and other puffs.

**pâte brisée** (French)   *Cookery.* flaky pie pastry.

**pâté de foie gras** (French)   *Cookery.* pâté made with liver from specially fattened geese, considered a great delicacy.

**pâte de verre** (French)   *Antiques.* a decorative glass made by a technique in which powdered glass of various colors is mixed and refired.

**pâte dure** (French)   *Ceramics.* hard paste, made with mineral clay, used in making high-quality porcelain. See also **pâte tendre.**

**pâte feuilletée** (French)   *Cookery.* puff pastry dough. Also **feuilletée.**

217

pâté maison (French)    a pâté as prepared by a particular restaurant.

pater (Latin)   father.

paterfamilias (Latin)   father of the household; patriarch of the family.

Pater Noster (Latin)   the Our Father, the first two words and Latin title of the Lord's Prayer.

pater patriae (Latin)   father of his country.

pâtes fraîches (French)    fresh pasta.

pâte sucrée (French)    *Cookery.* a sweet pie pastry.

pâte sur pâte (French)    a technique for decorating porcelain using colored pottery slip. Also **pâte-sur-pâte**.

pâte tendre (French)    *Ceramics.* soft paste, made with artificial clay, used in lesser quality porcelain. See also **pâte dure**.

patetico (Italian)    *Music.* pathetic.

pathétique (French)    *Music.* full of pathos.

pâtisserie (French)    1. a pastry; a confection. 2. a pastry shop.

pâtissier (French)    a pastry chef.

patois (French)    1. a regional dialect peculiar to one area of a country. 2. a pidgin or mixture of two languages. 3. cant; argot.

patres conscripti (Latin)    (lit., 'conscript fathers') *Roman history.* formal mode of address for the Roman Senate. Originally *patres et conscripti* 'fathers and conscripted ones.'

patria potestas (Latin)    (lit., 'paternal power') *Roman law.* authority held by a Roman father over his family.

patris est filius (Latin)    (lit., 'he is his father's son') he takes after his father.

patron, *fem.* patronne (French)    1. the owner of an inn or restaurant. 2. *Architecture.* teacher; master.

patrón (Spanish)    1. a boss; head man.    2. an owner, especially of land.

paucas pallabris (pseudo-Latin)    a few words (corruption of **paucis verbis**; from *Taming of the Shrew*, Scene I).

paucis verbis (Latin)    in a few words; briefly.

paupiette (French)    *Cookery.* a thin slice of meat or fish, rolled and stuffed.

pausa (Italian)    *Music.* a rest, as opposed to a **fermata**.

pavé (French)    1. pavement. 2. a jewelry setting in which the stones are placed very close together.

pavillon (French)    *Music.* the bell-shaped part of a wind instrument.

pavillon chinois (French)    *Music.* a noise-making instrument used especially in military music.

pax (Latin)   peace.

218

**Pax Britannica** (Latin)  British peace, as imposed upon the nations of the British empire, especially India.

**pax ecclesiae** (Latin)  (lit., 'peace of the church')  sanctuary or truce as provided by a church.

**pax in bello** (Latin)  (lit., 'peace in war')  a period of reduced fighting in the middle of a war.

**pax regis** (Latin)  (lit., 'peace of the king')  good order and civil tranquillity as maintained by government.

**Pax Romana** (Latin)  Roman peace, as that forcefully imposed within the Roman Empire.

**pax tecum** *or* **vobiscum** (Latin)  peace be with you (singular or plural).

**payadores** (Spanish)  gaucho minstrels.

**payess** (Hebrew)  *Judaism.* the long sideburn locks worn by Orthodox Jewish men.

**paysage** (French)  1. *Fine Arts.* landscape painting. 2. a landscape.

**pays de cocagne** (French)  a land of plenty.

**peag.**  See **wampum.**

**peau de soie** (French)  (lit., 'pelt of silk') a satinlike fabric of silk or rayon. Also **peau-de-soie.**

**peccavi** (Latin)  (lit., 'I have sinned') a confession of guilt.

**pêche** (French)  peach.

**péché mortel** (French)  (lit., 'deadly sin') *Antiques.* a chaise longue formed of an upholstered armchair and a matching upholstered stool.

**pecora** (Italian)  a baby sheep, used for Easter feasts.

**pecorino** (Italian)  a hard, sharp cheese made of sheep's milk. See also **romano.**

**pecunia non olet** (Latin)  money doesn't smell; the source of money does not matter. Also **non olet.**

**pedregal** *or* **pedrigal** (Spanish)  an area covered with rocks.

**Pedro Ximénez** (Spanish)  a variety of Spanish grape used for winemaking in the Montilla region and as a sweetening agent for sherry in Malaga and Jerez. *Abbr.* **PX.**

**peignoir** (French)  a woman's dressing gown.

**peine, à.**  See **à peine.**

**peinture** (French)  *Fine Arts.* the painting technique characteristic of an artist or school of artists.

**peinture à la colle** (French)  *Fine Arts.* 1. a painting technique employing opaque, colored powder suspended in a gum solution. 2. poster-color painting.

**peinture à l'essence** (French)  *Fine Arts.* a painting method using oil paints with the excess oil removed.

**peinture claire** (French)   *Fine Arts.* a technique, employed by Manet and others, in which the academic style of gradations from light to dark was replaced by sharp contrasts.

**pelado** (Spanish)   (lit., 'hairless; stripped') a person of a lower social or economic class.

**pelota** (Spanish)   1. ball.    2. a Basque game from which **jai alai** developed.    3. *Mexico.* the game of **jai alai.**    4. *Cookery.* a dumpling used in Spanish-style stews.

**pelure** (French)   a hard, thin paper used for postage stamps.

**peña** (Spanish)   a cliff.

**penates** (Latin)   household gods. See also **lares et penates.**

**penco** (Spanish)   1. a poor horse; nag.    2. a country bumpkin.

**pendente lite** (Latin)   (lit., 'with the suit pending') *Law.* during litigation.

**Penedés** (Spanish)   a wine district of Catalonia in northeastern Spain.

**penetralia** (Latin)   the innermost parts.

**penetralia mentis** (Latin)   the secret recesses of the mind.

**penne** (Italian)   (lit., 'feathers') short lengths of tubular, hollow **pasta** cut on the diagonal.

**pensée,** *pl.* **pensées** (French)   *Literature.* a collection of thoughts or reflections, as the *Pensées* of Pascal.

**Penseur, Le.**   See **Le Penseur.**

**pensieroso** (Italian)   *Music.* pensive; musing.

**pension** (French)   a boardinghouse in Europe where lodgings are rented at a weekly or monthly rate.

**pensione** (Italian)   a private hotel; boarding house.

**pentimento** (Italian)   (lit., 'repentance') *Fine Arts.* details painted over by the artist that become visible again as the paint becomes translucent with age.

**peón** (Spanish)   1. a laborer; landless peasant.    2. *Bullfighting.* a capeman.

**peperino** (Italian)   *Geology.* a volcanic rock produced by the fusion of sand and cinders.

**peperonata** (Italian)   *Cookery.* a dish made with bell peppers, onions, and tomatoes, cooked and served cold as an appetizer.

**peperoncino,** *pl.* **peperoncini** (Italian)   small, cone-shaped green peppers preserved in vinegar.

**peperoni, pepperoni** (Italian)   1. sausage made with hot peppers, often used as a topping on pizza.    2. red, green, or yellow bell peppers.

**pepitas** (Spanish)   toasted pumpkin seeds.

**per accidens** (Latin)   (lit., 'by accident') *Logic.* by virtue of an external cause or nonessential factor. See also **per se.**

**per ambages** (Latin)   by circuitous means; beating around the bush.

**per annum** (Latin)   by the year; annually. *Abbr.* **p.a.; per an.**

**per ardua ad astra** (Latin)   through hardship to the stars (motto of the British Royal Air Force). See also **per aspera ad astra.**

**per aspera ad astra** (Latin)   through hardship to the stars. See also **per ardua ad astra.**

**per capita** (Latin)   (lit., 'by the heads') for or by each individual; individually.

**per centum** (Latin)   by the hundred; percent.

**perciatelli** (Italian)   a variety of pasta the same shape as **spaghetti** but much thicker.

**per contra** (Latin)   on the contrary; on the other hand.

**per curiam** (Latin)   (lit., 'by the court') *Law.* indicating an opinion of the whole court or the presiding judge rather than one given by a lesser judge.

**perdendo, perdendosi** (Italian)   (lit., 'losing') *Music.* gradually dying away.

**perdendo le forze** (Italian)   (lit., 'losing strength') *Music.* a direction indicating a gradual softening and a slight slowing down.

**per diem** (Latin)   1. by the day; daily.   2. a daily allowance for living expenses.

**perdreau** *or* **perdrix** (French)   partridge.

**perdu,** *fem.* **perdue** (French)   (lit., 'lost') 1. hidden away. 2. watching from an ambush.

**père** (French)   1. father. 2. a priest.

**perestroika** (Russian)   economic modernization, an effort of the Soviet government to update and add efficiency to its national industrial capacity.

**per fas et** (*or* **aut**) **nefas** (Latin)   by right and wrong; justly or unjustly.

**per favore** (Italian)   please.

**perfide Albion** (French)   treacherous Albion, Napoleon's epithet for England.

**pergamo** (Italian)   a pulpit.

**per gradus** (Latin)   step by step.

**per impossibile** (Latin)   as though it were possible; by means of something that is impossible.

**per incuriam** (Latin)   through negligence or carelessness.

**peripeteia** (Greek)   *Literature.* a sudden change of fortune or reversal in the action, especially in a drama.

**perito,** *pl.* **periti** (Italian)   an expert, especially one of the technical experts summoned by the Second Vatican Council.

**per mensem** (Latin)   by the month; monthly.

**permesso** (Italian)  may I pass?;  may I come in? (an expression of politeness).  See also **con permesso.**

**per minas** (Latin)  by threats.

**Pernod** (French)  an anise-flavored **apéritif.**

**per os** (Latin)  *Prescriptions.* by mouth; orally. *Abbr.* **p.o.**

**perpetuum mobile** (Latin)  a perpetual motion machine; something in perpetual motion.

**per procurationem** *or* **procuratorem** (Latin)  by an agent; by proxy; by the action of. *Abbr.* **p.p.** or **per pro.**

**per quod** (Latin)  whereby.

**per saltum** (Latin)  (lit., 'by a leap')  by a sudden advance.

**per se** (Latin)  **1.** in, for, or by itself.  **2.** *Logic.* by virtue of intrinsic cause.  See also **per accidens.**

**perseverando** (Latin)  by persevering.

**persiflage** (French)  banter; mockery; frivolity.

**persifleur** (French)  a person who speaks in a bantering or mocking way.

**persil** (French)  parsley.

**persillade** (French)  *Cookery.* a garnish consisting of chopped parsley, often mixed with garlic.

**persona** (Latin)  **1.** an assumed role.  **2.** a character in a play.  See **dramatis personae.**

**persona grata,** *pl.* **personae gratae** (Latin)  *Diplomacy.* an acceptable person.  See also **persona non grata.**

**persona muta** (Latin)  (lit., 'a silent person')  *Drama.* an actor with a non-speaking part.

**persona non grata,** *pl.* **personae non gratae** (Latin)  an unacceptable person; a diplomat who is no longer welcome in the country of his assignment.  Also **persona ingrata.**

**perspectif cavalière** (French)  *Architecture.* a linear perspective in which the projection is distorted by tilting the plane of the picture.

**perstetur** (Latin)  *Prescriptions.* it may be continued. *Abbr.* **pt.**

**per stirpes** (Latin)  (lit., 'by stems or race')  *Law.* term used in dividing an inheritance among the descendants of a deceased legatee.

**per totam curiam** (Latin)  by the entire court; unanimously.

**per viam** (Latin)  by way of.

**Pesach** (Hebrew)  *Judaism.* the Passover holiday.

**pesante** (Italian)  (lit., 'weighing')  *Music.* heavy.

**pescaditos** (Spanish)  small fish.

**pescado** (Spanish)  fish.

**pesce** (Italian)  fish.

**peso** (Spanish)  the monetary unit of various South American countries.

**pesto** (Italian)  *Cookery.* a paste-like sauce for pasta in which the prime ingredient is basil.

**petate** (Spanish)  1. a mat of straw or palm leaves.  2. a sack made of this material.

**pétillant** (French)  *Wine.* slightly sparkling.

**petit beurre** (French)  *Cookery.* a small butter cookie.

**petit bourgeois,** *fem.* **petit bourgeoise** (French)  a member of the lower middle class.

**petit caporal, le.**  See **le petit caporal.**

**petit déjeuner** (French)  breakfast.

**petite bourgeoisie** (French)  the lower middle class.

**petite marmite** (French)  (lit., 'little kettle')  *Cookery.* a broth made from beef and vegetables, served in a small pot.

**petite pièce** (French)  *Theater.* a minor or brief production.

**petites entrées** (French)  the first courses in a meal.

**petites gens** (French)  1. people with very little money.  2. people of no importance from an aristocratic perspective.

**petites morales** (French)  small details of politeness and courtesy.

**petit feu** (French)  *Ceramics.* a firing at low temperature.  See also **grand feu.**

**petit four,** *pl.* **petits fours** (French)  *Cookery.* fancy decorated cookies of various shapes and flavors.

**petitio principii** (Latin)  (lit., 'resorting to the principle')  *Logic.* begging the question; using a premise dependent upon or equivalent to the conclusion.

**petit-lait** (French)  whey.

**petit-maître** (French)  a man who is fastidious about his dress and appearance.

**petit mal** (French)  the milder form of epilepsy.  See also **grand mal.**

**petit monde** (French)  (lit., 'the little world') the lower social classes.

**petit point** (French)  *Applied Arts.* 1. fine needlework done on canvas.  2. fine lace.

**petits droits** (French)  *Copyright Law.* all rights pertaining to copyright and performing right, except those in stage performance.

**petits jeux** (French)  social games.

**petit souper** (French)  a light, informal supper for an intimate group.

**petits pois** (French)  small green peas.

**petits tours** (French)  *Ballet.* small turns.

**petit sujet** (French)  *Ballet.* a minor dancer in a ballet troupe.

**petits vins** (French)  local or country wines of France.

**petit tours.**  See **tours chaînés.**

**petit verre** (French)    a small glass of liqueur.

**peu à peu** (French)    little by little.

**peu de chose** (French)    a trifling matter.

**peut-être** (French)    perhaps.

**peu, un.**    See **un peu.**

**peyote** (Spanish)    a cactus common to the southwestern U.S. and northern Mexico whose dried tubercles are chewed as a hallucinogen.

**pezzo,** *pl.* **pezzi** (Italian)    *Music.* a piece.

**pezzonovante** (Italian)    (lit., '.90 caliber gun') an important person; a self-important person; equivalent to English *big shot.*

**Phantasiebild** (German)    fantasy; fantasy picture.

**Phantasiestück** (German)    fantasy piece.

**Philosophiae Doctor** (Latin)    the academic degree of Doctor of Philosophy. *Abbr.* **Ph.D.**

**phyllo** (Greek)    *Cookery.* a type of very thin pastry dough used in Greek dishes. Also **filo.**

**piacere, a.**    See **a piacere.**

**piacevole** (Italian)    *Music.* agreeable.

**pia mater** (Latin)    (lit., 'pious mother') *Anatomy.* the innermost of the coverings of the brain.

**pianamente** (Italian)    *Music.* softly.

**piangendo, piangente** (Italian)    (lit., 'weeping') *Music.* plaintively.

**piangevolmente** (Italian)    *Music.* sadly; mournfully.

**pianissimo** (Italian)    *Music.* very soft; very softly. *Abbr.* **pp.**

**piano** (Italian)    *Music.* soft; softly. *Abbr.* **p.**

**pianoforte** (Italian)    *Music.* a piano, especially one that is an antique. *Abbr.* **pf.**

**piano nobile** (Italian)    *Architecture.* the principal story of a formal residence, usually one story above the ground floor.

**piazza** (Italian)    **1.** a public square in a city.    **2.** a covered gallery or veranda.

**pibroch** (Scots Gaelic)    bagpipe music of the Scottish highlands.

**picadillo** (Spanish)    *Cookery.* a stuffing made of ground or minced meat.

**picador** (Spanish)    *Bullfighting.* a mounted bullfighter who vexes the bull with a lance.

**pícaro,** *fem.* **pícara** (Spanish)    **1.** a rogue or vagabond.    **2.** a rascal; petty crook. See also **novela picaresca.**

**piccata** (Italian)    *Cookery.* a designation for a dish made with veal cooked in butter and seasoned with lemon and chopped parsley.

**picot** (French)    one of the small loops of thread that forms the edging on lace or ribbon.

**pièce à thèse** (French)   *Theater.* a play with a thesis, intended to be instructive.

**pièce bien faite** (French)   *Theater.* a play that is well constructed but rather shallow.

**pièce de circonstance** (French)   an artistic work created for a special occasion.

**pièce de résistance** (French)   1. *Cookery.* the featured dish of a meal. **2.** the main feature or event in a series.

**pièce de spectacle** (French)   a creative work intended to dazzle the viewer with its special effects.

**pièce de théâtre** (French)   a dramatic work.

**pièce d'occasion** (French)   a work written to commemorate a special occasion.

**pièce montée** (French)   1. a set piece. 2. *Cookery.* a decorative preparation.

**pièce noire** (French)   *Theater.* a play in which tragic events and pessimism dominate.

**pièce rose** (French)   *Theater.* a play with an optimistic spirit that ends happily.

**pied, à.**   See **à pied.**

**pied, être de.**   See **être de pied.**

**pied-à-terre** (French)   an apartment or other residence maintained as a convenience for occasional visits away from home.

**pied de biche** (French)   *Furniture.* a hoof foot, a decorative leg that resembles a cloven hoof.

**pied en cap, de.**   See **de pied en cap.**

**pied noir** (French)   a French or European inhabitant of Algeria.

**pieds, cinq positions des** (French)   *Ballet.* the five positions of the feet with which every classical ballet step begins or ends.

**pierre fendre, à.**   See **à pierre fendre.**

**Pietà** (Italian)   1. *Fine Arts.* any depiction of the Virgin Mary holding the slain Jesus, the most famous example being Michelangelo's sculpture.   **2.** *Music.* (*l.c.*) pity.

**pietas** (Latin)   loyal devotion, as to family, country, or friends.

**piétiner** (French)   (lit., 'to trample') *Ballet.* designating accented movements performed on the points.

**pietosamente** (Italian)   *Music.* piteously.

**pietra dura** (Italian)   *Fine Arts.* the hard stones used in Italian mosaics.

**piffero** (Italian)   *Music.* a fife.

**pilaf** (Turkish)   *Cookery.* a dish of rice cooked in meat broth, containing seasonings and often meat or fish. Also **pilaff; pilau; pilaw.**

**pilau** *or* **pilaw.**   See **pilaf.**

**pilón** (Spanish)   *Southwestern U.S. and Mexico.* an extra portion or measure added to a purchase or bargain for good will. See also **lagniappe.**

**piloncillo** (Spanish)   *Southwestern U.S. and Mexico.* a type of sugar candy.

**pilpul** (Hebrew)   *Judaism.* rabbinical disputation over fine points of Talmudic rules.

**piña** (Spanish)   **1.** a pineapple.   **2.** a pine cone.

**piña colada** (Spanish)   a cocktail made with pineapple juice and rum.

**piñata** (Spanish)   *Mexico.* a decorated ceramic or paper container filled with candy and toys, featured at Mexican Christmas celebrations.

**pincé** (French)   *Music.* **1.** designating stringed instruments that are plucked rather than bowed. See also **pizzicato. 2.** an ornament created by rapidly alternating one note with a lower one.

**pince-nez** (French)   eyeglasses that are held in place by a small noseclip.

**pinchos** (Spanish)   *Cookery.* pieces of meat or mushrooms broiled and served on skewers as an appetizer.

**pinole** (Spanish)   *Mexico.* a drink made of sweetened corn.

**piñon** (Spanish)   **1.** a pine nut.   **2.** a pine cone.

**pinot noir** (French)   a variety of red burgundy wine.

**pinto** (Spanish)   (lit., 'painted') a spotted horse; a "paint" horse.

**pinxit** (Latin)   *Fine Arts.* he (*or* she) painted (it) (written with the artist's name on a work of art). *Abbr.* **pinx.**

**piperade** (French)   *Cookery.* a Basque-style omelet with tomatoes and peppers.

**piperno** (Italian)   *Geology.* a rough, ash-colored volcanic rock used in paving.

**piqué** (French)   **1.** a fabric woven with a pattern of raised cords. **2.** ornamentation with patterns of punching and inlay, as of gold or tortoise shell. **3.** *Ballet.* a movement performed by stepping directly on the point or half-point of the working foot while the other foot is raised in the air. **4.** *Music.* a staccato effect, as a bouncing movement of the bow in violin playing.

**piquet** (French)   a card game for two players, using a deck of 32 cards, with points scored for different combinations.

**piragua** (Spanish)   a small Indian boat with one sail.

**pirogi** (Russian)   *Cookery.* small dumplings containing a filling of meat, fruit, etc. Also **pirogen; piroshki.**

**piroshki.**   See **pirogi.**

**pirouette** (French)   a complete turn of the body on one foot, as in dancing.

**pis aller** (French)   a last resort; a course of action to be followed only in extreme necessity. Also **pis-aller.**

**Pisces** (Latin)   the Fishes, a constellation and sign of the zodiac.

**pisco** (Spanish)   an Andean alcoholic beverage.

**pise de terre** (French)   the rammed earth method of building, in which clay, gravel, etc., are packed hard in forms to make a building material. Also **pisé de terre.**

**piselli** (Italian)   peas.

**pissaladière** (French)   *Cookery.* a style of pizza popular in Nice, made with onions, black olives, and anchovies.

**pissoir** (French)   a public urinal of France, usually situated on a sidewalk.

**pisto** (Spanish)   *Cookery.* a Spanish dish that varies from region to region, made with vegetables and sometimes including eggs and ham.

**pistolet.**   See **ailes de pigeons.**

**pistou** (French)   *Cookery.* a mixture of tomatoes, garlic, basil, and olive oil, often used in making vegetable soups.

**pita** (Greek)   bread baked in round, flat pieces with a hollow pocket inside; pocket bread.

**pittura metafisica** (Italian)   *Fine Arts.* a style of dreamlike, melancholy painting that developed early in the 20th century as a reaction against futurism.

**più** (Italian)   *Music.* more.

**più allegro** (Italian)   *Music.* quicker.

**più lento** (Italian)   *Music.* slower.

**più mosso** (Italian)   *Music.* more animated.

**pizzaiola, alla.**   See **alla pizzaiola.**

**pizza rustica** (Italian)   *Cookery.* a type of pie containing cheese, ham, sausage, and hardboiled eggs layered between pastry dough.

**pizzicato,** *pl.* **pizzicati** (Italian)   *Music.* 1. plucked, referring to the technique of plucking the strings of a violin with the fingers instead of using the bow.   2. *n.* a passage played in this way. See also **coll'arco.**

**placé** (French)   *Ballet.* correctly aligned, referring to a dancer's body.

**place, sur.**   See **sur place.**

**placet** (Latin)   (lit., 'it pleases (me)') a vote of assent.

**plaisir, à.**   See **à plaisir.**

**plané** (French)   (lit., 'soaring') *Ballet.* designating steps in which the dancer tries to remain in mid-air for as long as possible.

**plata** (Spanish)   silver.

**plat du jour** (French)   the special meal or dish of the day in a restaurant.

**plat mijoté** (French)   *Cookery.* a carefully prepared, long-simmered dish.

**Plattdeutsch** (German)   Low German, the more informal dialects of northern Germany.   See also **Hochdeutsch.**

**playa** (Spanish)  1. a beach.  2. a shallow desert depression where water may collect during rainy seasons. See also **tinaja, 1.**

**plaza de toros** (Spanish)  *Bullfighting.* the large outdoor arena where bullfights take place. See also **ruedo.**

**plebs** (Latin)  the masses; the common people.

**plein air** (French)  (lit., 'the open air') the outdoors, especially in reference to atmosphere and the quality of light.

**plein-air** (French)  *Fine Arts.*  1. designating painting done outdoors rather than in a studio.  2. designating a style of painting that captures the effects of natural light in outdoor scenes. See also **en plein air.**

**plein jeu** (French)  (lit., 'full play') *Music.*  1. the full power of an organ or harmonium.

**pleno jure** (Latin)  with full right or authority.

**plenum** (Latin)  (lit., 'full') a full meeting of an assembly.

**plié** (French)  *Ballet.* a bending of the knees with the back kept straight.

**plique à jour** (French)  an enameling technique in which translucent enamel is reinforced by metal ribbing, producing a stained-glass window effect.

**plisse** *or* **plissé** (French)  (lit., 'pleated') a fabric with a puckered finish.

**plumbum** (Latin)  the metallic element lead. *Abbr.* **Pb.**

**pobrecito,** *fem.* **pobrecita** (Spanish)  poor dear; poor little thing.

**pochade** (French)  *Fine Arts.* a rough sketch done in oils that is preliminary to a more finished version of the subject.

**poché** (French)  *Architecture.* the areas representing wall sections in a plan, usually shown blackened.

**pochette** (French)  (lit., 'little pocket') *Music.* a small stringed instrument, similar to a violin, formerly used by dancing masters.

**pochissimo** (Italian)  *Music.* very little; the least possible. Also **pochetto.**

**pochoir** (French)  *Fine Arts.* a stencil.

**poco** (Italian)  *Music.* a little; rather.

**poco** (Spanish)  a little; a small amount; a bit.

**poco allegro** (Italian)  *Music.* somewhat quick.

**poco a poco** (Italian)  little by little. Also **a poco a poco.**

**poco curante,** *pl.* **poco curanti** (Italian)  (lit., 'caring little') a careless, indifferent person. Also **pococurante.**

**poco forte** (Italian)  *Music.* somewhat loud.

**poco più lento** (Italian)  *Music.* somewhat slower.

**podestà** (Italian)  the chief magistrate in medieval Italian towns.

**poêle** (French)  a frying pan.

**poelée** (French)  *Cookery.* soup stock for boiling fowl.

**poema sinfonico** (Italian)   *Music.* a symphonic poem, a one-movement work with literary, dramatic, and pictorial elements.

**poème symphonique** (French)   *Music.* a continuous, one-movement work containing literary, dramatic, and pictorial elements.

**poète manqué** (French)   a poet of little talent; would-be poet. See also **poète maudit**.

**poète maudit** (French)   (lit., 'cursed poet') *Literature.* a poet who is not understood or appreciated by his contemporaries. See also **artiste maudit; poète manqué**.

**pogrom** (Russian)   *Russian history.* an organized massacre of a minority group, as of Russian Jews.

**poi** (Hawaiian)   *Cookery.* a Hawaiian dish of taro root made into a paste.

**poilu** (French)   an infantryman.

**point** (French)   1. a stitch. 2. a type of lace. See also **petit point**.

**point, à.**   See **à point**.

**point, au.**   See **au point**.

**point coupé** (French)   (lit., 'cut stitch') a type of lace with open areas cut out for added ornamentation.

**point d'Alençon** (French)   Alençon lace, a delicate lace with an outline of twisted yarn.

**point d'Angleterre** (French)   English lace, made using thread that is woven around a framework of pins.

**point d'appui** (French)   1. point of support; fulcrum. 2. a base of military operations.

**point de France** (French)   handmade lace produced in France prior to 1665.

**point de gaze** (French)   (lit., 'gauze stitch') a delicate lace with floral patterns on a net ground.

**point de Hongrie** (French)   (lit., 'Hungarian stitch') flame stitch, with a pattern of ogees in the fabric.

**point de repère** (French)   reference or guide mark.

**point d'esprit** (French)   a decorative net with fine dots woven into it.

**pointe,** *pl.* **pointes** (French)   *Ballet.* the tip of the pointed toes.

**pointé** (French)   *Music.* pointed; detached.

**pointe d'archet, à la.**   See **à la pointe d'archet**.

**pointes, sur les.**   See **sur les pointes**.

**pointes, temps de.**   See **temps de pointes**.

**pointillé** (French)   designating a decoration of tooled dots, as on a book cover.

**pointillisme** (French)   *Fine Arts.* a form of Impressionism in which dots of pure colors are juxtaposed to create an effect.

**pointilliste** (French)    *Fine Arts.* an artist using **pointillisme.**

**poire** (French)    a pear.

**poireau** (French)    a leek.

**pois** (French)    pea; peas.

**poisson** (French)    fish.

**poitrine** (French)    breast.

**poivrade** (French)    *Cookery.* a pepper sauce.

**poivre** (French)    pepper. See also **au poivre.**

**polenta** (Italian)    *Cookery.* a cornmeal mush served with sauces or used as a bed for roast poultry or game.

**polis,** *pl.* **poleis** (Greek)    an ancient Greek city-state.

**politburo** (Russian)    an executive committee of a national Communist party.

**politesse** (French)    politeness.

**politico** (Italian)    a politician.

**político** (Spanish)    **1.** *n.* a politician.    **2.** *adj.* political.

**pollame** (Italian)    poultry.

**pollice presso** (Latin)    (lit., 'with thumb closed') a sign of approbation.

**pollice verso** (Latin)    (lit., 'with thumb turned') thumbs down; rejection of a suggestion.

**pollo** (Italian, Spanish)    chicken.

**polo** (Spanish)    a dance of southern Spain accompanied by castanets and rhythmic clapping.

**polpette,** *sing.* **polpetta** (Italian)    meatballs.

**Polska** (Polish)    **1.** the Polish name for Poland.    **2.** (*l.c.*) designating something Polish.

**poltergeist** (German)    spirit said to manifest itself by making loud noises and displacing objects.

**pomme** (French)    an apple.

**pomme de terre** (French)    a potato.

**pommes frites** (French)    fried potatoes.

**pomodoro,** *pl.* **pomodori** (Italian)    a tomato. See also **fileto di pomodoro.**

**pomodoro, al.**    See **al pomodoro.**

**pompier** (French)    (lit., 'fireman') *Fine Arts.* a 19th-century school of art taking as its subject matter allegorical, religious, and mythological themes, and treating them in a technically skillful but uninspired way.

**pomposo** (Italian)    *Music.* pompous.

**ponderoso** (Italian)    *Music.* heavy; ponderous. Also **pondoroso.**

**ponentino** (Italian)    a westerly breeze.

**pons asinorum** (Latin)   (lit., 'bridge of asses')   any problem considered difficult for a beginner or a simpleton (from the designation for Euclid's fifth geometric proposition: if a triangle has two sides equal, the angles opposite those sides are also equal).

**ponticello** (Italian)   (lit., 'little bridge')   *Music.* the bridge of a stringed instrument.

**pontifex maximus** (Latin)   (lit., 'supreme priest')   **1.** *Roman religion.* an official priestly position at Rome.   **2.** (*cap.*) one of the titles of the pope.

**Pont l'Evêque** (French)   a semi-soft, strong-flavored yellow cheese of Normandy.

**porc** (French)   pork.

**porchetta** (Italian)   suckling pig.

**porcini** (Italian)   a type of wild mushroom.

**por favor** (Spanish)   please.

**portamento** (Italian)   (lit., 'carrying')   *Music.* the carryover of one note into the next in singing or in playing a bowed instrument.

**portando** (Italian)   *Music.* carrying, especially in the sense of **portamento**.

**portato** (Italian)   *Music.* carried. See also **portamento**.

**port de bras** (French)   *Ballet.* a movement or series of movements of the arms.

**port de voix** (French)   *Music.* carrying the voice smoothly from one note to another.

**Port du Salut** (French)   a variety of soft, creamy cheese (named for the Trappist monastery where it was first produced). Also **Port Salut**.

**porté**, *fem.* **portée** (French)   *Ballet.* **1.** designating a step that is carried from one spot to another. **2.** the raising and carrying of a female dancer by a male dancer.

**porte-cochere** (French)   a covered porch at the door of a building for sheltering people as they enter or leave their vehicles. Also **porte-cochère**.

**porte-monnaie** (French)   a purse; pocketbook.

**portiere** (French)   a curtain at a doorway. Also **portière**.

**posada** (Spanish)   an inn.

**posé** (French)   *Ballet.* a posed position of the body.

**Posillipo, alla.**   See **alla Posillipo**.

**position fermée** (French)   (lit., 'closed position')   *Ballet.* a position in which the feet touch each other.

**position ouverte** (French)   (lit., 'open position')   *Ballet.* a position in which the feet are held apart.

**positions de bras** (French)   *Ballet.* the basic positions of the arms from which all arm movements begin.

**positions des pieds, cinq.**   See **pieds, cinq positions de**.

**positions soulevées** (French)    *Ballet.* the open positions of the feet.

**posizione** (Italian)    *Music.* the shifting of the left hand in the playing of a stringed instrument to produce a different set of notes. Also **manica.**

**posse comitatus** (Latin)    (lit., 'the power of the county') forces gathered by the sheriff to preserve law and order. *Abbr.* **posse.**

**post bellum auxilium** (Latin)    (lit., 'help after the war') assistance offered too late.

**post cibos** *or* **cibum** (Latin)    *Prescriptions.* after meals. *Abbr.* **p.c.**

**post diem** (Latin)    (lit., 'after the day') *Law.* said of a payment made after the due date.

**post facto** (Latin)    after the event; after the fact. Also **ex post facto.**

**post hoc, ergo propter hoc** (Latin)    (lit., 'after this, therefore on account of this') the illogical reasoning that something resulted from a certain preceding fact or event merely because one followed the other in time.

**post litem motam** (Latin)    *Law.* after the suit commenced.

**post meridiem** (Latin)    after midday; between noon and midnight. *Abbr.* **p.m., P.M.** See also **ante meridiem.**

**post mortem** (Latin)    (lit., 'after death') 1. an examination of a corpse after death.    2. a review and evaluation of an incident or set of events.

**post obitum** (Latin)    after death.

**post partum** (Latin)    after childbirth.

**postre** (Spanish)    a dessert.

**post scriptum** (Latin)    (lit., 'after what has been written') a note added at the end of a letter after the signature; postscript. *Abbr.* **P.S.**

**post tenebras lux** (Latin)    after darkness comes the dawn (said especially of a sudden realization).

**potage** (French)    soup.

**potage du jour** (French)    the special soup of the day in a restaurant.

**pot-au-feu** (French)    *Cookery.* a dish of beef simmered in vegetables, usually with the broth served separately.

**potée** (French)    *Cookery.* a soup of meat and vegetables.

**potiche** (French)    a porcelain vase.

**potiron** (French)    pumpkin.

**potpourri** (French)    1. a fragrant mixture of dried flower petals, herbs, and spices. 2. a medley; a collection of miscellaneous elements. 3. a confused mixture. 4. *Cookery.* a stew. Also **pot-pourri.**

**potro** (Spanish)    a colt; young horse.

**pouding** (French)    pudding.

**poudre** (French)    powder.

**Pouilly-Fuissé** (French)    a select variety of dry white wine from Burgundy.

232

**Pouilly-Fumé** (French)    a variety of dry white wine from the Loire valley.

**poularde** (French)    a fat pullet; capon.

**poule au pot** (French)    (lit., 'chicken in the pot') a stewed chicken, the Sunday meal that Henry IV of France promised to the common people.

**poulet** (French)    a young chicken.

**poult-de-soie** (French)    a fine, ribbed silk.

**pourboire** (French)    a gratuity.

**pour le mérite** (French)    for merit (used on medals).

**pourparler** (French)    an informal preliminary meeting.

**pour passer le temps** (French)    to pass the time.

**pourquoi?** (French)    why?

**pousse-café** (French)    1. a liqueur served after coffee. 2. a drink in which several different liqueurs are layered in a glass.

**poussin** (French)    a chick; a just-hatched chicken.

**Poussinisme** (French)    *Fine Arts.* the doctrine of the French Academy during the 17th century that stressed linear elements and design as the criteria of artistic excellence.

**pou stō** (Greek)    (lit., 'where I may stand') a place of leverage; a good base of operations.

**pow wow** (Algonquian)    1. a North American Indian tribal gathering. 2. a meeting of any sort.

**pozo** (Spanish)    a well; natural spring.

**pozzolana** (Italian)    *Geology.* a volcanic rock used to prepare concrete that can cure under water.

**praemissis praemittendis** (Latin)    with preliminaries omitted.

**praemonitus praemunitus** (Latin)    forewarned (is) forearmed.

**praenomen** (Latin)    1. first name; given name.    2. the first name in the Roman system for naming individuals, designating the personal name, as *Gaius* in *Gaius Julius Caesar.* See also **cognomen, 3; nomen, 3.**

**praeteriti anni** (Latin)    bygone years.

**praliné** (French)    containing or flavored with nuts boiled in sugar.

**pranzo** (Italian)    dinner.

**Pravda** (Russian)    (lit., 'truth') the official newspaper of the Soviet Communist party.

**précieux,** *fem.* **précieuse** (French)    1. affected in manners and speech. 2. (*fem.*) a member of the woman's literary group of 17th-century France whose goal it was to refine language and manners.

**préciosité** (French)    affectation in manners and language.

**precipitando** (Italian)    *Music.* hurrying. Also **precipitandosi.**

**precipitato, precipitoso** (Italian)    *Music.* hurried.

**précipité** (French)    *Ballet.* a hurried glissade step.

**precipitosamente** (Italian)   *Music.* hurriedly.

**précis** (French)   a summary or abstract.

**precisione** (Italian)   *Music.* precision, in regard to time.

**preciso** (Italian)   *Music.* precise, in regard to time.

**predella** (Italian)   an altar platform.

**prego** (Italian)   1. please.   2. you're welcome.

**preludio** (Italian)   *Music.* a prelude.

**premier coup** (French)   the first blow or stroke.   See also **au premier coup.**

**premier cru** (French)   a select, superior wine made from the first growth of the vine.

**premier danseur étoile,** *fem.* **première danseuse étoile** (French)   *Ballet.* the title of the most prestigious dancer in the Paris ballet company.

**premier danseur,** *fem.* **première danseuse** (French)   *Ballet.* the leading dancer in a ballet company.

**première** *or* **premiere** (French)   the opening performance of a play, movie, or other entertainment.

**première partie** (French)   *Furniture.* the primary inlay or ground in inlaid work.

**première position** (French)   *Ballet.* the first position, a basic position of the feet or arms, used in teaching.

**premier pas, le.**   See **le premier pas.**

**premier venue, le.**   See **le premier venue.**

**prensa, la** (Spanish)   the press.

**préparation** (French)   *Ballet.* the movement used to prepare for a step or turn.

**presa** (Italian)   (lit., 'taking; seizure')   *Music.* a mark indicating the point in a canon at which each successive voice is to take up the theme.

**pré-salé** (French)   young sheep raised in salt meadows.

**presidente** (Spanish)   1. a president.   2. *Southwestern U.S. and Mexico.* a local government official.

**presidio** (Spanish)   a prison; fortress.

**pressando, pressante** (Italian)   *Music.* accelerating.

**prestezza, con.**   See **con prestezza.**

**prestissimo** (Italian)   *Music.* very quick.

**presto** (Italian)   *Music.* quick.

**prie-dieu** (French)   a kneeling stand, for use during prayer.

**prima.**   See **primo.**

**prima ballerina** (Italian)   the leading female dancer in a ballet company.

**prima ballerina assoluta** (Italian)   a title of great honor bestowed upon a distinguished female ballet dancer.

**prima buffa** (Italian)   *Opera.* the principal female comic singer or actress.

**prima colazione** (Italian)    breakfast.

**prima donna** (Italian)    1. a person with a haughty or self-righteous manner. 2. *Opera.* the leading female singer in an opera company. See also **diva**.

**prima donna assoluta** (Italian)    *Opera.* a title of great honor bestowed on a distinguished female performer.

**prima facie** (Latin)    (lit., 'at first appearance')   1. *Law.* presumed true unless disproved by other evidence.    2. clear and apparent at first glance.

**prima inter pares.**    See **primus inter pares**.

**primavera** (Italian)    1. spring.    2. *Cookery.* a designation for a **pasta** dish with a sauce of finely cut spring vegetables sauteed in olive oil.

**prima vista, a.**    See **a prima vista**.

**prima volta** (Italian)    *Music.* the first time.

**primo,** *fem.* **prima** (Italian)    1. first in rank; chief.    2. *Music.* *n.* the first or principal part, as in a duet.

**primo basso** (Italian)    *Music.* the chief bass singer.

**prim'omo** (Italian)    *Opera.* the principal actor or male singer. Also **primo uomo**.

**primo nomo** (Italian)    *Theater.* the best performer.

**primo tempo** (Italian)    *Music.* the first tempo, that indicated at the beginning of a piece.

**primo tenore** (Italian)    *Music.* the leading tenor singer.

**primo uomo.**    See **prim'omo**.

**primum mobile** (Latin)    (lit., 'first moving thing') the prime mover; in ancient cosmology, the outermost sphere of the concentric spheres forming the universe, whose movement drove the others.

**primus inter pares** (Latin)    first among equals, said of a designated leader or chairman in a group of peers. Also, *fem.*, **prima inter pares**.

**primus motor** (Latin)    the first mover; the cause of all movement.

**princeps** (Latin)    1. *Roman history.* the official designation for the emperor.    2. a prince.

**principe** (Italian)    a prince.

**principessa** (Italian)    a princess.

**principium,** *pl.* **principia** (Latin)    1. principle.    2. (*pl.*, *cap.*) title given to a basic, fundamental work of scholarly inquiry.

**printanier,** *fem.* **printanière** (French)    *Cookery.* designating a dish prepared with early spring vegetables. See also **primavera**.

**printanière, à la.**    See **à la printanière**.

**Priorato** (Spanish)    a strong, amber-colored white wine from Tarragona in northeastern Spain.

**prise** (French)    a pinch of snuff.

**prisiadka** (Russian)    a step in Slavic folk-dancing in which a male dancer squats and kicks out each foot alternately.  See also **kazachok.**

**prix fixe** (French)    the fixed menu of a restaurant, from which courses may be selected for a set price.  See also **à la carte; table d'hôte.**

**probatum est** (Latin)    it is or has been proved or tried.

**pro bono publico** (Latin)    for the public good, said of goods or services provided without charge.  Frequently shortened to **pro bono.**

**procès-verbal** (French)    an official report of proceedings or facts; minutes of a meeting.

**proemium** (Latin)    introduction; prologue.

**pro et contra** (Latin)    for and against.  *Abbr.* **pro et con.**

**profanum vulgus** (Latin)    the common rabble.  See also **odi profanum vulgus.**

**profil perdu** (French)    *Fine Arts.* a severe profile, in which the head of the subject is turned from view.

**profiterole** (French)    *Cookery.* a cream puff filled with ice cream, whipped cream, or custard, often served with chocolate sauce.  Also **profiterolle.**

**profondo** (Italian)    *Music.* deep, referring to a bass voice.

**pro forma** (Latin)    as a matter of form; as a formality to satisfy legal or procedural requirements.

**progressivamente** (Italian)    *Music.* progressively.

**pro hac vice** (Latin)    for this occasion (only).

**projet** (French)    1. *Architecture.* the main elements of a design.  2. a draft of a treaty or other document.

**prolegomenon,** *pl.* **prolegomena** (Greek)    1. an introductory essay or prologue to a longer work.  2. any introductory portion or preliminary phase.

**prolétaire** (French)    a person of the working class.

**pro memoria** (Latin)    in memory of; as a reminder.

**promenade, en.**    See **en promenade.**

**promotor fidei.**    See **advocatus diaboli.**

**pronto** (Italian)    *Music.* ready; prompt.

**pronto** (Spanish)    now; immediately; right away.

**pro nunc** (Latin)    for the time being.

**pronunciamiento** (Spanish)    a public decree or proclamation, especially a declaration of rebellion.

**pro patria** (Latin)    for one's country.

**proprio motu** (Latin)    by one's own motion; spontaneously.

**proprio vigore** (Latin)    1. by its own strength; because of its intrinsic meaning.  2. by one's own strength; through independent action.

**propter hoc** (Latin)    on account of this.

**pro rata** (Latin)   according to a rate or proportion; proportionately.

**pro re nata** (Latin)   (lit., 'for the thing that is born')   **1.** adapted for the occasion or to meet a sudden development.   **2.** *Prescriptions.* as needed. *Abbr.* **p.r.n.**

**prosciutto** (Italian)   spiced pressed ham, served as a cold cut.

**prosit** (Latin)   (lit., 'may it benefit you')   to your health (said as a toast).

**pro tanto** (Latin)   for so much; to that extent; as far as it goes.

**protégé,** *fem.* **protégée** (French)   a person being trained or supported by another, usually in regard to career or vocation.

**pro tempore** (Latin)   for the time; temporarily.   *Abbr.* **pro tem.**

**Provençal** (French)   designating something from Provence, as the people or their language.   See also **langue d'oc.**

**provençale, á la.**   See **à la provençale.**

**provolone** (Italian)   a hard-ripened light-colored cheese, often smoked, put up in tear-shaped balls that are wrapped in twine for hanging.

**proxime accessit.**   See **accessit.**

**proximo** (Latin)   of or during the next month.   *Abbr.* **prox.**   See also **ultimo.**

**pruneau** (French)   a prune; French plum.

**publici juris** (Latin)   (lit., 'of public right')   *Law.* referring to property common to all, as air and light.

**puchero** (Spanish)   *Cookery.* a stew that usually includes meat, chicken, and vegetables, and, in countries of Spanish America, bananas.

**pucka.**   See **pukka.**

**pudenda,** *sing.* **pudendum** (Latin)   the genitals.

**pueblito** (Spanish)   a small **pueblo.**

**pueblo** (Spanish)   **1.** a village or town.   **2.** a people.   **3.** an Indian village, especially one consisting of a group of communal dwellings built of **adobe.**

**puerto** (Spanish)   **1.** a seaport.   **2.** a mountain pass.

**pugaree.**   See **pugree.**

**pugnis et calcibus** (Latin)   (lit., 'with fists and heels')   with all one's means or strength.

**pugree** (Hindi)   **1.** a turban worn by natives of India.   **2.** a cloth wound around a hat and trailing behind as a protection against the sun.   Also **pug(g)aree; puggree.**

**pukka** (Anglo-Indian)   sound; reliable; genuine.   Also **pucka; pakka.**

**Pulcinella** (Italian)   *Theater.* a big-nosed clown that speaks Neapolitan dialect, one of the stock figures of the **commedia dell'arte,** the model for the English Punch.

**pulque** (Spanish)   *Mexico.* an alcoholic beverage made from the **maguey.**

**pulquería** (Spanish)   *Mexico.* a bar or shop serving **pulque.**

**punctatim** (Latin)    point for point.

**punctum** (Latin)    1. point; small area. 2. *Music.* a note.

**punctum saliens** (Latin)    salient point; key feature.

**Punica fides.**    See **fides Punica.**

**punkah** (Hindi)    a large swinging fan suspended from a ceiling and pulled back and forth with a rope to create a draft.

**puntilla** (Spanish)    1. *Bullfighting.* a short dagger used to finish off the bull.    2. fine lace edging.

**purdah** (Hindi)    1. a screen or curtain for secluding females from sight. 2. the practice of secluding females.

**purée** (French)    *Cookery.* 1. an ingredient that has been creamed by passing through a sieve or by mashing. 2. a creamy soup made of meat and vegetables that have been boiled and then passed through a sieve.

**purgatorio** (Italian)    purgatory.

**purpureus pannus** (Latin)    a purple patch, an excessively ornate literary passage (Horace, *Ars Poetica* 15).

**pur sang** (French)    (lit., 'pure blood') genuine beyond a doubt.

**Putsch** (German)    *Politics.* a coup d'état.

**putto,** *pl.* **putti** (Italian)    *Fine Arts.* representations of children of angelic or cupidlike appearance.

# Q

**qua** (Latin)   as; in the capacity of; considered as; as far as.

**quadratista** (Italian)   *Fine Arts.* an artist whose specialty is **trompe l'oeil** perspective painting. Also **quadraturista.**

**quadrennium** (Latin)   a period of four years.

**quadriga** (Latin)   a chariot drawn by four horses.

**quadrille** (French)   1. a type of square dance for couples. 2. *Ballet.* a term for a group of dancers.

**quadrivium** (Latin)   the advanced division of the seven liberal arts, comprising arithmetic, geometry, astronomy, and music. See also **trivium.**

**quaere** (Latin)   (lit., 'inquire')   a query or question; a call for an investigation.

**quae vide** (Latin)   which see (used in cross references). *Abbr.* **q.v.; qq.v.**

**quaglia,** *pl.* **quaglie** (Italian)   quail.

**Quai d'Orsay** (French)   the address of the French Foreign Ministry, metonymic for the ministry itself.

**quantum libet** (Latin)   *Prescriptions.* as much as one pleases. *Abbr.* **q.l.; q. lib.**

**quantum meruit** (Latin)   as much as one deserved.

**quantum mutatus ab illo** (Latin)   how different from what he was.

**quantum placet** (Latin)   *Prescriptions.* as much as one pleases. *Abbr.* **q. pl.; q.p.**

**quantum sufficit** (Latin)   *Prescriptions.* as much as is sufficient. *Abbr.* **q.s.; quant. suff.**

**quantum vis** (Latin)   as much as you wish.

**quaque hora** (Latin)   *Prescriptions.* every hour. *Abbr.* **qq. hor.**

**quart** (French)   *Ballet.* a quarter or fourth part of a movement.

**quarte** (French)   a defensive position in fencing.

**quartetto** (Italian)   *Music.* 1. a quartet. 2. the music composed for such a group.

**quartier** (French)   neighborhood.

239

**Quartier Latin** (French)  the area near the University of Paris, on the left bank of the Seine, frequented by students, writers, artists, and intellectuals. See also **Rive Gauche.**

**quass.**  See **kvass.**

**quater in die** (Latin)  *Prescriptions.* four times a day. *Abbr.* q.i.d.

**quatre** (French)  four.

**quatre mains, à.**  See **à quatre mains.**

**quatre-quarts** (French)  *Cookery.* pound cake, so called because a classic recipe for it lists four four-ounce parts each of eggs, butter, flour, and sugar.

**quatrième position** (French)  *Ballet.* the fourth position, a basic position of the feet or arms, used in teaching.

**quattrini,** *sing.* **quattrino** (Italian)  small coins.

**quattro** (Italian)  four.

**quattrocento** (Italian)  the 15th century or the 1400's, especially in reference to Italian fine arts or literature.

**quattro mani** (Italian)  *Music.* four hands.

**quattro voci** (Italian)  *Music.* four voices.

**Quebecois** (French)  a person from Quebec. Also **Québecois.**

**quebrada** (Spanish)  1. a dry ravine that may fill with water after a heavy rain.  2. rough country broken by gullies and ravines.

**qué dice?** (Spanish)  what do you say? what do you think about it?

**quel courage!** (French)  what courage! how brave!

**quel dommage!** (French)  what a pity! too bad! (an expression of disappointment).

**quelque chose** (French)  something.

**quelqu'un** (French)  somebody; someone.

**quem quaeritis** (Latin)  whom do you seek? (question of the angel to the women who visited the tomb of the risen Christ).

**quenelle** (French)  *Cookery.* a type of dumpling made of forcemeat, served in a sauce or used as a garnish.

**qué pasa?** (Spanish)  what's happening? what's up?

**querido,** *fem.* **querida** (Spanish)  1. dear; sweetheart.  2. a lover, especially in an extramarital affair.

**quesadilla** (Spanish)  *Cookery.* a turnover made of **tortilla** dough, filled with cheese or a mixture of cheese and meat.

**quesados** (Spanish)  *Cookery.* triangle-shaped corn chips filled with cheese, onions, and **guacamole.**

**que será será** (Spanish)  what will be, will be.

**queso** (Spanish)  cheese.

**qu'est-ce que c'est?** (French)  what is it? what is this?

**questura** (Italian)    police headquarters; a police station.

**qué tal?** (Spanish)    1. what's up?    2. how are you?

**queue fourché** (French)    *Heraldry.* a forked or double tail, as on a depiction of a lion.

**quibus** (Latin)    *Prescriptions.* from which.

**quiche** (French)    *Cookery.* a dish consisting of a pielike pastry shell filled with a custard mixture and other ingredients and baked. Also **quiche Lorraine.**

**quid faciendum** (Latin)    what is to be done?

**quid novi** (Latin)    what's new?

**quid nunc** (Latin)    what now?

**qui docet discit** (Latin)    he who teaches, learns.

**quid pro quo** (Latin)    (lit., 'something for something (else)') something given in return for something else; compensation.

**quién sabe?** (Spanish)    who knows?

**quinquennium** (Latin)    a period of five years.

**quintetto** (Italian)    *Music.* 1. a quintet.    2. the music composed for such a group.

**quisque** (Latin)    *Prescriptions.* each; every. *Abbr.* **q.; qq.**

**quis separabit** (Latin)    who shall separate us?

**quite** (Spanish)    *Bullfighting.* the action by which the **matador** lures the bull away from the **picador** and his horse.

**qui transtulit sustinet** (Latin)    he who transplanted sustains (motto of Connecticut).

**qui va là?** (French)    who goes there?

**qui vive** (French)    (lit., 'who goes there?') alert; watchful (used in the expression *on the qui vive*).

**quoad hoc** (Latin)    1. as much as this. 2. with respect to this.

**quo animo** (Latin)    with what intention?

**quod avertat Deus** (Latin)    may God prevent it.

**quod erat demonstrandum** (Latin)    that which was to be demonstrated or proven, used at the end of a proof of a theorem. *Abbr.* **Q.E.D.**

**quod erat faciendum** (Latin)    that which was to be done or made. *Abbr.* **Q.E.F.**

**quod erat inveniendum** (Latin)    that which was to be found.

**quod est** (Latin)    which is.

**quod nota** (Latin)    which note; make note of this.

**quod vide** (Latin)    which see (used in a cross reference). *Abbr.* **q.v.**

**quoi bon, à.**    See **à quoi bon.**

**quo iure** *or* **jure** (Latin)    by what law? by what right?

**quo modo** (Latin)    by what means? in what way?

**quondam** (Latin)   former; formerly.

**quoties opus sit** (Latin)   *Prescriptions.* as often as necessary. *Abbr.* **quot. op. sit.**

**quo vadis** (Latin)   whither thou goest? where are you going? (question supposedly asked by St. Peter upon meeting Jesus when leaving Rome; used as the title of a novel by Sienkiewicz).

**Quran.**   See **Koran.**

# R

**râble** (French)   the back and loins of a quadruped such as a hare or a rabbit; saddle cut.   See also **selle**.

**raccourci** (French)   *Ballet.* a position in which the thigh of the working leg is raised and the knee bent while the pointed toes rest on the knee of the supporting leg.

**race, de.**   See **de race**.

**raclette** (French)   *Cookery.* a Swiss specialty consisting of melted cheese served with small boiled potatoes and gherkins.

**raconteur,** *fem.* **raconteuse** (French)   a person skilled at storytelling.

**raddolcendo, raddolcente** (Italian)   (lit., 'sweetening')   *Music.* becoming calmer.

**radeau,** *pl.* **radeaux** (French)   (lit., 'raft') an armed barge, used during the American Revolution.

**radicchio** (Italian)   wild or cultivated chicory, used in salads or cooked.

**radici** (Italian)   radishes.

**radix malorum** (Latin)   the root of all evil.

**raffiné** (French)   (lit., 'refined; polished') 1. designating a person of impeccable taste. 2. designating an elegant dresser.

**raffrenando** (Italian)   *Music.* restraining the speed.

**rafraîchissements** (French)   refreshments; cool drinks.

**ragoût** (French)   *Cookery.* a thick stew of meat or fish.

**ragù** (Italian)   *Cookery.* 1. a thick, spicy tomato-meat sauce.   2. a meat stew with garlic, tomatoes, and spices.

**raifort** (French)   horseradish.

**raisiné** (French)   *Cookery.* a jam or jelly made from grape juice or wine must.

**raison** (French)   reason; cause; justification.

**raison d'état,** *pl.* **raisons d'état** (French)   a reason of state, invoked by a government in defending an action or position.

**raison d'être** (French)   reason for being; justification for existence.

243

**raisonné** (French)    organized; systematically arranged. See also **catalogue raisonné.**

**raisonneur** (French)    *Theater.* a commentator or character in a play who presents the author's message.

**rajah** (Hindi)    1. a king or prince in India. 2. an honorary Hindu title. 3. a title of rulers in the Malay archipelago. Also **raja.**

**raki** (Greek)    an anise-flavored **liqueur.**

**râle de la mort** (French)    death rattle.

**rallentando** (Italian)    *Music.* gradually slowing down. Also **retardando, rilasciando, rilasciante, ritardando, ritenendo, ritenente.**

**rallentato** (Italian)    *Music.* gradually slowed. Also **ritardato; ritenuto.**

**ramada** (Spanish)    a shelter made of branches. Also **ramaje.**

**Ramadan** (Arabic)    *Islam.* the ninth month of the Islamic calendar, observed as a holy month by daily fasting from dawn till sunset.

**ramal** (Spanish)    a short whip made of thongs and attached to the reins or saddle. Also **romal.**

**ramassé** (French)    *Ballet.* picked up, referring to a step.

**rambla** (Spanish)    1. a dry ravine. 2. a boulevard; avenue.

**ranchería** (Spanish)    *Southwestern U.S. and Latin America.* a group of humble dwellings, especially an Indian village. See also **rancho.**

**ranchero** (Spanish)    1. a herdsman; stockman. 2. *Cookery.* a sauce made with onions, peppers, tomatoes, and spices.

**rancho** (Spanish)    1. a ranch.    2. group of huts or dwellings. See also **ranchería.**

**ranee** (Hindi)    the wife of a **rajah.** Also **rani.**

**rani.**    See **ranee.**

**rape,** *sing.* **rapa** (Italian)    turnips.

**rapidamente** (Italian)    *Music.* rapidly.

**rapido** (Italian)    *Music.* rapid.

**rapport** (French)    a relationship characterized by understanding and a spirit of cooperation.

**rapporteur** (French)    a person designated to compile a report on a specific subject, or to prepare an account of a meeting or discussion.

**rappresentativo, stile.**    See **stile rappresentativo.**

**rapprochement** (French)    a reconciliation or re-establishment of good relations between once hostile parties.

**rara avis,** *pl.* **rarae aves** (Latin)    (lit., 'a rare bird') a rarely seen or remarkable object or person.

**ratatiné** (French)    (lit., 'shriveled, shrunken') a rough-surfaced fabric.

**ratatouille** (French)    *Cookery.* a vegetable casserole containing eggplant, zucchini, and onions.

**Rathaus** (German)   town hall.

**Rathskeller** (German)   **1.** cellar of a town hall used as a beer hall or restaurant.   **2.** restaurant located below street level.   Also **Ratskeller**.

**rattenendo** (Italian)   *Music.* gradually holding back.

**rattenuto** (Italian)   *Music.* held back gradually.

**ravigote** (French)   *Cookery.* a highly seasoned white sauce.

**ravioli,** *sing.* **raviolo** (Italian)   *Cookery.* small squares of **pasta** stuffed with a meat or cheese filling.

**raviolini** (Italian)   tiny **ravioli**.

**ravissant** (French)   ravishing; delightful.

**ravvivando** (Italian)   *Music.* quickening.

**ravvivato** (Italian)   *Music.* quickened.

**re** (Latin)   **1.** concerning; with regard to.   **2.** *Law.* in the case of.   Also **in re**.

**real** (Spanish)   an old Spanish monetary unit of small value.

**realia** (Latin)   (lit., 'real things')   **1.** objects, such as coins or tools, used to illustrate the everyday life of a culture.   **2.** *Philosophy.* things of substance.

**Realpolitik** (German)   *Politics.* political realism, especially referring to policy based on power rather than ideals.

**reata** (Spanish)   a rope used for tying or catching stock; a lariat.

**rebbe** (Yiddish)   *Judaism.* **1.** a rabbi.   **2.** a teacher in a Jewish school.

**rebocillo** (Spanish)   a linen headdress for women.   Also **rebociño**.

**rebours, à.**   See **à rebours**.

**rebozo** (Spanish)   a scarf worn by women that covers the head and shoulders, and can be used to cover the face.   Also **reboso, rebosa, riboza**.

**rebus sic stantibus** (Latin)   as long as things remain as they are; until circumstances change.

**recette** (French)   a recipe.

**réchaud** (French)   a chafing dish or portable stove.

**réchauffé** (French)   **1.** *Cookery.* a dish prepared from reheated leftovers.   **2.** something that is a rehash or reuse of familiar material, as in literature or the arts.

**recherché** (French)   **1.** sought after.   **2.** extremely rare; arcane; obscure.   **3.** highly refined; elegant.

**recherches** (French)   inquiries; investigations.

**recibiendo** (Spanish)   (lit., 'receiving')   *Bullfighting.* the act of killing the bull from in front, without moving the feet.

**règita** (Italian)   *Music.* a performance; recitation.

**recitando, recitante** (Italian)   (lit., 'reciting')   *Music.* singing in **recitativo**.

245

**récitatif.**   See recitativo.

**recitativo,** *pl.* **recitativi** (Italian)   *Music.* recitative, a style of vocal composition that seeks to imitate the natural inflections of speech and is used for narrative and dialogue in opera and **oratorio.**

**recitativo accompagnato** (Italian)   *Music.* accompanied **recitativo.**

**recitativo parlando** (Italian)   *Music.* **recitativo** that very closely resembles speech.

**recitativo secco** (Italian)   (lit., 'dry recitative')   *Music.* a quick-moving **recitativo** that has only a few chords as background.

**recitativo stromentato** (Italian)   *Music.* **recitativo** accompanied by full orchestra.

**recoupé** (French)   (lit., 're-cut') a diamond or other gem with 36 facets.

**recto** (Latin)   (lit., 'on the right') the right-hand page of an open book, the front side of a single leaf. See also **verso.**

**rectus in curia** (Latin)   (lit., 'right in court')   *Law.* a person within the law and with an honest case.

**recueil** (French)   a collection or compilation of various writings or documents.

**recueil choisi** (French)   a choice collection of writings.

**recuerdo** (Spanish)   1. a souvenir; keepsake.   2. *pl.* greetings; regards.

**reculant, en.**   See en reculant.

**reculons, à.**   See à reculons.

**redivivus** (Latin)   1. renewed; reborn.   2. brought back to life.

**redolet lucernam.**   See olet lucernam.

**redondillo** (Spanish)   *Literature.*   1. an eight-syllable quatrain with an *abba* rhyme scheme.   2. an eleven-syllable quatrain with an *abab* rhyme scheme.

**redoute** (French)   a public masked ball, very popular in the 18th century.

**reductio ad absurdum** (Latin)   (lit., 'a reduction to the absurd') 1. refutation of an argument by showing the absurdity of its logical conclusion.   2. taking something to an absurd extreme.

**reductio ad impossibile** (Latin)   (lit., 'reduction to the impossible') 1. refutation of an argument by showing that its conclusion is impossible.   2. an impossible conclusion.

**redux** (Latin)   brought back; returned.

**reflet** (French)   iridescence or luster on the surface of ceramics. Also **reflet nacré.**

**reflet métallique** (French)   metallic luster on the surface of ceramics.

**refritos.**   See frijoles refritos.

**régalade, à la.**   See à la régalade.

**Régence** (French)    *Antiques.* furniture and decoration of the French Regency period, between Louis XIV and Louis XV (ca. 1700–1720).

**regime** (French)    1. a system of government or ruling party, often tyrannical. 2. a style of living that is necessary for health or disciplinary reasons. Also **régime.**

**regina** (Latin)    queen.

**regina coeli** (Latin)    queen of heaven (reference to the Virgin Mary).

**regina scientiarum** (Latin)    queen of sciences, epithet given by the scholastics to philosophy.

**régisseur** (French)    a stage director.

**Regius** (Latin)    (lit., 'belonging to the king') in British universities, title of professorships established or maintained by the crown.

**règle, de.**    See **de règle.**

**règle du jeu, la.**    See **la règle du jeu.**

**regnat populus** (Latin)    the people rule (motto of Arkansas).

**Reich** (German)    the German state, especially referring to three particular eras of government.

**Reichsführer** (German)    title of Nazi leader Heinrich Himmler, second-in-command to Adolph Hitler.

**Reichstag** (German)    the lower house of the German parliament during the Second and Weimar Republics.

**re infecta** (Latin)    with the matter unfinished; without reaching one's goal.

**Reinheitsgebot** (German)    (lit., 'purity law') *Brewing.* law regulating the formulation of German beer.

**rejón** (Spanish)    *Bullfighting.* a long-handled lance.

**rejoneador** (Spanish)    *Bullfighting.* a bullfighter who fights from horseback, using a **rejón.**

**réjouissance** (French)    (lit., 'rejoicing') *Music.* a light, quick movement, similar to a **scherzo.**

**relâche** (French)    1. *Theater.* a sign indicating that no performance is to be given. 2. respite; pause.

**relâché** (French)    *Music.* loosened, referring to the snare of a drum.

**relai** (French)    one of a chain of simple, moderately priced hotels in France.

**relevé** (French)    (lit., 'raised') 1. *Ballet.* a rising up to the point or half-point position of the feet during the execution of a step. Also **temps relevé.** *Architecture.* 2. a measured drawing of old work. 3. a restoration.

**relevé de potage** (French)    *Cookery.* a dish served after the soup.

**relievo.**    See **rilievo.**

**religio loci** (Latin)    the feeling of solemnity evoked by a place (Vergil, *Aeneid* VIII.349).

**religiosamente** (Italian)    *Music.* religiously; devoutly.

**religioso** (Italian)    *Music.* religious; devout.

**reliquiae** (Latin)    remains, especially the fossils of animals or plants.

**rem acu tetigisti** (Latin)    (lit., 'you have touched the thing with a needle') you have hit the nail on the head.

**remanet** (Latin)    (lit., 'it remains')    *Law.* a case left unsettled at the end of a judicial term.

**remanié assemblage** (French)    *Geology.* a group of fossils that have been removed from an older bed and redeposited in a new one by the action of the elements.

**remis velisque** (Latin)    (lit., 'by oars and sails')    with all one's effort; using all available means.

**remonta.**    See **caballada.**

**remontant, en.**    See **en remontant.**

**rémoulade** (French)    *Cookery.* a type of mayonnaise to which mustard and herbs have been added, used as a sauce or dressing.

**remplissage** (French)    *Music.* 1. the filling or padding of a composition. 2. ornamentation.

**remuda.**    See **caballada.**

**renaissance** (French)    1. revival; rebirth. 2. (*cap.*) a revival in art or literature, a period of intense vitality following one of mediocrity.

**rencontre** (French)    1. a battle or contest. 2. a casual meeting.

**rendezvous** (French)    1. a meeting agreed upon by two or more parties. 2. a place agreed upon for a meeting. —*v.* 3. to meet at a fixed time and place. Also **rendez-vous.**

**rendu** (French)    1. an architectural rendering. 2. the coloring of an architectural drawing.

**renga** (Japanese)    Japanese linked-verse poetry.

**renovetur semel** (Latin)    *Prescriptions.* it may be renewed once (only). *Abbr.* **ren. sem.**

**rente** (French)    revenue or income.

**rentes sur l'état** (French)    French government bonds.

**rentrée** (French)    1. the period in the fall when schools open and people return from their summer vacations. 2. *Music.* re-entry.

**renversé,** *fem.* **renversée** (French)    *Ballet.* the bending of the body sideways and back during a turn.

**repartimiento** (Spanish)    1. a division, distribution.    2. a grant of conquered territory given by a Spanish explorer to one of his followers. See also **encomienda.**

**repas maigre** (French)    a meal of fish, suitable for fast days or for dieting. See also **jour maigre; maigre.**

**repertoire** (French)   1. *Performing Arts.* the works that a performer, company, or orchestra is prepared to perform for an audience.   2. the entire stock of works in an artistic field. Also **répertoire.**

**repetatur** (Latin)   *Prescriptions.* let it be repeated. *Abbr.* **rept.**

**répéter** (French)   *Ballet.* to rehearse.

**répétiteur** (French)   *Music.* the chorus master of an opera house.

**répétition** (French)   rehearsal of a ballet, opera, or other stage performance.

**répétition générale** (French)   *Theater.* a performance or full dress rehearsal not open to the public.

**repetitore** (Italian)   *Opera.* the choral director of an opera house.

**replicato** (Italian)   *Music.* repeated; doubled.

**repli sur soi** (French)   retreat into onself for examination and evaluation.

**répondez, s'il vous plaît** (French)   please reply (used with invitations). *Abbr.* **R.S.V.P..**

**reportage** (French)   1. a documentary style of reporting, as for television, usually on a timely or controversial subject.   2. a particular style of reporting.

**repoussage** (French)   the technique of working **repoussé.**

**repoussé** (French)   *Fine Arts.* a designation for a relief produced on metal by hammering from the reverse side.

**repoussoir** (French)   *Fine Arts.* a figure or object placed in the extreme foreground of a picture to enhance the illusion of depth.

**requiescat in pace** (Latin)   may he (*or* she) rest in peace. Also, *pl.*, **requiescant in pace.** *Abbr.* **R.I.P.**

**res** (Latin)   *Law.* 1. thing; object; matter.   2. a cause for action; a case.

**res adjudicata.**   See **res judicata.**

**res alienae** (Latin)   the property of others.

**res angusta domi** (Latin)   straitened conditions at home (Juvenal, *Satires* 3.165).

**réseau,** *pl.* **réseaux** (French)   (lit., 'network') 1. *Astronomy.* a network of fine lines imposed on a photograph of stars for measurement.   2. *Applied Arts.* a fine netted ground or foundation for lacemaking.   3. *Photography.* a screen with colored filters, used in color work.

**reserva** (Spanish)   high-quality wine, aged from eight to ten years in oak barrels.

**res gestae** (Latin)   (lit., 'things done') 1. deeds; accomplishments.   2. *Law.* incidental matters or remarks that are admissible in a suit.

**residuum** (Latin)   (lit., 'that which remains') the balance; residue.

**res integra** (Latin)   (lit., 'an entire matter') *Law.* an entirely new matter of law, without precedent.

**res inter alios** (Latin)   (lit., 'a matter between others')   something beyond the scope of the issue at hand.

**res ipsa loquitur** (Latin)   (lit., 'the matter speaks for itself')   *Law.* an inference that the mere happening of an injury shows negligence.

**Résistance, La.**   See **La Résistance**.

**res judicata** (Latin)   (lit., 'a matter decided')   *Law.* a point or case that has been settled by a judicial decision. Also **res adjudicata**.

**res nihili** *or* **nullius** (Latin)   (lit., 'a thing of nothing or of nobody')   1. a matter or person of no importance.   2. *Law.* something that belongs to no person.

**res nova,** *pl.* **res novae** (Latin)   (lit., 'a new thing')   1. an innovation.   2. *Roman history.* a political revolution.

**respice finem** (Latin)   1. consider the end (of life).   2. consider the consequences of an action.

**res publica** (Latin)   (lit., 'the public thing')   1. the Roman republic.   2. a republic.   3. the commonwealth.

**ressaut** (French)   *Architecture.* the projection or recession of one component part, in contrast to an adjoining part.

**restaurateur** (French)   the owner or manager of a restaurant.

**résumé** (French)   a summary or abstract, especially one detailing personal background and achievements. Also **resume, resumé**.

**resurgam** (Latin)   I shall rise again.

**retablo** (Spanish)   *Fine Arts.*   1. a series of figures or paintings that represent a story or event.   2. an altarpiece.

**retardando.**   See **rallentando**.

**reticella** (Italian)   (lit., 'little net')   *Needlework.* a pattern of stitching creating a net-like effect.

**retiré** (French)   *Ballet.* a movement in which the dancer raises the working leg to second position with toes pointed at the knee of the supporting leg, then returns to fifth position. Also **temps retiré**.

**retroussage** (French)   *Fine Arts.* the technique of smearing an etching during printing in order to create richer tones.

**retroussé** (French)   turned up, referring to a nose.

**retsina** (Greek)   a Greek wine flavored with resin. Also **retzina**.

**reus** (Latin)   *Law.*   1. defendant.   2. party to a contract or a suit.

**réveil** (French)   awakening.

**re vera** (Latin)   in truth; in fact.

**révérence** (French)   *Ballet.* a bow; a curtsey.

**rêverie** (French)   1. a daydream; a spell of musing.   2. *Music.* a composition evoking daydreaming or musing.

**rex** (Latin)   king.

**rex bibendi** (Latin)    (lit., 'king of the drinking')   master of the revels.   Also arbiter bibendi; magister bibendi.

**Rex Iudaeorum.**    See **Iesus Nazarenus** . . . .

**Reyes, día de los** (Spanish)    (lit., 'day of the Kings')   Epiphany; Twelfth Night.

**rez-de-chaussée** (French)    *Architecture.* the ground floor.

**Rialto** (Italian)    1. the former trading and business section of Venice.     **2.** a well-known Venetian bridge.     3. any theatrical district, such as Broadway.

**Ribeiro** (Spanish)    a variety of white and red wines produced in Galicia in northwestern Spain.

**ric-à-ric** (French)    rigorously; down to the last penny.

**ricercare** (Italian)    (lit., 'to seek out')   *Music.* a type of composition in the fugue style, with the theme developed in many elaborate ways.

**richettato** (Italian)    *Music.* 1. a staccato effect.     2. See **spiccato**.

**rickshaw.**    See **jinriksha**.

**ricotta** (Italian)    a very soft, unripened white cheese.

**ridotto** (Italian)    1. *Music.* an adaptation of a piece from the full score of a work.     2. an 18th-century entertainment that included music and dancing by a masked company.

**rien ne va plus** (French)    *Roulette.* the call of the **croupier** indicating that the wheel is about to spin and no more wagers may be placed.

**rien sans Dieu** (French)    Nothing without God.

**rifacimento** (Italian)    a re-working of a literary or musical composition.

**riffioramenti** (Italian)    *Music.* embellishments added by a performer. See also **fioritura**.

**rigatoni** (Italian)    tubular, hollow **pasta** cut in short lengths.

**rigolet** (French)    (lit., 'ditch, channel')   *Geology.* in the Mississippi River valley, a small stream, creek, or rivulet.

**rigore** (Italian)    *Music.* exactitude of tempo.

**rigor mortis** (Latin)    (lit., 'the stiffness of death')   the stiffening of the body that occurs within a few hours after death.

**rigoroso** (Italian)    *Music.* exact, in regard to tempo.

**rigueur, à la.**    See **à la rigueur**.

**rigueur, de.**    See **de rigueur**.

**rijstafel** (Dutch)    (lit., 'rice-table')   *Cookery.* a meal at which plain boiled rice is served with a variety of other foods in small dishes.

**rikshaw.**    See **jinriksha**.

**rilasciando.**    See **rallentando**.

**rilasciante.**    See **rallentando**.

**rilievo** *or* **relievo** (Italian)    *Fine Arts.* in sculpture, the projection of figures from a flat surface. See also **alto rilievo; basso rilievo; cavo rilievo; mezzo rilievo; schiacciato rilievo.**

**rillettes** (French)    *Cookery.* a spread made of finely cut-up meat, usually pork, simmered many hours in broth and then mashed to spreading consistency.

**rima chiusa** (Italian)    (lit., 'closed rime')    *Prosody.* a rime scheme in which the two outer lines and the two inner lines of a quatrain rime.

**Rinascimento** (Italian)    the Renaissance.

**rinceau** (French)    *Architecture.* a strip pattern in low relief showing an undulating vine with leaves, fruits, and flowers.

**rinforzando** (Italian)    (lit., 're-enforcing')    *Music.* applying stress to individual notes or chords.

**rinforzato** (Italian)    (lit., 're-enforced')    *Music.* stressed, referring to individual notes or chords.

**rinzaffato** (Italian)    *Fine Arts.* a coarse plaster used to spackle a wall being prepared for **fresco** painting.

**rio** (Italian)    a small canal in Venice.

**río** (Spanish)    a river.

**Rioja** (Spanish)    a variety of red and white wines produced in the Rioja district in north-central Spain.

**ripetizione** (Italian)    *Music.* a rehearsal.

**ripieno** (Italian)    (lit., 'full')    *Cookery.* 1. *n.* stuffing. 2. *adj.* filled; stuffed. 3. *Music.* an indication once used for passages played by the full orchestra, in contrast to **concertato,** those played by a solo performer or a group of performers.

**ripopée** (French)    1. wine slops. 2. a medley. 3. a confusing mixture.

**riposatamente** (Italian)    *Music.* restfully.

**ris de veau** (French)    sweetbreads.

**riserva** (Italian)    a classification for select, vintage Italian wines that are at least three years old.

**risi e bisi** (Italian)    *Cookery.* a dish of rice cooked in broth with fresh peas.

**riso** (Italian)    rice.

**risolutamente** (Italian)    *Music.* resolutely.

**Risorgimento** (Italian)    the 19th-century movement led by Mazzini and Garibaldi for the unification and independence of Italy.

**risotto** (Italian)    *Cookery.* designating a dish containing rice combined with other ingredients.

**risqué** (French)    1. beyond the limits of propriety. 2. off-color; sexually suggestive.

**rissolé** (French)    *Cookery.* browned, as by frying.

**rissoles** (French)   *Cookery.* thin pancakes filled with minced pork or veal, dipped in batter and baked.

**ristringendo** (Italian)   (lit., 'tightening') *Music.* quickening.

**risvegliato** (Italian)   (lit., 'awakened') *Music.* animated.

**ritardando.**   See **rallentando.**

**ritardato.**   See **rallentato.**

**ritardo** (Italian)   (lit., 'delay') *Music.* the act of gradually lessening the speed of a piece.

**rite de passage,** *pl.* **rites de passage** (French)   a ritual or special act that indicates the transition from one stage of life to another.

**ritenendo.**   See **rallentando.**

**ritenente.**   See **rallentando.**

**ritenuto.**   See **rallentato.**

**ritornello** (Italian)   *Music.*   1. the return to full orchestra after a vocal or solo passage.   2. See **da capo.**   3. a type of old Italian folk song with rime repeated in the first and third lines of three-line stanzas, thought to be the precursor of **terza rima.**

**ritournelle** (French)   *Music.*   1. anything returned to.   2. a short melody played between the scenes of an opera.   3. symphonic music occurring before and after vocal passages in a chant or anthem.

**Rive Gauche** (French)   the left bank of the Seine in Paris, known for its bohemian character. See also **Quartier Latin.**

**Rivero** (Spanish)   a district in Galicia that produces fruity red wines.

**rivière** (French)   a necklace of diamonds or other jewels, often consisting of several strings.

**rivolgimento** (Italian)   *Music.* the reversal of voices in double counterpoint.

**riz** (French)   rice.

**robe de chambre** (French)   a dressing gown; a housecoat.

**robe de cour** (French)   a court dress.

**robe de nuit** (French)   a nightdress. See also **negligée.**

**robe de style** (French)   a gown with a full skirt.

**robusto** (Italian)   1. hearty; robust.   2. *Music.* a tenor suited to play strong masculine roles in opera.

**rocaille** (French)   *Antiques.* a lavish type of decoration that flourished in the time of Louis XV, inspired by the forms of shells and rocks.

**roche moutonnée** (French)   (lit., 'fleecy rock') *Geology.* protruding bedrock that has been sculpted by glacial action so that it resembles a grazing sheep.

**rodillas** (Spanish)   (lit., 'knees') *Bullfighting.* passes executed by the bullfighter while kneeling.

**rognon** (French)    kidney.

**Roi Soleil, Le.**    See **Le Roi Soleil.**

**rôle de l'équipage** (French)    a list of the crew of a ship.

**rollatine,** *sing.* **rollatina** (Italian)    *Cookery.* thin cutlets of veal that are stuffed and simmered in stock or sauteed.

**romal.**    See **ramal.**

**roman** (French)    a novel.

**roman à clef** (French)    (lit., 'novel with a key') a novel in which real persons and incidents appear under a thin fictional disguise.  Also **livre à clef.**

**roman à thèse** (French)    a novel that seeks to prove a thesis or promote a cause.

**roman bourgeois** (French)    a middle-class novel, having popular rather than intellectual appeal.

**romance** (French)    *Music.* a ballad.

**romance** (Spanish)    a Spanish ballad recounting the exploits of legendary figures.

**romance sans paroles** (French)    *Music.* a song without words.

**romanesque** (French)    *Music.* **1.** a type of **galliard. 2.** name for a melody used as a ground bass in the 17th century. **3.** a type of song.

**roman expérimental** (French)    a novel in which new techniques are tried.

**roman-fleuve** (French)    a very long novel or a sequence of several complete novels following one character or group of characters over a long period.

**romano** (Italian)    a sharp, aged Italian cheese made from sheep's milk, usually served grated.

**roman poétique** (French)    a novel in which the author uses techniques usually associated with poetry.

**roman policier** (French)    a detective novel.

**romanza** (Italian)    *Music.* **1.** a song; ballad. **2.** an instrumental composition suggestive of a love song.

**romanzo** (Italian)    *Literature.* the genre of the Italian romantic epic, a long poem in **ottava rima** recounting the loves and adventures of the knights of Charlemagne and King Arthur.

**romesco** (Spanish)    *Cookery.* a peppery sauce of the Tarragona region of Spain, served mainly with fish.

**ron** (Spanish)    rum.

**rond** (French)    *Ballet.* **1.** *adj.* circular. **2.** *n.* a circle.

**rond, en** (French)    *Ballet.* in a circle.

**rond de bras** (French)    *Ballet.* a circular movement of the arms.

**rond de jambe** (French)    *Ballet.* a circular movement of the leg.

**ronde** (French)    *Music.* 1. the whole note or semi-breve. 2. a round dance, the music for which is sung by the dancers.

**rondeau,** *pl.* **rondeaux** (French)    *Music.* a dance-song form of the Middle Ages in which solo singing was alternated with choral response.

**rondino** (Italian)    *Music.* a short **rondo.**

**rondo** (Italian)    1. *Music.* a composition or movement having its main theme stated three or more times in the same key with minor themes interwoven. 2. See **rondeau.**

**rondoletto** (Italian)    a short **rondo.**

**Roquefort** (French)    a blue-veined cheese made from sheep's milk, aged in the Roquefort caves in south-central France.

**roquette** (French)    a type of wild lettuce.

**rosado** (Spanish)    a rosé wine.

**rosalia** (Italian)    *Music.* a type of sequence in which a phrase or motif is exactly repeated in another key.

**rosato** (Italian)    a rosé wine.

**rosbif** (French)    roast beef.

**rosé** (French)    a pink-colored wine, produced from black grapes.

**rose du Barry** (French)    *Antiques.* a rose-pink ground color used on Sèvres porcelain.

**Rosh Hashanah** (Hebrew)    *Judaism.* the high holy day celebrating the Jewish New Year.

**rosso** (Italian)    a designation for red wine.

**rosso antico** (Italian)    (lit., 'antique red') a type of red marble with white veins.

**rosticceria** (Italian)    an Italian snack bar.

**Rota** (Latin)    *Roman Catholic Church.* the supreme ecclesiastical tribunal at Rome. Also **Sacra Romana Rota.**

**rotation** (French)    *Ballet.* rotation of the leg at the hip.

**rôti** (French)    a roast; roasted meat.

**rotini** (Italian)    (lit., 'little wheels') **pasta** in the shape of wheels.

**rôtisserie** (French)    1. a shop or restaurant specializing in roast meat or poultry. 2. a spit that turns automatically within an oven, used for roasting meats and poultry.

**rôtissoire** (French)    a Dutch oven.

**rotolo** (Italian)    *Cookery.* a type of thin pancake rolled around a filling.

**rotondo** (Italian)    1. *Music. adj.* full in tone. 2. see **rotunda.**

**rotunda** (Italian)    *Architecture.* a circular room, hall, or building covered with a dome. Also **rotondo.**

**rouble.**   See **ruble.**

**roué** (French)   a person who pursues pleasure to the point of total debauchery.

**rouelle de veau** (French)   a **filet** of veal.

**rouge** (French)   1. a designation for a red wine. 2. *Roulette.* any one of the red areas on which one may wager. See also **noir.**

**rouge à lèvres** (French)   lipstick.

**rouge et noir** (French)   *Games.* a card game played on a table marked with red and black diamonds. Also **rouge-et-noir, rouge-et-noire.** Also called **trente-et-quarante.**

**rouille** (French)   (lit., 'rust')  *Cookery.* a mixture of bread crumbs, garlic, and olive oil, served with **bouillabaisse.**

**roulade** (French)   1. *Music.* an ornamental vocal passage sung with one syllable, popular in 17th- and 18th-century music. 2. *Cookery.* a thin slice of meat filled with forcemeat and rolled, then simmered in broth.

**rouleau** (French)   1. a roll or coil. 2. a cylindrical roll of coins, packaged in paper.

**roux** (French)   *Cookery.* a blend of butter and flour used as a binding for sauces and soups.

**royale** (French)   *Ballet.* a type of **changement** step in which the calves are beaten together before the feet change position.

**royale double** (French)   *Ballet.* a type of **changement** step in which the calves are beaten together twice before the feet change position.

**ruana** (Spanish)   a woolen cape with an opening for the head, worn in Colombia and Venezuela.

**ruat caelum** (Latin)   (lit., 'though the heavens fall')  consequences be damned; come what may.

**rubato** (Italian)   (lit., 'stolen')  *Music.* the lengthening of one note at the expense of another to add expression.

**ruble** (Russian)   the basic monetary unit of the Soviet Union. Also **rouble.**

**rudement** (French)   *Music.* roughly.

**rue** (French)   street.

**Rueda** (Spanish)   a white wine of northern Spain.

**ruedo** (Spanish)   *Bullfighting.* the bullring; arena. See also **plaza de toros.**

**rugola** (Italian)   field lettuce, somewhat bitter in taste.

**ruiné,** *fem.* **ruinée** (French)   1. designating someone who has lost money, health, and happiness. 2. destroyed; spoiled.

**rupee** (Hindi)   the basic monetary unit of India, Pakistan, and other countries.

**rurales** (Spanish)   the Mexican rural mounted police force.
**rus in urbe** (Latin)   (lit., 'the country in the city') an urban place with rural amenities (Martial, *Epigrams* 12.57).
**russe, à la.**   See à la russe.

# S

**sabe?** (Spanish)  do you understand?  Also **savy; savez.**

**sabot** (French)  a wooden shoe.

**sabra** (Hebrew)  a native-born Israeli.

**sacate.**  See **zacate.**

**sacatón.**  See **zacatón.**

**sacchetto** (Italian)  a satchel-type woman's purse.

**sachem** (Narragansett)  1. a chief of a tribe or confederation.  2. a political leader.

**Sacra Romana Rota.**  See **Rota.**

**sacré** (French)  1. sacred; holy.  2. damned; cursed.

**sacré bleu** (French)  curse it!  damn it!  Also **sacrebleu.**

**sacre rappresentazioni** (Italian)  (lit., 'sacred representations')  *Music.* Italian mystery or miracle plays, entirely sung during their last phase in the mid-16th century, considered precursors of opera.

**Sacrum Romanum Imperium** (Latin)  the Holy Roman Empire.

**saeva indignatio** (Latin)  fierce indignation.

**safari** (Swahili)  an expedition for the purposes of hunting, photography, or exploration, especially in eastern Africa.

**saggia vino** (Italian)  a pipette or wine thief for taking samples of wine from a barrel.

**Sagittarius** (Latin)  the Archer, a constellation and sign of the zodiac.

**sahib,** *fem.* **sahibah** (Urdu)  a title of respect for Europeans, used by Indian natives during the colonial period.  Also **saheb.**

**saignant** (French)  (lit., 'bloody') rare; underdone (said of meat).

**Saint-Emilion** (French)  a variety of red wine from **Bordeaux.**

**Saint-Julien** (French)  a variety of red wine from one of the Médoc regions of **Bordeaux.**

**sake** (Japanese)  a Japanese alcoholic beverage made from rice.

**sal** (Latin)  salt.

**sala** (Spanish)  a large room; the living room; parlor.

**salaam** (Arabic)    (lit., 'peace') **1.** a common expression of greeting in Arabic countries. **2.** a gesture of greeting consisting of a bow with the right hand on the forehead. Also **salam.**

**salaam aleikum** (Arabic)    (lit., 'peace be unto you') a Muslim greeting.

**salade niçoise** (French)    *Cookery.* a hearty salad of tuna fish, potatoes, and string beans, served with **vinaigrette** dressing.

**salambô** (French)    a type of **éclair** topped with caramel.

**salami** (Italian)    a spicy sausage of Italian origin, used as a cold cut.

**salamini** (Italian)    a small salami.

**sal Atticum** (Latin)    (lit., 'Attic salt') **1.** the characteristically brilliant, refined wit of the Athenians. See also **acetum Italum; merum sal. 2.** intellectual wittiness.

**sale** (Italian)    salt.

**salé** (French)    **1.** salted, as for preservation. **2.** coarse, referring to talk or narrative.

**salina** (Spanish)    **1.** a salt deposit. **2.** a body of water having a high salt concentration.

**salle, autour de la** (French)    *Ballet.* around the room.

**salle à manger** (French)    a dining room.

**salle d'armes** (French)    a fencing or weapons school.

**salle d'attente** (French)    a waiting room.

**salle de danse** (French)    **1.** a dance hall. **2.** a dancing school.

**salle de jeu** (French)    a gambling hall.

**salle privée** (French)    a room in a gambling house for private play.

**salmis** (French)    *Cookery.* a dish prepared from partially cooked game stewed in juices, seasonings, and wine. Also **salmi.**

**salon** (French)    **1.** a large reception room in a hotel or on a ship. **2.** a shop in the fashion industry, as for a dressmaker or hairdresser. **3.** (*cap.*) an annual exhibit in Paris of the work of living artists and sculptors. **4.** a gathering for casual discussion of cultural or intellectual issues.

**Salon d'Automne** (French)    *Fine Arts.* an annual autumn exhibit in Paris.

**Salon des Indépendants** (French)    *Fine Arts.* an annual exhibit of the works of artists deemed too radical for the Salon. See also **salon, 3.**

**Salon des Refusés** (French)    *Fine Arts.* **1.** a special exhibition ordered by Napoleon III in 1863 to show the works of artists rejected by the conservative Academy of Fine Arts. **2.** any exhibition of works of art not accepted by an official organization.

**saloperie** (French)    **1.** coarseness; sluttishness. **2.** bad-tasting food or wine.

**salpicon** (French)    *Cookery.* a stuffing for roast meats.

**salpicón** (Spanish)    *Cookery.* a spicy condiment made of tomatoes, **chiles,** onions, avocados, and coriander.

**salsa** (Italian)   sauce.

**salsa** (Spanish)  1. *Cookery.* sauce.   2. *Music.* a kind of lively, rhythmic Caribbean dance music.

**salsa colorada** (Spanish)  *Cookery.* red chile sauce.

**salsa cruda** (Spanish)  *Cookery.* a pungent sauce made from green chiles, tomato, onion, and coriander.

**salsa verde** (Italian, Spanish)  *Cookery.* a sauce made of parsley and herbs, used especially with chicken or seafood.

**salsiccia** (Italian)   fresh, uncooked sausage.

**saltarello,** *pl.* **saltarelli** (Italian)  *Music.* a lively Italian dance.

**saltimbocca** (Italian)   *Cookery.* a designation for a dish made with thin cutlets of veal and **prosciutto** sauteed in butter.

**salud** (Spanish)   health; to your health (used as a toast).

**saludos** (Spanish)   greetings.

**salumeria** (Italian)   an Italian delicatessen specializing in pork products.

**salus populi suprema lex esto** (Latin)   the welfare of the people shall be the supreme law (motto of Missouri).

**salut** (French)   cheers! greetings! (used as a toast).

**salute** (Italian)   (to your) health! (used as a toast).  Also **alla vostra salute; a vostra salute.**

**salve,** *pl.* **salvete** (Latin)   hail! greetings!

**salvia** (Italian)   the herb sage.

**salvo conducto** (Spanish)   a safe-conduct pass.

**sal volatile** (Latin)   smelling salts.

**salyut** (Russian)   salute.

**sama** (Japanese)   a Japanese title of respect for exalted personages, placed after the name.  See also **san.**

**samba** (Portuguese)   a rhythmic Brazilian dance.

**Sambuca** (Italian)   an Italian **liqueur** flavored with anise.

**samisen** (Japanese)   a Japanese musical instrument similar to a guitar, having an elongated neck and three strings.

**samizdat** (Russian)   illegal, underground publishing in the Soviet Union.

**sampan** (Chinese)   a small Oriental boat propelled by a single scull.

**samshu** (Chinese)   a Chinese **liqueur** made from millet or rice.

**samurai** (Japanese)   1. (*cap.*) a member of a hereditary warrior class in feudal Japan, often a retainer of a **daimio.** 2. *adj.* characteristic of or used by a Samurai.

**san** (Japanese)   a Japanese form of address used after a name, equivalent to *Mister.* See also **sama.**

**sanbenito** (Spanish)   a colored tunic worn by those accused of heresy during the Spanish Inquisition.  Also **sambenito.**

261

**Sancerre** (French)    a dry, fruity white wine from the Loire region of central France.

**sancta simplicitas** (Latin)    (lit., 'holy simplicity') charming innocence or naivety.

**sanctum** (Latin)    1. a holy place.    2. a private room.

**sanctum sanctorum** (Latin)    (lit., 'the holy of holies')    1. *Judaism.* the innermost chamber of the temple.    2. a secluded, personal place of retreat.

**Sanctus** (Latin)    (lit., 'holy')    *Christian liturgy.* prayer at the conclusion of the Preface to the Mass.

**sandhi** (Sanskrit)    *Linguistics.* the modification of sounds in words spoken rapidly together, as *gotcha* for *got you.*

**Sandinismo** (Spanish)    a political and social movement in Nicaragua, named after guerilla leader Augusto Sandino (1895–1934).

**Sandinista** (Spanish)    a follower of the Nicaraguan **Sandinismo** movement.

**sandolino** (Italian)    a type of canoe rowed with one double-bladed oar.

**sang-de-boeuf** (French)    (lit., 'ox-blood') a dark-red color characteristic of Chinese porcelain.

**sang-froid** (French)    (lit., 'cold blood') self-composure in difficult circumstances; lack of emotionalism.

**sanglier** (French)    a boar; wild boar.

**sangre** (Spanish)    blood.

**Sangre de Toro** (Spanish)    (lit., 'blood of the bull') a robust red wine from Catalonia.

**sangría** (Spanish)    a punch made of wine and fruit juice.

**Sanhedrin** (Hebrew from Greek)    *Jewish history.* the assembly of elders of ancient Jerusalem, having secular and ecclesiastical authority.

**sans-culotte** (French)    1. a scornful name given by aristocrats to republicans during the French Revolution, derived from the fact that the latter wore pantaloons instead of breeches.    2. a radical; revolutionary.

**sans Dieu, rien.**    See **rien sans Dieu.**

**sans doute** (French)    no doubt; doubtless.

**Sansei** (Japanese)    a grandchild of Japanese immigrants to the United States.  See also **Issei; Kibei; Nisei.**

**sans mélange** (French)    (lit., 'unmixed') pure; unalloyed.

**sans pareil** (French)    without equal; peerless.

**sans peur et sans reproche** (French)    without fear and without reproach, a term used to describe Bayard, one of Charlemagne's knights, in the *Chanson de Roland.*

**sans souci** (French)    carefree; easy-going (often used in the names of resorts).

**santé** (French)    health.

**santo,** *fem.* **santa** (Italian, Spanish)    1. *n.* saint. 2. *adj.* holy; sainted.

**santon** (French)    one of the clay figurines in a **crèche.**

**Santo Padre** (Italian)    (lit., 'holy father') the pope.

**Santo Spirito** (Italian)    the Holy Spirit.

**sapristi** (French)    good God! (a mild oath).

**sarabande** (French)    *Music.* a dance of Spanish origin, its music in triple time and with many ornaments.

**sarape** (Spanish)    a blanket, usually of a colorful woven pattern, worn over the shoulders or used as bedding. Also **serape; zarape.**

**sarde** *or* **sardine** (Italian)    sardines.

**sari** (Hindi)    the traditional outer garment of Hindu women, consisting of a long piece of cotton or silk wrapped around the body.

**Sartor Resartus** (Latin)    (lit., 'the tailor reclothed') title of a book by Thomas Carlyle.

**sasquatch** (Salish)    a large, hairy mammal said to inhabit the wilderness of the Pacific Northwest. Also **Sasquatch.** See also **yeti.**

**satis superque** (Latin)    enough and too much; more than enough (Catullus 7.10).

**Saturnalia** (Latin)    1. *Roman history.* the festival of Saturn, in December. 2. a period of revelry.

**sauce au beurre** (French)    *Cookery.* a butter sauce.

**sauce béarnaise.**    See **béarnaise.**

**sauce blanche** (French)    *Cookery.* a white sauce.

**sauce financière** (French)    *Cookery.* a Madeira wine sauce with truffles.

**sauce meunière** (French)    *Cookery.* a sauce of browned butter, lemon juice, and parsley.

**sauce piquante** (French)    *Cookery.* a sauce based on brown meat stock, to which herbs and wine are added.

**sauce relevée** (French)    *Cookery.* a highly seasoned sauce.

**sauce verte** (French)    *Cookery.* a green sauce.

**saucier** (French)    a sauce-maker, one of the culinary ranks.

**saucisse** (French)    1. sausage. 2. a long tube filled with gunpowder, used as an emergency fuse. 3. a large bundle of sticks used in fortification.

**saucisson** (French)    a large sausage used for cold cuts.

**Sauerbraten** (German)    *Cookery.* a type of pot roast marinated in a vinegar-based sauce.

**Sauerkraut** (German)    *Cookery.* cabbage cut fine and fermented in a salt solution.

**saumon** (French)    salmon.

**saut de basque** (French)    (lit., 'Basque jump') *Ballet.* a step involving a leap and a turning of the body.

**saut de chat.**    See **pas de chat.**

**saut de flèche** (French)    (lit., 'arrow step') *Ballet.* a step in which one leg shoots out like an arrow away from the other. Also **temps de flèche.**

**sauté** (French)    1. *Cookery.* fried quickly in a small amount of butter or oil.   2. *Ballet.* jumped or jumping.

**Sauternes** (French)    a sweet, white wine of the **Bordeaux** region.

**sauvage** (French)    1. wild; savage.   2. unsociable; shunning society.

**sauve qui peut** (French)    (lit., 'save (himself) who can') a disorderly rout; stampede.

**savant** (French)    a scholar; a learned person. See also **les savants.**

**savarin** (French)    *Cookery.* a small, molded yeast cake, cooked in rum or kirsch, often served hot.

**savate** (French)    a type of boxing in which both the hands and the feet are used.

**savoir faire** (French)    (lit., 'knowing what to do') a facility for knowing how to react in the best way to any situation. Also **savoir-faire.**

**savoir vivre** (French)    (lit., 'to know how to live') knowledge of the world and of how to live the good life. Also **savoir-vivre.**

**sayonara** (Japanese)    farewell; goodbye.

**scagliola** (Italian)    *Antiques.* a type of imitation marble produced with ground plaster of Paris and a glue solution.

**Scala, La.**    See **La Scala.**

**scaloppine,** *sing.* **scaloppina** (Italian)    *Cookery.* a designation for a manner of preparation using thin slices of meat, usually veal, with various ingredients.

**scalpellino,** *pl.* **scalpellini** (Italian)    *Fine Arts.* 1. a worker who prepares stone for sculpting.   2. an inferior sculptor.

**scamorza** (Italian)    a mild, light-yellow, semi-soft cheese.

**scampi** (Italian)    1. large shrimp or prawns.   2. *Cookery.* a designation for a dish of shrimp marinated in a garlic sauce and broiled.

**Scaramouche** (Italian)    *Theater.* the boastful coward, one of the stock figures of the **commedia dell'arte.**

**scelta, a.**    See **a scelta.**

**scemando** (Italian)    *Music.* lessening, referring to volume or tone; **diminuendo.**

**scena** (Italian)    *Music.* 1. a scene in an opera.   2. a recitative with melodic passages interspersed.

**scène** (French)    1. *Opera.* a movement for a solo voice, differing from ordinary recitative and **aria** by its length and intensity.    2. *Ballet.* the stage.

**scène à faire** (French)    *Theater.* a key scene in a play, often the climax.

**scène d'action** (French)    *Ballet.* a mimed scene or episode in a story ballet.

**sch-.**    See at sh- for Yiddish terms.

**Schadenfreude** (German)    malicious enjoyment of the discomfiture of others.

**scherzando** (Italian)    *Music.* playfully; jokingly.  Also **scherzante, scherzevole, scherzevolmente.**

**scherzante.**    See **scherzando.**

**scherzetto** (Italian)    *Music.* a short **scherzo.** Also **scherzino.**

**scherzevole, scherzevolmente.**    See **scherzando.**

**scherzino.**    See **scherzetto.**

**scherzo,** *pl.* **scherzi** (Italian)    (lit., 'joke') *Music.* a light, cheerful movement in a symphony, **sonata,** or quartet.

**scherzosamente** (Italian)    *Music.* playfully.

**scherzoso** (Italian)    *Music.* playful.

**schiacciato rilievo** (Italian)    (lit., 'squashed relief') *Fine Arts.* relief sculpture in which the projection of the figures from the background is minimal. See also **alto rilievo; basso rilievo.**

**schiuma** (Italian)    the frothy foam produced by the hot milk used in making **cappuccino.**

**schizzo** (Italian)    (lit., 'sketch') *Music.* 1. a brief composition, generally for piano, evocative of a picture.    2. a composer's rough draft of a work.

**Schlacht** (German)    battle.

**Schlagobers** (German)    whipped cream.

**Schlagwort** (German)    catchword; catchphrase.

**Schloss** (German)    castle.

**Schmierkäse** (German)    *Cookery.* a soft, white cheese similar to cottage cheese.

**Schnapps** (German)    a type of distilled spirits, especially a clear, white, flavored **liqueur.**

**schnell** (German)    quick.

**Schnitzel** (German)    (veal) cutlet.

**schola cantorum** (Latin)    1. a school of singers; choir shool.    2. a section of a church for the choir.

**scholium,** *pl.* **scholia** (Latin)    a scholarly note on a classical text; an explanatory note on a mathematical work.

**schöne Welt, die** (German)    fashionable society.    See also **geistige Welt, die.**

**schuss** (German)    *Skiing.* 1. *n.* unchecked, straight descent down a steep slope. 2. *v.* to execute a schuss.

**Schutzstaffel** (German)    the elite Nazi military service that swore personal loyalty to Adolph Hitler.    *Abbr.* **S.S.**

**Schwarzwald** (German)    the Black Forest, in SW West Germany.

**Schweinehund** (German)    *Derogatory.* filthy swine; a term roughly equivalent to English *son of a bitch.*

**scientia** (Latin)    knowledge; an organized body of knowledge.

**scilicet** (Latin)    (lit., 'it is clear (that)')    to wit; that is to say; namely. *Abbr.* **sc.**

**scintillante** (Italian)    *Music.* sparkling.

**scioltamente** (Italian)    *Music.* in a free and easy manner.

**scioltezza, con.**    See **con scioltezza.**

**sciolto** (Italian)    *Music.* free; easy. See also **con scioltezza.**

**scire facias** (Latin)    (lit., 'you may make (him) know')    *Law.* a judicial writ requiring that cause be shown why a judgment, record, etc., should not be executed or annulled.

**scirocco.**    See **sirocco.**

**scivolando** (Italian)    *Music.* sliding; **glissando.**

**scordato** (Italian)    *Music.* out of tune.

**scordature** (Italian)    *Music.* abnormal tuning of a stringed instrument in order to produce unusual effects.

**Scorpio** (Latin)    the Scorpion, a constellation and sign of the zodiac.

**scorrendo, scorrevole** (Italian)    (lit., 'running through')    *Music.* 1. gliding from note to note; **glissando.**    2. in a flowing manner.

**scripsit** (Latin)    he (*or* she) wrote (it) (used with the name of the author).

**scriptorium** (Latin)    a room used for writing.

**scugnizzi** (Italian)    the street waifs of Naples.

**sculpsit** (Latin)    he (*or* she) carved (it) (written with the name of the sculptor or engraver).

**scungilli** (Italian)    conch.

**scusa** (Italian)    excuse me; I beg your pardon.    Also **scusate; scusatemi; scusi.**

**sdegnoso** (Italian)    *Music.* disdainful.

**sdrucciolando** (Italian)    *Music.* sliding; **glissando.**

**séance** (French)    1. a gathering at which people seek to communicate with the spirits of the dead. 2. a session; a committee or society meeting.

**séance d'essai** (French)    *Auto racing.* a practice run that allows drivers to test the course.

**seawan.**   See **wampum.**

**sec** (French)   *Wine.* dry; not sweet.

**secco** (Italian)   **1.** a designation for a dry wine.   **2.** without instrumentation, referring to recitative. See also **recitativo secco.**   **3.** See **staccato.**

**secento** (Italian)   the 17th century or the 1600's, especially in reference to Italian fine arts or literature.

**sechs** (German)   six.

**Sechzehntelnote** (German)   *Music.* sixteenth note.

**secondando.**   See **colla voce.**

**seconda volta** (Italian)   *Music.* a second time.

**seconde, à la.**   See **à la seconde.**

**seconde position** (French)   *Ballet.* the second position, a basic position of the feet or arms, used in teaching.

**secrétaire** (French)   **1.** *Furniture.* a writing-desk, especially one with small drawers, pigeonholes, and a fall-front. Also **secrétaire à abattant. 2.** a secretary.

**secrétaire à abattant.**   See **secrétaire, 1.**

**Section d'Or, La.**   See **La Section d'Or.**

**secundum artem** (Latin)   (lit., 'following the art')   **1.** in accordance with the rules of the art; skillfully.   **2.** in accordance with the accepted practice.

**secundum bonos mores** (Latin)   (lit., 'according to good usages') in accordance with established custom; in orderly fashion.

**secundum legem** (Latin)   according to the law.

**secundum naturam** (Latin)   according to nature; not artificially.

**secundum ordinem** (Latin)   according to order; in order.

**secundum quid** (Latin)   (lit., 'in accord with something') in some respect; in a qualified or limited way.

**secundum regulam** (Latin)   according to rule; by the rule.

**secundum usum** (Latin)   according to usage or custom.

**secundum veritatem** (Latin)   in accord with truth.

**se defendendo** (Latin)   (lit., 'in defending oneself') *Law.* in self-defense, hence excusable.

**Seder** (Hebrew)   *Judaism.* a ceremonial dinner held in Jewish homes at Passover, commemorating the deliverance of the Jews from bondage in Egypt. See also **Haggadah.**

**Seele** (German)   **1.** soul.   **2.** mind.   **3.** heart.

**Sefer Torah** (Hebrew)   (lit., 'book of law') the scroll containing the **Torah** or biblical Books of Moses, kept in the Holy Ark (**Aron Kodesh**) in a synagogue or temple. Also **Sepher Torah.**

**segarrito.**   See **cigarrito.**

**segno** (Italian)    *Music.* a sign that indicates the beginning or end of a repeated passage. See also al segno; da capo al segno; dal segno.

**segue** (Italian)    *Music.* 1. here follows, indicating a passage that is to be played without pause. See also **attacca**.    2. *n.* a transition from one piece to another.

**seguendo, seguente** (Italian)    *Music.* following.

**seguidilla** (Spanish)    a Spanish dance and style of music in triple time, popular both with folk musicians and classical composers.

**seguro** (Spanish)    sure; surely; safety.

**se habla español.**    See aquí se habla español.

**sehr gut** (German)    very good.

**sei** (Italian)    six.

**seigneur** (French)    1. a feudal lord. See also **jus primae noctis**. 2. *Canada.* one of the landed gentry.

**seigneurie** (French)    *Canadian history.* one of the large grants of land made to French officers for settlement of discharged veterans.

**seis** (Spanish)    six.

**Seite** (German)    1. side. 2. page.

**sel** (French)    1. salt. 2. wit.

**selle** (French)    the saddle, the part of the hindquarters from the ribs to the leg, as of lamb. See also **râble**.

**selvaggina.**    See cacciagione.

**Semana Santa** (Spanish)    Holy Week.

**semis** (Latin)    *Prescriptions.* half. *Abbr.* **ss.**

**semiseria** (Italian)    (lit., 'half-serious')    *Opera.* a designation for an opera with several comic scenes, as distinguished from an **opera seria**.

**semolina** (Italian)    a coarse flour milled from durum wheat, used in making pasta.

**semper eadem** (Latin)    ever the same (motto of Queen Elizabeth I).

**semper et ubique** (Latin)    always and everywhere.

**semper felix** (Latin)    always fortunate.

**semper fidelis** (Latin)    always faithful (motto of the U.S. Marine Corps).

**semper idem** (Latin)    always the same.

**semper paratus** (Latin)    always prepared (motto of the U.S. Coast Guard and of the Boy Scouts).

**semplicità, con.**    See con semplicità.

**semplice** (Italian)    *Music.* simple; without embellishments.

**sempre** (Italian)    (lit., 'always')    *Music.* an indication that a piece is to be played in the same manner throughout.

**senatus consultum** (Latin)    *Roman history.* a decree or resolution of the Roman senate.

268

**Senatus Populusque Romanus** (Latin)   the senate and the Roman people. *Abbr.* **S.P.Q.R.**

**senda** (Spanish)   path; trail.

**señor** (Spanish)   1. a term of address, equivalent to *Mister* or *sir*. *Abbr.* **Sr.** 2. a gentleman.

**señora** (Spanish)   1. a term of address, equivalent to *Mrs*. *Abbr.* **Sra.** 2. a married woman or older woman.

**señorita** (Spanish)   1. a term of address, equivalent to *Miss*. *Abbr.* **Srta.** 2. a young woman.

**señorito** (Spanish)   1. a term of address for a young man, often used by servants.   2. a wealthy, young aristocrat or land owner.

**sensibile** (Italian)   *Music.* sensitive. See also **nota sensibile.**

**sensu bono** (Latin)   in a good sense.

**sensu lato** (Latin)   in a broad or extended sense.

**sensu malo** (Latin)   in a bad sense.

**sensu obscaeno** (Latin)   in an obscene sense.

**sensu proprio** (Latin)   in its proper sense.

**sensu stricto** (Latin)   in a strict sense; strictly speaking.

**sentito** (Italian)   *Music.* with expression; with feeling.

**senza accompagnamento** (Italian)   *Music.* without accompaniment, referring to an **aria.**

**senza replica** (Italian)   *Music.* without repetition.

**senza sordini,** *sing.* **senza sordino** (Italian)   *Music.* 1. without mutes, referring to bowed instruments.   2. without dampers, referring to the piano.

**senza stromenti** (Italian)   *Music.* without instruments.

**senza tempo** (Italian)   *Music.* without strict time.

**se offendendo** (pseudo-Latin)   (facetiously, 'in offending onself')   the gravedigger's garbled version of **se defendendo** in *Hamlet* V.1.

**separatio a mensa et t(h)oro** (Latin)   *Law.* separation from bed and board; legal separation. Also **a mensa et t(h)oro; mensa et t(h)oro.**

**séparé** (French)   *Music.* separated; uncoupled.

**Sephardi,** *pl.* **Sephardim** (Hebrew)   the Jews of Spain and Portugal and their descendants, distinct from the **Ashkenazim** in customs and language.

**Sepher Torah.**   See **Sefer Torah.**

**sepoy** (Anglo-Indian)   a native Indian soldier in the service of the British during the colonial period.

**seppia** (Italian)   a small cuttlefish, similar to a squid.

**seppuku.**   See **hara-kiri.**

**sept** (French)   seven.

**septennium** (Latin)   a period of seven years.

**septetto** (Italian)   *Music.* 1. a group of seven performers; a septet.   2. a composition for such a group.

**sequens,** *pl.* **sequentia** (Latin)   the following item(s).   *Abbr.* **seq.;** *(pl.)* **seqq.**

**sequitur** (Latin)   (lit., 'it follows')   a logical conclusion.

**sérac** (French)   an irregularly shaped formation of ice on the surface of a glacier caused by melting or shifting of the glacier.

**serai** (Turkish)   a resting place for travelers; caravansary.

**serape.**   See **sarape.**

**serenata** (Italian)   *Music.* 1. a serenade.   2. a type of dramatic **cantata,** popular in 18th-century European courts.   3. an orchestral or band suite, similar to a **divertimento.**

**serenatella** (Italian)   *Music.* a short **serenata.**

**Serenissima, La.**   See **La Serenissima.**

**seriamente, seriosamente** (Italian)   *Music.* seriously.

**seriatim** (Latin)   in series; one by one in succession.

**sérieux,** *fem.* **sérieuse** (French)   1. serious-minded; not trivial.   2. *Music.* serious.

**serinette** (French)   a small hand organ used to train birds to sing.

**serrando** (Italian)   (lit., 'pressing')   *Music.* getting quicker.

**serranilla** (Spanish)   *Literature.* a poem about the shepherd's life.

**serrato** (Italian)   (lit., 'pressed')   *Music.* quickened.

**serré** (French)   *Ballet; Music.* concise; quickened.

**serrer les reins** (French)   *Ballet.* an instruction to tighten the muscles of the buttocks and abdomen.

**service compris** (French)   service included in the price; no tipping necessary.

**serviette** (French)   a napkin.

**Servus Servorum Dei** (Latin)   (lit., 'servant of the servants of God')   a title of the pope.

**sesquihora** (Latin)   *Prescriptions.* an hour and a half.   *Abbr.* **sesquih.**

**sesquipedalia verba** (Latin)   (lit., 'words a foot and a half long')   excessively long words used to impress (Horace, *Art of Poetry* 97).

**sestetto** (Italian)   *Music.* 1. a group of six performers; a sextet.   2. a composition for such a group.

**se tirer d'affaire** (French)   to extricate oneself from a difficult situation.

**sette** (Italian)   seven.

**settecento** (Italian)   the 18th century or the 1700's, especially in reference to Italian fine arts or literature.

**severamente** (Italian)   *Music.* severely.

270

**sevillana** (Spanish)  1. designating something from Seville in southern Spain.  2. *Music.* a type of seguidilla from Seville.

**sewan.**   See **wampum.**

**Sezession** (German)  *Fine Arts.* a style associated with Art Nouveau. Also **Jugendstil.**

**sfinge** (Italian)  (lit., 'sphinx') a type of pastry filled with a mixture of ricotta cheese, sugar, candied citron, and chocolate.

**sfogato** (Italian)  (lit., 'poured forth') *Music.* free and unstrained in style.

**sfogliata** (Italian)  puff pastry.

**sfogliatelli** (Italian)  puff pastry filled with various sweet, creamy fillings.

**sforzando** (Italian)  *Music.* forcing, that is, playing a note or chord with emphasis. *Abbr.* **sf.**

**sforzato** (Italian)  *Music.* forced, each note or chord being played with emphasis.

**sfregazzi** (Italian)  *Fine Arts.* a technique of shading color on a painting by using the finger instead of the brush.

**sfumatezza** (Italian)  *Fine Arts.* the process of blending and harmonizing two colors or shades into one another.

**sfumato** (Italian)  1. *Fine Arts.* vague outlines and shadowy colors in a painting.  2. *Music.* played in an indistinct way.

**sgraffito.**   See **graffiti.**

**Shabbas** (Hebrew)  *Judaism.* the Sabbath. Also **Shabbes.**

**Shabbas goy** (Hebrew)  *Judaism.* a Gentile who, as a service to Jews, performs tasks on the Sabbath that are forbidden to them.

**shadchen** (Yiddish)  *Judaism.* a person who arranges marriages; matchmaker. Also **shadchan.**

**shah** (Persian)  the title of the former ruler of Iran.

**shalom** (Hebrew)  (lit., 'peace') a traditional Jewish expression of greeting or farewell.

**shalom aleichem** (Hebrew)  (lit., 'peace to you') a traditional Jewish expression of greeting, the reply to which is **aleichem shalom.**

**shaman** (Turkic)  a medicine man or high priest of a northern Asian tribe.

**shaygets,** *pl.* **shkotzim** (Yiddish)  a Gentile man or boy. Also **shegets.**

**shaytl.**   See **sheitel.**

**shegets.**   See **shaygets.**

**sheik** (Arabic)  a village or tribal leader in Arab countries. Also **sheikh.**

**sheitel** (Yiddish)  *Judaism.* a wig worn by Orthodox women after marriage. Also **shaytl.**

**sherif.**   See **amir, 2.**

**Shiah** (Arabic)   the smaller of the two major divisions of Islam, regarding Ali, the son-in-law of Muhammad, as his successor. Also **Shia**. See also **Sunna**.

**shibah.**   See **shivah**.

**shiksa** (Yiddish)   a Gentile woman or girl. Also **shikseh**.

**shish kebab** (Turkish)   *Cookery.* small pieces of meat (**kabobs**) and vegetables roasted on a skewer.

**shivah** (Hebrew)   a prescribed seven-day period of mourning for dead relatives. Also **shibah**.

**shlemiel** (Yiddish)   an unlucky, clumsy, or foolish person.

**shlep** (Yiddish)   1. to carry or lug. 2. See **shlepper**.

**shlepper** (Yiddish)   an insignificant, inept, or untidy person. Also **shlepp**.

**shlimazel** (Yiddish)   a chronically unlucky person for whom nothing turns out well. Also **shlimazl**.

**shlock** (Yiddish)   1. *adj.* cheap; shoddy. 2. *n.* something of inferior quality; junk.

**shmaltz** (Yiddish)   1. cooking fat, especially chicken fat. 2. exaggerated sentimentality in a theatrical or musical performance.

**shmatte** (Yiddish)   1. a small cloth or rag. 2. something cheap or shoddy. 3. a person deserving no respect.

**shmo** (Yiddish)   a foolish or boring person.

**shmooze** (Yiddish)   1. a friendly conversation. 2. to talk in a friendly way; chat.

**shmuck** (Yiddish)   1. *Vulgar.* a penis. 2. a detestable person; dope; jerk.

**shmutz** (Yiddish)   dirt; soil, as on clothes.

**shnook** (Yiddish)   a meek, pathetic person.

**shnorrer** (Yiddish)   a beggar; moocher; chiseler.

**shnozzle** (Yiddish)   nose.

**shochet** (Hebrew)   *Judaism.* a person certified to slaughter animals in accord with Jewish law. Also **shohet**.

**shofar** (Hebrew)   *Judaism.* a ram's horn used as an instrument to signal religious occasions and, formerly, as a signal for battle. Also **shophar**.

**shogun** (Japanese)   *Japanese history.* one of the military lords who held sway in Japan from the 8th century into the 19th century.

**shoji** (Japanese)   a light screen or panel made of paper stretched over a frame, used as a room divider in Japanese houses.

**shophar.**   See **shofar**.

**shtetl** (Yiddish)   a Jewish village or community of eastern Europe prior to World War I.

**shtick** (Yiddish)   1. a bit; piece. 2. a prank; trick; device.

**shul** (Yiddish)   a synagogue.

**shuto** (Japanese)    a **karate** chop made with the side of the hand.

**sì** (Italian)    yes.

**sí** (Spanish)    yes.

**sic** (Latin)    thus (placed in parentheses after a doubtful or inaccurate passage or phrase to indicate that it is taken unchanged from the original).

**siccatif** (French)    *Fine Arts.* a paint drier.

**siciliana, alla.**    See **alla siciliana.**

**siciliano** (Italian)    (lit., 'Sicilian') *Music.* an old dance of Sicilian origin marked by slow tempo and a swaying rhythm.

**sic passim** (Latin)    thus throughout (placed in parentheses to indicate that an apparent error usually or often appears thus in the original).

**sic semper tyrannis** (Latin)    thus always to tyrants (motto of Virginia; quoted by John Wilkes Booth as he assassinated Lincoln).

**sic transit gloria mundi** (Latin)    thus passes the glory of the world.

**sicut ante** (Latin)    as before.

**sieben** (German)    seven.

**siècle** (French)    century; age.

**siècle d'or** (French)    the golden age, often referring to the period of Louis XIV.

**Sieg** (German)    victory.

**Sieg heil!** (German)    (lit., 'hail to victory!') a salute used by the Nazis.

**sierra** (Spanish)    a mountain range.

**siesta** (Spanish)    an afternoon nap.

**siete** (Spanish)    seven.

**si fortuna iuvat** (Latin)    if fortune favors.

**siglo de oro** (Spanish)    the golden age; a term generally applied to the period of Spanish history from 1500 to 1650, especially with reference to literature.

**signora** (Italian)    1. the equivalent of the title *Mrs.* 2. a married woman.

**signore** (Italian)    1. the equivalent of the title *Mr.* 2. a man. Also **signor.**

**signorina** (Italian)    1. the equivalent of the title *Miss.* 2. an unmarried young woman.

**signorino** (Italian)    1. the equivalent of the title *Master.* 2. a young boy.

**silenzio** (Italian)    silence.

**s'il vous plaît** (French)    if you please; please. *Abbr.* **S.V.P.**

**similia similibus curantur** (Latin)    likes are cured by likes (the principle of homeopathic medicine).

**similis simili gaudet** (Latin)    like takes pleasure in like.

**similiter** (Latin)    likewise.

**simpatico,** *fem.* **simpatica** (Italian)    pleasant; likeable.

**simpático** (Spanish)    congenial; friendly.

273

**simple** (French)    *Ballet.* simple or ordinary, used to describe a step.

**simplex munditiis** (Latin)    simple in elegance (Horace, *Odes* I.5).

**simulacrum** (Latin)    an image, likeness, or representation of someone or something.

**sine anno** (Latin)    without the year (given).

**sine cura** (Latin)    without care or duties.

**sine die** (Latin)    (lit., 'without a day') adjourned with no day fixed for re-assembly or resumption. *Abbr.* **s.d.**

**sine dubio** (Latin)    without doubt.

**sine invidia** (Latin)    without envy.

**sine ira et studio** (Latin)    without anger and partiality (Tacitus, *Annals* I.1).

**sine legitima prole** (Latin)    without legitimate offspring. *Abbr.* **s.l.p.**

**sine loco, anno, vel nomine** (Latin)    without place, year, or name (said of a book that has no notice of publication). *Abbr.* **s.l.a.n.**

**sine loco et anno** (Latin)    without place and year (said of a book that does not give the place and year of publication).

**sine mascula prole** (Latin)    without male offspring.

**sine mora** (Latin)    without delay.

**sine nomine** (Latin)    without a name. *Abbr.* **s.n.**

**sine prole** (Latin)    without offspring. *Abbr.* **s.p.**

**sine qua non** (Latin)    (lit., 'without which not') an indispensable condition; a necessary precondition. See also **causa sine qua non.**

**sinfonia** (Italian)    a symphony.

**singerie** (French)    *Fine Arts.* the depicting of monkeys in human situations or tasks, a type of satire popular in the 18th century.

**singhiozzando** (Italian)    *Music.* sobbingly.

**Singspiel** (German)    *Music.* type of comic opera.

**sinistra** (Italian)    *Music.* left, referring to the hand.

**Sinn Fein** (Irish)    (lit., 'we ourselves') a political organization advocating Irish nationalism and independence from Great Britain.

**sino al segno** (Italian)    *Music.* an indication to continue playing to the segno.

**sinopia** (Italian)    *Fine Arts.* a preliminary sketch for a **fresco** painting, made in red crayon on plaster.

**si opus sit** (Latin)    *Prescriptions.* if there is need. *Abbr.* **s.o.s.**

**si parla italiano** (Italian)    Italian spoken here.

**sirocco** (Italian)    1. a hot, humid southerly wind of Italy that originates in the Sahara.    2. any hot, humid southerly wind. Also **scirocco.**

**sissonne** (French)    *Ballet.* a step consisting of a jump from two feet onto one foot (named for its inventor, Comte de Sissonne). Also **pas sissonne.**

**sissonne soubresant.**   See **pas de poisson.**

**sistema** (Italian)   *Music.* a stave, the lined form on which the signs for musical notation are written.

**siste viator** (Latin)   pause, traveler (frequently used on Roman tombstones).

**sitar** (Hindi)   a stringed instrument of India resembling a guitar, having a small body, a very long neck, and sympathetic strings that create a distinctive sound.

**Sitzkrieg** (German)   period of relative inactivity during a declared war.

**six** (French)   six.

**skål.**   See **skoal.**

**skoal** (Scandinavian)   a word used as a toast. Also **skål.**

**slargando, slargandosi** (Italian)   *Music.* slowing up; **rallentando.**

**slegato** (Italian)   (lit., 'unbound')   *Music.* the opposite of **legato,** that is, notes not smoothly connected. See also **staccato.**

**slentando** (Italian)   *Music.* slowing; **rallentando.**

**slivovitz** (Serbo-Croatian)   a plum-flavored brandy of eastern Europe.

**smalto,** *pl.* **smalti** (Italian)   *Fine Arts.* a small piece of colored glass or enamel employed in mosaic work.

**smaniante** (Italian)   *Music.* frenzied; passionate.

**smanioso** (Italian)   *Music.* with great intensity; furiously.

**sminuendo** (Italian)   *Music.* diminishing in power; **diminuendo.**

**sminuito** (Italian)   *Music.* lessened in power; diminished.

**smorendo** (Italian)   *Music.* becoming slower and softer by degrees.

**smorzando** (Italian)   *Music.* dying away. *Abbr.* **smorz.**

**snellamente** (Italian)   *Music.* nimbly.

**soave** (Italian)   1. *Music. adj.* gentle; tender.   2. *n. (cap.)* a light-bodied white wine produced in the Veneto region.

**soavemente** (Italian)   *Music.* tenderly; gently.

**sobresaliente** (Spanish)   *Bullfighting.* a standby substitute, either a bull or a bullfighter.

**sobriquet** (French)   a nickname; a pseudonym.

**socca** (French)   *Cookery.* a type of pancake made of chick-pea flour, a specialty of Nice.

**Sociedad Anónima** (Spanish).   See **Société Anonyme.**

**Società Anonima** (Italian).   See **Société Anonyme.**

**Société Anonyme** (French)   a designation for a French publicly owned stock company. *Abbr.* **S.A.**

**Société des Vingt** (French)   (lit., 'Society of the Twenty')   *Fine Arts.* an association of artists formed in Brussels in 1884, the aim of which was to promote unconventional art. Also **Les Vingt.**

275

**société en commandite** (French)   a corporation in which some of the partners contribute capital without being involved in the direction.

**socius criminis** (Latin)   partner in crime.

**soffione** (Italian)   a type of fumarole or volcanic vent giving off steam. See also **solfatara.**

**sofrito** (Spanish)   (lit., 'lightly fried')  *Cookery.* the base of many Spanish sauces, consisting of chopped onion fried in olive oil, to which chopped garlic and tomatoes are added.

**soga** (Spanish)   a rope.

**soggetto** (Italian)   1. *Music.* the subject of a fugue. 2. *Theater.* the scenario of a **commedia dell'arte** play.

**sogliola,** *pl.* **sogliole** (Italian)   filet of sole.

**soi-disant** (French)   1. self-styled; pretended. 2. so-called.

**soie** (French)   silk.

**soigné,** *fem.* **soignée** (French)   1. well-groomed. 2. prepared or tended with care.

**soirée** (French)   a social gathering in the evening. Also **soiree.**

**sola.**   See **solo.**

**solennemente** (Italian)   *Music.* solemnly.

**solera** (Spanish)   *Wine.* a system by which fortified wines, especially sherry, are progressively blended by transferring them from higher to lower barrels.

**solfatara** (Italian)   a type of fumarole or volcanic vent giving off sulfurous gases. See also **soffione.**

**solfeggio,** *pl.* **solfeggi** (Italian)   *Music.* a singing or sight reading exercise using the sol-fa system of naming the tones of a scale.

**soli.**   See **solo.**

**sollecitando** (Italian)   *Music.* hurrying forward.

**solo,** *fem.* **sola** (Italian)   *Music.* alone.

**solus,** *fem.* **sola** (Latin)   *Drama.* alone on the stage.

**solvitur ambulando** (Latin)   (lit., 'it is solved by walking')  the solution is (to be) found by trial and error.

**sombrée** (French)   *Music.* a designation for a voice of a dark, veiled quality.

**sombrero** (Spanish)   a Mexican hat with a very wide, circular brim.

**sommelier** (French)   the person in charge of wines in a restaurant or club.

**sonata** (Italian)   *Music.* a composition for one or two instruments consisting of several movements in different rhythms and speeds.

**sonatina** (Italian)   *Music.* a form of the **sonata** with fewer than four movements.

**son et lumière** (French)    (lit., 'sound and light') a dramatic spectacle set in a historic site to re-enact its history.

**sonnerie** (French)    *Music.* a sounding, as of bells or a trumpet.

**sopa** (Spanish)    soup.

**sopaipillas** (Spanish)    *Cookery.* Mexican fried sweet bread, served with butter and honey.

**sopra** (Italian)    *Music.* on; above.

**sopra bianco.**    See bianco sopra bianco.

**soprano** (Italian)    *Music.* the highest female voice.

**soprano acuto** (Italian)    *Music.* a high soprano.

**soprano leggiero** (Italian)    *Music.* a light, adaptable soprano.

**soprano sfogato** (Italian)    *Music.* a very high, light soprano.

**soprassata,** *pl.* **soprassate** (Italian)    a type of pressed salami.

**sorbet** (French)    sherbet.

**sordamente** (Italian)    *Music.* in a muffled style; softly.

**sorda.**    See sordo.

**sordino,** *pl.* **sordini** (Italian)    *Music.* 1. a mute for an instrument. Also sordina, sordine.    2. *(pl.)* dampers on a piano. See also con sordino. 3. a small, boat-shaped Italian violin.

**sordo** (Italian)    *Music.* dull; muffled.

**soror** (Latin)    sister.

**sorteo** (Spanish)    (lit., 'lottery')    *Bullfighting.* the assignment of the bulls to the matadors who will fight them.

**sortes Biblicae** (Latin)    divination by random selections from the Bible.

**sortes Homericae** (Latin)    divination by random selections from the works of Homer.

**sortes Vergilianae** (Latin)    divination by random selections from the works of Vergil.

**sortie** (French)    *Music.* a closing piece.

**sortita** (Italian)    *Opera.* the first aria sung by the prima donna.

**sospirando** (Italian)    *Music.* sighing; sorrowful. Also sospirante, sospirevole, sospiroso.

**sostenendo** (Italian)    *Music.* sustaining. Also sostenente.

**sostenuto** (Italian)    *Music.* 1. *adj.* sustained.    2. *n.* the middle pedal on a piano, used to sustain the sound.

**sottoaceti** (Italian)    cucumbers or other vegetables pickled in vinegar.

**sotto in su** (Italian)    *Fine Arts.* a technique of perspective used in ceiling painting that makes a cornice figure appear vertical to the viewer from below.

**sotto portico** (Italian)    *Architecture.* the area under a portico, used as a public walk.

**sotto voce** (Italian)   1. with a soft or subdued voice.   2. *Music.* in a barely audible way.

**sou** (French)   a former French coin of very small value.

**soubise** (French)   a **purée** of onions and rice, often used as an accompaniment to meat.

**soubresaut** (French)   *Ballet.* a sudden spring or jump, from which the dancer lands on both feet.

**soubrette** (French)   1. *Theater.* the part of lady's maid or a similar coquettish role for a young woman.   2. *Opera.* a secondary female part in comic opera, often that of a flirtatious and lively lady's maid.   3. a young woman who performs such roles.

**soufflé** (French)   *Cookery.* a light, puffy dish made with stiffly beaten egg whites and various ingredients and baked in a casserole.

**souffleur** (French)   *Theater.* prompter.

**soupçon** (French)   (lit., 'suspicion') a very small amount; a trace.

**soupe** (French)   *Cookery.* soup.

**soupe au pistou** (French)   a vegetable soup of Provence.  See also **pistou**.

**soupe de l'Inde** (French)   *Cookery.* mulligatawny soup.

**soupe grasse** (French)   (lit., 'fat soup') *Cookery.* a soup containing meat.

**soupe maigre** (French)   (lit., 'thin soup') *Cookery.* a soup made without meat.

**souper** (French)   supper.

**soupière** (French)   a covered classical urn, often seen in decorative motifs.

**soupirant** (French)   1. *Music.* sighing.   2. a wooer; lover.

**sourdine, à la.**   See **à la sourdine.**

**sous-chef** (French)   the assistant chef, one of the culinary ranks.

**sous-sus** (French)   (lit., 'under-over') *Ballet.* a movement combining a raising of the body with a springing motion.  Also **temps de cou-de-pied.**

**soutache** (French)   an ornamental braid, such as that used on a military uniform.

**soutenu** (French)   *Ballet; Music.* sustained.

**soutenu en tournant** (French)   *Ballet.* a turn on both feet.

**souvlaki** (Greek)   *Cookery.* cubes of marinated beef, pork, or lamb cooked on a skewer.

**soviet** (Russian)   an administrative council with local or regional jurisdiction, culminating in the Supreme Soviet.

**sowar** (Urdu)   a native Indian who served as a cavalryman.

**soyuz** (Russian)   union.

**spaghetti** (Italian)   1. a variety of **pasta** shaped in long, round strands.   2. *Cookery.* a dish of such **pasta** with sauce, usually a tomato-meat sauce.

**spanakopitta** (Greek)   *Cookery.* a type of pie made of **phyllo** with a filling of chopped spinach and various cheeses, especially **feta.**

**spandendo** (Italian)   *Music.* expanding in forcefulness.

**Spanna** (Italian)   a robust red wine produced in Piedmont. Also called **Gattinara.**

**spasibo** (Russian)   thank you.

**Spätzle** (German)   *Cookery.* a kind of noodle made fresh from batter.

**spécialité de la maison** (French)   the specialty of the house, a dish recommended by a restaurant because of special skill used in preparing it.

**spediendo** (Italian)   *Music.* hurrying; speeding.

**sperdendosi** (Italian)   *Music.* fading out.

**spes** (Latin)   hope.

**spezzatino,** *pl.* **spezzatini** (Italian)   *Cookery.* **1.** a stew of braised beef or veal cubes in gravy.   **2.** cubes of meat.

**spianato,** *fem.* **spianata** (Italian)   *Music.* smooth; even.

**spiccato** (Italian)   *Music.* a technique for playing the violin in which the bow is made to bounce on the strings. Also **richettato.**

**spiedo, allo.**   See **allo spiedo.**

**spiegando** (Italian)   (lit., 'unfolding')   *Music.* becoming louder.

**Spiel** (German)   play; game.

**spinaci** (Italian)   spinach.

**spinto** (Italian)   *Music.* a dramatic **soprano.**

**spirante** (Italian)   *Music.* expiring; dying away.

**spirito, con.**   See **con spirito.**

**spiritoso** (Italian)   *Music.* spirited.

**spirituel,** *fem.* **spirituelle** (French)   intellectual; witty.

**spiritus asper** (Latin)   *Greek grammar.* rough breathing (before a vowel); aspiration.

**spiritus frumenti** (Latin)   (lit., 'spirit of the grain')   whiskey.

**spiritus lenis** (Latin)   *Greek grammar.* smooth breathing (before a vowel); absence of aspiration.

**splendide mendax** (Latin)   nobly untruthful; deceitful for a good purpose (Horace, *Odes* III.11.35).

**splendor formae** (Latin)   excellence of form; outstanding beauty.

**spolia opima** (Latin)   (lit., 'choice spoils')   *Roman history.* the arms or booty taken from the person of a defeated general, considered a great achievement.

**spongata** (Italian)   *Cookery.* a confection of candied fruit, nuts, and honey covered with shortbread.

**sponte sua.**   See **sua sponte.**

**sposa** (Italian)   a bride.

**Sprachgefühl** (German)   feeling for language, especially sensitivity to the idiom of a language.

**sprechen sie deutsch?** (German)   do you speak German?

**sprezzatura** (Italian)   *Fine Arts.* the effortless manner of a great artist.

**spumante** (Italian)   a designation for a sparkling wine, usually white.

**spumone, spumoni** (Italian)   a frozen molded dessert containing different flavors of ice cream and candied fruits.

**sputnik** (Russian)   an earth satellite of the Soviet Union, especially the first one, launched in 1957.

**Stabat Mater** (Latin)   (lit., 'the mother was standing')   *Christianity.* title of a Latin hymn about the Virgin Mary at the Cross.

**staccato** (Italian)   1. *Music.* played so that the notes are as short and detached as possible, the opposite of **legato.**   2. consisting of distinct, abrupt units of sound. Also **secco.**

**Stahlhelm** (German)   (lit., 'steel helmet') a nationalist German veterans organization formed after World War I.

**Stalag** (German)   German prisoner-of-war camp.

**stannum** (Latin)   tin. *Abbr.* **Sn.**

**statim** (Latin)   *Medicine.* immediately. *Abbr.* **stat.**

**statu quo** (Latin)   in the state it was. See also **status quo.**

**statu quo ante bellum.**   See **status quo ante bellum.**

**status belli** (Latin)   a state of war.

**status in quo.**   See **status quo.**

**status quo** (Latin)   (lit., 'the state in which')   the existing state of affairs.

**status quo ante** (Latin)   (lit., 'the state in which before')   the conditions existing before a certain event.

**status quo ante bellum** (Latin)   the situation as it was before the war. See also **uti possidetis.**

**stecco.**   See **graffiti, 3.**

**stendendo** (Italian)   *Music.* spacing notes out; **rallentando.**

**stentato** (Italian)   (lit., 'labored')   *Music.* held back, with every note stressed.

**stesso,** *pl.* **stessi;** *fem.* **stessa,** *pl.* **stesse** (Italian)   *Music.* the same, often referring to speed. Also **istesso.**

**stet** (Latin)   let it stand (direction to a proofreader or typesetter to retain or restore something that had been queried or deleted).

**stiacciato** (Italian)   a Renaissance technique of very low **basso rilievo,** often used on coins. Also **sticciato.**

**stibium** (Latin)   antimony. *Abbr.* **Sb.**

**stichomythia** (Greek)   *Greek tragedy.* an exchange of dialogue, often emotional or argumentative, in alternating lines between two characters.

**stigmata** (Greek)    marks, corresponding to the wounds of Jesus Christ, said to appear on the bodies of certain devout individuals.

**Stijl, De.**    See **De Stijl.**

**stile rappresentativo** (Italian)    *Opera.* the use of **recitativo** as a representation of the human speaking voice rather than as a musical form.

**stilnovisti** (Italian)    *Literature.* a group of late 13th-century Tuscan poets who introduced a style, favored by Dante, that broke from the courtly love tradition.

**Stimmung** (German)    1. mood.    2. atmosphere.    3. *Music.* pitch.

**stinguendo** (Italian)    *Music.* fading away.

**stiracchiando** (Italian)    (lit., 'tugging; pulling') *Music.* making the music last; ritardando.    Also **stiracchiato; stirando; stirato; straccinato.**

**Stollen** (German)    *Cookery.* Christmas fruit loaf.

**stracchino** (Italian)    a soft, creamy white cheese produced in Lombardy.

**stracciatelle** (Italian)    *Cookery.* a soup made with eggs, flour, and grated parmesan cheese.

**straccinato.**    See **stiracchiando.**

**strada** (Italian)    a road.

**strascicando.**    See **strascinando.**

**strascinando** (Italian)    *Music.* dragging or slurring, said of bowing or singing **portamento.**    Also **strascicando.**

**Strasse** (German)    street.

**strata** (Italian)    *Cookery.* a dish consisting of layers of bread and cheese covered with a sauce of beaten eggs, then baked.

**Strega** (Italian)    a dry, vanilla-based Italian **liqueur.**

**strepitosamente** (Italian)    *Music.* noisily.

**strepitoso** (Italian)    *Music.* noisy.

**stretto** (Italian)    (lit., 'narrow') *Music.* 1. overlapping that occurs in a fugue when the subject and answer are drawn together.    2. in opera or oratorio, a quickening of tempo at the end of a movement.

**stricto sensu.**    See **sensu stricto.**

**stringendo** (Italian)    (lit., 'squeezing') *Music.* progressively quickening the tempo.

**stromenti da arco** (Italian)    *Music.* instruments played with a bow.

**stromenti da fiato** (Italian)    *Music.* wind instruments.

**stromenti da percossa** (Italian)    *Music.* percussion instruments.

**stromenti da tasto** (Italian)    *Music.* keyboard instruments.

**stromenti di corda** (Italian)    *Music.* stringed instruments.

**stromenti di legno** (Italian)    *Music.* wood instruments.

**stromento,** *pl.* **stromenti** (Italian)    a musical instrument.    Also **strumento.**

**Strudel** (German)  *Cookery.* pastry consisting of a filling rolled inside a thin layer of dough and baked.

**stucco lustro** (Italian)  stucco with a shiny surface.

**Stück** (German)  piece; piece of music; play.

**stukach** (Russian)  a government informer.

**stupor mundi** (Latin)  (lit., 'the wonder of the world') an incredible genius.

**Sturmabteilung** (German)  the Nazi militia known as the Brown Shirts or Storm Troopers. *Abbr.* **S.A.**

**Sturm und Drang** (German)  (lit., 'storm and stress') *Literature.* a German romantic literary movement of the second half of the 18th century; key figures were Schiller, Goethe, and Herder.

**style champêtre** (French)  *Fine Arts.* a type of painting in which rustic pastoral scenes are the subject matter.

**style de perruque** (French)  *Music.* a mediocre or antiquated style.

**style galant** (French)  *Music.* the rococo style of the 18th century.

**style mécanique** (French)  *Fine Arts.* an angular, industrial style of painting, sculpture, and architecture, popular in the 1920s and 1930s.

**sua sponte** (Latin)  of one's own will; voluntarily.

**subadar** (Urdu)  1. a governor of a province in the Mogul Empire. 2. a native Indian officer of a company of native troops in the British service. Also **subahdar.**

**sub anno** (Latin)  (lit., 'under the year') occurring in a particular year. *Abbr.* **s.a.**

**sub conditione** (Latin)  conditionally.

**sub Iove** *or* **Jove** (Latin)  (lit., 'under Jove') outdoors.

**subito** (Italian)  *Music.* suddenly; at once. Also **subitamente.**

**sub judice** (Latin)  *Law.* before the judge or court; under judicial consideration.

**sub modo** (Latin)  under a qualification; in a qualified or conditional sense.

**sub poena** (Latin)  under penalty (of law).

**sub rosa** (Latin)  (lit., 'under the rose') under cover; in secret; in confidence (from the use of a rose as a symbol of confidence among participants in a meeting).

**sub sigillo** (Latin)  under the seal of silence or confession; in confidence.

**sub silentio** (Latin)  in silence, as when a matter is passed over tacitly or without formal notice.

**sub specie** (Latin)  under the appearance of.

**sub specie aeternitatis** (Latin)  (lit., 'under the aspect of eternity') 1. considered with relation to God's perfection (Spinoza, *Ethics* 5.29). 2. taken in perspective.

**substratum,** *pl.* **substrata** (Latin)   an underlying layer, substance, or influence.

**sub verbo** (Latin)   (lit., 'under the word')   a direction to find a reference under a specified word or heading.  Also **sub voce.** *Abbr.* **s.v.**

**sub voce.**   See **sub verbo.**

**succès de mouchoir** (French)   (lit., 'handkerchief success') an artistic work that is popular because it evokes emotion.

**succès de ridicule** (French)   an artistic work that succeeds because people take it as a joke.

**succès de scandale** (French)   an artistic work that gains great attention because of its shocking qualities.

**succès de snobisme** (French)   an artistic work that succeeds because of its highbrow appeal.

**succès d'estime** (French)   an artistic work that wins critical acclaim but is not popular.

**succès fou** (French)   an artistic work that is received with great public enthusiasm.

**succubus** (Latin)   1. a female demon believed to have sexual intercourse with men while they sleep.  See also **incubus.**   2. a mistress or paramour. Also **succuba.**

**sucre** (French)   *Cookery.* sugar.

**sucre en morceaux** (French)   *Cookery.* sugar cubes.

**sucrier** (French)   a sugar bowl.

**sudadero** (Spanish)   *Southwestern U.S.* a seeping fissure in a water tank.

**suédoise, à la.**   See **à la suédoise.**

**sueño** (Spanish)   sleep; dream.

**suerte** (Spanish)   1. chance; lot.   2. luck.

**sufficit** (Latin)   it is sufficient.

**suggestio falsi** (Latin)   deliberate misrepresentation.

**sui generis** (Latin)   (lit., 'of its own species')   in a class by itself; in a class by oneself.

**sui juris** (Latin)   (lit., 'of one's own right')   *Law.* of full age and capacity; not subject to the authority of another.  See also **alieni juris.**

**suisse, à la.**   See **à la suisse.**

**suite, de.**   See **de suite.**

**suivez** (French)   *Music.* a direction to the accompanist to follow the soloist.

**sujet** (French)   1. *Music.* a tune or musical theme that recurs in a composition, or is used as the first theme in a fugue.  2. *Ballet.* a soloist of the company.

**sukiyaki** (Japanese)    *Cookery.* a Japanese dish of meat seasoned with soy sauce, tofu, and greens, usually cooked at the table.

**sulla tastiera** (Italian)    *Music.* in violin playing, bowing on or near the fingerboard. Also **sul tasto.**

**sul ponticello** (Italian)    *Music.* in violin playing, bowing close to the bridge.

**sul tasto.**    See **sulla tastiera.**

**sumi** (Japanese)    black ink used by Japanese calligraphers and painters.

**sumi-e** (Japanese)    *Fine Arts.* a style of Japanese painting done in black ink or **sumi.**

**summa** (Latin)    1. a comprehensive synthesis or summary.    2. (*cap.*) the *Summa Theologica* of Thomas Aquinas.

**summa cum laude** (Latin)    with the highest honor, the highest level of distinction on academic degrees. See also **cum laude; magna cum laude; maxima cum laude.**

**summum bonum** (Latin)    the supreme good; the highest good (Cicero, *On Duties* I.2).

**summum ius** *or* **jus** (Latin)    (lit., 'the highest law or right')    strict application of the law.

**sumo** (Japanese)    a Japanese style of wrestling contested between specially trained men of great size.

**Sunna** (Arabic)    1. the larger of the two major sects of Islam, believed to be based on Muhammad's sayings.    2. traditional Muslim law, said to be based on the words and actions of Muhammad. Also **Sunnah.** See also **Shiah.**

**Sunni** (Arabic)    a follower of the **Sunna** division of Islam. Also **Sunnite.**

**sunt lacrimae rerum** (Latin)    (lit., 'there are tears for things')    there are sorrows for mortal sufferings (Vergil, *Aeneid* I.462).

**suo iure** *or* **jure** (Latin)    in one's own right.

**suo loco** (Latin)    in its proper place; in one's rightful place.

**suo Marte** (Latin)    (lit., 'by one's own Mars')    by one's own prowess.

**suo motu** (Latin)    under its own power; by one's own power.

**suono,** *pl.* **suoni** (Italian)    *Music.* sound.

**suo nomine** (Latin)    in his own name.

**suo periculo** (Latin)    at one's own peril or risk.

**suo tempore** (Latin)    in its own time; at one's own pace.

**supercherie** (French)    a deliberate fraud or deception.

**supplicando** (Italian)    *Music.* begging; imploring. Also **supplichevole.**

**supplichevolmente** (Italian)    *Music.* imploringly.

**suppressio veri** (Latin)    concealment of the truth or of facts.

**supra** (Latin)   above; mentioned previously (used to refer to a previous passage in a book).

**suprema lex** (Latin)   the highest law.

**suprême** (French)   (lit., 'ultimate') *Cookery.* **1.** a designation for an especially intricate way of preparing certain dishes. **2.** chicken or fish filets served in a rich cream sauce.

**sura** (Arabic)   *Islam.* one of the 114 chapters of the **Koran.** Also **surah.**

**sur canapé** (French)   served on toast.

**Sûreté** (French)   the criminal investigation department of the French police system.

**sur fond réservé** (French)   See **en plein.**

**sur le cou de pied** (French)   *Ballet.* an indication that the heel of one foot is to rest on the lower part of the leg just above the **ankle.**

**sur les pointes** (French)   *Ballet.* on the **pointes** or tips of the toes.

**sur le vif** (French)   *Fine Arts.* painted from life.

**sur place** (French)   *Ballet.* a term indicating that the dancer is to stay in one place.

**sursum corda** (Latin)   lift up your hearts.

**surtout** (French)   above all; especially.

**sushi** (Japanese)   *Cookery.* a manner of Japanese preparation for raw fish, usually wrapped with rice in bite-size pieces.

**Süsschen** (German)   darling.

**susurrando** *or* **susurrante** (Italian)   *Music.* whispering.

**suum cuique** (Latin)   to each his own.

**suum cuique pulcrum** (Latin)   to each his own (idea of what is) beautiful.

**suus cuique mos** (Latin)   to each his own way; everyone has his own customs, observances, or viewpoint.

**svegliando** (Italian)   (lit., 'awakening') *Music.* becoming brisk.

**svegliato** (Italian)   (lit., 'awakened') *Music.* brisk; sprightly.

**svolgimento** (Italian)   *Music.* the development of a composition through its use of themes.

**swami** (Sanskrit)   *Hinduism.* a religious teacher.

**sympathique** (French)   arousing feelings of warmth and friendship in others.

**Symphonische Dichtung** (German)   *Music.* symphonic poem.

# T

**tabac** (French)    tobacco. Also **tabac à fumer**.

**tabatière** (French)    a snuff box.

**tabi** (Japanese)    a covering for the foot similar to a sock, worn with a **zori**.

**tablaos** (Spanish)    Spanish nightclubs featuring **flamenco**.

**table à manger** (French)    dining table.

**tableau,** *pl.* **tableaux** (French)    1. *Theater; Ballet.* a still representation of a scene or picture by a group of performers. 2. a scene or incident having the quality of suspended animation. Also **tableau vivant**. 3. a graphic scene or picture.

**tableau vivant.**    See **tableau, 2**.

**table de toilette** (French)    a dressing table.

**table d'hôte** (French)    (lit., 'host's table') a restaurant bill of fare of specified courses served at a fixed time and price.

**table d'instrument** (French)    *Music.* the sounding board of an instrument.

**tablier** (French)    an apron or pinafore.

**tabula rasa** (Latin)    (lit., 'a scraped writing tablet') 1. a clean slate; a blank surface. 2. an unsophisticated mind ready for new experiences.

**tacet** (Latin)    (lit., 'it is silent') *Music.* a direction that an instrument or voice is to be silent for a specified time.

**tachisme** (French)    *Fine Arts.* a form of abstract art in which paint is spilled, poured, or smeared onto the canvas, forming blots or splotches (*taches*) of color.

**tachiste** (French)    *Fine Arts.* an artist who practices **tachisme**.

**taci** (Italian)    *Music.* a direction that certain instruments are not to play. Also **taciasi**.

**taco** (Spanish)    *Cookery.* a **tortilla** that is folded and filled, usually with meat flavored with **chile**, cheese, and other condiments.

**tactus** (Latin)    (lit., 'touched') *Music.* a metrical beat.

**t(a)edium vitae** (Latin)    weariness of living; a disgust with life.

287

**tae kwon do** (Korean)    a Korean style of martial arts similar to **karate**.

**Tafelmusik** (German)   *Music.* mealtime music.

**tagliatelli** (Italian)   *Cookery.* a flat **pasta** made in various widths.

**taglierini** (Italian)   *Cookery.* a flat, narrow **pasta** used in soups and with sauces.

**tai chi** (Chinese)   a Chinese discipline of programmed physical movements and exercises that are intended to promote physical and spiritual well-being.

**taille** (French)   1. *French history.* a tax levied by a king or **seigneur** on his subjects. 2. *Fashion.* the waist or bodice. 3. *Music.* the tenor part; a tenor instrument.

**taille d'épargne.**   See **champlevé**.

**taille douce** (French)   *Fine Arts.* 1. the process of engraving on a copper or another metal surface. 2. a work created by this process.

**tailleur** (French)   1. a woman's tailored suit. 2. *Gambling.* a card dealer.

**tajo** (Spanish)   1. a trench.    2. a cut or gash.

**tallith,** *pl.* **tallithim** (Hebrew)   *Judaism.* a shawl with fringes at the four corners, worn by Jewish men during prayer services. Also **talit(h); tal(l)is; tallit.**

**tallith katan.**   (Hebrew) See **arba kanfoth.**

**talmouse** (French)   *Cookery.* a type of flaky pastry.

**Talmud** (Hebrew)   *Judaism.* the collection of non-biblical Jewish law and tradition, made up of the **Mishnah** and the **Gemara.**

**tamale, tamal** (Spanish)   *Cookery.* a Mexican dish made of corn, ground meat, and **chile**, usually wrapped in corn husks.

**tambourin** (French)   *Music.* 1. a long, narrow drum of Provence. 2. an old dance of Provence in two-in-a-measure time.

**tameshiwara** (Japanese)   the destruction of inanimate objects, such as boards and bricks, by means of **karate** blows.

**Tanach** (Hebrew)   *Judaism.* the whole of Jewish Scripture; the Old Testament. See also **Hagiographa; Nebiim; Torah.**

**tango** (Spanish)   1. a ballroom dance of Spanish American origin consisting of dramatic movements and poses and rapid changes of direction. 2. the music for this dance.

**Tannenbaum** (German)   a Christmas tree.

**tant mieux** (French)   so much the better.

**tanto** (Italian)   *Music.* so much; as much.

**tant soit peu** (French)   ever so little.

**Tantum Ergo** (Latin)   *Christianity.* title of a Latin hymn by Thomas Aquinas.

**tapa** (Spanish)   *Cookery.* an appetizer; hors d'oeuvre. Also **entremés.**

**tapadero** (Spanish)   a leather stirrup cover.

**tapaojos** (Spanish)   a blindfold used on unruly pack or saddle animals.

**tapenade** (French)   a condiment containing olives, anchovies, and capers.

**tapis vert** (French)   (lit., 'green carpet') *Landscape design.* an expanse of lawn.

**tapotement** (French)   tapping or patting with the hand in massage.

**taqueté** (French)   (lit., 'pegged') *Ballet.* designating small, quick steps that are danced on the **pointes** and strike the floor sharply.

**tarallo** (Italian)   a kind of ring-shaped biscuit flavored with anise.

**tarantella** (Italian)   *Music.* 1. a lively dance originating in southern Italy near Taranto.   2. the music for this dance.

**tardamente** (Italian)   *Music.* slowly.

**tardando** (Italian)   *Music.* gradually slowing.  See also **rallentando**.

**tarole** (French)   *Music.* a shallow type of side drum. Also **tarole grégoire**.

**tarole grégoire.**   See **tarole**.

**tarsia.**   See **intarsia**.

**tarte tatin** (French)   *Cookery.* an upside-down apple tart with a caramelized top.

**tartine** (French)   1. a slice of bread spread with butter and jam, served for breakfast or as a snack.   2. a small tart.

**tartufi,** *sing.* **tartufo** (Italian)   1. truffles.   2. a confection, often made with chocolate.

**TASS** (Russian)   the official Soviet news agency (an acronym).

**tastevin** (French)   a cup used by a **sommelier**, often worn around the neck.

**tatami** (Japanese)   a thick, woven floor mat used in Japanese homes.

**tatons, à.**   See **à tatons**.

**tauromaquía** (Spanish)   bullfighting and its related activities, skills, and lore; tauromachy.

**Taurus** (Latin)   the Bull, a constellation and sign of the zodiac.

**Tavel** (French)   a rosé wine produced in the Rhone Valley.

**taverna** (Italian)   a small, simple pub that may also serve food.

**tavola calda** (Italian)   a short-order restaurant that serves dishes from a steam table.

**tazza** (Italian)   1. *Antiques.* a tall drinking cup with a wide, shallow bowl. 2. the raised basin of a fountain.

**tedesca, alla.**   See **alla tedesca**.

**tedesco, al.**   See **al tedesco**.

**Te Deum** (Latin)   *Christianity.* title of an ancient liturgical hymn.

**tefillin** (Hebrew)  *Judaism.* the phylacteries, small, black, leather cubes, one strapped to the forehead and another to the left arm of Jewish men during prayer, each containing parchment inscribed with certain biblical verses. Also **tephillin.**

**te iudice** *or* **judice** (Latin)  (lit., 'you being the judge') in your judgment.

**tejano,** *fem.* **tejana** (Spanish)  Texan.

**tel quel** (French)  as is.

**tema** (Italian)  *Music.* the main subject of a composition.  Also **thema.**

**tema con variazioni** (Italian)  1. *Music.* an air with variations.  2. *Literature.* humorous verse or parody.

**tema fondamentale.**  See **motivaguida.**

**tempestosamente** (Italian)  *Music.* tempestuously.

**tempête** (French)  (lit., 'tempest')  *Music.* an exuberant dance in two-in-a-measure time.

**tempo alla breve.**  See **alla breve.**

**tempo a piacere** (Italian)  *Music.* tempo as the performer pleases.

**tempo comodo** (Italian)  *Music.* 1. moderate tempo.  2. tempo convenient to the player.  Also **tempo commodo.**

**tempo di ballo** (Italian)  *Music.* in dance time.

**tempo di cappella** (Italian)  *Music.* in the tempo of church music.

**tempo di gavotta** (Italian)  *Music.* in the tempo of a gavotte.

**tempo di marcia** (Italian)  *Music.* in the tempo of a march.

**tempo di minuetto** (Italian)  *Music.* in the tempo of a minuet.  Also **tempo di menuetto.**

**tempo di prima parte** (Italian)  *Music.* in the tempo of the first part.

**tempo di valse** (Italian)  *Music.* in waltz time.

**tempo frettevole** (Italian)  *Music.* in quicker tempo; hurrying.  Also **tempo frettoloso.**

**tempo giusto** (Italian)  *Music.* in strict time.  Also **a tempo giusto.**

**tempo maggiore.**  See **alla breve.**

**tempo ordinario** (Italian)  *Music.* 1. tempo that is neither fast nor slow.  2. an indication to resume the tempo of a previous passage.  Also **tempo primo.**  3. tempo in which the beats have their normal value, in contrast to **alla breve.**

**tempo perduto** (Italian)  *Music.* a tempo that is irregular, interrupted, or lost.

**tempo primo** (Italian)  1. the first or original tempo of a passage.  2. See **tempo ordinario, 2.**

**temporada** (Spanish)  *Bullfighting.* the season for the fights.

**tempore** (Latin)  in the time of (used with the name of a person).

**tempo reggiato** (Italian)    *Music.* an indication that the tempo is to accommodate the soloist.

**tempo rubato** (Italian)    (lit., 'stolen time') *Music.* irregular tempo, caused by slowing one note and quickening another without altering the time of each measure as a whole. See also **a tempo rubato**.

**tempranillo** (Spanish)    a variety of grape grown in the **Rioja** district of Spain, valued for the deep ruby color it gives to wine.

**temps** (French)    1. *Music.* tempo; beat. 2. *Ballet.* a movement (originally referring to the timing of a step to a rhythm).

**temps de cou-de-pied.**    See **sous-sus**.

**temps de flèche.**    See **saut de flèche**.

**temps de l'ange** (French)    (lit., 'angel's movement') *Ballet.* a soaring step in which the back is arched and the legs are bent like those of angels in old paintings.

**temps d'élévation** (French)    (lit., 'elevation movement') *Ballet.* any step that involves springing or jumping. Also **pas d'élévation**.

**temps de pointes** (French)    *Ballet.* any step or movement executed on the toes or **pointes**.

**temps de poisson.**    See **pas de poisson**.

**temps échappé.**    See **échappé**.

**temps frappé** (French)    *Music.* the downbeats or parts that are accented.

**temps levé** (French)    1. *Music.* the upbeats or parts that are not accented. 2. *Ballet.* a movement in which the body is raised by an upward spring from one foot or both feet.

**temps lié** (French)    (lit., 'linked movements') *Ballet.* a series of connected movements involving all parts of the body, used as an exercise.

**temps plané** (French)    *Ballet.* a soaring movement.

**temps relevé.**    See **relevé**.

**temps retiré.**    See **retiré**.

**tempura** (Japanese)    *Cookery.* seafood or vegetables dipped in batter and deep-fried.

**tempus edax rerum** (Latin)    time, devourer of (all) things (Ovid, *Metamorphoses* XV.234).

**tempus fugit** (Latin)    time flies.

**tempus ludendi** (Latin)    a time for playing.

**tempus omnia revelat** (Latin)    time reveals all things.

**tendu,** *fem.* **tendue** (French)    *Ballet.* stretched.

**Tenebrae** (Latin)    (lit., 'darkness') *Christian liturgy.* the extinguishing of candles, part of the ritual of Holy Week, to commemorate the Crucifixion.

**tenebrosi** (Italian)    (lit., 'shadowy') *Fine Arts.* a school of Venetian painters who used strong lights and shadows for effect.

291

**tenebroso** (Italian)    *Music.* dark; gloomy.

**tenendo** (Italian)    *Music.* sustaining.

**teneramente** (Italian)    *Music.* tenderly.

**tenerezza, con.**    See **con tenerezza.**

**tenore,** *pl.* **tenori** (Italian)    *Music.* a tenor. Also **tenorista.**

**tenore buffo** (Italian)    *Music.* a tenor who does comic roles.

**tenore di grazia** (Italian)    *Music.* a lyric tenor.

**tenore leggiero** (Italian)    *Music.* a light tenor.

**tenore primo** (Italian)    *Music.* a first tenor.

**tenore ripieno** (Italian)    *Music.* a tenor of a large chorus.

**tenore robusto** (Italian)    *Music.* a strong tenor.

**tenorista.**    See **tenore.**

**tenu,** *fem.* **tenue** (French)    *Music.* held.

**tenutavinicola** (Italian)    a large wine-making estate.

**tenuto,** *pl.* **tenuti;** *fem.* **tenuta,** *pl.* **tenute** (Italian)    *Music.* held, referring to notes or chords that are to be sustained for their full time.

**tepee** (Siouan)    a conical tent of the Indians of the North American plains.

**tephillin.**    See **tefillin.**

**tepidamente** (Italian)    *Music.* in an unimpassioned way.

**tepido** (Italian)    *Music.* tepid; unimpassioned.

**tequila** (Spanish)    an alcoholic beverage made from the juice of the agave.

**ter in die** (Latin)    *Prescriptions.* three times a day. *Abbr.* **t.i.d.**

**teriyaki** (Japanese)    *Cookery.* a designation for a Japanese dish of meat or fish that has been marinated in a soy sauce mixture and broiled.

**terme** (Italian)    sulphur baths.

**terminé** (French)    *Ballet.* ended; concluded.

**terminus ad quem** (Latin)    (lit., 'the end toward which') finishing point; goal. See also **terminus ante quem.**

**terminus ante quem** (Latin)    (lit., 'the end before which') the date before which an event must have occurred. See also **terminas a quo; terminus ad quem.**

**terminus a quo** (Latin)    (lit., 'the end from which') 1. the point of departure. 2. the date after which an event must have occurred. See also **terminus ante quem.**

**ter quaterque beatus** (Latin)    three and four times blessed (adapted from Vergil, *Aeneid* I.94).

**terra alba** (Latin)    (lit., 'white earth') white clay or other natural material, as used in ceramics.

**terra cotta** (Italian)    (lit., 'cooked earth') 1. a fired clay, brownish-red or yellowish-red in color, used in ceramics and ornamental work.    2. a brownish-red color. Also **terra-cotta, terracotta.**

**terrae filius** (Latin)   (lit., 'son of the earth')   a person of undistinguished parentage.

**terra es, terram ibis** (Latin)   dust thou art, to dust wilt thou return (Genesis 3:19).

**terra firma** (Latin)   solid earth; dry land.

**terra incognita** (Latin)   (lit., 'unknown land')   1. unexplored territory.   2. a subject about which nothing is known.

**terra irredenta** (Italian)   1. areas inhabited by an Italian majority but controlled by Austria until the Treaty of Versailles in 1919.   2. any region under the control of a power that does not represent its ethnic majority.

**terra rossa** (Italian)   a type of soil, reddish-brown in color, covering limestone bedrock in areas around the Adriatic Sea.

**terra verde** (Italian)   *Fine Arts.*   a grayish-green pigment used in painting; green earth.

**terrazzo** (Italian)   *Architecture.*   a flooring surface made of marble chips set in white or colored concrete.

**terre, à.**   See à terre.

**terre, par.**   See à terre.

**terre à terre** (French)   (lit., 'ground to ground')   *Ballet.*   designating steps performed close to the floor with very slight elevation.

**terre de pipe** (French)   *Ceramics.*   earthenware made with a white paste and covered with a transparent glaze.

**terre pisée.**   See pise de terre..

**terre verte** (French)   1. a grayish-green color.   2. *Fine Arts.*   green earth pigment.

**terribilità** (Italian)   *Fine Arts.*   qualities or features of a work that cause awe and fear in the viewer.

**terroir** (French)   (lit., 'soil')   an earthy taste present in certain wines produced on heavy soil.

**tertium quid** (Latin)   (lit., 'a third something')   something intermediate between or related to two things, but distinct from both.

**tertius gaudens** (Latin)   (lit., 'rejoicing third')   a third party who gains an advantage from the conflict of two others.

**terza rima** (Italian)   *Literature.*   a verse form consisting of a series of tercets with the middle line of each riming with the first and third lines of the next, used by Dante in *The Divine Comedy*.

**terzetto** (Italian)   *Music.*   a trio, used especially of singers.

**terzi tuoni** (Italian)   *Music.*   third tones, sounds heard after two loud notes sound together.

**tessera**, *pl.* **tesserae** (Latin)   *Fine Art.* a small piece of marble or other stone used in mosaic work.

**tessitura** (Italian)   *Music.* the texture of the vocal line in a song, considered best if an excessive number of high or low notes is avoided.

**testudo** (Latin)   (lit., 'tortoise')   *Warfare.* a Roman defensive tactic in which a closely formed unit placed their shields overhead, as when attacked by archers.

**tête-à-tête** (French)   (lit., 'head-to-head')   **1.** *n.* an intimate conversation between two people.   **2.** *adv.* privately; intimately.   **3.** *adj.* of a private or confidential nature.   **4.** *n.* an S-shaped seat on which two people can sit facing each other.

**tête-bêche** (French)   *Philately.* designating stamps printed upside down or sideways in relation to one another.

**tête de cuvée** (French)   choice wine made from the initial crushing of the grapes.

**tête-de-pont** (French)   *Fortification.* a bridgehead.

**tête de veau** (French)   *Cookery.* calf's head, often cooked in a sauce and served with a **vinaigrette** dressing.

**tetrazzini** (Italian)   *Cookery.* a designation for a dish consisting of diced chicken in a cream and mushroom sauce served over **pasta** (named to honor the opera singer, Luisa Tetrazzini).

**textus receptus** (Latin)   the accepted text; the standard text.

**Théâtre-Français.**   See **Comédie Française.**

**thé dansant** (French)   a tea party at which there is dancing.

**thema.**   See **tema.**

**thé musical**, *pl.* **thés musicaux** (French)   a tea party at which music is performed.

**thermae** (Latin)   hot springs; hot baths.

**thon** (French)   tuna.

**tiempo** (Spanish)   **1.** time.   **2.** weather.

**tienta** (Spanish)   *Bullfighting.* the testing of young bulls and sometimes of their mothers at a bullranch.

**tiers état** (French)   the third estate; the commoners.

**timbale** (French)   *Cookery.* **1.** a custard-like dish containing meat, fish, or vegetables, baked in a drum-shaped mold.   **2.** a drum-shaped pastry shell.

**timbre** (French)   the characteristic quality of a sound besides its pitch and loudness.

**timbre-poste** (French)   a postage stamp.

**timeo Danaos et dona ferentes** (Latin)   I fear the Greeks even when they bring gifts (Vergil, *Aeneid* II.49).

**timidezza, con.**   See **con timidezza.**

**timorosamente** (Italian)   *Music.* fearfully.

**timoroso** (Italian)   *Music.* fearful.

**timpani**, *sing.* **timpano** (Italian)   *Music.* kettledrums.

**timpani coperti** (Italian)   *Music.* kettledrums muffled by means of a cloth covering. See also **timpani sordi**.

**timpani sordi** (Italian)   *Music.* kettledrums muted either by being covered with a cloth or by being struck with sponge-headed drumsticks. See also **timpani coperti**.

**timpanista** (Italian)   *Music.* a player of kettledrums.

**tinaja** (Spanish)   1. *Southwestern U.S.* a hole in which water collects, especially one formed by a waterfall. See also **playa, 2.**   2. a very large earthenware jar.

**tinto** (Italian)   *Music.* color; expression.

**tinto** (Spanish)   1. red wine.   2. *South America.* black coffee served in small cups; demitasse.

**Tío Pepe** (Spanish)   (lit., 'Uncle Joe')   *Wine.* a variety of very dry sherry.

**tirailleur** (French)   *French history.* an infantry unit of native troops in a French-controlled territory.

**tire-bouchon, en.**   See **en tire-bouchon**.

**tiropitta** (Greek)   *Cookery.* a type of pie made of **phyllo** with a filling of various cheeses, especially **feta**.

**tisane** (French)   an herbal tea, taken for digestive or medicinal purposes.

**tisane de champagne** (French)   a light champagne.

**toccata** (Italian)   *Music.* a prelude for organ or harpsichord, played with great rapidity, the hands seeming to barely touch the keyboard.

**toccatella** *or* **toccatina** (Italian)   *Music.* a short **toccata**.

**tocco, il.**   See **il tocco**.

**toches** (Yiddish)   the buttocks. Also **tochis; tuches; tuchis**.

**Todentanz** (German)   *Music.* dance of death.

**tofu** (Japanese)   *Cookery.* processed soybean curd, used as a basic ingredient.

**toga candida** (Latin)   *Roman history.* the all-white toga worn by candidates for public office.

**toga praetexta** (Latin)   *Roman history.* the purple-bordered toga worn by magistrates and freeborn children.

**toga virilis** (Latin)   *Roman history.* 1. the manly toga, assumed by Roman boys on reaching the age of 14.   2. any mark of physical or intellectual maturity.

**toile** (French)   1. a type of linen or cotton cloth. 2. *Music.* a stage curtain. 3. *Fine Arts.* canvas for painting.

**toile de Jouy** (French)    a cotton or linen fabric with a print pattern on a light background (originating in the French town of Jouy-en-Josar).

**tombant** (French)    (lit., 'falling')    *Ballet.* designating a step with the action of falling down.

**tombé**, *fem.* **tombée** (French)    (lit., 'fallen')    *Ballet.* designating a movement that involves falling forward, backward, or sideways onto the working leg.

**ton** (French)    1. high fashion; elegance.    2. a current vogue.

**Ton**, *pl.* **Töne**    (German)    *Music.*    1. tone.    2. pitch.    3. key.    4. note.

**Tondichtung** (German)    *Music.* tone poem.

**tondo** (Italian)    *Music.* full-toned; rounded.

**ton doux** (French)    *Music.* a soft, sweet tone.

**Tonfarbe** (German)    *Music.* tone color; theory of interrelationship between visual and aural impression.    Also **Farbeton**.

**tonica** (Italian)    *Music.* the name of the first note of the scale; the keynote.

**tonitruone** (Italian)    *Music.* a hanging sheet of iron that is shaken to create the effect of loud noise.

**Tonkunst** (German)    *Music.* music; musical art.

**tonnato vitello** (Italian)    *Cookery.* a dish consisting of sliced veal covered with a mixture of tuna and mayonnaise.

**tonneau**, *pl.* **tonneaux** (French)    1. a rear seating compartment on a car.    2. a metric ton. Also **millier**.    3. a large cask of wine.    4. in Bordeaux, 900 liters of wine or 100 cases of 12 bottles.

**tonnelet** (French)    *Ballet.* a short hoop skirt once worn by male dancers.

**tonno** (Italian)    tuna. See also **al tonno**.

**tono**, *pl.* **toni** (Italian)    *Music.*    1. a tone; sound.    2. the key or mode.    3. Gregorian tone.    Also **tuono**.

**Tonsatz** (German)    *Music.* musical composition.

**tonto**, *fem.* **tonta** (Spanish)    1. foolish; stupid.    2. *n.* a fool; dimwit.

**Tonwissenschaft** (German)    *Music.* the science of music.

**topos** (Greek)    *Literature.* an oft-repeated scene or situation; type; cliché.

**Torah** (Hebrew)    *Judaism.*    1. the Pentateuch or Books of Moses, the first five books of Jewish Scripture, containing biblical law. See also **Hagiographa**; **Nebiim**; **Tanach**.    2. the entire body of Jewish law as contained in Scripture and the **Talmud**.

**torchère** (French)    a tall stand for holding a candelabrum or lamp.

**tordion.**    See **tourdion**.

**toreador** (Spanish)    *Bullfighting.* a generic term for a bullfighter.

**toreo** (Spanish)    bullfighting.

**torero** (Spanish)    *Bullfighting.* a generic term for a bullfighter.

**torii** (Japanese)    a decorative gateway at the entrance to Shinto temples.

**toril** (Spanish) *Bullfighting.* the pen where the bull is kept before entering the ring. Also **encierro.**

**tornando** (Italian) *Music.* returning.

**toro** (Spanish) bull.

**torreja de maíz** (Spanish) a corn fritter.

**torreón** (Spanish) **1.** a high tower. **2.** a vantage point; lookout.

**torres** (Spanish) *History.* coastal lookout towers built in Spain after the Christian reconquest.

**torrone** (Italian) nougat.

**torta** (Italian) a dessert cake; **torte.**

**torta al ron** (Spanish) rum cake.

**Torte** (German) *Cookery.* a rich cake; tart.

**tortelli** (Italian) *Cookery.* a dish made with two layers of **pasta** that are filled and cut into various shapes. Also **tortelloni.**

**tortellini** (Italian) *Cookery.* small, stuffed rings of **pasta.**

**tortelloni** (Italian) *Cookery.* **1.** large **tortellini. 2.** See **tortelli.**

**tortilla** (Spanish) *Cookery.* a flat, unleavened corn or wheat cake, usually served with various fillings and seasoning.

**tortillon** (French) *Fine Arts.* a small cylinder made of paper twisted to a point, used for shading chalk and pencil drawings.

**tortina** (Italian) *Cookery.* a type of pie containing various cooked vegetables.

**tortue** (French) turtle.

**tortue claire** (French) *Cookery.* clear turtle soup.

**tostado** (Spanish) (lit., 'toasted') *Cookery.* a flat **tortilla** on which are layered refried beans, meat or chicken, lettuce, tomatoes, onions, and sour cream.

**tostamente** (Italian) *Music.* quickly.

**tostissimamente** (Italian) *Music.* with utmost rapidity.

**tostissimo** (Italian) *Music.* most rapid.

**tosto** (Italian) *Music.* quick; rapid.

**tostón** (Spanish) **1.** *Cookery.* roast suckling pig. **2.** *Mexico.* a fifty-cent coin.

**totidem verbis** (Latin) in just so many words; in these words.

**toties quoties** (Latin) as often as occasion arises.

**totis viribus** (Latin) with all one's might.

**toto caelo** (Latin) (lit., 'by the whole heaven') diametrically opposed; worlds apart.

**totum** (Latin) the whole.

**touché** (French) (lit., 'touched') **1.** *Fencing.* a hit. **2.** a word said in acknowledgement of a telling remark.

**toujours** (French)    always.

**toujours l'amour** (French)    love always; love forever.

**tour** (French)    *Ballet.* a turning movement of the body.

**tour de force,** *pl.* **tours de force** (French)    1. a feat of exceptional skill or intelligence in the arts or another field. 2. a difficult technique or maneuver that is well executed. 3. *(pl.) Music.* bravura passages.

**tour de main** (French)    a magician's trick.

**tourdion** (French)    *Music.* an early French dance in triple time. Also **tordion.**

**tourelle** (French)    a turret.

**tour en l'air** (French)    *Ballet.* a virtuoso display of a male dancer in which he rotates his body while in the air.

**tour jeté** (French)    *Ballet.* a step in which the dancer leaps from one foot, turns in the air, and lands on the other foot.

**tournant, en.**    See **en tournant.**

**tournedos** (French)    *Cookery.* small slices from the beef filet, variously prepared.

**tours chaînés** (French)    *Ballet.* a series of small turning steps consisting of a half-turn of the body on each step. Also **petit tours; déboulés.**

**tourte** (French)    *Cookery.* a tart or pie, often filled with meat.

**tourtière** (French)    a meat pie with many variations, a specialty of Quebec Province.

**tout à coup** (French)    suddenly.

**tout à fait** (French)    entirely.

**tout à l'heure** (French)    1. very soon. 2. just now; just a moment ago.

**tout à vous** (French)    sincerely yours.

**tout court** (French)    1. only; with nothing else. 2. abruptly.

**tout de suite** (French)    immediately; at once.

**tout ensemble** (French)    1. *n.* the overall effect; the whole. 2. *adv.* taken as a whole; all together.

**toutes jambes, à.**    See **à toutes jambes.**

**tout le monde** (French)    all the world; everybody.

**tout prix, à.**    See **à tout prix.**

**tovarich** (Russian)    comrade, a standard form of address among Soviet Communists. Also **tovarish; tovarishch.**

**trabajo** (Spanish)    work.

**tradiciones** (Spanish) (lit., 'traditions')    *Literature.* short sketches blending history, anecdote, and satire, a form originated by the Peruvian writer Ricardo Palma.

**tradolce** (Italian)    *Music.* very soft; sweet.

**traduction** (French)    1. a translation. *Music.* **2.** an arrangement. **3.** a transposition.

**tragédienne** (French)    *Theater.* an actress who plays tragic roles.

**train à grande vitesse** (French)    the high-speed train of France. *Abbr.* **TGV.**

**trait de chant** (French)    *Music.* a melodic passage or phrase.

**trait d'harmonie** (French)    *Music.* chords following each other in succession; a harmonic sequence.

**traje de luces** (Spanish)    (lit., 'suit of lights') *Bullfighting.* the customary uniform of the bullfighter, made of silk and brocade and decorated with sequins.

**tranche de vie** (French)    (lit., 'slice of life') *Fine Arts; Literature.* a realistic, often harsh representation of scenes and incidents from life.

**tranquillamente** (Italian)    *Music.* quietly; calmly.

**tranquillo** (Italian)    *Music.* tranquil.

**trapunto** (Italian)    *Needlework.* a form of decorative quilting.

**trascinando** (Italian)    *Music.* holding back; **rallentando.**

**trattenuto** (Italian)    *Music.* **1.** held back. **2.** sustained.

**tratto** (Italian)    *Music.* dragged. See also **non tratto.**

**trattoria** (Italian)    a small, simple restaurant, often run by a family.

**travesti, en.**    See **en travesti.**

**trayf** (Yiddish)    *Judaism.* not **kosher.** Also **treyf.**

**tre** (Italian)    three. See also **a tre.**

**Trebbiano** (Italian)    a dry white wine produced in several regions of Italy.

**trecento** (Italian)    the 14th century or the 1300's, especially in reference to Italian fine arts or literature.

**tre corde** (Italian)    (lit., 'three strings') *Music.* in piano playing, a direction to play without using the pedals. Also **tutte le corde** ('all the strings').

**tremando** (Italian)    *Music.* with **tremolo.** Also **tremante, tremolando.**

**tremendismo** (Spanish)    *Literature.* the technique of creating fear and horror in the reader by offering many gory details, employed by contemporary Spanish writers.

**tremolo** (Italian)    *Music.* **1.** an effect created by the rapid repetition of a single note or the alternation of two notes. **2.** in singing, a pitch-fluctuating effect similar to **vibrato.** See also **ondeggiamento.**

**trente-et-quarante.**    See **rouge et noir.**

**tres** (Spanish)    three.

**très** (French)    very.

**très animé** (French)    *Music.* very lively.

**très bien** (French)    very well; all right.

**très cher** (French)    very expensive.

**très fort** (French)   *Music.* very loud.

**très lentement** (French)   *Music.* very slowly.

**très vif** (French)   *Music.* very brisk.

**très vite** (French)   *Music.* very fast.

**triclinium** (Latin)   a Roman dining couch for three reclining people.

**tricolore.**   See **drapeau tricolore.**

**triduum** (Latin)   1. *Prescriptions.* for three days. *Abbr.* **trid.**   2. a period of three days.

**triennium** (Latin)   a period of three years.

**trillando** (Italian)   *Music.* trilling.

**trio** (Italian)   *Music.* 1. a group of three, especially three performers.   2. a composition for three instruments or voices.

**tripas** (Spanish)   1. entrails; guts.   2. belly.

**triste** (French, Spanish)   sad; melancholy.

**tristesse** (French)   sadness; melancholy.

**tristezza** (Italian)   *Music.* sadness.

**tristo** (Italian)   *Music.* sad.

**trivium** (Latin)   the lower division of the seven liberal arts, consisting of grammar, rhetoric, and logic.   See also **quadrivium.**

**troika** (Russian)   1. a carriage or wagon drawn by three horses.   2. any group of three acting in concert.

**trois** (French)   three.

**trois, à.**   See **à trois.**

**troisième en avant** (French)   *Ballet.* an arm position in which one arm is curved in front of the body and the other opened to the side.

**troisième en haut** (French)   *Ballet.* an arm position in which one arm is curved above the head and the other is held out to the side.

**troisième position** (French)   *Ballet.* a basic position of the feet in which they are pointed outward and crossed over.

**trois-quarts** (French)   *Ballet.* three-quarters, as in describing a turn.

**tromba** (Italian)   *Music.* a trumpet.

**trompe de chasse** (French)   a hunting horn.

**trompe l'oeil** (French)   (lit., 'trick of the eye') 1. *Fine Arts.* a graphic depiction intended to create an illusion of space or of a real object.   2. a deceptive appearance. Also **trompe-l'oeil.**

**tronco** (Italian)   *Music.* an indication that the sounds should be cut short.

**trop** (French)   too many; very much. See also **de trop.**

**troppo** (Italian)   *Music.* too much. See also **non troppo.**

**trouvaille** (French)   a lucky find.

**trouvères** (French)   *Music.* the poet-composers who traveled through France during the Middle Ages. Also **trouveur.**

**truditur dies die** (Latin)  one day drives out another; time rushes on (Horace, *Odes* II.18.15).

**truffe,** *pl.* **truffes** (French)  truffle.

**truffé** (French)  garnished with truffles.

**truite** (French)  trout.

**truité** (French)  a designation for porcelain that has a crackled glaze.

**tsar.** See **czar.**

**tsarevitch.** See **czarevitch.**

**tsarevna.** See **czarevna.**

**tsarina.** See **czarina.**

**tsunami** (Japanese)  a tidal wave produced by an underwater geologic disturbance.

**tsurugi.** See **ken.**

**tubetti** (Italian)  (lit., 'little tubes')  small, tubular **pasta** used mainly in soups.

**tuches.** See **toches.**

**tuebor** (Latin)  I will defend (motto on the coat-of-arms of Michigan).

**tulle** (French)  a fine net of silk or other sheer material used for wedding veils and formal gowns.

**tulwar** (Hindi)  a type of Indian saber.

**tumultuoso** (Italian)  *Music.* tumultuous; agitated.

**tuono,** *pl.* **tuoni** (Italian)  1. See **tono.**  2. thunder.

**tu quoque** (Latin)  (lit., 'you, too') a reply to an accusation, implying that the accuser is guilty of the same offense.

**Turquerie** (French)  1. *Antiques.* Turkish-style objects.  2. *Fine Arts.* painting that depicts pseudo-Turkish scenes, popular in the 18th century.

**turrón** (Spanish)  *Cookery.* a Spanish confection containing marzipan, nougat, cream cake, chocolate, honey, and hazelnuts.

**tutta forza** (Italian)  *Music.* as loud and strong as possible.  Also **tutta la forza.**

**tutte le corde.** See **tre corde.**

**tutti** (Italian)  *Music.* designating a passage to be played by all the performers together.

**tutti frutti** (Italian)  (lit., 'all the fruits')  1. a confection, usually ice cream, made with several kinds of fruit or fruit flavorings.  2. a collection of different ideas or objects.  Also **tutti-frutti.**

**tutti unisoni** (Italian)  *Music.* all in unison.

**tutu** (French)  *Ballet.* a short skirt worn by female dancers.

**tuum est** (Latin)  it is yours.

**tzar.** See **czar.**

# U

**Übermensch** (German)   (lit., 'superman') Nietzsche's term for an ideal of a superior human being.

**uberrima fides** (Latin)   (lit., 'most abundant faith')   *Law.* complete openness and honesty, without hint of concealment or misrepresentation of fact.

**ubique** (Latin)   everywhere.

**ubi sunt** (Latin)   (lit., 'where are they?')   an expression of dismay over the loss of those who have died (opening words of several medieval songs; fully, *ubi sunt qui ante nos fuerunt* 'where are they who lived before us?').

**ubi supra** (Latin)   where (mentioned) above; in the place or book mentioned above. *Abbr.* **u.s.**

**uccello,** *pl.* **uccelli** (Italian)   small song birds.

**uhuru** (Swahili)   freedom.

**uisge beatha** (Gaelic)   (lit., 'water of life')   whiskey.

**ukelele** (Hawaiian)   a small, stringed instrument similar to a guitar. Also **ukulele.**

**ukiyo-e** (Japanese)   a genre of Japanese painting and printmaking of the 17th through 19th centuries.

**ultima ratio** (Latin)   the final argument; the last resort. See also **ultima ratio regum.**

**ultima ratio regum** (Latin)   (lit., 'the final argument of kings')   the use of hostile force (motto inscribed on the cannons of Louis XIV).

**ultima Thule** (Latin)   (lit., 'farthest Thule')   **1.** the land believed by the ancients to be the farthest northern point accessible.   **2.** a very far-off or exceedingly remote place.   **3.** a very lofty or hard-to-reach goal.

**ultime** (Latin)   lastly; finally. *Abbr.* **ult.**

**ultimo** (Latin)   of or during the previous month. *Abbr.* **ult.; ulto.** See also **proximo.**

**ultimum vale** (Latin)   a final farewell.

303

**ultimus Romanorum** (Latin)  (lit., 'the last of the Romans')  an epithet used of notable personalities who epitomize Roman qualities.

**ultra vires** (Latin)  (lit., 'beyond the powers')  *Law.* beyond the bounds of a charter or legally authorized limit.

**Umlaut** (German)  the character ¨ , printed over a vowel to show that it is sounded differently from normal.

**umore** (Italian)  *Music.* humor; playfulness.

**un** (French)  one.

**una corda** (Italian)  (lit., 'one string')  *Music.* 1. the soft pedal on a piano. 2. a direction to use the soft pedal in playing the piano.  3. Also **a una corda.** a direction to use one string only in playing a stringed instrument.

**una voce** (Latin)  with one voice; unanimously.

**una volta** (Italian)  *Music.* once.

**und so weiter** (German)  and so on, equivalent to *etc.* **Abbr. usw.**

**unguibus et rostro** (Latin)  (lit., 'with claws and beak')  with all one's might; with no holds barred.

**unisoni, aria all'.**  See **aria all'unisono.**

**uniti** (Italian)  *Music.* united; often used to revoke the direction **divisi.**

**uno** (Italian, Spanish)  one.

**uno animo** (Latin)  of one mind; unanimously.

**uno ictu** (Latin)  with a single blow.

**uno saltu** (Latin)  with one leap; at a single bound.

**un peu** (French)  a little; a very tiny bit.

**un poco** (Italian)  *Music.* a little; rather. Also **un po'.**

**Unterseeboot** (German)  a German U-boat or submarine.

**uomo universale** (Italian)  a man of many interests and abilities; a Renaissance man.

**uovo,** *pl.* **uova** (Italian)  an egg.

**urbi et orbi** (Latin)  to the city (of Rome) and the world (used in papal bulls).

**Ursprache** (German)  original language, used especially in reference to proto-Indo-European.

**Urtext** (German)  source; text that is a basis for derivative versions.

**usque ad aras** (Latin)  (lit., 'up to the altars')  1. to the last extremity.  2. up to the point of conflict over religion. See also **amicus usque ad aras.**

**usque ad nauseam** (Latin)  (lit., 'even to nausea')  to the point of disgust. See also **ad nauseam.**

**usus loquendi** (Latin)  usage in speech.

**utile dulci** (Latin)  the useful with the pleasant.

**ut infra** (Latin)  as cited below; see further below (a direction in a book).

**uti possidetis** (Latin)   (lit., 'as you possess')   *Diplomacy.*  the principle that parties to a treaty may keep whatever territory was occupied at a particular time, usually at the end of hostilities.  See also **status quo ante bellum**.

**ut supra** (Latin)   as cited above; see above (a direction in a book).

**uva** (Italian)   grapes.

**uxor** (Latin)   wife.

# V

va (Italian)    (lit., 'it goes on')   *Music.* a direction to continue.

vache (French)    cow.

vache à lait (French)    a milch cow.

vacherie (French)    (lit., 'cowbarn') an island in the Louisiana swamps.

vacherin (French)    1. a very creamy, white cheese of the Jura region. 2. a dessert made of meringue circles filled with whipped cream or fruit.

vacillando (Italian)    *Music.* wavering; in irregular time.

vade mecum (Latin)    (lit., 'go with me')   1. a handbook carried for ready reference.    2. something kept handy for frequent use.

vae victis (Latin)    woe to the conquered! (Livy, *History* V.48).

Valdepeñas (Spanish)    a wine district of La Mancha in central Spain.

Valdostana, alla.    See **alla Valdostana.**

vale, *pl.* valete (Latin)    farewell; goodbye.

valet (French)    a manservant who attends to the personal needs of his employer.

valet de chambre (French)    1. a personal servant; **valet.** 2. in a royal household, the groom of the bed-chamber.

valet de pied (French)    a footman; flunkey.

valet de place (French)    a servant who waits on guests and often acts as a courier.

valete ac plaudite (Latin)    *Roman drama.* farewell and applaud (said by actors at the end of the play).

válgame Diós (Spanish)    (lit., 'save me, God') an expression of disbelief or surprise similar to *God almighty!*

Valpolicella (Italian)    a fruity red wine produced in northern Italy.

valse à deux temps (French)    *Music.* a quick waltz in which the dancers execute two steps to a measure.

vámonos (Spanish)    let's go. See also **vamos.**

vamos (Spanish)    (lit., 'we go') go!; get out!

vanitas vanitatum (Latin)    vanity of vanities.

307

**vapeur, à la.**  See à la vapeur.

**vaquero** (Spanish)  a cowboy.

**vargueños** (Spanish)  *Antiques.* mahogany or boxwood chests, inlaid with ivory and containing many drawers.

**varia lectio** (Latin)  *Textual criticism.* a variant reading for an ancient text, as when two manuscripts differ.

**variamente** (Italian)  *Music.* in a varied, free style of performance. Also **variamento.**

**variatim** (Latin)  variously; in various ways.

**variation** (French)  *Ballet.* any solo dance in a classical work.

**variazioni, con.**  See con variazioni.

**variorum** (Latin)  (lit., 'of various persons') used of texts containing notes or emendations by several scholars. Also **variorum notae** ('notes of various scholars'). See also **cum notis variorum.**

**varium et mutabile semper femina** (Latin)  woman is ever fickle and changeable (Vergil, *Aeneid* IV.569).

**vasco,** *fem.* **vasca** (Spanish)  Basque.

**Vaterland** (German)  fatherland.

**Vater Unser** (German)  the Lord's Prayer.

**vates sacer** (Latin)  sacred seer; the inspired poet.

**vaya con Diós** (Spanish)  (lit., 'go with God') goodbye; farewell.

**veau** (French)  calf; veal.

**vecchio additivo** (Italian)  a small quantity of a previous vintage of **Marsala** used in preparing a new batch of the wine.

**Veda** (Sanskrit)  *Hinduism.* the entire body of Hindu sacred writings.

**veduta,** *pl.* **vedute** (Italian)  (lit., 'view') *Fine Arts.* a painting of a recognizable place or scene.

**vega** (Spanish)  a fertile lowland.

**vellutato,** *fem.* **vellutata** (Italian)  *Music.* in a soft, velvety way.

**veloce** (Italian)  *Music.* swift; rapid.

**velocemente** (Italian)  *Music.* swiftly; rapidly. See also **con velocità.**

**velocità, con.**  See con velocità.

**velouté** (French)  (lit., 'smooth; creamy') 1. *Cookery.* a white sauce made with meat or fish stock, used as a base for sauces and soups. 2. a designation for wines that are exceptionally mellow and fine-textured. 3. *Music.* velvety.

**venaison** (French)  venison.

**vendemmia** (Italian)  a harvest of grapes for winemaking.

**vendetta** (Italian)  a hereditary blood feud, common in Corsica and southern Italy.

**venire facias** (Latin)   (lit., '(cause to) come')   *Law.* a writ requiring the sheriff to summon qualified persons for a jury.

**veni Sancte Spiritus** (Latin)   come, Holy Spirit.

**venite adoremus** (Latin)   *Music.* come, let us adore (Him); the refrain of the hymn "Adeste Fideles."

**veni, vidi, vici** (Latin)   I came, I saw, I conquered (Julius Caesar's terse announcement of his victory over Pharnaces of Pontus in 47 B.C.).

**venta** (Spanish)   **1.** a sale.   **2.** *Southwestern U.S.* a brand on an animal indicating that it has been sold.

**ventis secundis** (Latin)   with favoring winds.

**verbatim et literatim** (Latin)   word for word and letter for letter.

**Verbi Dei Minister** (Latin)   Minister of the Word of God. *Abbr.* **V.D.M.**

**verboten** (German)   prohibited; forbidden.

**verbum sapienti sat(is) est** (Latin)   a word to the wise is sufficient. *Abbr.* verb(um) sap.; verb(um) sat. Also **verbum sapienti; dictum sapienti sat(is) est.**

**verde antico** (Italian)   (lit., 'antique green') a deep-green ornamental marble with lighter-colored veins.

**Verdicchio** (Italian)   a white table wine produced in the foothills of the Appenines.

**verdura,** *pl.* **verdure** (Italian)   green vegetables.

**Verein** (German)   society; club.

**Verfasser** (German)   writer; author; composer.

**verghetta** (Italian)   (lit., 'a little switch') *Music.* the tail or ending of a note. Also **vergette.**

**verglas** (French)   a thin layer of hard, smooth ice on a rock surface.

**verismo** (Italian)   the realist movement in Italian arts, as in literature of the late 19th and early 20th centuries.

**veritas** (Latin)   truth (motto of Harvard University).

**veritas vos liberabit** (Latin)   the truth shall make you free (John 8:32).

**vérité** (French)   (lit., 'truth') stark realism, as in documentary films. See also **cinéma vérité.**

**Verlag** (German)   publishing house.

**vermicelli** (Italian)   very thin spaghetti.

**Vernaccia** (Italian)   a dry, aromatic white wine from Sardinia.

**vernis laque** (French)   a type of nail polish.

**vernis Martin** (French)   *Antiques.* a lacquer finish for furniture developed by the Martin brothers in 18th-century France.

**vernissage** (French)   *Fine Arts.* a private showing and reception preceding the opening of an exhibition.

**verroterie cloisonné** (French)     *Antiques.* a type of **cloisonné** in which the cells are filled with bits of glass or stone cut to fit.

**vers de société** (French)     light, mildly satirical poetry, intended for polite society.

**vers libre** (French)     *Prosody.* free verse; poetry that disregards formal rime and meter.

**verso** (Latin)     (lit., 'on a turned (leaf)') the left-hand page of an open book; the back side of a single leaf. See also **recto.**

**verso pollice.**     See **pollice verso.**

**verte** (Latin)     turn (the page).

**vertu, objet de.**     See **objet de vertu.**

**vesica piscis** (Latin)     (lit., 'bladder of a fish') *Fine Arts.* a pointed elliptical form with a figure of Christ, used especially in early Christian art. See also **mandorla.**

**vespera** (Latin)     *Prescriptions.* in the evening. *Abbr.* **vesp.**

**Vesperbrot** (German)     snack; afternoon tea.

**Vesuvio** (Italian)     a dry white wine produced near Mt. Vesuvius.

**vetro di Trina** (Italian)     *Antiques.* lace-like glass produced by the latticinio technique.

**vexata quaestio** (Latin)     a disputed question.

**vezzosamente** (Italian)     *Music.* tenderly; softly.

**Via Crucis** (Latin)     *Christianity.* the Way of the Cross.

**Via Dolorosa** (Latin)     (lit., 'the sorrowful road') *Christianity.* the path taken by Jesus to his crucifixion.

**via media** (Latin)     a middle course.

**viaticum** (Latin)     1. provisions for a journey.     2. a travel allowance.     3. *Roman Catholicism.* the Eucharist administered to a person in danger of death.

**vibrante** (Italian)     *Music.* 1. vibrating; tremulous.     2. resonant in tone.

**vibrato** (Italian)     *Music.* a tremulous or wavering effect in a note produced by slight variations in pitch. See also **ondeggiamento; tremolo.**

**vice** (Latin)     in place of; instead of; in succession to.

**vice mea** (Latin)     in my place.

**vice versa** (Latin)     conversely; with the order reversed.

**vicolo,** *pl.* **vicoli** (Italian)     a small, narrow street; alley.

**victor ludorum** (Latin)     (lit., 'the winner of the games') a champion competitor.

**vide** (Latin)     see (used in cross references).

**vide ante** (Latin)     see earlier (in the text).

**vide et crede** (Latin)     see and believe.

**vide infra** (Latin)     see below (in the text).

**videlicet** (Latin)   to wit; namely; that is to say. *Abbr.* **viz.**
**vide post** (Latin)   see further (in the text).
**vide supra** (Latin)   see above (in the text).
**vide ut supra** (Latin)   see as (it is stated) above (in the text).
**vie de Bohème** (French)   the stereotypical life of an artist, unconventional and informal.
**vier** (German)   four.
**Viertelnote** (German)   *Music.* quarter-note.
**vi et armis** (Latin)   by force of arms.
**vieux,** *fem.* **vieille** (French)   an old person.
**vif** (French)   (lit., 'lively') a winetaster's term for a fresh, light, young wine.
**vigneron** (French)   a vineyardist; wine-grower.
**vigorosamente** (Italian)   *Music.* vigorously.
**vigoroso** (Italian)   *Music.* vigorous.
**villageoise, à la.**   See **à la villageoise.**
**villancico** (Spanish)   a Christmas carol. Also **villancejo, villancete.**
**villanella** (Italian)   *Music.* a type of simple street song, popular in 16th-century Italy, in which the same music is repeated for many verses. Also **villota.**
**vin** (French)   wine.
**viña** (Spanish)   a vineyard.
**vinagreta** (Spanish)   *Cookery.* a vinegar sauce, a specialty of Catalonia.
**vinaigre** (French)   vinegar.
**vinaigre de toilette** (French)   aromatic vinegar.
**vinaigrette** (French)   *Cookery.* a dressing of vinegar, oil, and herbs.
**Viña Sol** (Spanish)   a crisp, dry white wine of Spain.
**vin blanc** (French)   white wine.
**vincet amor patriae** (Latin)   love of one's country will win, that is, will outweigh other considerations (Vergil, *Aeneid* VI.823).
**vincit omnia veritas** (Latin)   truth overcomes all things.
**vin coupé** (French)   blended wine.
**vinculum** (Latin)   (lit., 'fetter') *Mathematics.* a line placed over two or more terms to indicate that they are to be considered together.
**vinculum matrimonii** (Latin)   the bond of marriage.
**vin de paille** (French)   (lit., 'straw wine') white wine made from grapes dried on straw mats, very sweet and having a high alcoholic content.
**vin de table** (French)   (lit., 'table wine') a wine sold without indication of its origin, suitable for drinking with daily meals. Also **vin ordinaire.**
**vin d'honneur** (French)   (lit., 'wine of honor') 1. a reception for an honored guest. 2. a toast offered to such a guest.
**vin du pays** (French)   a local wine consumed where it is produced.

**Vingt, Les.**    See Société des Vingt.

**vingt-et-un** (French)    the card game blackjack or twenty-one.

**vin léger** (French)    a light wine.

**vin mousseux** (French)    a designation for any sparkling wine besides champagne.

**vino** (Italian, Spanish)    wine.

**vino bianco** (Italian)    a white wine.

**vino corriente** (Spanish)    a young, inexpensive wine, often served in a carafe.

**vino da arrosto** (Italian)    any full-bodied red wine that goes well with meat.

**vino da tavola** (Italian)    a table wine, as distinct from an aperitif or dessert wine. Also **vino da pasta.**

**vino de mesa** (Spanish)    table wine.

**vino de yema** (Spanish)    a superior quality wine, made from lightly pressed grapes.

**vino di lusso** (Italian)    a deluxe wine, such as a sparkling or fortified wine.

**vin ordinaire.**    See vin de table.

**vino rosato** (Italian)    a rosé wine.

**vino rosso** (Italian)    a red wine.

**Vino Santo** (Italian)    a dessert wine produced mainly in Tuscany, golden in color and quite sweet. Also **Vin Santo.**

**vino tipico** (Italian)    a wine controlled by law as to origin, grape variety, and method of production.

**vin pur** (French)    pure wine, not diluted with water.

**vin rosé** (French)    wine of pinkish color, made from black grapes fermented in a special way.

**vin rouge** (French)    red wine.

**viola bastarda** (Italian)    *Music.* a smaller bass viol intended for playing chordal and contrapuntal works. Also **viola di fagotto.**

**viola da braccio** (Italian)    (lit., 'viola of the arm') *Music.* the tenor viol, similar in range to the viola.

**viola da gamba** (Italian)    (lit., 'viola of the leg') *Music.* the bass viol, similar to the cello.

**viola d'amore** (Italian)    (lit., 'viola of love') *Music.* a member of the viol family, not widely in use, having sympathetic strings that produce a characteristic tone.

**viola di bordone** (Italian)    *Music.* a type of bass viol with sympathetic strings. Also **viola paradon.**

**viola di fagotto.**    See viola bastarda.

**viola paradon.**    See viola di bordone.

**viola pomposa** (Italian)   (lit., 'magnificent viol')   *Music.* a five-string violin developed by J. S. Bach to play high violincello passages.

**violentamente** (Italian)   *Music.* violently.

**violetta** (Italian)   *Music.* a member of the viol family, smaller and higher in pitch than the **viola d'amore.**

**violini unisoni** (Italian)   *Music.* a direction that the violins should play in unison.

**violino principale** (Italian)   *Music.* the first violin.

**violone** (Italian)   *Music.* **1.** a double bass. **2.** an organ stop yielding tones similar to a cello.

**violotta** (Italian)   *Music.* a tenor violin of size and pitch midway between the viola and the cello.

**vires.** See **vis.**

**vir et uxor** (Latin)   husband and wife.

**virginibus puerisque** (Latin)   for girls and boys (from Horace, *Odes* III.1.4; title of a book of essays by Robert Louis Stevenson).

**Virgo** (Latin)   the Virgin, a constellation and sign of the zodiac.

**viribus totis** (Latin)   with all one's might.

**viribus unitis** (Latin)   with forces united.

**virtù** (Italian)   *Fine Arts.* **1.** utmost ability as an artist. **2.** the qualities belonging to a connoisseur of fine art.

**virtuoso,** *pl.* **virtuosi** (Italian)   **1.** *Music.* a person with exceptional ability for playing an instrument or singing. Also **curioso. 2.** any highly regarded practitioner of a craft or skill. **3.** *adj.* showing or demanding great skill.

**virtute et armis** (Latin)   by valor and arms (motto of Mississippi).

**virtute officii** (Latin)   by virtue of one's office.

**vis,** *pl.* **vires** (Latin)   strength; force; power.

**vis a fronte** (Latin)   a frontal attack.

**vis a tergo** (Latin)   an attack from the rear.

**vis-à-vis** (French)   **1.** *adv.* face-to-face; opposite. **2.** *prep.* regarding; in relation to. **3.** *n.* the person opposite another. **4.** a person of rank or position equal to another.

**vis comica** (Latin)   comic power.

**vis inertiae** (Latin)   *Physics.* the force of inertia; resistance to change or progress.

**vis major** (Latin)   (lit., 'major force') *Law.* a natural, unpreventable force that is the cause of damage or loss. See also **force majeure.**

**vis medicatrix naturae** (Latin)   the healing power of nature.

**vis mortua** (Latin)   (lit., 'dead force') a force that has no effect.

**vis nova** (Latin)   new power; new energy.

**vis poetica** (Latin)   poetic power or genius.

**vis unita fortior** (Latin)   united force is stronger.

**vis vitae** (Latin)   the life force; the vigor of life.

**vis viva** (Latin)   living force.

**vita brevis, ars longa.**   See **ars longa, vita brevis.**

**vitam impendere vero** (Latin)   to devote one's life to truth (Juvenal, *Satires* 4.91; motto of Rousseau).

**vite** (French)   *Music.* **1.** *adj.* lively; quick. **2.** *adv.* quickly.

**vitella** (Italian)   very young, milk-fed veal.

**vitello** (Italian)   veal.

**viticulteur** (French)   a grower of grapes for wine.

**vitrail**, *pl.* **vitraux** (French)   a stained-glass window.

**viva** (Spanish)   an expression of enthusiastic approval, e.g., *Viva Mexico!*, 'Long live Mexico!'

**viva aqua** (Latin)   running water from a natural source.

**vivace** (Italian)   *Music.* vivacious; lively. Also **vivido.**

**vivacissimo** (Italian)   *Music.* most lively.

**viva il papa!** (Italian)   long live the pope!

**vivamente** (Italian)   *Music.* in a lively way.

**vivamus atque amemus** (Latin)   let's live and love (Catullus 5.1).

**vivat regina** (Latin)   long live the queen!

**vivat respublica** (Latin)   long live the republic!

**vivat rex** (Latin)   long live the king!

**viva voce** (Latin)   (lit., 'with the living voice') orally (as contrasted with *in writing*), in reference to an oral examination or vote.

**vive la bagatelle** (French)   long live frivolity!

**vive la différence** (French)   hooray for the difference! (between men and women).

**vive l'amour** (French)   long live love!

**vive la république** (French)   long live the republic!

**vive l'empereur** (French)   long live the emperor!

**vive le roi** (French)   long live the king!

**vivere parvo** (Latin)   (lit., 'to live on little') to live with limited means.

**vive ut vivas** (Latin)   live so that you may live hereafter.

**vive vale(que)** (Latin)   live (long) and prosper.

**vivido.**   See **vivace.**

**vivo** (Italian)   *Music.* brisk; animated.

**vixit** (Latin)   he (*or* she) lived (used on gravestones with the number of years of life).

**vocalise** (French)   *Music.* the singing of melodies only on the vowels, done as a vocal exercise.

**vocalizzo,** *pl.* **vocalizzi** (Italian)    *Music.* melodies sung only on vowels as a vocal exercise.

**voce,** *pl.* **voci** (Italian)    *Music.* voice.

**voce bianca** (Italian)    (lit., 'white voice')  *Music.* the voice of women and children.

**voce di petti** (Italian)    *Music.* 1. the chest voice. 2. the lowest register of the voice.

**voce di testa** (Italian)    *Music.* 1. the head voice, that used in **falsetto.** 2. the upper register of the voice.

**voce granita** (Italian)    (lit., 'granite voice')  *Music.* a firm, powerful voice.

**voce mista** (Italian)    *Music.* a voice displaying more than a single characteristic; a mixed voice.

**voce pastosa** (Italian)    *Music.* a soft, mellow voice.

**voce spiccata** (Italian)    *Music.* a voice that enunciates clearly.

**voce velata** (Italian)    *Music.* a veiled, slightly obscured voice.

**voci.**    See **voce.**

**voilà** (French)    there!; there it is!; look! (an exclamation used to point to a success or achievement).

**voile** (French)    1. a thin fabric with an open weave. 2. *Music.* the cloth used for muffling a drum.

**vois forte, à.**    See **à vois forte.**

**voix blanche** (French)    *Music.* a clear-toned female voice.

**voix céleste** (French)    (lit., 'heavenly voice') *Music.* an organ stop producing stringlike tones.

**volaille** (French)    poultry; fowl.

**volante** (Italian)    *Music.* 1. *adj.* swift and light; flying. 2. *n.* slurred staccato in playing a bowed instrument.

**volare** (Italian)    to fly, used in a popular Italian song to describe a carefree attitude toward life.

**volata** (Italian)    (lit., 'flight')  *Music.* a rapid series of notes.

**vol-au-vent** (French)    (lit., 'flight in the wind') *Cookery.* a light pastry shell with a filling of meat, fish, or poultry.

**volcanello** (Italian)    a small active cone inside the central crater of a volcano.

**volé,** *fem.* **volée** (French)    *Ballet.* flown; flying.  See also **de volée.**

**volens et potens** (Latin)    willing and able.

**volente Deo.**    See **Deo volente.**

**Volk** (German)    a people; nation.

**Völkerwanderung** (German)    the migration of entire ethnic populations.

**Volksdeutscher** (German)    term used of Europeans of German ethnic origin but living outside of Germany.

**Volkskammer** (German)   chief legislature of the German Democratic Republic.

**Volkssturm** (German)   a people's army of old men and young boys formed toward the end of World War II to defend Germany.

**volonté, à.**   See **à volonté.**

**volost** (Russian)   a rural administrative division of the Soviet Union.

**volta,** *pl.* **volte** (Italian)   (lit., 'time')   *Music.* 1. the ending of a section to be repeated. 2. a rapid dance in triple time, popular in the early 17th century.

**volte-face** (French)   an about-face, especially referring to a reversal of opinion or attitude.

**volteggiando** (Italian)   *Music.* crossing the hands in piano playing.

**volti** (Italian)   *Music.* turn over (direction found at the bottom of a page of sheet music).

**volti subito** (Italian)   *Music.* turn over quickly (direction found at the bottom of a page of sheet music).

**volubilmente** (Italian)   *Music.* volubly.

**volventibus annis** (Latin)   (lit., 'with years rolling on')   as years go by; in passing years.

**vongole** (Italian)   clams. See also **alle vongole.**

**vorlage** (German)   *Skiing.* a stance in which one leans far forward yet keeps the heels in contact with the skis.

**Vorspiel** (German)   *Music.* prelude; overture.

**Vortrag** (German)   1. lecture. 2. performance; recital.

**vospitanie** (Russian)   education of children's character.

**votre santé, à.**   See **à votre santé.**

**Vouvray** (French)   a white wine produced on the northern bank of the Loire River.

**vox,** *pl.* **voces** (Latin)   voice.

**vox angelica** (Latin)   (lit., 'angelic voice')   *Music.* an organ stop that produces a tremulous effect. Also called **vox caelestis.**

**vox barbara** (Latin)   an unconventional term; a barbarism.

**vox clamantis in deserto** (Latin)   the voice of one crying in the wilderness (Matthew 3:3). Also **vox clamans in deserto** ('a voice crying in the wilderness,' motto of Dartmouth College).

**vox et praeterea nihil** (Latin)   a voice and nothing more; a sound without meaning or substance.

**vox faucibus haesit** (Latin)   (lit., 'his voice stuck in his throat')   he was struck dumb with amazement (Vergil, *Aeneid* II.774).

**vox humana** (Latin)   (lit., 'a human voice')   *Music.* an organ stop that produces human-like sounds.

**vox populi** (Latin)　the voice of the people; popular opinion. *Abbr.* vox pop.

**vox populi, vox Dei** (Latin)　the voice of the people is the voice of God.

**voyageur** (French)　*Canada.* an expert frontier guide.

**voyagé,** *fem.* **voyagée** (French)　*Ballet.* moving across the stage by a series of small jumps while holding a pose.

**voyeur** (French)　one who spies on the sexual activities of others.

**voyez** (French)　see!; look!

**vraisemblance** (French)　the quality of appearing true or plausible; verisimilitude.

**vue, à.**　See à vue.

**vue d'oeil, à.**　See à vue d'oeil.

**vuelta al ruedo** (Spanish)　*Bullfighting.* a tour of the arena by the victorious bullfighter.

**vulgo** (Latin)　popularly; in the vernacular.

**vulnerant omnes, ultima necat** (Latin)　all (hours) wound, the final one kills (inscription seen on clocks).

**vulneratus, non victus** (Latin)　wounded, not conquered; bloody but unbowed.

# W

**wadi** (Arabic)    1. a watercourse that is dry except during rainy periods. 2. an oasis.

**wahine** (Hawaiian)    a woman.

**Waldglas** (German) *Antiques.* a colored glass made in medieval Germany; natural forest glass.

**wallah** (Hindi)    1. a designation for a person in charge of a thing or performing a particular activity. 2. a person; fellow. Also **walla.**

**Walpurgisnacht** (German)    the evening before May Day, on which witches were tradionally thought to celebrate a sabbath.

**wampum** (Narragansett)    beads made from seashells, used for barter by North American Indians. Also **wampumeag; peag; seawan; sewan.**

**wampumeag.**    See **wampum.**

**Wanderjahre** (German)    a period set aside for travel, especially as a part of one's education.

**wanderlust** (German)    passion for traveling; desire to see the world.

**was ist das?** (German)    what is that?

**Wasser** (German)    water.

**wedeln** (German) *Skiing.* a technique that consists of a rapid descent following a wavy course.

**Wehrmacht** (German)    the German armed forces prior to and during World War II.

**Weinstube** (German)    wine tavern; wineshop.

**Weltanschauung** (German)    philosophy of life; world view.

**Weltansicht** (German)    world view; an attitude toward or conception of reality as a whole.

**Weltbild** (German)    one's conception of the world; worldview.

**Weltburger** (German)    1. a citizen of the world. 2. an international celebrity.

**Weltgeist** (German)    the prevailing temperament of the world.

**Weltgeschichte** (German)    world history.

**Weltkrieg** (German)    world war.

**Weltpolitik** (German)    the policy of a nation with respect to the rest of the world.

**Weltschmerz** (German)    distress at the condition of the world; sentimental pessimism.

**Werk,** *pl.* **Werke** (German)    work of music or art; production.

**wie geht's?** (German)    how goes it?;   how are you?

**Wiener Schnitzel** (German)    *Cookery.* breaded veal cutlet.

**wigwam** (Algonquian)    a hut of the North American Indians, made of poles overlaid with animal skins or mats.

**Wilhelmstrasse** (German)    a street in Berlin on which German foreign ministry offices were located, formerly metonymic for German foreign policy.

**Wissenschaft** (German)    knowledge; science; the product of learned research.

**wok** (Chinese)    *Cookery.* a large cooking pan with a smoothly curved inner surface designed for stir-frying.

**won ton** (Chinese)    *Cookery.* Chinese-style stuffed dumplings, often served in soup.

**wunderbar** (German)    wonderful.

**wunderkind** (German)    child prodigy.

**wurst** (German)    sausage.

# X, Y

**xató** (Spanish)   *Cookery.* a salad of curly endive with a peppery sauce, a specialty of Catalonia.

**Yahweh** (Hebrew)   a transliteration of the Hebrew symbols for the holiest name of God.

**yanqui** (Latin American Spanish)   designating a person or thing from the United States.

**yarmulke** (Yiddish)   *Judaism.* a skullcap worn by Jewish males and at Jewish services. Also **yarmelke; yarmulkah.**

**yashmak** (Turkish)   the facial veil worn in public by Muslim women. Also **yashmac.**

**yassou** (Greek)   a Greek exclamation of greeting or farewell.

**yen** (Japanese)   the basic monetary unit of Japan.

**yenta** (Yiddish)   an annoying, gossipy woman.

**yerba mate** (Spanish)   a plant of the Río de la Plata region of Argentina whose leaves are used to make a kind of tea. See also **mate.**

**yeshiva** (Hebrew)   1. a Jewish elementary school. 2. a Jewish school of higher learning for the training of rabbis.

**yeti** (Tibetan)   the abominable snowman. See also **sasquatch.**

**yin yang** (Chinese)   *Chinese philosophy.* the two conflicting principles of the universe, one the negative, dark, and feminine (**yin**), the other the positive, bright, and masculine (**yang**).

**Yodel**   See **Jodel.**

**yoga** (Hindi)   1. a Hindu discipline of mind and body that strives for union with the Supreme Being. 2. the physical and meditative exercises that are derived from this discipline.

**yogi,** *fem.* **yogini** (Hindi)   one who practices **yoga.**

**Yom Kippur** (Hebrew)   *Judaism.* the Day of Atonement, a high holy day observed with fasting and prayer.

**yontif** (Yiddish)   a general term for a Jewish holiday.

**yucca** (Spanish)   a plant, common to the southwestern U.S. and Latin America, having stiff, spiny leaves, a tall central stem, and white flowers.

# Z

zabaglione, *pl.* zabaglioni (Italian)   *Cookery.* a custard dessert flavored with **Marsala** wine.   Also **zabaione; Marsala all'uovo.**

zacate (Spanish)   a type of wild grass used for fodder.

zacatón (Spanish)   a tough, fibrous grass found in the Southwestern U.S. and Mexico, used for making baskets, brooms, etc.

zaftig (Yiddish)   pleasingly plump; buxom.

zaibatsu (Japanese)   a large Japanese commercial conglomerate, usually family-controlled.

zambomba (Spanish)   *Music.* a primitive musical instrument consisting of parchment stretched over an earthen jar, through which a stick is inserted and rubbed to create sound.

zampogna (Italian)   *Music.* a type of bagpipe from Calabria.

zampone (Italian)   a variety of pork sausage, a specialty of Modena.

zapateado (Spanish)   *Music.* a Spanish dance in which the dancer marks time by stamping his or her heels.

zarape.   See **sarape.**

zarzuela (Spanish)   **1.** *Music.* a type of Spanish comic opera with spoken dialogue and often a topical theme.   **2.** *Cookery.* a dish of assorted fish in a pepper sauce.

zdrávstvui(te) (Russian)   a multipurpose Russian salutation, equivalent to *good day.*

zeffiroso (Italian)   *Music.* very light; zephyr-like.

zehn (German)   ten.

Zeitgeist (German)   spirit of the time(s).

Zeitschrift (German)   periodical; magazine.

Zeitung (German)   newspaper; journal.

zelosamente (Italian)   *Music.* zealously.

zeloso (Italian)   *Music.* zealous.

zeppela (Italian)   a type of cream-filled pastry.

ziggurat (Assyrian)    an ancient Assyrian temple of pyramidal construction.

zingaresa (Italian)    *Music.* in the style of gypsy music.

Zion (Hebrew)    a hill in Jerusalem on which the Temple was built, focal point for the movement to establish the Jewish homeland of Israel.

ziti (Italian)    a variety of pasta shaped in short, hollow tubes.

zoccolo, *pl.* zoccoli (Italian)    a clog; wooden shoe.

zonam solvere (Latin)    to untie the girdle (worn by a maiden until her wedding); to marry a virgin.

Zopfstil (German)    *Fine Arts.* a conventional mechanical style common in 18th-century Germany.

zoppa, alla.    See alla zoppa.

zori (Japanese)    a Japanese sandal fastened to the foot with thongs and worn over a **tabi.**

zuccotta (Italian)    *Cookery.* a confection made of sponge cake, whipped cream, chocolate, and candied fruits.

zufolo (Italian)    *Music.* a small flute or flageolet, often used to teach birds to sing.

zum Beispiel (German)    for example.    *Abbr.* z.B.

zuppa (Italian)    soup.

zuppa inglese (Italian)    *Cookery.* a dessert made of sponge cake soaked in Marsala wine and combined with cream filling and candied fruits.

zwei (German)    two.

Zwischenmusik (German)    1. *Music.* incidental music. 2. *Chess.* waiting move.

Zwischenstück (German)    1. transition piece. 2. *Theater.* interlude.